ENTREPRENEURIAL DEVELOPMENT

DR. NUZHATH KHATOON
Associate Professor,
PRR College of Commerce and Management,
Gandipet Road, Narsingi,
Hyderabad.

First Edition : 2012
Reprint : 2023

Published by : Mrs. Meena Pandey
for **HIMALAYA PUBLISHING HOUSE PVT. LTD.,**
"Ramdoot", Dr. Bhalerao Marg, Girgaon, Mumbai - 400 004.
Phone: 022-23860170, 23863863; **Fax:** 022-23877178
E-mail: himpub@bharatmail.co.in; **Website:** www.himpub.com

Branch Offices :

New Delhi : "Pooja Apartments", 4-B, Murari Lal Street, Ansari Road, Darya Ganj, New Delhi - 110 002. Phone: 011-23270392, 23278631; Fax: 011-23256286

Nagpur : Kundanlal Chandak Industrial Estate, Ghat Road, Nagpur - 440 018. Phone: 0712-2721215, 2721216

Bengaluru : Plot No. 91-33, 2nd Main Road, Seshadripuram, Behind Nataraja Theatre, Bengaluru - 560 020. Phone: 080-41138821; Mobile: 09379847017, 09379847005

Hyderabad : No. 3-4-184, Lingampally, Besides Raghavendra Swamy Matham, Kachiguda, Hyderabad - 500 027. Phone: 040-27560041, 27550139

Chennai : No. 34/44, Motilal Street, T. Nagar, Chennai - 600 017. Mobile: 09380460419

Pune : "Laksha" Apartment, First Floor, No. 527, Mehunpura, Shaniwarpeth (Near Prabhat Theatre), Pune - 411 030. Phone: 020-24496323, 24496333; Mobile: 09370579333

Cuttack : Plot No. 5F-755/4, Sector-9, CDA Markat Nagar, Cuttack - 753 014, Odisha. Mobile: 09338746007

Kolkata : 3, S.M. Bose Road, Near Gate No. 5, Agarpara Railway Station, North 24 Parganas, West Bengal - 700 109. Mobile: 09674536325

DTP by : Prerana Enterprises, Mumbai.

Printed at : Trinity Academy, Mumbai. On behalf of HPH

Prof. Mohd. Akbar Ali Khan
M.Com., LLB, M.Phill, FDP (IIMA),
PGD (FTM), AICPB(USA), Ph.D.
PROFESSOR & HEAD

(Accredited with 'A' Grade by NACC)

DEPARTMENT OF COMMERCE
OSMANIA UNIVERSITY
HYDERABAD - 500 007. A.P.
Off.: 040 - 27097693, 27682308,
Fax: 091-040-27097693
Res: 040-23343585, Cell: 09849457014
e-mail: ouhodcoms@yahoo.com,
e-mail: maakhan1155@gmail.com

FOREWORD

It is believed that we can positively change the world through entrepreneurship education. Entrepreneurship for the 21st Century is an utmost necessity of every educated youth for the competitive sustenance of the existing businesses and for new venture creation. Many courses are launched for entrepreneurship development programmes in almost all the Universities/Institutions in the globe. We are committed to helping colleges and universities develop creative and innovative entrepreneurship curricula, to increase teaching effectiveness, and to develop the teaching skills of entrepreneurs who are engaged in full-time or part-time teaching.

In view of the above, this book on the topic "Entrepreneurship Development is an important outcome focused on the basics of entrepreneurship development and different procedures and dimensions of institutional support. The book is written on the basis of contents of material coverage in the syllabus of different courses in A.P. and in India. I am sure that the book will be of great help to train the teacher so as to cultivate skills of entrepreneurship among the students.

sd/-
Prof. Mohd. Akbar Ali Khan
Vice Chancellor Telangana University

PREFACE

This book is about enterprise and entrepreneurship and their relationship to small business. The world has been changing, and the role of the individual has become increasingly more important, with individual entrepreneurship becoming even more necessary for economic success. This process has been referred to as the development of an enterprise culture and its benefits have been widely sought. Enterprise and its associated concepts of entrepreneurship and small business have therefore all been widely promoted and their development supported.

It is recognized that Small Scale Enterprises are increasingly important in economic growth, job creation, regional and local development, and social cohesion, that entrepreneurship and a dynamic small scale sector are important for restructuring economies and combating poverty, globalization, the acceleration of technological change and innovation create opportunities for Small Scale Enterprises but also involve transition costs and new challenges, and so Small Scale Enterprises policies need to be tailored to the circumstances and priorities of individual countries and sectors, while contributing to sustainable development and progress.

Universities have incorporated Entrepreneurship and Small Business Management in their course curriculum so as to provide necessary exposure to the students about the entrepreneurial and industrial climate of the country. This book Entrepreneurial Development is an endeavor to help the students of Business Management. It is written in the simple and lucid language so that the students may understand the concept of the topic clearly. Latest information and techniques has been introduced in various topics with examples of present scenario.

The Book's Overview:

The book is divided into six chapters.

- Chapter1: introduces the concept, qualities, characteristic, theories, importance, and development of entrepreneurship.
- Chapter 2: deals with motivation, competencies, and mobility of entrepreneurs and EDP.
- Chapter 3: provides the detail study of the small enterprises, its importance, objectives, problems, and formation.
- Chapter 4: cover the entire facets of the marketing areas of small enterprises.
- Chapter 5: assess the sources of institutional help for small enterprises.
- Chapter 6: describes the venture capital financing for business.

For each chapter there are learning questions, exercises to solve and at the end of each chapter, fill in the blanks, exercises are given with an appropriate choice of words for self assessment, and to confirm the understanding of the subject. The text is scripted with simple illustrations, diagrams, and tables to increase the level of understanding. The cases selected or written are from the Indian business environment.

It is my hope that the book "Entrepreneurship Development will contribute to higher learning and understanding of the subject.

Perfection cannot be achieved in a single literature, but there is always scope for improvement. Hence I will be grateful for any suggestion and corrections for the improvement of this book.

Nuzhath Khatoon

nuzhathkhatoon@gmail.com

ACKNOWLEDGEMENT

My sincere thanks to Prof. Akbar Ali Khan, Vice Chancellor Telangana University, for writing the foreword of this book and for his guidance and continues encouragement.

I am also thankful to my father Dr. Babu Khan, my mother Mrs. Zubaida Khatoon, my brothers, and my son Master Shahbaaz Khan for their inspiration, support, encouragement, and patience.

Finally I am grateful to Mr. Krishna Poojari and his entire team members of Himalaya Publishing House for helping and guiding me for the compilation of this book.

Nuzhath Khatoon

nuzhathkhatoon@gmail.com

CONTENTS

Entrepreneur and Entrepreneurship

1

Chapter

CHAPTER OUTLINE

- Concept of Entrepreneur
- Characteristics of Entrepreneur
- Quality of Entrepreneur
- Distinction between an Entrepreneur and a Manager
- Functions of Entrepreneur
- Types of Entrepreneur
- Concept of Entrepreneurship
- Theories of Entrepreneurship
- Characteristics of Entrepreneurship

- **Scope of Entrepreneurship**
- **Growth of Entrepreneurship in India**
- **Scope of Entrepreneurship in India**
- **Role of Entrepreneurship in Economic Development**
- **Barriers of Entrepreneurship**
- **Problems of Entrepreneurship**
- **Recent trends of Women Entrepreneurs**
- **Problems faced by Women Entrepreneurs**
- **Remedies to solves the problems of Women Entrepreneurs**
- **Rural Entrepreneurship**
- **Training and Development of Rural Entrepreneurship in India**
- **Major problems/challenges faced by Rural Entrepreneurship**

Entrepreneur: An entrepreneur is an individual who is willing to take financial risks and undertakes new financial ventures. The word derived from the French word "entre" (to enter) and "prendre" (to take), and in a general sense applies to any person starting a new project or trying a new opportunity.

Many societies place great value on the entrepreneur. To encourage their activity, they may be offered access to inexpensive capital, tax exemptions and management advice. An entrepreneur has the greatest chance of success by focusing on a market niche, either too small or too new to have been noticed by established businesses. To help new technologies come to market, many universities establish *business incubators* for entrepreneurs hoping to turn leading edge research into marketable products

Entrepreneur is an Economic Agent who plays a vital role in the economic development of a country. Economic development of a country refers steady growth in the income levels. This growth mainly depends on its entrepreneur. An entrepreneur is an individual with knowledge skills, initiative, drive and spirit of innovation who aims at achieving goals. An entrepreneur identifies opportunities and seizes opportunities for economic benefits.

Entrepreneurs are generally highly independent, which can cause problems when their ventures succeed. In a small company the entrepreneur is able to personally manage most aspects of the business, but this is not possible once the company has grown beyond a certain size. Management conflicts often arise when the entrepreneur does not recognize that running a large stable company is different from running a small growing company. The problem is often resolved by the entrepreneur either leaving to start a new venture or being forced out by shareholders

An entrepreneur is a person who organizes and manages a business undertaking and assumes a risk for the sake of profit. Operating a business takes certain skills, few of the people have all the skills needed to run a business and some may compensate their skill by hiring staff or consultants and by obtaining education and training in the concerned skills.

Concept of Entrepreneur

The word "Entrepreneur" is derived from the French verb entreprendre, it means to undertake. In the early 16th century the Frenchmen who organized and led military expeditions were referred as "Entrepreneur". In the 18th century French economist **Richard Cantillo,** used the term entrepreneur as business. Since that time the word entrepreneur means one who takes the risk of starting a new organizations or introducing a new idea product or service to society.

According to **J.B. Say,** "An Entrepreneur is the economic agent who unites all means of production – land of one, labor of another and the capital of yet another and thus, produce a product. By selling the product in the market he pays rent of land, wages to labor, interest on capital and what remains is his profit". Thus an Entrepreneur is an organizer who combines a various factors of production to produce a socially valuable/viable product.

According to **Joseph Schumpeter,** "An entrepreneur in an advanced economy is an individual who introduces something in the economy, a method of production not yet listed by experience in the branch of manufacture concerning a product with which consumers are not yet familiar, a new source of raw materials or of new markets and the like". The functions of an entrepreneur according to Schumpeter are:

1. **Introduction of a new product.**
2. **Developing new markets and finding fresh source of raw materials and**
3. **Making changes.**

According to **Cantillon,** "An entrepreneur is the agent who buys factors of production at certain prices in order to combine them into a product with a view to selling it at uncertain prices in future".

According to **Peter Drucker,** "Entrepreneurs need to search for the source of innovation, change and their symptom which indicate opportunities for successful innovation", such changes might increase scope for economic and social innovation. According to him three conditions have to be fulfilled.

1. Innovation at work. It requires knowledge and ingenuity. It makes great demands on diligence, persistence and commitment.
2. To succeed, innovation must build on their strengths.
3. Innovation always has to be close to the market, focused on the market and indeed market driven.

Specially, systematic innovation means monitoring seven sources for innovative opportunities.

1. The unexpected:

- The unexpected success.
- The unexpected failure.
- The unexpected outside event

That is unseen opportunity, problem, success, failure and growth.

2. The incongruity:

Between reality as it actually is and reality as it assured to be or as it "right to be." That is difference between actual and standard.

3. Innovation based on process needs:

Needs, wants, desire and expectation

4. Changes in industry structure or market structure:

- That catches everyone unaware
- Identified the awareness.

The second set of sources for innovation opportunities, a set of these, involves changes outside the enterprise or industry.

5. Demographics: (Population changes, age, income, religion and region)

6. Change in perception: (Mood and meaning, stimuli)

7. New Knowledge: (Both scientific and non-scientific)

These seven sources require separates analysis for each has its own distinct character.

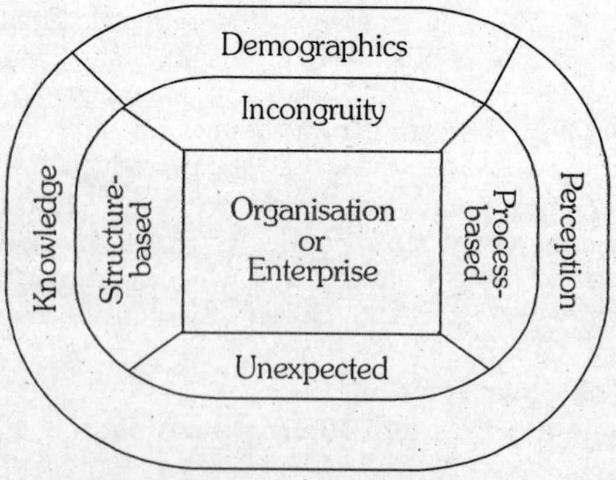

Fig. 1.1: Seven sources of innovative opportunity

Marketing Concept of Entrepreneur

The marketing concept of entrepreneurs includes knowing what a market consists of understanding of marketing research, the development of a marketing plan and the proper approach to a pricing strategy. A market is a group of consumers (potential customers) who have purchasing power and unsatisfied needs. A new venture will survive only if a market exists for its product or service. This is so obvious that it would seem every entrepreneur would prepare thoroughly the market analysis need to establish a target market. However, many entrepreneurs know very little about their market, and some even attempt to launch new ventures without identifying any market.

A number of techniques and strategies can assist entrepreneurs to effectively analyze a potential market. By using them entrepreneurs can gain in-depth knowledge about the specific market and can translate this knowledge into a well-formulated business plan. Effective marketing analysis also can help a new venture position itself and make changes that will result in increased sales. The key to this process is marketing research.

Common elements in the marketing skills of great entrepreneurs are:

1. They possess unique environmental insight, which they use to spot opportunities that others overlook or view as problems.
2. They develop new marketing strategies that draw on their unique insights. They view the *status quo* and conventional wisdom as something to be challenged.
3. They take risks that others, lacking their vision, consider foolish.
4. They live in fear of being preempted in the market.
5. They are fiercely competitive.
6. They think through the implications of any proposed strategy, screening it against their knowledge of how the marketplace functions. They identify and solve problems that others do not even recognize.
7. They are meticulous about details and are always in search of new competitive advantages in quality and cost reduction, however small or big.
8. They lead from the front, executing their management strategies enthusiastically and autocratically. They maintain close information control when they delegate.
9. They drive themselves and their subordinates.
10. They are prepared to adapt their strategies quickly and to keep adapting them until they work. They persevere long after others have given up.
11. They have clear visions of what they want to achieve next. They can see further down the road than the average manager can see.

To conclude, an entrepreneur is one who bears risk, unites various factors of production, to exploit the perceived opportunities in order to evoke demand, create wealth and employment.

Characteristic of Entrepreneur

An entrepreneur is a highly achievement-oriented, enthusiastic and energetic individual who has following characteristics.

1. Entrepreneurs are action-oriented, highly motivated individual who takes risks to achieves goals.
2. Entrepreneur will have unwavering determination and commitment. They are creative and result-oriented. They work hard in return for personal and financial rewards.
3. Entrepreneur accepts responsibilities with enthusiasm and endurance.
4. Entrepreneurs have self-confidence, dedicated, setting self-determined goals and markets for their ideas responding to existing market.
5. Entrepreneurs are thinkers and doers, planners and workers.

6. Entrepreneur depends on the intelligence, imagination and strength of purpose of an individual.
7. Entrepreneurs can foresee the future as a salesman's persuasiveness, a financial talent for manipulating funds, as an auditor precision etc.

A review of the literature related to entrepreneurial characteristics reveals the existence of a large number of factors that can be consolidated into a much smaller set of profile dimensions. For example, the following is one of common characteristics that has been compiled:

- Total commitment, determination and perseverance
- Drive to achieve and grow
- Opportunity and goal orientation
- Taking initiative and personal responsibility
- Persistent problem-solving
- Realism and a sense of humor
- Seeking and using feedback
- Internal focus of control
- Calculated risk taking and risk seeking
- Low need for status and power
- Integrity and reliability

Howard H. Strevenson and David E. Gumpert have presented an outline of the entrepreneurial organization that reveals such characteristics as imagination, flexibility and willingness to accept risks. William G. Gartner examined the literature and found a diversity of reported characteristics. John Hornaday examined various research sources and formulated a list of 42 characteristics often attributed to entrepreneurs.

Characteristics Often Attributed to Entrepreneurs

1.	Confidence	22.	Responsibility
2.	Perseverance, determination	23.	Foresight
3.	Energy, diligence	24.	Accuracy, thoroughness
4.	Resourcefulness	25.	Cooperativeness
5.	Ability to take calculated risks	26.	Profit orientation
6.	Dynamism, leadership	27.	Ability to learn from mistakes
7.	Optimism	28.	Sense of power
8.	Need to achieve	29.	Pleasant personality
9.	Creativity	30.	Egotism
10.	Ability to influence others	31.	Courage
11.	Ability to get along with people	32.	Imagination
12.	Initiative	33.	Perceptiveness
13.	Flexibility	34.	Tolerance for ambiguity
14.	Intelligence	35.	Aggressiveness
15.	Orientation to clear goals	36.	Ability to trust workers
16.	Positive response to challenges	37.	Efficacy
17.	Independence	38.	Commitment
18.	Responsiveness to suggestion and criticism	39.	Capacity for enjoyment
19.	Time competence, efficiency	40.	Sensitivity to others
20.	Ability to make decisions quickly	41.	Honesty, integrity
21.	Versatility, knowledge of product, market, machinery, technology.	42.	Maturity, balance

Fig. 1.2: Characteristics of Entrepreneurs

Research done by Southern Methodist University's Cox School of Business came up with common characteristics of over 200 successful entrepreneurs. Successful was defined as being in business for at least 5 years and who has gross revenues of at least $1 million.

Common Traits in a Successful Entrepreneur: Written by Judith L. Glick-Smith

1. Good Health: Successful entrepreneurs must work long hours for extended periods of time. When they get sick, they recover quickly.

2. A Need to Control and Direct: They prefer environments where they have maximum authority and responsibility and do not work well in traditionally structured organizations. This is not about power, though. Entrepreneurs have a need to create and achieve by having control over events.

3. Self-confidence: Findings showed that as long as entrepreneurs were in control, they were relentless in pursuit of their goals. If they lost control, they quickly lost interest in the undertaking.

4. Sense of Urgency: They have a never-ending sense of urgency to do something. This corresponds with a high energy level. Many enjoy individual sports rather than team sports. Inactivity makes them impatient.

5. Comprehensive Awareness: They have a comprehensive awareness of a total situation and are aware of all the ramifications involved in a decision.

6. Realistic Outlook: There is a constant need to know the status of things. They may or may not be idealistic, but they are honest and straightforward and expect others to be the same.

7. Conceptual Ability: They have superior conceptual abilities. This helps entrepreneurs identify relationships in complex situations. Chaos does not bother them because they can conceptualize order. Problems are quickly identified and solutions offered. The drawback is that this may not translate well to interpersonal problems.

8. Low Need for Status: Their need for status is met through achievement not through material possessions.

9. Objective Approach: They take an objective approach to personal relationships and are more concerned with the performance and accomplishment of others than with feelings. They keep their distance psychologically and concentrate on the effectiveness of operations.

10. Emotional Stability: They have the stability to handle stress from business and from personal areas in their lives. Setbacks are seen as challenges and do not discourage them.

11. Attraction to Challenges: They are attracted to challenges but not to risks. It may look like they are taking high risks, but in actuality they have assessed the risks thoroughly.

12. Describing with Numbers: They can describe situations with numbers. They understand their financial position and can tell at any time how much they have in receivables and how much they owe.

Quality of an Entrepreneur

Being an entrepreneur is about more than just starting a business or two, it is about having attitude and the drive to succeed in business. All successful Entrepreneurs have a similar way of thinking and posses several key personal qualities that make them so successful in business. Essential qualities of entrepreneur are as follows:

1. Success and Achievement: The entrepreneurs are self determined to achieve high goals in business, suppress anxieties, repair misfortunes and desire expedients, to run a successful business.

2. Risk Bearer: Entrepreneur accepts risk they select a moderate risk situation rather than gambling or avoiding risk, they understand and manage risk.

3. Opportunity Explorers: Always entrepreneur identifies opportunities. He seizes opportunity and converts them into realistic achievable goals.

4. Perseverance: Entrepreneur makes extreme efforts and work hard till the goal is successfully accomplished. They are deterred by uncertainties risks and difficulties coming in the way of achievement of ultimate goal.

5. Facing Uncertainty: Achievement-oriented people tend to tackle an unfamiliar but interesting situation. They go ahead with solutions for the problems even without the guidelines.

6. Feedback: Entrepreneur likes to have prompt immediate feedback of their performance.

7. Independence: Entrepreneur likes to be their own master and want to be responsible for their own decision. An entrepreneur is a job giver and not a job seeker.

8. Flexibility: Entrepreneur makes decisions based on the prevailing situation. Successful entrepreneur do not hesitate in revising their decision. Entrepreneur is a person with open minds not rigid.

9. Planner: Entrepreneur frames realistic business plans and follows them rigorously to achieve the objectives in a stipulated time limit.

10. Self-confidence: Entrepreneur directs his abilities towards the accomplishment of goals with the help of his strengths and weakness.

11. Stress Taker: Entrepreneur as a focal point he will make many right decisions which may involve lot of physical and emotional stress. He keeps cool under a lot of tension while decision making.

12. Motivator: Entrepreneur influence and initiate people and make them think in his way and act accordingly.

All these qualities are born not made. In other words business family background, knowledge and skills, education and experience are essential for a successful entrepreneur. It is a great idea to want to start a business, but a person has to analyze and estimate if he has the qualities that are essential for being a successful entrepreneur.

Qualities of a Successful Entrepreneur:

Entrepreneurs are persevering, are lovers of challenges, are action-oriented and are quick to learn, and adopt techniques to perform better as well as improve their business. They are independent extroverts who have the ability to lead people, manage them effectively, and steer their business toward its success. They are intelligent and able to utilize their skills, time, resources, and energy effectively. They are emotionally stable and healthy. They set reasonable, realistic goals and determine the ways to achieve the goals without fuss, have good communication skills as well as the ability to judge people and trust them accordingly. They have business acumen even without attending any business school and have the right instinct to make the right decision at the right time. They have the ability to make maximum use of the available resources and do not fear failure and are able to solve problems and seek solutions to existing problems easily.

Some Other Traits of Entrepreneurs:

- **Leadership:** An entrepreneur is a natural leader with the vision and the drive to do things right and steer his company toward success with ease.
- **Confidence:** He has to be self-confident, confident in his plans as he has carefully researched them and has mastered the skills necessary to implement them carefully.
- **Energetic:** They have amazing capacity for hard work and are energetic, motivating those that come in contact with them on account of their drive and determination.
- **Creative and Innovative:** This will be an essential criterion to design and sell products that are interesting which offer several benefits and have a competitive edge, making sure they capture the target market on launch without much difficulty.
- **Organized:** Entrepreneurs have to be highly organized and systematic, making it possible to achieve things in a much shorter time. The ability to deliver anything that has been

promised on time and the ability to stick to schedules are necessary for a person to be a successful entrepreneur.

- **Have Trouble Being Subordinates:** They usually are strong-willed and have trouble working under someone else.
- **Highly Competitive:** They are very competitive and will strive offer better services and products than the competition.
- **Will Not Hesitate To Take Risks:** Risks are part of any business, and a successful entrepreneur will have the knack of taking calculated risks that will only benefit the business.
- **Will Not Hesitate To Seek Help When Necessary:** They will hire necessary staff to help them in areas where they are not very confident.

These are some of the traits of entrepreneurs, which can be used as a checklist to determine if someone has the capability to be an entrepreneur. If you do start your own business, be sure to use the services as well as products offered by some firms to help new entrepreneurs like you succeed.

Distinction between Entrepreneur and a Manager

An entrepreneur is someone who seeks new and original ways of doing something, often used to describe a businessperson who finds a new way of advertising or advancing a new product or the product itself. A manager is someone who organizes the members of a workforce and delegates responsibility to those who can do the job

Distinction between an Entrepreneur and a Manager

Point of Distinction	Entrepreneur	Manager
1. Goal Management	An entrepreneur starts a venture by setting up a new enterprise for his personal gratification.	But the main aim of a manager is to render his service in an enterprise already set up by someone.
2. Status	Entrepreneur is the owner of enterprise.	A manager is the servant in the enterprise.
3. Risk	An entrepreneur bears all risks and uncertainty involved in the enterprise.	A manager being a servant does not bear any risk involved in the enterprise.
4. Rewards	Entrepreneur for his risk bearing role receives profits. It is not only uncertain and irregular but can at times be negative.	Regular can never be negative.
5. Innovation	As an innovator he is called as change agent who introduces goods and services to meet changing needs of the customers.	A manager executes the plans of the entrepreneur. Thus, a manager translates the ideas into practice.

Fig. 1.3: Distinction between an Entrepreneur and a Manager

At the heart of every new venture and start-up, company is a "structural conflict", which often poses a threat to the continued existence of the organization. This conflict can be summed up by the following statement: "The very qualities necessary to set up a new business, are the qualities which will adversely affect the smooth running of that business, sometimes, fatally".

The "structural conflict" arises from the fact that the entrepreneur, who has taken significant personal and commercial risks to set up the business, who has worked day and night to strengthen and promote it, at some point discovers that the business is working well and he can sit back, relax, and enjoy the fruits of his labors. But the typical entrepreneur is not the type to take things easy; he continues to be actively involved in the day-to-day activities of the company, which is growing quickly and now requires well-organized administration. His involvement can lead to hostility and tension, which damage the organization's ability to function and even to survive.

Let's summarize the significant differences between the entrepreneur and the manager:

1. Behavioral Differences: The typical entrepreneur wants to "be in control" of his life (which is often the reason why he started the business), of his business and especially of his employees. The professional manager, on the other hand, enters a company which needs to delegate authority, since it has reached the stage in its development where the entrepreneur can no longer "do it all himself".

2. Management Style: The entrepreneurial management style is very demanding, leaving very little room for error, and none at all for actual failures, since in most cases the business is a "one man show", even if there are other employees. The professional manager, however, must be tolerant of failure (and see it as a basis for learning) and develop an administrative team, since a basic assumption is that responsibility in the organization must pass from the "all-knowing" entrepreneur to people who still have to learn about the business.

3. The Moving Force: Entrepreneurial management is characterized by concepts such as "entrepreneurship", "creativity", "innovation", and so on, indicators of the desire to create "something from nothing". Professional management is characterized by concepts such as "order", "organization", "procedures", and so on, indicating the desire to organize and maintain what exists.

4. Growth: Entrepreneurial management is noted for its ability to react quickly and effectively to new business opportunities. This ability is the foundation for rapid growth of the company in its entrepreneurial stage. Professional management is noted for medium and long term strategic planning, which leads to controlled growth of the company during the process of establishment.

5. Organizational Structure: The entrepreneurial organization is characterized by its informal, flexible structure, which allows it to adapt to changes required by its rapid growth. Professional management, on the other hand, requires a formal and fairly rigid organizational structure, which leaves no room for rapid reactions to business opportunities, but protects the organization from sudden collapse.

6. Decision Making: The entrepreneur usually makes decisions, even those of critical importance for his business, on the basis of his own personal intuition and "gut feelings". The professional manager makes decisions after collecting detailed information and reaching operative conclusions, while relying on experts both from within and outside the organization.

7. Definition of Aims: The entrepreneur describes his organization in terms of "vision", "dream" and "mission" and manages to give his employees the feeling that they are working for a higher aim than just marketing a product and/or service.

The professional manager describes the company aims in terms of market segments, yield per worker and profitability.

8. Attitude to Money: Although the accepted myth is that entrepreneurs are driven by the desire for power and money, both theoretical and empirical studies have shown that typical entrepreneurs are in fact driven by the desire for success rather than power. This means that, in the eyes of most entrepreneurs, while money is a welcome by-product of their efforts, it is not the reason for their efforts.

The professional *business manager,* on the other hand, looks at the business he manages through "financial eyes" and defines its aims (usually in the short term only) purely in financial terms.

9. Attitude to Risk: The myths describe entrepreneurs as "wild risk-takers", although many studies have shown that in fact the typical entrepreneur is very good at assessing risks. On the other hand, the professional manager, who sees his task as strengthening and maintaining the company, is naturally afraid of risks and tries to maintain the status quo.

Characteristic	Entrepreneur	Manager
Behavior Characterized by	Desire for Control	Delegation of Authority
Management Style	One-man Show	Management Team
Driving Force	Creativity – Innovation	Establish and Preserve the *Status Quo*
Organizational Growth	Rapid Reaction	Strategic Planning
Organization Structure	Informal, Flexible	Organized
Decision-Making	Intuitive	Collect Information and Seek Advice
Definition of Aims	In terms of "Vision"	In Commercial Terms
Attitude to Money	A By-product	Measure of Success
Attitude to Risk	Calculated Risks	Avoidance of Risks
Organizational Culture	"Entrepreneurial Culture"	"Management Culture"

Fig. 1.4: Functions of an Entrepreneurs and a Manager related to Business Activities

10. Company Culture: The typical entrepreneur does not usually try to define a "culture" for the organization he sets up, since in most cases he himself is the organization. The literature defines this situation as "the entrepreneurial organizational culture", characterized by large doses of charisma and "manipulativeness". The professional manager does try to establish a well-defined company culture, based on company values on one hand and commercial aims on the other.

In the light of the foregoing, we can conclude that there is a world of difference between the "entrepreneurial manager" and the professional manager, and indeed this was true until the last decade. But, it has become clear in recent years that the ideal manager will be one who knows how to combine certain traits of the professional manager, such as order and discipline, with entrepreneurial characteristics such as quick reaction to business opportunities, creativity and the ability to fill employees with a sense of vision and challenge.

Functions of Entrepreneurs

The entrepreneur can identify opportunities to start a business either as a manufacturer or as a distributor, for entrepreneurship exists in every field of economic endeavor. Manufacturing activities require a relatively high capital investment and a greater degree of entrepreneurial abilities than distribution activities. Entrepreneurship has also been developed in the trading sector. A manufacturing entrepreneur demonstrates his entrepreneurial talents by bringing out new products while a trading entrepreneur performs his entrepreneurial functions in creating demand for the business in which he deals.

Entrepreneur performs various primary functions from the stage of starting an enterprise to its success level. These functions are in the sequential manner.

1. ***Planning:*** Planning is the first step in the direction of setting up of an enterprise. He prepares blue print of proposed project in a formal systematic format it is submitted to the authorities concerned for obtaining the legal sanction for the venture.

Planning process involves the following steps:

(a) Scanning of the best and suitable idea.
(b) Selection of product line.
(c) Determination of type of business organization. (Individual or partnership or corporate)
(d) Estimation of the capital needed.
(e) Selection of capital resources.
(f) Selection of location.
(g) Studying the government, rules, regulation and policies.
(h) Selecting the way to fulfill the government formalities.
(i) Study of availability of labor force.
(j) Study of market and market strategy to be adopted

Functions of Entrepreneur

I. Primary function	II. Other functions	III. Functions important for developing countries
1. Planning	1. Diversification of production.	1. Management of share resources.
2. Organization	2. Expansion of the enterprise.	2. Dealing with public bureaucracy.
3. Decision making	3. Maintaining cordial employer and employee relations	3. Acquiring and assembly of the factory.
4. Management	4. Tackling labor problem.	4. Engineering.
5. Innovation	5. Co-ordination with outside organizer	5. New product.
6. Risk bearing		6. Parallel opportunities.
7. Uncertainty bearing.		7. Marketing.
		8. Management.
		9. Customer relation.
		10. Public bureaucracy.

Fig. 1.5: Functions of an Entrepreneur

2. ***Organization:*** An entrepreneur co-ordinates, assembles and supervises land, labor and capital during the promotion stage and at the performance stage for optimum utilization of the resources. Efficient expansion and growth of the enterprise largely depends on the efficiency of the organizational networks employed and monitored by the entrepreneur.

3. ***Decision Making:*** Arther H. Cole has described the entrepreneur as a decision maker. As a decision maker he takes various decisions regarding following matters;
   (a) Determination of the business objective of the enterprise.
   (b) Decision regarding procurement of machine, material, men, money and market.
   (c) Decision regarding requisition of efficient technology and new equipments.
   (d) Decision regarding development of a market for the product.
   (e) Maintenance of good relations with public authorities and with society at large.

4. ***Management:*** The management with reference to entrepreneur stands for not only the working of the venture but also managing of the day-to-day problems. In includes future

expansion and policies in the long run. Direction of men, machine, material, money, organizing land, labor and capital for the enterprise.

5. ***Innovation:*** Implies "doing of new things or doing of things that are already being done in a new way", Schumpeter considered economic development as a desire dynamic change brought by entrepreneur by instituting new combinations of production. According to him innovation may occur in any one of the following five forms.
   (a) Launching of new product in the market.
   (b) Introduction of new technology in the production.
   (c) Creation of new market.
   (d) Discovery of new and better source of raw material.
   (e) Creation

6. ***Risk Bearing:*** An entrepreneur undertakes the responsibility for loss that may arise due to unforeseen contingencies in future. He guarantees interest to creditors, wages to labor, and rent to the landlord and risk can be insured.

7. ***Uncertainty Bearing:*** Risk which cannot be insured against and it is incalculable. Entrepreneur bears uncertainty refers to the uncertain trends of market; trade credits, etc., which by its nature cannot be insured or capitalized or salaried too.

Types of Entrepreneurs

Types of Entrepreneur / Classification

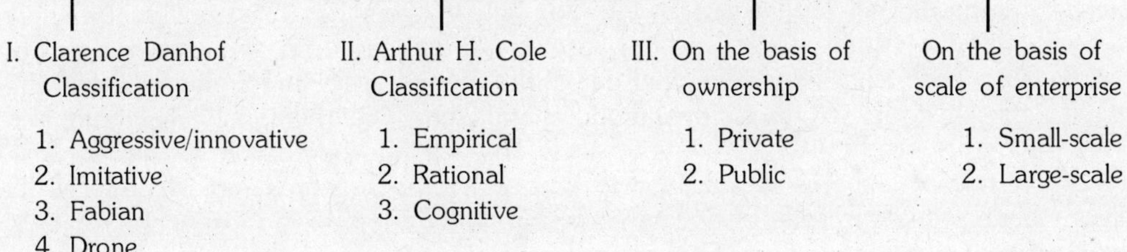

Fig. 1.6: Types of Entrepreneurs

I. Clarence Danhof Classification

He classified entrepreneur into four types.

1. ***Innovative:*** Innovative entrepreneur is one who assembler and synthesis information and introducer new combination of factors of production. Example of innovative entrepreneur who has innovated in a replicate industry is Nand Kishore Chaudhary. He brought automation, supply-chain management, and professional business practices to the mundane process of carpet weaving and distribution in the desert state of Rajasthan, India. By implementing modern production practices and ERP technology, he was able to grow a small business, **Jaipur Rugs,** that he would run from his home into a world-class production and distribution company, which employed 40,000 workers and generated $21 million in revenue in 2008. This is in a land where PCs were, until recently, as scarce as rainwater.

2. ***Imitative:*** Imitative entrepreneur is also known as adoptive entrepreneur. He simply adopts successful innovation introduced by other innovator. These entrepreneurs are most suitable for developing countries because such countries prefer to imitate the technology, knowledge and skill already available in more advanced countries. The Cochin Shipyard is a good example of the result of imitative entrepreneurship. The Shipyard has been constructed using the innovative technology provided by the Mitsubishi

Heavy Industries Ltd. of Japan. Imitative entrepreneurs are most suitable for the underdeveloped nations because in these nations people prefer to imitate the technology, knowledge and skill already available in more advanced countries. In highly backward countries there is shortage of imitative entrepreneurs also. People who can imitate the technologies and products to the particular conditions prevailing in these countries are needed. Sometimes, there, is a need to adjust and adopt the new technologies to their special conditions. Imitative entrepreneurs help to transform the system with the limited resources available. However, these entrepreneurs face lesser risks and uncertainty than innovative entrepreneurs. While innovative entrepreneurs are creative, imitative entrepreneurs are adoptive. One more examples is Walton has introduced its motorbikes, refrigerators, televisions and other electronic appliances in Bangladesh not being the original inventor of those products.

3. ***Fabian:*** The Fabian entrepreneur is timid and cautious. He imitates other innovations only if he is certain that failure to do so may not damage his business. Kodak, a company that happened to be the market leaders in producing analog cameras but they did not realize the change and the introduction of the Digicam. For that they lost their leadership, having lost the leadership they have diversified the business in producing the Digicams instead of producing Analog cameras.
4. ***Drone:*** His entrepreneur activity may be restricted to just one or two innovations. He refuses to accept or adopt changes in production even at the risk of reduced returns. Such entrepreneurs may even suffer losses but they do not make changes in production methods. They are laggards as they continue to operate in their traditional way and resist changes. When their product loses marketability and their operations become uneconomical they are pushed out of the market. They are conventional in the sense that they stick to conventional products and ideas. The traditional industries of Kerala are characterized by drone entrepreneurs. The coir and bamboo industries are still in the hands of laggards who refuse to innovate. One more example is Citycell Telecom Bangladesh, in spite of having knowledge they didnt do innovation.

II. Arthur H. Cole Classification

He classifies entrepreneurs as:

1. **Empirical**: He is an entrepreneur hardly introduces anything revolutionary and follows the principles of rule of thumb.
2. **Rational**: The rational entrepreneur is well informed about the general economic conditions and introduces changes which took more revolutionary.
3. **Cognitive**: Cognitive entrepreneur is well informed, draws upon the advice and services of experts and introduces changes that reflects complete break from the existing scheme of enterprise.

III. Classification on the Basis of Ownership

1. **Private:** Private entrepreneur is motivated by profit and it would not enter those sectors of the economy in which prospects of monetary rewards are not very bright
   - *(a)* **Founder entrepreneurs:** Those entrepreneurs who are the founder of the business. They are the ones who conceptualize a business plan and then put in efforts to make the plan a success. (Example, Dirubhai Ambani of the Reliance Group)
   - *(b)* **Second generation operators of family owned business:** They are entrepreneurs who have inherited the business from their fathers or forefathers (Mukesh Ambani and Anil Ambani sons of Dirubhai Ambani)

(c) **Franchises:** It is a method of doing business wherein the parent owner licenses his trademarks and tried and proves methods of doing business to a franchisee in exchange for a recurring payment. Example: MacDonalds has given its franchisee operation to local players after thorough scrutiny and proper training.

(d) **Owner manager:** When a person buys a business from the founder and then invests his time and resources in it then he is called as owner manager.

2. **Public Entrepreneurship:** In the underdeveloped countries government will take the initiative to share enterprises.

IV. Classification Based on the Scale of Enterprise

(a) **Small-scale:** This classification is especially popular in the underdeveloped countries. Small entrepreneurs do not possess the necessary talents and resources to initiate large-scale production and introduce revolutionary technological changes.

(b) **Large-scale:** In the developed countries most entrepreneurs deal with large-scale enterprises. They possess the financial and necessary enterprise to initiate and introduce new technical changes. The result is the developed countries are able to sustain and develop a high level of technical progress.

V. Classification Based on the Development Angle

1. **Prime mover:** This entrepreneur sets in motion a powerful sequence of development, expansion and diversification of business.
2. **Manager:** Such an entrepreneur contributes does not initiate expansion and is content just staying in business.
3. **Minor innovator:** This entrepreneur contributes to economic progress by finding better use for existing resources.
4. **Satellite:** This entrepreneur assumes a supplier's role and slowly moves towards a productive enterprise.
5. **Local trading:** Such an entrepreneur limits his enterprise to the local market.

VI. Classification Based on Types of Entrepreneurial Business

1. **Manufacturing:** An entrepreneur who runs such a business actually produces the products that can be sold using resources and supplies. For example, apparel and other textile products, chemical and related products, electronics and other electrical equipment, fabricated metal products, industrial machinery and equipment , printing and publishing, rubber and miscellaneous plastic products, clay etc.
2. **Wholesale:** An entrepreneur with such a business sells products to the middle man.
3. **Retailing:** An entrepreneur with such a business sells products directly to the people who use or consume them.
4. **Service:** An entrepreneur in this business sells services rather than products.

TYPES OF ENTREPRENEURS

I. Intrapreneur: A person within a large corporation who takes direct responsibility for turning an idea into a profitable finished product through assertive risk-taking and innovation. Intrapreneurship is known as the practice of a corporate management style that integrator risk taking and innovation approaches, as well as the reward and traditionally thought of as being the province of entrepreneurship.

Companies benefit from Intrapreneurship because it can function as a means of overcoming aspects of corporate bureaucracy that impede innovation allowing companies to remain creative and hence competitive. Moreover, Intrapreneurship can remedy the loss of challenging and rewarding jobs, which can lead to greater job satisfaction and productivity.

Workers who are given freedom to experiment are often associated with the innovation process and the development of new products, services, or businesses within corporations. Intrapreneurship researchers refer to this freedom to experiment as innovative culture. According to Howard Oden in *Managing Corporate Culture Innovation, and Intrapreneurship,* research indicates that Intrapreneurship succeeds when companies provide their innovators with support, encouragement, and an atmosphere that promotes innovation. Specifically, Oden enumerated a host of attributes often found in innovative cultures, including:

1. Long-term strategic and cultural leadership: Upper-level management provides long-term strategies and challenging goals for the company's innovation.

2. Promotion of innovation and intrapreneurship: The company encourages new ideas and new ways of doing things at all levels and promotes risk taking.

3. Flexibility and adaptability: The company does not have a hierarchical structure, rather a flat structure, and the innovation process involves different team of workers, not different levels of management.

4. Collaboration and teamwork: The company encourages teamwork and collaborative innovation.

5. Ongoing learning: Workers are expected to improve their skills and learn new ones continuously.

6. Toleration of failure: Since some innovations fail to bear fruit, companies must accept failure as part of the innovation process in order to keep intrapreneurs free from the fear of failure.

Companies that foster innovation usually possesses these and other related characteristics that allow intrapreneurs to seek solutions and generate new ideas, processes, products, or services, while not disrupting the regular flow of business. Although innovation can and does occur in any environment, too rigid and authoritarian corporate culture definitely can stifle the initiative and creativity of Intrapreneurs.

Intrapreneurs are entrepreneur who took in an existing business. Most big business do well because there are employees who manage there business in a unique way. They have characteristics that set them apart from other employees. They apply their entrepreneurial skills to turn the business into a competitive business and because they work in big businesses, they are called Intrapreneur. They do not own a business but rather manager a business and is paid a salary. Examples of Intrapreneurship are:

A lot of companies are known for their efforts towards nurturing their in-house talents to promote innovation. The prominent among them is "Skunk Works" group at Lockheed Martin. This group formed in 1943 to build **P-80 fighter jets**. Kelly Johnson was the director of the project, a person who gave "14 rules of intrapreneurship".

At "**3M**" employees could spend their 15% time working on the projects they like for the betterment of the company. On the initial success of the project, 3M even funds it for further development.

Genesis Grant is another 3M intrapreneurial program which finances projects that might not end up getting funds through normal channels. Genesis Grant offers $85,000 to these innovators to carry forward their projects.

Robbie Bach, J Allard and team's XBOX might not have been feasible without the Microsoft's money and infrastructure. The project required 100s of millions of Dollars and quality talent to make the product.

Example of Intrapreneurship: A classic case of intrapreneurs is that of the founders of Adobe, John Warnock and Charles Geschke. They both were employees of Xerox. As employees of Xerox, they were frustrated because their new product ideas were not encouraged. They quit

Xerox in the early 1980s to begin their own business. Currently, Adobe has an annual turnover of over $3 billion.

Features of Intrapreneurship: Entrepreneurship involves innovation, the ability to take risk and creativity. An entrepreneur will be able to look at things in novel ways. He will have the capacity to take calculated risk and to accept failure as a learning point. An intrapreneur thinks like an entrepreneur looking out for opportunities, which profit the organization. Intrapreneurship is a novel way of making organizations more profitable where imaginative employees entertain entrepreneurial thoughts. It is in the interest of an organization to encourage intrapreneurs. Intrapreneurship is a significant method for companies to reinvent themselves and improve performance.

In a recent study, researchers compared the elements related to entrepreneurial and intrapreneurial activity. The study found that among the 32,000 subjects who participated in it, five percent were engaged in the initial stages of a business start-up, either on their own or within an organization. The study also found that human capital such as education and experience is connected more with entrepreneurship than with intrapreneurship. Another observation was that intrapreneurial startups were inclined to concentrate more on business-to-business products while entrepreneurial startups were inclined towards consumer sales.

Another important factor that led to the choice between entrepreneurship and intrapreneurship was age. The study found that people who launched their own companies were in their 30s and 40s. People from older and younger age groups were risk averse or felt they have no opportunities, which makes them the ideal candidates if an organization is on the look out for employees with new ideas that can be pursued.

II. Techno-preneurs: Entrepreneurs who combines their technological and entrepreneurial skills are known as techno-preneurs. They are currently taking the world by storm. They are mostly found in IT, engineering technology and biotechnology industries.

III. Co-preneurs: When couples such as husband and wife to work together as co-workers, or co-owners of their entrepreneurial business they are known as co-preneurs. These couples combine their expertise. They rely on each other's strengths in running the business. Both members of a couple will have equal say in the business.

IV. Corporate Cast-offs and Dropouts: People who are retrenched or who voluntarily resign from the corporate sector are sometimes known as corporate cast-offs and dropouts. Such people often decide to start their own businesses. These people have the advantage of management and working experience. They often became consultants and workshop facilitators.

V. Social Entrepreneurs: People or organizations that start an entrepreneurial business to develop and benefit the community are called social entrepreneurs. They may make a profit, but their motivation is to give a service that will uplift and improve the lives of a specific society. The benefits they provide are, for example, services, buildings, scholarship and employment.

VI. Women Entrepreneurs: Modern day women who are stepping beyond their traditional roles into the so-called men's world by starting and running successful entrepreneurial enterprises are known as women entrepreneurs. In the past, women were marginalized and their talents and abilities not recognized. They mostly did household work or held inferior positions in the work place.

CONCEPT OF ENTREPRENEURSHIP

Entrepreneurship is the indivisible process flourishes when the interlinked dimensions of individual psychological entrepreneurship, entrepreneur traits, social encouragement, business opportunities, government policies, availability of plenty of resources and opportunities coverage towards the common good, development of the society and economy.

Entrepreneurship is the process of identifying opportunities in the market place, arranging the resources, required to pursue these opportunities and investing the resources to exploit the opportunities for long-term gains. It involves creating wealth by bringing together resources in new ways to start and operate an enterprise.

According to **Cole,** "Entrepreneurship is the purposeful activity of an individuals undertaken to initiate, maintain and aggrandize profit by production or distribution of economic goods and services.

According to **Higgins,** "It is meant the function of foreseeing investment and production opportunities organizing an enterprise to undertake a new production process, raising capital, hiring labor, arranging the supply of raw materials finding site, introducing a new technique, discovering new resources or raw materials or selecting top managers for day to day operations of the enterprise.

Many definitions of entrepreneurship can be found in the literature describing business processes. The earliest definition of entrepreneurship, dating from the eighteenth century, used it as an economic term describing the process of bearing the risk of buying at certain prices and selling at uncertain prices. Other, later commentators broadened the definition to include the concept of bringing together the factors of production. This definition led others to question whether there was any unique entrepreneurial function or whether it was simply a form of management. Early this century, the concept of innovation was added to the definition of entrepreneurship. This innovation could be process innovation, market innovation, product innovation, factor innovation, and even organizational innovation. Later definitions described entrepreneurship as involving the creation of new enterprises and that the entrepreneur is the founder.

Considerable effort has also gone into trying to understand the psychological and sociological wellsprings of entrepreneurship. These studies have noted some common characteristics among entrepreneurs with respect to need for achievement, perceived locus of control, orientation toward intuitive rather than sensate thinking, and risk-taking propensity. In addition, many have commented upon the common, but not universal, thread of childhood deprivation, minority group membership and early adolescent economic experiences as typifying the entrepreneur.

Entrepreneurship vs. Small Business

Many people use the terms "Entrepreneurs" and "Small business owner" synonymously. While they may have much in common, there are significant differences between the entrepreneurial venture and the small business. Entrepreneurial ventures differ from small business in these ways;

1. **Amount of wealth creation:** Rather than simply generating an income stream that replaces traditional employment, a successful entrepreneurial venture creates substantial wealth, typically in excess of several million dollars of profit.
2. **Speed of wealth creation:** While a successful business can generate several million dollars of profit over a lifetime, entrepreneurial wealth creation often is rapid, for example, within 5 years.
3. **Risk:** The risk of an entrepreneurial venture must be high, otherwise, with the incentive of sure profits many entrepreneurs would be pursuing the ideas and the opportunity no longer would exist.
4. **Innovation:** entrepreneurship often involves substantial innovation beyond what a small business might exhibit. This innovation gives the venture the competitive advantage that results in wealth creation. The innovation may be in the product or service itself, or in the business processes used to deliver it.

To conclude entrepreneurship is set of activities performed by an entrepreneur thus, entrepreneur proceeds entrepreneurship. The relationship between an Entrepreneur and Entrepreneurship.

Entrepreneur	Entrepreneurship
Person	Process
Visualiser	Vision
Organizer	Organization
Decision maker	Decision making
Innovator	Innovation
Risk bearer	Risk bearing
Motivator	Motivation
Creator	Creation
Leader	Leadership
Manager	Management
Initiator	Initiation
Planner	Planning
Technician	Technology
Communicator	Communication
Administrator	Administration

Fig. 1.7: Relationship between an Entrepreneur and Entrepreneurship

THEORIES OF ENTREPRENEURSHIP

The theory of entrepreneurship is particularly interesting in that it sees the entrepreneur as the "driving force" behind the economic process. When a market requires agents to interact with only limited knowledge and in a state of genuine ignorance as to the eventual outcomes, there is a constant need for coordination. In a competitive open market process, entrepreneurs play just such a role through the discoveries they make. Even more importantly, competition and entrepreneurship promote long-term growth and development.

A consistent universal theory does not exist in entrepreneurship, but rather it consists of several different approaches including psychology, sociology, anthropology, regional science and economics. No common theoretical framework, even if demanded for rigorously, exists to synthesize the different points of views. Some trials to develop multidimensional approach to entrepreneurship study the problems also mainly from perspective of the above mentioned well-established disciplines.

Economic theory intrinsically paints entrepreneurial individuals as self-interested economic actors, issuing from the same mold as **Adam Smith's** butcher, brewer, and baker. The alternative would be to assume that entrepreneurs are motivated by benevolence or altruism, and neither economics (see Becker 1976) nor sociobiology, offers a theory of motivations that does not relate in some way to self-interest. Accordingly, economics posits implicitly that entrepreneurs maximize some subjective utility function in which pecuniary wealth and income (the objectives most commonly associated with entrepreneurship) are but two among many disparate variables. Other utility variables include such intangibles as status and ideological preferences.

Innovation Theory of Joseph Schumpeter, whose "creative destruction" (of stationary equilibrium) metaphor (1942) has become synonymous with entrepreneurship. Innovating new and improved goods and services, new and expanded markets, and improved production methods, organizational structures, and supply sources were the functions that Schumpeter attributed to the entrepreneur, (1937). Influential theory of the firm added transaction-cost minimization to Schumpeter's function list, implying that "in the absence of transactions costs, there is no economic basis for the existence of the firm" (Coase 1988), and, consequently, no role for the business entrepreneur. A refined list of entrepreneurial functions can be assembled now from books written by entrepreneurs such as Donald Trump (1987), by executives such as Jack Welch (2005), and by economists such as marketing guru Michael Porter (1980, 1985). Schumpeter anticipated that the separation between business ownership and control (see Berle and Means 1932) would eventually transform these functions into routine institutional tasks. Despite considerable specialization since Schumpeter's time, however, individuals continue to produce sparkling examples of entrepreneurship.

Schumpeter saw entrepreneurial functions as occupying a small part of the entrepreneur's overall time and effort, the remaining time being spent on mundane and routine matters, such as office and personnel management, purchasing, marketing, and dealing with constraining laws and regulations (a less time-consuming task in Schumpeter's day). The Schumpeterian entrepreneur did not make a career out of entrepreneurship *per se*. Instead, he mixed entrepreneurship with other activities within the firm, earning a normal return on most labor and human capital as well as a separate, residually determined return on entrepreneurial capital. Schumpeter's entrepreneur was motivated not only by pecuniary profit and perquisites, but also by the intangible rewards stemming from a love for the game and a desire for recognition and respect.

Harvey Leibenstein's X-efficiency Theory has recently applied to analyze the role of the entrepreneur. Basically, X-efficiency is the degree of inefficiency in the use of resources within the firm; it measures the extent to which the firm fails to realize its productive potential. Productive potential is identified with the point on Neo classical production frontiers. X-efficiency arises either because the firm's resources are used in the wrong way or because they are wasted, that is, not used at all. He also stresses that the supply of entrepreneurship "depends on alternate opportunities available to potential entrepreneurs, as well as on the value society places on entrepreneurship as an activity versus the alternative occupations available to the entrepreneurs. In some cases employment in the civil service, the professions, political careers, careers in church organizations, [and] military organizations may carry greater prestige than entrepreneurship, and this will influence the supply"

Leibenstein identified two main roles for the entrepreneurs. The first role is input completion, which involves making available inputs that improve the efficiency of existing production methods or facilitate the introduction of new ones. The role of the entrepreneur is to improve the flow of information in the market. The second role, is filling, is closely asking to the arbitrage function emphasized by Kirzner. Leibenstein provides a very vivid description of gap filling, visualizing the economy as a net made up of nodes and pathways.

According to **Theory of Market Equilibrium** (Hayek), the absence of entrepreneurs in Neo-classical economics is intimately associated with the assumption of market equilibrium. The elasticity of bank credit causes a disparity between the natural and market rate of interest. The ultimate cause of instability in the business world in the elasticity of bank credit but the trace the consequences are not through variations in consumers expenditures, but through the change in volume of real investment by entrepreneurs. This theory tells us that sectoral balance in economic system is essential steady economic development.

The role of the entrepreneur is one of the most pivotal elements in the economic theories of the Austrian School. Instead of a set of static equilibrium models with pristine assumptions, the Austrians elucidate an emergent market revolving around the dynamic actions of entrepreneurs in an uncertain environment, a perpetual state of disequilibrium. Professors Joseph Schumpeter and Israel Kirzner, two of the most prominent entrepreneurial theorists, both agree on the fundamental role of the entrepreneur in the market process, and that economics ought to focus on disequilibrium. However, they interpret the function and purpose of the entrepreneur in two starkly contrasting ways. Schumpeter argued that it is a small cluster of entrepreneur-innovators that cause disequilibrium in the market with revolutionary new inventions, and that this unstable process will ultimately morph capitalism out of existence. Kirzner both incorporates the entrepreneurial nature of the market to a broader range of human action, and takes an optimistic approach, arguing that the entrepreneur instead alleviates disequilibrium and brings the market closer to equilibrium and economic harmony.

According to **Harward School Theory** (Cole, 1949), "entrepreneurship comprises any purposeful activity that initiate, maintain or develop a profit-oriented business, in interaction with internal, economic, political and social circumstances of business". This approach emphasized two types of activities like organizational and the sensitivity to the environmental characteristic that affect decision making. So, entrepreneurs operate under fairly uncertain circumstance.

Despite its stress on the human factor in the production system, the Havard tradition never explicitly challenged the equilibrium – obsessed orthodox economic theory. This was challenged by the neo-Austrian School who argued that disequilibrium, rather than equilibrium, was the likely scenario and as such, entrepreneurs operate under fairly uncertain circumstances. The essence of entrepreneurship consists in the alertness of market participants to profit opportunities. A typical entrepreneur, according to Kirzner (1979), is the arbitrageur, the person who discovers opportunity at low prices and sells the same items at high prices because of intertemporal and interspatial demands.

Risk Bearing Theory Frank Knight (1885-1972), first introduced the dimension of risk-taking as a central characteristic of entrepreneurship. He adopts the theory of early economists such as Richard Cantillon and J. B. Say, and adds the dimension of risk-taking. This theory considers uncertainty as a factor of production, and holds the main function of the entrepreneur as acting in anticipation of future events. The entrepreneur earns profit as a reward for taking such risks.

Alfred Marshall in his *Principles of Economics* (1890), held land, labor, capital, and organization as the four factors of production, and considered entrepreneurship as the driving factor that brings these four factors together. The characteristics of a successful entrepreneur are, thorough understanding of the industry, good leadership skills and foresight on demand and supply changes and the willingness to act on such risky foresights Success of an entrepreneur however depends not on possession of these skills, but on the economic situations in which they attempt their endeavors. Many economists have modified Marshall's theory to consider the entrepreneur as the fourth factor itself instead of organization, and which coordinates the other three factors.

The sociological theory entrepreneurship holds social cultures as the driving force of entrepreneurship. The entrepreneur becomes a role performer in conformity with the role expectations of the society, and such role expectations base on religious beliefs, taboos, and customs. **Max Weber** (1864-1920), held religion as the major driver of entrepreneurship, and stressed on the spirit of capitalism, which highlights economic freedom and private enterprise. Capitalism thrives under the protestant work ethic that harps on these values. The right combination of discipline and an adventurous free-spirit define the successful entrepreneur.

McClellands Theory of Achievement Motivation holds that people have three motives for accomplishing things: the need for achievement, need for affiliation, and need for power. Need for achievement and need for power drive entrepreneurship. He considers entrepreneurs as people who do things in a better way and makes decisions in times of uncertainty. The dream to achieve big things overpowers monetary or other external incentives. His experiment revealed that traditional beliefs do not inhibit an entrepreneur, and that it is possible to internalize the motivation required for achievement orientation through training.

Peter Drucker (1909-2005), holds innovation, resources, and an entrepreneurial behavior as the keys to entrepreneurship. According to him entrepreneurship involves. (1) Increase in value or satisfaction to the customer from the resource. (2) Creation of new values and (3) Combination of existing materials or resources in a new productive combination

Psychological theories such as those developed by **McClelland** pay attention to personal traits, motives and incentives of an individual and conclude that entrepreneurs have a strong need for achievement. A similar focus is found in locus of control theories that conclude that an entrepreneur will probably have strong internal locus of control. This means that an entrepreneur believes in his or her capabilities to commence and complete things and events through his or her own actions. **Brockhaus** (1982), suggests that an internal locus of control, even if it fails to distinguish entrepreneurs, may serve to distinguish the successful entrepreneur from the unsuccessful one. How do we measure success of entrepreneur? Success is a relative concept that can also be measured differently in different contexts. If success is measured in relation to the fulfillment of the goals and objectives of a particular entrepreneur, self-employed could also be classified as successful if their businesses generate continuously a satisfactory (in relation to their goals) level of living. On the other hand, high-growth ventures may be considered unsuccessful if they are not able to offer high enough ROI to their investors.

According to Shaver and Scott (1991, 31) Murray (1938), saw a need as a force "in the brain region" and the specific need for achievement was defined as:

"To accomplish something difficult, to master, manipulate, or organize physical objects, human beings, or ideas, to do this as rapidly and as independently as possible, to overcome obstacles and attain a high standard, to excel oneself to rival and surpass others and to increase self-regard by the successful exercise of talent".

Entrepreneurship: An Integrative Behavioral Framework

The key elements identified are Personal Resourcefulness, Achievement Orientation, Strategic Vision, Opportunity Seeking and Innovativeness.

Personal Resourcefulness

The root of the entrepreneurial process can be traced to the initiative taken by some individuals to go beyond the existing way of life. The emphasis is on initiative rather than reaction, although events in the environment may have provided the trigger for the person to express initiative. This aspect seems to have been subsumed within 'innovation' which has been studied more as the 'change' or 'newness' associated with the term rather 'proactiveness'.

'Personal resourcefulness' in the belief in one's own capability for initiating actions directed towards creation and growth of enterprises. Such initiating process requires cognitively mediated self regulations of internal feelings and emotions, thoughts and actions as suggested by Kanungo and Misra (1992).

Achievement Orientation

While personal initiative and purposeful behaviour can be view as a good starting point of an entrepreneurial effort, many such initiatives fail. The archetype successful entrepreneur is supposed to epitomize achievement motivation (McClelland, 1961), which facilitates the creation and development of enterprises in competitive environments. While critics have raised serious questions regarding the unique or overarching significance of n-Ach in the emergence of entrepreneurship (Smelser, 1976), this element of personality has continued in the mainstream of entrepreneurship theory (Shaver and Scott, 1991). People with high n-Ach are known to seek and assume high degree of personal responsibility, set challenging but realistic goals, work with concrete feedback, research their environment and choose partners with expertise in their work (Kanungo and Bhatnagar, 1978). Such characteristics of high n-Ach people contribute to successful completion of tasks that they venture to take up. Hence, we see achievement orientation as a set of cognitive and behavioural tendencies that are oriented towards ensuring that outcomes such as enterprise creation, survival and growth are realized.

Opportunity Seeking

The context in which an individual brings to bear his/her initiative, achievement orientation and visioning have a strong bearing on what it produces; when these forces are directed towards realizing surplus or value in a market environment, over a period of time, we see the creation of enterprises. This perspective of the entrepreneur as a merchant adventurer, who in Cantillon's view balances out imperfections in the market (Gopakumar, 1995), in pursuit of what Bentham terms wealth, provided the historical basis for the development of entrepreneurship. The wealth is seen as the reward the entrepreneurial individual gains for the risk taken or exercise of judgment where there is greater possibility for error; this distinguishes between certain return from wage labour, and return from risk-oriented production for the market. Hence, 'opportunity seeking' would include one's ability to see situations in terms of unmet needs, identifying markets or gaps for which product concepts are to be evolved, and the search for creating and maintaining a competitive advantage to derive benefits on a sustained basis.

Innovativeness

Schumpeter (1949), went on to conceptualize entrepreneurs as persons who are not necessarily capitalists or those having command over resources, but as ones who create new combinations of the factors of production and the market to derive profit. Innovativeness refers to creation of new products, markets, product-market combinations, methods of production and organization, and the like that enable the enterprise to gain competitive advantage in the market.

It is evident that each of the dispositions referred to may be found in all types of individuals (entrepreneurs and non-entrepreneurs). Then how can we relate these dispositions to entrepreneurship? We propose that when these five elements converge at high intensities, in non-restrictive environments, it is likely to give rise to enterprise formation. Therefore, one may find individuals who had created enterprises in the past now turning weak because they may no longer be proactive enterprise creators; instead they may be content to play the role of managers in their stable business, or turn to community leadership, and the like. Hence, this perspective lends to a process view of entrepreneurship.

Characteristics of Entrepreneurship

1. ***Ability to create enterprise*:** Entrepreneurship is primarily an economic activity because it involves creation and operation of an enterprise. It is basically concerned with satisfying the needs of customer with the help of production and distribution of goods and services.
2. ***Organizing function:*** An entrepreneur brings together various factors of production for an economic use. He co-ordinates and controls the factors of production, efforts of use the persons engaged in his enterprise.
3. ***Innovation:*** Entrepreneurship is an automatic spontaneous and creative response to changes in the environment. It involves innovation of something new to cause dynamic change and spectacular success in the economy and create conditions for growth of the economy.
4. ***Risk bearing capacity:*** Risk is an inherent and inseparable element of entrepreneurship. He assumes the uncertainty of future. Entrepreneur's guarantees rent to the landlord, wages to employees and interest to the investors in the hope of earning more than the expenses.
5. ***Managerial and leadership functions:*** An industrial entrepreneur must have additional personality traits such as managerial and leadership skills. These qualities predominant orientation in the direction of productivity, working relation and creative integration along with desire to make profit. Entrepreneurship demands tactful handling of risk and uncertainties because new commodity and its acceptability is uncertain.
6. ***Gap filling:*** The gap filling between human needs and the available products and services lead to entrepreneurship. An entrepreneur identifies the gap and takes necessary corrective measures to fill the gap, to achieve his action oriented motive in the enterprise as an entrepreneur with the help of entrepreneurship process.

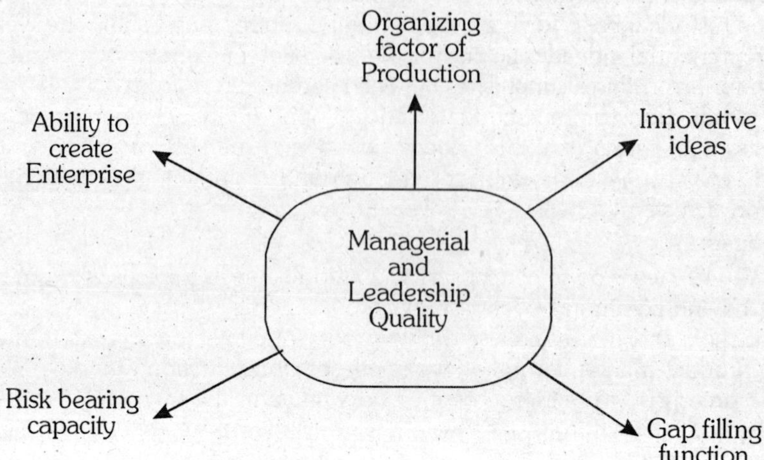

Fig. 1.8: Characteristic of Entrepreneurship

SCOPE OF ENTREPRENEURSHIP

Entrepreneurship and the economic development compliment each other. An economic system of country determines the nature and scope of entrepreneurship. It can bring about drastic changes in the very structure of the economy.

Entrepreneurship works in different ways in different economic system such as capitalism, socialism and mixed economy.

Capitalism: A capitalist economy represents free enterprise, means freedom to save and invest free competition, consumer sovereignty and very less interference from the government.

Price of the product will be determined on the basis of the force of demand and supply with reference to cost of production.

Socialism: Private entrepreneurship is absent in a socialist economic system. Economic and financial experts play important role in the development of entrepreneurship in the system. Such entrepreneurship mainly wants to serve the society not to make money or to make profit only.

Here central authority is appointed by the government make policies, frame plan and procedures for the proper and efficient mobilization of resources and allocation of resources into those industries of national prominence.

Mixed Economy: It is characterized by co-existence of both the public and private sectors in the same line of production and consumer goods are left to the private enterprises. Government undertakes the production of capital goods.

In a mixed economy restrictions are placed by the government to eliminate the problems of monopoly capitalism. Government under this type of economy curbs the growth of monopolies and encourages competition.

Thus entrepreneurship plays a great and vital role in all major economic system. Its importance stands beyond challenges and making of huge profit in every economic system.

GROWTH OF ENTREPRENEURSHIP IN INDIA

Before the arrival of the British India was a self-sufficient rural economy. Agriculture was the main source of livelihood. But there existed a well organized and well developed rural industry consisting of handicraft marble work and metal work.

The establishment of the British rule in India dealt a revere blow to the growth of trade and industry.

Lessons from Entrepreneurial History

From the foregoing historical review of entrepreneurship in India, the following conclusions may be drawn.

1. Before independence, most of the entrepreneurs emerged from a few business communities like Banias (Hindu and Jain), Parsis, Gujaraties, Chettiars etc. Entrepreneurship was in abundance among Indian but the climate was not conducive. In the absence of State assistance and institutional finance entrepreneurship became the close preserve of few wealthy families. After independence, the base of entrepreneurship has widened due to a series of measures, policies and programs of the government. Now entrepreneurs are drawn from various non-traditional cartel and communities.

2. This kind of entrepreneurial growth during the pre-independence period was quite in conformity with the experience of other countries. Initially trading community serves as the source of entrepreneurship. But once the roots of industrialization are laid entrepreneurial spatial permeate among other groups.

It is well known fact that when India won the political freedom. Its economy was quite stagnant, backward and underdeveloped. The country was facing the serious problem of poverty, unemployment and low levels of production, income and consumption. The government of free India had to face greater challenges and responsibilities for speedy growth of the economy for socio-economic welfare of the nation. As a matter of fact initially due to social backwardness and lack of education, the level of entrepreneurial ability in the country was very low. The government was very much keen to promote economic activities at a faster rate for maximum utilization of economic resources in order to attain economic progress and prosperity. The concept of mixed economy was adopted by the government and a very wide scope was left open for the activities in the private sector. Under such conditions, the government realized that without the active support of private entrepreneurs the tasks of speeding up the wheels of economic growth cannot be accomplished. Hence, the urgency of developing the entrepreneurship was recognized and several measures were taken by the government in this direction.

Sl. No	***Time Span***	***Growth of Entrepre-neurs***	***Factors leading to Growth of Entrepreneurship in India***
1.	1960 to 1970	10%	In 1948, immediately after Independence, Government introduced the Industrial Policy Resolution. This outlined the approach to industrial growth and development. It emphasised the importance to the economy of securing a continuous increase in production and ensuring its equitable distribution. After the adoption of the Constitution and the socio-economic goals, the Industrial Policy was comprehensively revised and adopted in 1956. To meet new challenges, from time to time, it was modified through statements in 1973, 1977 and 1980.Favorable policies for the development of entrepreneurship (two resources are most critical finance and managerial capabilities). Govt. started Industrial Investment corporations to support through credit schemes.
2.	1970 to 1980	5.7%	The Industrial Policy statement of 1973, *inter alia*, identified high-priority industries where investment from large industrial houses and foreign companies would be permitted. The Industrial Policy Statement of 1977, laid emphasis on the centralisation and on the role of small-scale, tiny and cottage industries. Reservation of some of the product to the SSI, Entrepreneurship Development Programs with well designed inputs for

			motivating, informing and skilling entrepreneurial individual started to spread entrepreneurship.
3.	1980 to 1990	8.5%	The Industrial Policy Statement of 1980, focussed attention on the need for promoting competition in the domestic market, technological upgradation and modernisation. The policy laid the foundation for an increasingly competitive export based and for encouraging foreign investment in high-technology areas. This found expression in the Sixth Five Year Plan which bore the distinct stamp of Smt. Indira Gandhi. It was Smt. Indira Gandhi who emphasised the need for productivity to be the central concern in all economic and production activities. The Govt. Support like, exemption, credit under priority sector lending from banks and financial institutions, marketing support through reservation of items for products from small scale industry sector for government purchases, providing infrastructure facilities like sheds, plots in industrial estates, technological support, new management techniques, training and entrepreneurship development programs.
4.	1990 to 2000	5.83%	Emerging entrepreneurs has to face challenges of competition from the opening up of economy to globalization, need for increasing exports and to meet World Trade Organization commitments. The policy support provided so far has acted a catalyst in promoting this sector. However, the planning commission felt an urgent need to review the policy measures so as to make this sector more growth oriented and enable it to withstand the pressure from global competition. Government will provide enhanced support to the small-scale sector so that it flourishes in an environment of economic efficiency and continuous technological upgradation. Foreign investment and technology collaboration will be welcomed to obtain higher technology, to increase exports and to expand the production base
5.	2000 to 2005	8.9%	The entrepreneurs are provided working capital by commercial banks and in some cases by cooperative banks and regional rural banks. Term loans are provided by SFCs, SIDCs, NSIC and NABARD. Financial assistance from NSIC and to some extent from SIDCs is available in the form of supply of machinery on hire purchase basis/deferred payment basis. Small sized SSI and tiny units also get some term loans from commercial banks along with working capital in the form of composite loans

Fig. 1.9: Growth of Entrepreneurship

The basic policy support of SSI sector had its roots in the Industrial Policy Resolution 1977, laid emphasis on reservation of items. The reservation economically viable and technologically feasible products to be exclusively manufactured by small-scale industry began with a list of 47 items which was gradually extended to too many products. At present 812 items are in the reserved list. The other policy support which could be listed are excise exemption, credit under priority sector lending from banks and financial institutions, marketing support through reservation of items for products from small-scale industry sector for government purchases, providing infrastructure facilities like sheds, plots in industrial estates, technological support, new management techniques, training and entrepreneurship development programmes. There were about 20 lakhs small-scale industry units in 1990-91 providing goods. Worth ₹ 1,55,340 crores exports order of ₹ 9,661 crores and providing employment to about 125 lakhs persons. The achievement of SSI sector in 1999-2000 were 32.25 lakh SSI units providing production of ₹ 5,78,299 crores, exports of ₹ 53,995 crores and providing employment to 177.30 lakh persons.

Though this sector has shown substantial progress, its major problems like inadequate credit flow from banks and financial institutions, inadequate infrastructure facilities, low quality standards of products, use of technology, plant and machinery and equipments and inefficient management techniques, are still inhibiting the sector. In addition to these, this sector has to face challenges of competition from the opening up of economy to globalization, need for increasing exports and to meet World Trade Organization commitments. The policy support provided so far has acted a catalyst in promoting this sector. However, the planning commission felt an urgent need to review the policy measures so as to make this sector more growth oriented and enable it to withstand the pressure from global competition.

India's vision of emerging as an economic power in the 21st century can be realized through the promotion and development of the small and medium enterprises.

Liberalization and globalization are the order of the day. The market forces will determine the systems and manner of production. The allocation of resources with in the sector must be governed by the criteria of efficiency, productivity and competitiveness. The Small-scale Industries will have to move from a regime of protective environment to a competitive environment. Small-scale industrial units feel apprehensive about globalization and the impact of the agreements with World Trade Organization (WTO).

Recent Trends

Under planned economy India has achieved remarkable progress in all the spheres of economy. It has developed almost all the sectors of the economy and succeeded in achieving the high levels of production, income and consumption. The rate of capital formation has considerably increased and the levels of savings and investments have also improved. The industrial sector of the country has shown significant progress in the field of production, employment and income generation. As a result, of this, India has become the tenth largest industrialized nation of the world. With the help of concerted efforts made by the government the image of the country in respect fo entrepreneurship has changed. Now in addition to the traditional form of entrepreneurship such as Gujarati, Marwari entrepreneurship, the modern version of entrepreneurship has emerged and a good number of modern entrepreneur particularly in the fields of technology have shown better performance. After introduction of economic reforms and the policies of globalization, modernization, diversification and expansion has enlarged the fields of economic activities.

Rapid progress in the field of science and technology has expanded the scope of innovations in production, processes, and techniques. It has now become essential to adopt a more mature and finer approach towards the concept of entrepreneurship. The government's efforts for entrepreneurial development and motivation have resulted in good impact in the field of small business and industry.

In the changing business scenario, the major driving forces are the customer, competition and change and they are contributing a lot in the market oriented process. It has been well recognized that through appropriately designed entrepreneurship development programs the things may improved significantly. There programmer are now playing a very important role particularly in developing entrepreneurial motivation, sharpening entrepreneurial traits and behavior, providing guidance for project planning and executing and identifying larger scope for greater industrial and business opportunities incentives and facilities. With the rapid growth of technical manpower, it is necessary to attract potential entrepreneur to small business and industry.

Both the Central Government and various State Governments are taking increased interest in promoting the growth of entrepreneurship. Individuals are being encouraged to form new businesses and are being provided such government support as tax incentives, buildings, roads, and a communication system to facilitate this creation process. The encouragement by the central and state governments should continue in future as more lawmakers are realizing that new enterprises create jobs and increase the economic output of the region. Every state government should develop its own innovative industrial strategies for fostering entrepreneurial activity and timely development of the technology of the area. The states should have their own state-sponsored venture funds, where a percentage of the funds has to invested in the ventures in the states.

Society's support of entrepreneurship should also continue. This support is critical in providing both motivation and public support. A major factor in the development of this societal approval is the media. The media should play a powerful and constructive role by reporting on the general entrepreneurial spirit in the country highlighting specific success cases of this spirit in operation.

Finally, large companies should show an interest in their special form of entrepreneurship-intrapreneurship-in the future. These companies will be increasingly interested in capitalizing on their Research and Development in the hyper competitive business environment today.

SCOPE OF ENTREPRENEURSHIP DEVELOPMENT IN INDIA

In India there is a dearth of quality people in industry, which demands high level of entrepreneurship development programme through out the country for the growth of Indian economy.

The scope of entrepreneurship development in country like India is tremendous. Especially since there is widespread concern, that the acceleration in GDP growth in the post reforms period has not been accompanied by a commensurate expansion in employment. Results of the 57th round of the National Sample Survey Organization (NSSO) show that unemployment figures in 2001-02 were as high as 8.9 million. Incidentally, one million more Indian joined the rank of the unemployed between 2000-01 and 2001-02. The rising unemployment rate (9.2% 2004 est.) in India has resulted in growing frustration among the youth. In addition there is always problem of underemployment. As a result, increasing the entrepreneurial activities in the country is the only solace. Incidentally, both the reports prepared by Planning Commission to generate employment opportunities for 10 crore people over the next ten years have strongly recommended self-employment as a way-out for teaming unemployed youth.

We have all the requisite technical and knowledge base to take up the entrepreneurial challenge. The only thing that is lacking is confidence and mental preparation. We are more of a reactive kind of a people. We need to get out of this and become more proactive. What is more important than the skill and knowledge base is the courage to take the plunge. Our problem is we do not stretch ourselves. However, it is appreciative that the current generations of youth do not have hang-ups about the previous legacy and are willing to experiment. Theses are the people who will bring about entrepreneurship in India.

At present, there are various organizations at the country level and state level offering support to entrepreneurs in various ways. The Govt. of India and various State Govts. have been implementing various schemes and programs aimed at nurturing entrepreneurship over last four decades. For example, NISIET provides systematic training, dissemination of the information and data regarding all aspects of entrepreneurship and conducting research in entrepreneurship. Then there are various Govt. sponsored scheme for the budding entrepreneurs.

Various Chambers of Commerce and apex institutions have started organizing seminars and workshops to promote entrepreneurship. Incidentally, various management colleges have incorporated entrepreneurship as part of their curriculum. This is indeed a good development. This shows the commitment of the Govt. and the various organizations towards developing entrepreneurial qualities in the individuals.

Promoting Entrepreneurship

In India, where over 300 million people are living below the poverty line, it is simply impossible for any government to provide means of livelihood to everyone. Such situations surely demand for a continuous effort from the society, where the people are encouraged to come up with their entrepreneurial initiative.

Encouragement at attitudinal and social level

In the future, innovation and entrepreneurship needs to be encouraged at Social levels, Governmental levels and Managerial levels. There must be a social attitude that views innovations with positive attitude and reject an innovation only when it is not acceptable.

Encouragement at physical level

At this level the encouragement will refer to two aspects necessary for entrepreneurship to thrive, one is the provision of venture capital and the other being infrastructural support. A real example is Export Processing Zones which are performing extremely well when given the support.

What will be the qualities needed to succeed in this new world?

First and foremost, we need the entrepreneurial spirit. Outside India, this spirit has been very evident in the IT industry. 35% of the start-ups in Silicon Valley are by Indians. We need to have similar risk-taking ability within the country as well. Entrepreneurs need more than technical talent, more than business savvy. What they need is the indefatigable energy and incurable optimism that enables them to take the road less traveled and converts their dreams into reality. It is a force that beckons an individual to pursue countless opportunities. Entrepreneurs must learn how to overcome the risk of failure, or of vulnerability. The institutions can give them valuable insights and also support them in entrepreneurial activities.

Role of Entrepreneurship in Economic Development

Entrepreneurs play a significant role in the development of the economy. An entrepreneur affects the lives of many people as it creates new job, provides the product, develops the technology, and provides feasible solutions to the existing social and environmental problems. Entrepreneurship creates wealth for the person and for the country. It is the most powerful force of the economy.

Today, the business environment and technological advancements present complex challenges to an individual's entrepreneurial drive and determination. Most entrepreneurs prefer to outsource projects to save on operating cost. They even outsource the most critical process of their manufacturing or business operations.

Entrepreneurs need the right interest to initiate the right motivation for starting a small business or project. Interest comes from the dream to improve an individual's lifestyle, social status, control of future, and raise standard of living. Entrepreneurship is a natural medium to fulfill economic aspirations, channel drive and energy, and build something for themselves.

Economic development essentially means the process of upward change whereby the real per capital income of a country increases over a period of time.

Entrepreneurship plays a vital role in economic development. Entrepreneurs serve as the catalysts in the process of industrialization and economic growth.

Entrepreneurs are the keys to the creation of new enterprises that energize the economy and rejuvenate the established enterprises that make up the economic structure. Entrepreneurs initiate and sustain the process of economic development in the following ways:

1. ***Capital formation:*** Entrepreneurs mobilize the idle savings of the public through the issues of industrial securities. Investment of public savings in industry results in productive utilization of national resources. Rate of capital formation increases which is essential for rapid economic growth. Thus an entrepreneur is the creator of wealth.
2. ***Improvement in per capita income:*** Entrepreneur locate and exploit opportunities, they convert the latent and idle resources like land, labor and capital with national income and wealth in the form of goods and services. They help to increase in the country, which are important yardsticks for measuring economic growth.
3. ***Generation of employment:*** Entrepreneur generates employment both directly and indirectly. Directly, self-employment as an entrepreneur offers the best way for independent

and honorable life. Indirectly by setting up large and small scale business units they offer jobs to millions by this way entrepreneurs solved the unemployment problem in the country.

4. ***Balanced regional development:*** Entrepreneur in the public and private sectors help to remove regional disparities in economic development. They set up industries in backward areas to avail the various concession and subsidies offered by the Central and State Governments. Public sector steel plants and private sector industries by Modis, Tatas, Birlas and others have put the hitherto unknown places on the international park.
5. ***Improvement in living standards:*** Entrepreneurs set up industries which remove scarcity of essential commodities and introduce new products. Production of goods on mass scale and manufacture of handicrafts etc, in the small scale sector help to improve the standard of life of a common man. These offer goods at lower costs and increase variety in consumption.
6. ***Economic independence:*** Entrepreneurship is essential for national self reliance. Industrialists help to manufacture indigenous substitutes, to hitherto imported products there by reducing dependence on foreign countries. Businessmen also export goods and services on a large scale and thereby earn the scarce foreign exchange for the country such import substitution and export promotion help to ensure the economic independence of the country without which political independence has little meaning.
7. ***Backward and forward linkages:*** An entrepreneur initiator change which has a chain reaction. Setting up of an enterprise has several backward and forward linkages for example the establishment of a steel plant generates several ancillary units and expands the demand of iron ore, coal etc. these are backward linkages. By increasing the supply of steels, the plant facilitates the growth of machine building, tube making, utensil manufacturing and such other units are the forward linkage, thus entrepreneurial behavior is critical to the long term validity of every economy.
8. ***Growth of Entrepreneurs:*** In terms of benefiting the people, the development of small and medium scale industries and businesses offered many advantages. Most important perhaps, aimed the mounting un employment, are the small and medium enterprise, which generate more jobs and often use labor intensive methods of production industries and businesses of smaller size also work towards promoting better income distribution and development of entrepreneurship in addition to broader benefits as rural industrialization and increased export earnings.

One of the most potentially profitable areas of human resources development for small and medium sized enterprises is the training of entrepreneurs and managers such training programs should be as well rounded as possible, covering not only the basics of business, technology and so forth but also helping the trainees to identify their aptitudes motivating them, encouraging innovative thinking and helping to develop personalities and attitudes geared for success. Indeed, small industries and business are ideally suited for capitalizing on entrepreneurial skills, initiative and talent and thus assisting in building a dynamic private sector in developing countries.

The growth of entrepreneurship in the port planning period has been significant for ex: between 1960 and 1995, the number of private companies went up from 26,000 to nearly 3,25,000. It will be seen that the maximum increase in the number of factories was in the case of industries which by virtue of their being in the small / medium scale sector are less regulated than others. The increase in the number of factories in industries like tobacco and related products, wood and wood products, rubber and its products, jewellery, photographic and optical goods, watches and clothes, medical, surgical and scientific equipments, sports, equipment, cold storage etc was more than forty times during the period 1959-1995.

The growth in the number of small entrepreneurs has been encouraging. The small scale sector has grown in volume from 16,000 units in 1950, to over 26 lakh units by the end of 1995.

The range of items produced by the small scale sector ranges from consumer good to high precision items.

Not only the number of entrepreneurs grown over a period of time but also the scope of entrepreneurship is getting broad based. Earlier for a large proportion of firms in India, the basic unit of entrepreneurship was the extended family. This tendency is now getting dilated. A study conducted a few years back by the Economic and Scientific Research Foundation (ESRF) indicates that out of a sample of entrepreneurs studied by them around 1/5 of them were managers and engineers before they turned entrepreneurs. It was found that around 57% of the new entrepreneurs in starting small scale units were motivated by the experience of their previous employment. Entrepreneurship in these cases was not necessarily in born but largely acquired.

BARRIERS OF ENTREPRENEURSHIP:

Barriers to the development of the entrepreneurship: There are societies which have more entrepreneurial than others; such societies promote entrepreneurial behavior with the net result of more entrepreneurs in societies. In general, there are certain factors which either support entrepreneurship or act as barriers to the entrepreneurship, such factors can be (1) Economic, (2) Social (3) Political and (4) Psychological. The negative influence creates inhibiting milieu to the emergence of entrepreneurship. These barriers can be economic and non- economic

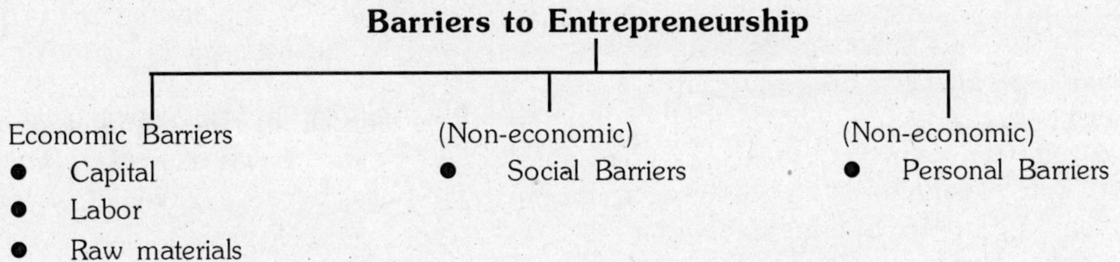

Fig. 1.10: Barriers to Entrepreneurship

1. **Economic Barriers:** These barriers are capital, labor and raw material.
   (a) **Capital:** Capital is the most important pre-requisite for setting up the new enterprise. Capital is a lubricant to the process of production. Money is the resource that helps mobilize other resources like men, materials and machines. Entrepreneurship in any society increases with the increase in the supply of capital. Thus, lack of availability of capital with any society or nation acts as a serious barriers for promoting entrepreneurship in that society
   (b) **Labor:** Cheap labor of a developing country may prima facie appear to be strength in promoting enterprises, but the fact of the cheap labor is often unproductive or has a low level of productivity. This unskilled and low productive labor acts as a barrier in setting up the modern enterprise. However, by using labor saving innovations, the innovative entrepreneurs have ability to overcome the disadvantages of high cost labor in developed economies.
   (c) **Raw Materials:** In the absence of raw material no enterprise can be established and in absence of enterprises the entrepreneurs do not emerge. The lack of raw material is normally the greatest economic barrier for the growth of entrepreneurship. Japanese society has been able to overcome the problem of lack of raw materials through innovative management systems.
2. **Non-economic Barriers:** A large number of sociological and psychological factors act as the non economic barriers. Many societies and regions endowed with skilled labor and

natural material have remained entrepreneurially backward because of such factors. The factors which prevent the emergence of entrepreneurs can be classified as social/ environmental and personal barriers.

(a) **Social Barriers:** People are bound by their cultural values. Every society lays down some unwritten norms of acceptable behavior. All members of that society are required to follow norms. If such norms are broken, the society does not approve of the resultant behavior and exert direct and indirect pressure in the individual to conform to a particular way, purely because it is customary. Some of the social behavior are:

(i) **Practical Values:** Most of the progressive societies discourage day dreaming, playfulness and fantasy by their adult members. Such behavior is considered childish and unsuitable for grown up persons. The adults are required to be functional in their thinking.

(ii) **Emotional Block:** Entrepreneurship involves risk, besides financial risk, it involves emotional risk. Every entrepreneur runs a risk of making mistakes and incurring losses in his venture. People usually understand two situation i.e., either a person is right or wrong. Throughout one's life one is trying to find right answer to the problems and avoid the wrong solutions. Right answer is considered as failure. A fear of being wrong, leads one to construct elaborate justification for own judgments and actions.

At work, people use a number of productive tools like sales forecast, market research, budgets etc., so that in case of failure their decisions are perceived as rational. In case the decision proves to be wrong one can defend it by claiming that high level of prudence was exercised. People are afraid of not only making mistakes but more so of appearing foolish because of such mistakes. This emotional fear is a barrier to entrepreneurship.

(b) **Personal Barriers:** In the given environment few people take up the career of entrepreneurship. Even among the societies which are considered entrepreneurially progressive only selected few venture to set-up their own enterprise. This indicates that personal barriers prevent people from launching their enterprises. The following factors as personal barriers to entrepreneurship development.

(i) **Lack of Sustainable Motivation:** Most people enjoy initiating a new product. People generally have a need for new experiences and involvements. Being a part of new development furthers their status need. They appreciate the idea of being a part of something new. Thus, it is easy to attain a high level of commitment, enthusiasm and motivation at the initiation stage of an enterprise. However, when the project is off the ground or faces first obstacle, the initial level of interest gradually wanes off. The entrepreneurship requires a sustained level of motivation and commitment and it is often difficult to sustain this motivation against the initial hurdles.

(ii) **Difficulty and Ambiguity:** Some people are very compulsive and become upset if the order of their physical life is violated. Such people prefer every thing to be at its right place. This is also true of mental processes and in certain cases of ability. A new structure or sequence may also be impaired because of lack of orderliness. Although orderliness provides the advantages of aesthetics and functionality, yet it is important to have an ability to cope with asymmetry. When a new method of working is initiated, it is not possible to forsee every eventually and predict the exact outcome. Some of the things cannot be simulated and have to be tested only by experience. In many situations the data collected will be imperfect and ultimately decisions

will be based upon opinion and value judgments. People who excessively depend on order will find it a hindrance.

(iii) **Inability to Dream:** It is a general experience that when a deadline is fixed for an assignment, the initial progress is slow and gains pace when the last minute approaches. Most people do their best work immediately prior to the final deadline as they allocate enough time in the early stages of the assignment to store up the information in their subconscious. The entrepreneur needs to use both parts of his intellect, the subconscious for incubation of ideas and conscious for solution of problems.

(iv) **Imitative Entrepreneurs:** Imitative entrepreneurship is characterized by readiness to adopt successful innovations by innovating entrepreneurs. They first imitate techniques and technology innovated by others.

(v) **Lack of Clean Perception:** Several times lack of perception creates lot of difficulties, the main difficulties are due to lack of knowledge of new techniques and new technology and products.

Problems of Entrepreneurship

The problems of entrepreneurship are divided into two groups external and internal.

External Problems: External problems are those which result from factors beyond the control of the entrepreneur the availability of power and other infrastructure facilities required for the smooth running of small scale industries (SSI).

1. Mega Businesses: The advent of much bigger competition, especially regional and national chains, into the same geographical area as the small businesses poses an immediate threat to the small business. With deeper pockets of money, they can outspend the smaller businesses in every aspect of their business and still charge lesser for their products. Big businesses control the entire supply chain and they can manipulate it to meet the customer needs dynamically. They also leverage high-end technology to keep costs under control in a way that cannot be emulated by the small-scale businesses. They also have several partnerships which allow them to bundle a wide variety of products and services for their customers.

2. Finding and retaining qualified workers: Small-scale businesses cannot pay the level of wages or benefits that can be offered by large-scale businesses. Another key factor is the visibility of the organization. With the death of the patriarchic organization that supported a life-long employment, employees are looking at employers to provide life-long employability. A smaller organization is unable to provide the depth of knowledge or experience that will enable an employee to make a major transition into another company or business entity easily. Hence most small businesses find it much more difficult to hire and retain skilled workers. They have to look for employees within a reduced pool of candidates, some of whom may be transient. Many small-scale businesses rely on family members to fill some of the roles. Lack of skilled employees or the inability to hire them can result in a lot of additional costs in terms of time (and money) spent in recruitment and retraining. When an employee leaves, the new employee must spend a non-trivial amount of time being trained so that he or she can replace the old employee.

3. City, State and Central regulations: Every business owner has to comply with a variety of regulations, including obtaining permits and licenses, and health and safety inspections. While necessary for the overall well-being of the community, this poses a burden on the business owner in terms of time and money that could have been spent growing the business. Environmental regulations, workplace rules and the paperwork associated with tax compliance contribute to most of the burden. Although all businesses have to bear the burden of regulations, small businesses are more affected. Research shows that small firms employing less than 20 employees have a higher annual regulatory burden per employee than firms employing more than 500 employees. A disproportionate amount of regulatory work has to be done by the employer and other owners which leave less time for management that would yield better results for the company.

4. Economic uncertainty: Many small business owners are at the mercy of economic conditions that they have no control on. This is particularly true in cities and towns dependent on large employers. When such employers decide to lay off hundreds of workers, it adversely affects several small scale businesses that were built around those employers. Recent developments such as globalization have affected small business owners drastically, particularly those manufacturing products that can now be imported at very low cost. Events such as multi-national treaties and new trade blocs happening elsewhere in the world have impact on small businesses affected by the new economic conditions.

5. Being up to date with technology: Small business owners are generally laggards in technology adoption. The primary reason is the high cost of keeping up with the latest technological innovations in the particular industry, especially in the last decade, when the pace of technological advancement has been phenomenal. The major risk with a small business living with outdated technology is that of competition leapfrogging over it and quickly reducing it to oblivion. Also new technology usually brings the promise of reduced costs and/or increased revenue. One cannot talk about new technology without mentioning the Internet. Most small businesses are not technically savvy enough to use the Web effectively. They also cannot afford to hire expert site designers to map out a good online strategy.

6.Access to adequate capital: Many small businesses find it very difficult to obtain finance, especially if they are starting up or if they are a relatively new business. Lenders require security for loans and many smaller businesses do not have adequate security to be accepted. Changes in banking organizations, particularly large mergers, have affected lending to small-scale entrepreneurs. During downturns in the economy, the capital crunch grows more severe as banks reduce lending to riskier borrowers, to which category small businesses belong.

Internal Problems:

Internal problems are those which are not influenced by external forces. The internal problems affecting the industries relate to organization, structure, production channel distribution channel, technical know-how, training industrial relations and inadequacy of management etc.

The problem of industries, whether in the small scale sector or in the organized sector are almost identical. However, the organized sector is financially very strong and its resources are large; it can face problems more effectively, whereas the small sector, because of its weak financial structure, and limited resources face many problems. Large sector proprietor employ trained and experienced managers, in small sector proprietor, director, owner has to take care of all the problems. The large sector can influence its raw material suppliers, its customers and at times even the government is framing its policies, but the small entrepreneur is helpless in this respect.

In general the internal problems faced by the entrepreneurs are:

1. **Finance:** One of the several problems faced by the entrepreneur is the non availability to carry out its operations. Generally a small business begins with a small base. Many of the units in the small sector lack the credit worthiness required to raise as capital from the capital markets. As a result, they heavily depend on local financial resources and are frequently the victims of exploitation by the money lenders. These units frequently suffer from the lack of adequate working capital, either due to delayed payment of dues to them or locking up of their capital in unsold stocks. Banks also do not lend money without adequate collateral security or guarantees and margin money, which many of them are not in a position to provide.
2. **Raw Materials:** Another major problem is the procurement of raw materials. If the required material are not available, they have to compromise on the quality or have to pay a high price to get the good quality materials. Their bargaining power is relatively low due to the small quantity of purchases made by them. Also, they cannot afford to

take the risk of buying in bulk as they have facilities to store the materials. Because of general scarcity of metals. Chemicals and extractive raw materials in the economy, the small scale sector suffers the most. This also means a waste of production capacity for the economy and loss of further units.

3. **Managerial Skills:** Small business is generally promoted and operated by a single person, who may not possess all the managerial skills required to run the business. Many of the small business entrepreneurs possess sound technical knowledge but are less successful in marketing the output. Moreover, they may not find enough time to take care of all functional activities. At the same time they are not in a position to afford professional managers.
4. **Labour:** Small business cannot afford to pay higher salaries to the employees, which affects employee willingness to work hard and produce more. Thus, productivity per employee is relatively low and employee turn over is generally high. Because of lower remuneration offered, attracting talented people is a major problem in small business organizations. Unskilled workers join for low remuneration but training them is a time consuming process. Also unlike large organizations, division of labour cannot be practiced, which results in lack of specialization and concentration.
5. **Marketing:** Marketing is one of the most important activities as it generates revenue. Effective marketing of goods requires a thorough understanding of the consumer's needs and requirements. In most cases, marketing is a weaker area of small organizations. These organizations have to depend excessively on middlemen, who at times exploit them by paying low price and delayed payments. Further, direct marketing may not be feasible for small business firms as they lack the necessary infrastructure.
6. **Quality:** Many small businesses do not adhere to desired standards of quality. Instead they concentrate on cutting the cost and keeping the prices low. They do not have adequate resources to invest in quality research and maintain standards of the industry, nor do they have the expertise to upgrade technology. In fact maintaining quality is their weakest point, when competing in global markets.
7. **Capacity Utilization**: Due to lack of marketing skills or lack of demand, many business firms have to operate below full capacity due to which their operating costs tend to increase. Gradually this leads to sickness and closure of the business.
8. **Technology:** Use of outdated technology is often stated as serious lacunae in the case of small industries, resulting in low productivity and uneconomical production.
9. **Sickness:** Prevalence of sickness in small industries has become a point of worry to both the policy makers and the entrepreneurs. The causes of sickness are both internal and external. Internal problems include lack of skilled and trained labour and managerial and marketing skills. Some of the external problems includes delayed payment, shortage of working capital, inadequate loans and lack of demand for their demands.

Environmental Factors Affecting Entrepreneurship

A complex and varying combination of financial, institutional, cultural and personality factors determines the nature and degree of entrepreneurial activity at any time. The personal backgrounds of the entrepreneurs are determined mainly by the environment in which they are born and brought up and work. A multitude of environmental factors determines the entrepreneurial spirit among people. The entrepreneurs in turn create an impact on the environment. The interaction between the entrepreneur and his environment is an ongoing process. At any given point of time, the entrepreneurs derive meanings from the environment prevailing at that time and try to adapt and change the environment to suit their needs.

The environment, particularly the external environment is dynamic. It keeps on changing and affects different organizations to a varying extent. The impact of environment on the organization depends largely on the degree to which the organization depends on the environment and organizational response to environmental changes. All the factors outside and inside (Individual, groups, machinery, equipment, procedures, rules, policies etc) an organization interact and affect the performance of the organization. Some of the environmental factors which hinder entrepreneurial growth are:

1. Sudden changes in Government policy.
2. Sudden political upsurge.
3. Outbreak of war or regional conflict.
4. Political instability or hostile Government attitude towards industry.
5. Excessive corruption among Government agencies.
6. Ideological and social conflicts.
7. Unreliable supply of power, material, finance, labour and other inputs.
8. Rise in the cost of inputs.
9. Unfavorable market fluctuation, recession and inflation.
10. Non cooperative attitudes of banks and other financial institutions.

Entrepreneurship is environmentally determined. The most important essential for the entrepreneurial growth is the presence of a favorable business environment. A healthy environment requires active social and cultural behavior of the people, efficient economic conditions, helpful and motivating Government policies, etc.

Recent Trends of Women Entrepreneurs

Women entrepreneur may be defined as the woman or a group of women, who initiate, organize and operate a business enterprise. According to the government of India, a woman entrepreneur is defined as "an enterprise owned and controlled by a woman and having a minimum financial interest of 51 per cent of the capital and giving at 51 per cent of the employment generated in the enterprise to women".

Women in general have been discriminated against male dominated society. Education beyond primary or at the most high school was rare. In general girls in rural and small towns are considered to be fit for cooking food and confine to home affairs. The participation of women in business is almost nil.

The report of the national committee on women status in society has made starting revelations. Major findings of the report are as:

(a) Decline in the sex ratio due to excessive mortality among women and female children.

(b) Disparity in access to healthcare and the widening gap between women and men literacy.

(c) Education and training facilities to women for employment is negligible.

(d) Sense of fear: Daily newspaper publishes reports about rape, bride burning, dowry death and wives beaten to death.

(e) Women are afraid of going out alone after dark and cannot go for shopping without male helpers.

Initially women tended to go in for traditional and home-based projects and the common perception even today is that women go in for garments, pickles, etc. This, however, is far from the truth. With the changing times a growing number of women are taking to non-traditional projects and succeeding as entrepreneurs. Female entrepreneurs quite often do not have technical knowledge, work experience and exposure to business world and there are certain other socio-cultural, environmental constraints, especially to women.

The growing economic power of women is difficult to measure. Statistics of women in management positions are scarce and unreliable. In many instances, a woman may run a company, but put her assets under the name of a male relative. But in specific industries, it is clear that women are making strides. In India, from 2006 to 2008, the number of women in the high-tech industry jumped nearly 60 per cent to about 671,000. Today, women make up about one-fourth of all information technology workers in India, according to the National Association of Software and Service Companies (NASSCOM), which collaborates with the Indian government to set policy and practices for the country's information technology industry.

Despite the hurdles, the next generation is expected to see even more women thrive in the work force. Several South Asian countries, including India, Bangladesh, Bhutan, Sri Lanka and the Maldives, have achieved gender parity at the primary school level, according to the World Bank. In Bangladesh, Sri Lanka, and the Maldives, gender parity has reached the secondary school level. In India, women make up more than 40 per cent of the students at engineering colleges, the steppingstones to stable, middle-class jobs, according to the Indian government. In the mid-1980s, no more than 8 per cent of engineering college students in India was women.

Example: Technology is one realm where women could break gender barriers and flourish as entrepreneurs, says Vinita Gupta, a prominent Indian-American businesswoman in California's Silicon Valley. She is best known as the first Indian-American woman to take a company public. Digital Link Corp., a telecommunications products company she founded in 1985, in Palo Alto, California, and ran as CEO, went public in 1994. She now sits on the boards of the Palo Alto Medical Foundation, the Indian School of Business and Maitri, a Silicon Valley nonprofit that assists women victims of domestic violence. (She was born in India, did her bachelor's in engineering in 1973, at the University of Roorkee (now the Indian Institute of Technology-Roorkee). She then went to the U.S. for her post-graduate master's education, to UCLA (the University of California, Los Angeles). She worked five years with GTE in its telecom group and eight years at Nortel (then called Bell Northern Research). She started Digital Link Corp. in 1985, where she was the CEO for about 20 years. She took the company public in 1994, re-privatized it in 1999 and continued until 2005, when she decided to retire, although she was its largest shareholder and continued as chairman).

The reasons of the slow progress of women entrepreneurs:

1. Women are known to have lower attachment to work and are, therefore, content with lower position;
2. They do not consider themselves as primary earners and withdraw from the labor force once family income reaches adequacy;
3. They lack education and training commensurate with men as marriages and home making take precedence;
4. They are less preferred to men in recruitment and selection because of legal and other problems.
5. Women are low paid, up keep is expensive. For example, a factory will have to appoint a doctor, a crèche and such other considerations.

Functions and Role of Women Entrepreneurs

Like a male entrepreneur a woman entrepreneur must perform five functions.

1. Explore the prospects of starting new enterprise.
2. Undertaking of risks and the handling of economic uncertainties.
3. Introduction of innovations.
4. Co-ordination, administration and control.
5. Routine supervision.

All these functions appear to be some what uneven in character for instance, risk taking and innovation are paramount for establishing or diversifying an enterprise. Coordination and supervision became increasingly important in improving the efficiency and assuming smooth, balanced operation of the undertaking. In women enterprises, usually the same lady performs all these functions. Most likely, she is also the owner of the enterprise.

Women entrepreneur can more easily undertake three types of industrial enterprises.

1. Operate purely as a sub contractor on raw materials provided by the customer.
2. Manufacture an item to the long or short term order of another enterprise, usually a large scale unit.
3. Manufacture the item for direct sale in the market.

Growth of Women Entrepreneur

In recent years women have made their mark in different walks of life and are competing successfully with men despite the social, psychological and economic barriers. This has been possible due to education, political awakening, urbanization, legal safeguards, social reforms etc.

In India women entrepreneur constitute a negligible proportion of the total entrepreneurs. Attitudinal constraints social traditions inhibits, the emergence of women entrepreneurs. "The typical women enterprises are the extension of kitchen activities i.e., the 3 Ps, pickle powder (Masala) and pappad, or the traditional cottage industries of basket making etc.

With the spread of education and the growing awareness among women they have entered into engineering, electronic, energy and many other industries. Various government agencies and voluntary bodies, like Mahila Mandals, have accelerated the growth of women entrepreneurs in the country.

PROBLEMS FACED BY WOMEN ENTREPRENEURS

1. ***Shortage of Finance:*** Women and small entrepreneur suffer from inadequate financial resources and working capital. They lack access to external funds due to absence of tangible security and credits in the market. They also face the problem of obtaining working capital for financing day to day operations of their enterprise. They often rely on personal savings and loans from family friends.
2. ***Inefficient Arrangements for Sales and Marketing:*** For marketing their products they are often at the mercy of the middlemen who exploit them, but the elimination of middlemen is difficult to run their business.
3. ***Shortage of Raw Materials:*** Women entrepreneurs find it difficult to obtain the raw material for their production, as the prices of most of the material high for them to purchase or they have buy in bulk which they cannot due to low finance.
4. ***Stiff Competition***: Most of the women entrepreneurs have to face stiff competition from the organized industries and male entrepreneurs, as they are not properly organized.
5. ***High Cost of Production:*** Another problem for women entrepreneurs is the high cost of production. Government assistance in from of grants and subsidies to some extent reduces this difficulty, but still it is necessary to increase efficiency and expand productive capacity and thereby reduce the cost.
6. ***Low Mobility:*** This is one of the biggest problems of the women entrepreneurs, they often tend to get accommodate in small town. In order to expand their business they have to come out and increase their mobility to understand the market.
7. ***Family Responsibilities:*** In India, its women's duty to take care of the family and children. Most of the married women entrepreneurs have to make a fine balance between business and home. Their success in this regard also depends on the support of their husband and family. Despite of modernization, tradition and family responsibilities slow down the movement and development of women entrepreneurs.
8. ***Social Attitudes:*** Despite of social equality, there is discrimination of the women in the society. In a tradition-bound society, women suffer from male reservations about a women's role and clarity.

9. ***Low Ability to Bear Risk:*** As women does not have property on their name and other financial institutions and family members also does not rely on the capacity of the women entrepreneurs, to spend the fund on their business. So they are having low ability to bear risk. Most of the women entrepreneurs lack entrepreneurial training, thus they lack growth and development in the field of their business.
10. ***Lack of Education:*** In India the literacy rate of women is low. Due to lack of education most of the women entrepreneurs are not aware of proper knowledge of the technological development. Lack of information and experience creates further problems in operating their business.
11. ***Low Need for Achievement:*** Women entrepreneurs lack the need for achievement, as they are proud to bask in the glory of their parent, husbands and sons etc. In the absence of urge to achieve, few women succeed as entrepreneurs.

Remedies to Solve the Problem of Women Entrepreneur

The following measures may be adopted to solve the problems faced by women entrepreneurs in India.

1. ***Finance Cells:*** In various public financial institutions and banks special cells may be opened for providing easy finance to women entrepreneurs. Effort should be made to provide finance at the local level. They must be provided at concessional rates of interest and on easy repayment basis.
2. ***Marketing Cooperatives:*** Encouragement and assistance must be provided to women entrepreneurs for setting up of their enterprises and marketing their products in the market. This will help them to eliminate the middlemen, who exploit their margin of profit.
3. ***Supply of Raw Materials:*** Scarce and imported raw materials may be made available to women entrepreneurs on priority basis.
4. ***Education and Awareness:*** It is necessary to change negative social attitudes towards women. Not only providing them education but also providing and encouraging them for their entrepreneurial activities.
5. ***Training Facilities:*** Training is essential for the growth and development of the entrepreneurship. Training schemes must be designed in such a way that women can take full advantage of it. Training is necessary for running successful enterprise.

Development of Women Entrepreneurs

Under 7th Five Year Plan special privilege was given to development of women. It suggested the following points.

(a) To treat women as specific target group in all development programs.

(b) To properly diversity vocational training facilities for women to suit their varied needs and skills.

(c) To encourage appropriate technologies, equipments and practice for reducing their drudgery and increase their productivity.

(d) To provide marketing assistance at the state level.

(e) To increase women's participation in decision making.

Associations of Women Entrepreneur

With the growth of women entrepreneurs a few association of women entrepreneurs have been set up both at international and national level. The main purpose of these association is to create a congenial environment for developing women entrepreneurs in rural and urban area they seek the following objectives.

1. To provide a meeting ground for women entrepreneurs.
2. To promote and develop feeling of unity and brotherhood among the entrepreneurs.
3. To develop self confidence and hope among women entrepreneurs.
4. To present the problems of women entrepreneurs before the concerned authorities for consideration and redressal.
5. To secure various concessions, subsidies and assistance for women entrepreneurs.
6. To conduct entrepreneurial development programs for women.
7. To organize seminar conference on entrepreneurship with the help of other national and international bodies.
8. To perform activities to improve the operational efficiency of women entrepreneurs.

Some of the Associations of Women Entrepreneurs are

1. Women entrepreneurs wings of NAYE. National Alliance of Young Entrepreneur.
2. Indian Council of Women Entrepreneur.
3. FICCI Ladies Organization (FLO).
4. National Commission on Self Employed Women in the Informal Sector.
5. World Association of Women Entrepreneur WAWE.
6. Associated Country Women of the World ACWW.

Rural Entrepreneurship

Since the Green Revolution there has been tremendous increase in the opportunities for development of farm entrepreneurship. If agricultural development program is to be speeded up farm entrepreneurship must be developed. According to Epstein, there are four characteristics of farm entrepreneurship, namely, social interaction, innovation and willingness to assume risk. The key factors affecting farm entrepreneurship are attitudes towards farming, pride in farming activities, upward striving and use of progressive techniques.

The cost of modern technology is beyond the means of small and marginal farmers. Cooperative credits societies and bank will have to provide institutional credits at subsidized rates. The government has to subsidize the cost of farms inputs. Farmers are unable to regulate the supply of food grains to the market. They suffer from shortage of finances and storage facilities. The Government of India has fixed procurement prices of essential farm products. The Food Corporation of India has established a network of foodgrain procurement centers all over the country. However, transport, communication, remittance and warehousing problems hinder its effort. There is need to develop infrastructural and electrification in rural areas.

Rural entrepreneurial development is a complex problem which can be tackled by the social, political and economic institutions. The sooner, they are established, the better it would be for the entrepreneurial development in the rural sector and the economic growth of the country

The problem is essentially both-sided which is development of one area at the cost of development of some other place, with concomitant associated problems of underdeveloped countries. For instance, we have seen unemployment or underemployment in the villages that has led to influx of rural population to the cities. What is needed is to create a situation so that the migration from rural areas to urban areas comes down. Migration *per se* is not always undesirable but it should be the minimum as far as employment is concerned. Rather the situation should be such that people should find it worthwhile to shift themselves from town sand cities to rural areas because of realization of better opportunities there. In other words, migration from rural areas should not only get checked but overpopulated towns and cities should also get decongested. The question is, is it really possible? If it is so, ways can always be found out. One is by forcibly stopping villagers from settling in the slums of towns and cities, making use of all powers to clear the slums so the villagers are forced to go back. But such practices have not achieved the desired results in the past. Apart from causing suffering to the poor people and adding to the expenditure for the Government, social tensions and economic hardships created by the government officials and their staff in every demolition of slums is not desirable from a same government. Moreover, when a slum is demolished people do not move out of urban locality. They only relocate to a nearby place because they are entrenched in the economy of the town or city. Though governments have tried out various schemes for generating incomes in the rural areas such government initiatives have not stopped people from moving out of villages to cities. This is because such government initiatives are not on their own capable of enabling people to earn adequately and ameliorate their conditions. There has to be some committed enterprising individual or a group of people who should be capable of making use of the government policies and schemes for the betterment of rural people. Some individuals who happen to be local leaders and NGOs and who are committed to the cause of the rural people have been catalystic agents for development. Though their efforts need to be recognized, yet much more needs to be done to reverse the direction of movement of people, i.e. to attract people to the rural areas. It means not only stopping the outflow of rural people but also attracting them back from the towns and cities where they had migrated. This is possible when young people consider rural areas as places of opportunities. Despite all the inadequacies in rural areas one should assess their strengths and build on them to make rural areas places of opportunities. This is much to do with the way one sees the reality of the rural areas. The way a survivor or a job seeker would see things would be certainly different from those who would like to do something worthwhile and are ready to go through a difficult path to achieve their goals. It isn't that there is a dearth of people with such mindset. But with time they change their minds and join the bandwagon of job seekers due to various compulsions. Enabling them to think positively, creatively and entrepreneurship purposefully is utmost for the development of rural areas. Young people with such perspective and with the help of rightly channelized efforts would usher in an era of rural entrepreneurship. In this country successful rural entrepreneurs would solve many of the chronic problems within a short time.

Constraints of Potential Rural Entrepreneurs and Development Inputs

Constraints	*Inputs*
1. Low self-image and confidence.	Motivational inputs, unfreezing and experience sharing by successful local entrepreneurs.
2. No faith on others includes friends.	Group building experiences
3. No exposure to industry/business.	Field visit to factories and big market.
4. Whom to contact for starting a venture, what formalities and procedures are to be followed.	Information inputs on procedures and formalities
5. How to know whether the identified business is a viable and sound proposition	Opportunity identification and guidance.
6. How to know whether the identified business is a viable and sound proposition	Market survey, project report preparation
7. How does one carry out bank-operations like filing up deposit and withdrawal slip etc.	Training in simple banking procedures
8. How to manage the business? simulation exercises.	Basic management orientation through
9. How to read and write accounts? Simple accounting in terms of writing income and expenditure.	Functional and numerical literacy.
10. Almost no technical skills.	Technical training (on-the-job training)

Training and Development of Rural Entrepreneur

A brief sketch of the training and support programs launched by the government is given to enable reader to get a comprehensive view of the effort of human resources development for rural entrepreneurship.

1. Training of Rural Youth for Self Employment (TRYSEM)

TRYSEM was launched by the Government of India in 1979, as a facilitating component of Integrated Rural Development Program (IRDP). Under this program rural youth are trained for self-employment in the field of agriculture and allied activities, industries and services. The basic components of the program are as follows:

(i) Identification of beneficiaries with entrepreneurial qualities
(ii) Identification of entrepreneurial opportunities
(iii) Training in motivation and skills
(iv) Provision of credits facilities
(v) Sharing of risk element by providing investment subsidy
(vi) Helping in provision of raw material and marketing and
(vii) Constant monitoring and follow up.

2. Prime Minister's Rozgar Yojana(PMRY)

PMRY was launched on 2nd October 1993 to assist educated unemployed youth to set up self-employment ventures. It relates to the setting up of the self employment ventures in all economically viable projects (except direct agricultural operations). The Schemes also seeks to associate reputed non government organizations in implementation of PMRY Scheme especially in the selection, training of the entrepreneurs and preparation of project profiles.

Schemes targeted for setting up of nearly 7 lakhs enterprises and consequent employment generation to more than one million educated unemployed youth in the last four years of the Eighth five Year Plan. The target for the year 2004-05 and 2005-06 under the Yojana has been enhanced from 2.20 lakhs beneficiaries to 2.50 lakh beneficiaries per annum for creation of additional employment opportunities in the rural non-farm sector.

3. Swaranjayanti Gram Swarozgar Yojana (SGSY)

SGSY was launched by Government of India in 1999, with a focus on providing effective self-employment through self-help group approach and activity cluster farmers and poor families below poverty line. The self-help groups are motivated through training and capacity building for taking up thrift and credit activity and start their own small rural enterprises through the financial assistance of Revolving Fund Assistance.

The Scheme also seeks to associate reputed non-governmental organizations in implementation of SGSY Scheme Rural Employment Generation Program (REGP): On the basis of recommendation of the High Power Committee submitted in May 1994, headed by the then Prime Minister of India, the KVIC launched Rural Employment Generation Program with effect from 1st Nov., 1995, for generation of two million jobs under the KVI sector in the rural areas of the country.

The main objectives of REGP are *(a)* to generate employment in rural areas *(b)* to develop entrepreneurial skill and attitude among rural unemployed youth *(c)* to achieve the goal of rural industries (d) to facilitate participation of financial institutions for credit flow to rural industries.

Need and Development of Rural Entrepreneurship

Innovative, workable, practical and functional paradigms of rural development are urgently required in the guest for sustainable rural communities–communities in which economic development is achieved in harmony with improvement in the quality of human life and where a healthy economy supports the quality of both human and ecological system. The need for and growth of rural industries has become essential in a country like India because of the following reasons:

1. Rural industries generate large-scale employment opportunities in the rural sector as most of the rural industries are labor intensive.
2. Rural industries are capable of checking rural urban migration by developing more and more rural industries.
3. Rural industries/entrepreneurship help to improve the per capita income of rural people thereby reduces the gaps and disparities in income of rural and urban people.
4. Rural entrepreneurship controls concentration of industry in cities and thereby, promotes balanced regional growth in the economy.
5. Rural entrepreneurship facilitates the development of roads, street lighting, drinking water etc. in the rural sector due to their accessibility to the main market.
6. Rural entrepreneurship can reduce poverty, growth of slums, pollution in cities and ignorance of inhabitants.
7. Rural entrepreneurship creates an avenue for rural educated youth to promote it as a career.

The majority of rural areas in India are vortices of unsustainably social and economic distress. A new development perspective is needed, which provides fresh insights and tools for improving a community's industry, commerce infrastructure and household behavior as a whole system. The goals of the project to develop rural area can be identified as follows:

1. To link mass of the population, tied to traditional means of production, into modern commercial sector of the economy.
2. To enhance the development of traditional agriculture by linking them to broader market and technological opportunities.
3. To bridge the gap between the development of the modern and the traditional sector of the economy.
4. To stimulate the development of entrepreneurship based on health and hygiene.

Institutions and individuals promoting rural development see entrepreneurship as a strategic development intervention that could accelerate rural development process.

The quantum of business and opportunities for socio-economic opportunities in the Indian rural sector are enormously enhanced level of attention of large corporation towards villages both for marketing of their product/services as well as part of CSR. (Corporate Social Responsibility) are noteworthy. Appropriate institutional framework promoter entrepreneurial development, practical mechanisms, for risk taking and risk sharing in the early and most uncertain stages of entrepreneurial ventures and the organizational system conducive to growing new and existing business.

Rural innovations not only improve the productivity and efficiency of local farmers or artisans, but also have significant environmental and social impact by developing eco friendly "appropriate" solution to local problems.

The development of rural entrepreneurs is a complex problem which can be tackled by the social, political and economic institutions. The sooner they are established the better it would be for the entrepreneurial development in the rural sector and the economic growth of the country.

1. Provide employment opportunities

Rural entrepreneurship is labor intensive and provide a clear solution to the growing problem of unemployment. Development of industrial units in rural areas through rural entrepreneurship has high potential for employment generation and income creation.

2. Check on migration of rural population

Rural entrepreneurship can fill the big gap and disparities in income rural and urban people. Rural entrepreneurship will bring in or develop infrastructural facilities like power, roads, bridges etc. It can help to check the migration of people from rural to urban areas in search of jobs.

3. Balanced regional growth

Rural entrepreneurship can dispel the concentration of industrial units in urban areas and promote regional development in a balanced way.

4. Promotion of artistic activities

The age-old rich heritage of rural India is preserved by protecting and promoting art and handicrafts through rural entrepreneurship.

5. Check on social evils

The growth of rural entrepreneurship can reduce the social evils like poverty, growth of slums, pollution in cities etc.

6. Awaken the rural youth

Rural entrepreneurship can awaken the rural youth and expose them to various avenues to adopt entrepreneurship and promote it as a career.

7. Improved standard of living

Rural entrepreneurship will also increase the literacy rate of rural population. Their education and self-employment will prosper the community, thus increasing their standard of living.

Major Problems/Challenges faced by Rural Entrepreneurship

1. ***Government Policies:*** Licensing, taxes and tariffs.
2. ***Management:*** In many small firms some individuals is responsible for the production and management.
3. ***Marketing and Finance Operations:*** The entrepreneur still has to make the decision relating to each of the above functions.
4. ***Technical Information:*** Lack of awareness on technology and processing.
5. ***Marketing:*** Large firms can afford transport, storage facility, advertising and product development efforts which an individual, more often, cannot.
6. ***Credit:*** Mostly forced to rely on personal savings, borrowing from friends and relatives and moneylenders.

Development of Rural Entrepreneurship

In **rural Indian economy** tiny and micro enterprises, creates huge employment opportunities; produces necessary goods and services to cater to the local requirements and contributes significantly to the development and growth of the nation. It helps inculcate growth with equity viz; both **women and men** alike mobilize savings and internal financial resources for entrepreneurial activities. In fact creations of micro enterprises are considered as an effective tool for sustainable livelihood, poverty alleviation and employment generation. Similarly, economics of micro finance makes it a compelling anti-poverty strategy. With a small amount, rural youth can establish a small business, repay the loan and still own the productive assets. Even in terms of narrow aims of increasing beneficiary incomes, micro-enterprise and micro finance development can succeed for vast majority of poor. The IISD model is a step towards a solution to a wide range of development problems with a main focus on wider strategy for poverty alleviation.

Pre-training Stage: under which the main activities are resource studies, campaigning and identification of potential entrepreneurs.

Training Stage: which focuses on the participants acquiring knowledge and skills in business opportunity, identification of activity, preparation of project report, market survey and feasibility, production and financial management etc. Through these phases and various other psychological and behavioral motivational exercises, case studies, role-plays, etc. the participants are motivated and trained how to successfully launch and manage their enterprises.

Post-training Stage: which aims at follow-up and regular monitoring of the trained potential entrepreneurs thus ensuring a good start-up rate. Post training Follow-up is an important activity after the completion of rural entrepreneurship development programs. In this context effective steps are taken to assist and guide to the trainees in setting-up their small enterprises for self-employment.

In encouraging entrepreneurship in rural areas, seeking leadership these characteristics are essential.

1. They can orchestrate people, strategies and technologies to fit caning environments.
2. They are usually creative risk takers.
3. They thrive on change and cope well with uncertainty.
4. They are determined and disciplined in implementing their visions and ideas.
5. They enjoy deciding and make forward looking decisions.

The following measures are suggested for developing entrepreneurship in the rural areas.

- Availability of the raw material is essential for any industries; policies should be made to strengthen the raw material base in rural areas.
- Funds made available at easy installment and less interest rate to the entrepreneurs of the rural area.
- In order to solve the problems of marketing for rural industries , common production-cum-marketing centers need to set up and developed with modern infrastructural facilities, in the areas having good production and growth potential.
- Lack of aptitude and competency hinders the growth of rural entrepreneurship, there is need to develop these aptitude and entrepreneurial competencies by providing Entrepreneurship Development Program.
- Proper provision needs to be made to impart the institutional training to orient entrepreneurs in specific products and trades, so that they can utilize local resources and financial availability.

Review Questions

1. Define Entrepreneurs. Explain in brief.
2. Explain the characteristics of Entrepreneurs.
3. Explain the qualities of the Entrepreneurs.
4. Compare and contrast between an Entrepreneur and a Manager.
5. What are the functions of the Entrepreneurs?
6. Explain different types of Entrepreneurs.
7. Explain Intrapreneurship.
8. Briefly explain the concept of Entrepreneurship.
9. Write in detail about the growth of Entrepreneurship in India?
10. Explain the Role of Entrepreneurship in Economic Development.
11. Define Women entrepreneurs.
12. What are the problems faced by the women entrepreneurs? What are the remedies?
13. Define Rural Entrepreneurship. What are the problems of Rural Entrepreneurship?
14. What are the steps taken to improve Rural Entrepreneurship?

Fill in the Blanks.

1. ______ is an economic agent who plays an important role in the economic development.
2. Who had given this definition of entrepreneur, "An entrepreneur is an economic agent who unites all means of production, land of one, labor of another and the capital of yet another and thus produce a product. By selling the product in the market he pays the rent, wages to labor, interest on capital and what remains is his profit.
3. The first step in the direction of setting up of an enterprise is __________
4. Arthur H. Cole has describe the entrepreneurs as a ______________
5. ____________ implies "doing of new things or doing of things that are already being done in a new way".
6. Clarence Danhof classified entrepreneurs into ________, ______, ________ and ____
7. On the basis of ownership types of entrepreneurs are _____________ and _______
8. This type of entrepreneur hardly introduces anything revolutionary and follow the principle of rule of thumb.
9. _____________ are entrepreneurs who work in an existing business, advice and manage the business activities.
10. People who voluntarily resign from the corporate sectors and start their own business are called as ______________
11. ____________ is the purposeful activity of an individual or a group of associated individuals undertaken to initiate, maintain and aggrandize profit by production.
12. ___________ and ________ are compliment to each other
13. It is characterized by the co-existence of both public and private sector in the same line of production.
14. In this type of economy the price of the product will be determined on the basis of the force of demand and supply with reference to cost of production.
15. Economic development essentially means the process of _____________ where real per capita income of the country increases.
16. __________ problems are those which are not under the control of the entrepreneur
17. Define women entrepreneur_______________________
18. ICWE stand for______________________
19. Write any three problem faced by the rural entrepreneurs_________, ________ and ___
20. Need for achievement theory was given by_______________
21. ______________ is based on the Govt. interest in the economic development of the society.
22. What are the internal factors of motivation for the entrepreneurs: ________, _______, _________, _________, _________
23. McClelland 's acquired need theory include the following needs________, ___________ and ___________
24. _____________ plays an important role in the economic development of the country.

Answers:

1. Entrepreneur
2. J. B. Say
3. Planning
4. Decision Maker
5. Innovation

6. Innovative, Imitative, Fabian and Drone
7. Private and Public
8. Empirical
9. Intrapreneurs
10. Corporate Castoff or Dropouts
11. Entrepreneurship
12. Entrepreneurship and Economic Development
13. Mixed Economy
14. Capitalistic Economy
15. Upward Change
16. External Problem
17. An enterprise owned and controlled by a woman and having a maximum financial interest of 51% of the capital and giving 51% of the employment generated in the enterprise to women
18. Indian Council of Women Entrepreneurs
19. Govt. Policies, Marketing, Technical and Credit
20. McClelland
21. Entrepreneurship Development
22. Desire to do something, Educational qualification, Technical background, Year of experience and Occupational background
23. Need for Affiliation, Need for Power and Need for Achievement
24. Entrepreneurship

◆◆◆

Factors Affecting Entrepreneurial Growth

Chapter 2

CHAPTER OUTLINE

- Factors Affecting Entrepreneurship
- Entrepreneurial Process
- Entrepreneurial Motivation
- Entrepreneurial Competencies
- Entrepreneurship Development Program
- Course Content of Entrepreneurship Development Program
- Phases of Entrepreneurship Development Program
- Evaluation of Entrepreneurial Development Programs (EDP)
- Entrepreneurial Behavior

The emergence and development of entrepreneurship is not a spontaneous one but a dependent phenomenon of economic, social, political, psychological factors often nomenclature as supporting conditions to entrepreneurship development. These conditions may be positive and may be negative on the emergence of entrepreneurship. Positive emergence constitutes facilitative and conducive conditions for the emergence of entrepreneurship, whereas negative emergence create inhibiting milieu to the development of entrepreneurship. The economist considers the structure of economic incentives found in the market environment as most relevant to entrepreneurial activity. The sociologist emphasizes society's value and status hierarchy as the main force governing entrepreneurial activity. On the other hand, the psychologist stresses certain inner, psychic concerns as the prime movers of risk taking and innovation.

Following are the factors of environment affecting entrepreneurial growth. These conditions are grouped under two categories.

I. Economic Condition: One of the most important factors affecting entrepreneurship is the economic environment. It includes the capital, labor, raw material and market.

1. **Capital:** It is the essence of enterprise. Availability of capital facilitates mobility of land, machine, material etc. is required to produce goods. Therefore, capital is a lubricant which smoothens the working of vehicle called enterprise. Increased capital investment, capital output ratio results in profits, which ultimately goes up to capital formation.
2. **Labor:** Quality and quantity of labor influence the entrepreneurship mobility, dexterity and immobility. Low cost labor and capital intensive technology oriented enterprises influence entrepreneurship. Entrepreneurs, therefore, often find difficulty to secure sufficient labour. They are forced to make elaborate and costly, arrangements to recruit the necessary labour. The problem of low-cost immobile labour can be circumvented by plunging ahead with capital-intensive technologies
3. **Raw Materials:** Availability of raw materials, nature of industrial establishment, technological innovation and mobility of raw materials encourages or curbs the development of entrepreneurship. Of course, in some cases, technological innovations can compensate for raw material inadequacies. The Japanese case, for example, witnesses that lack of raw material clearly does not prevent entrepreneurship from emerging but influenced the direction of entrepreneurship. In fact, the supply of raw materials is not influenced by themselves but becomes influential depending upon other opportunity conditions. The more favourable these conditions are, the more likely is the raw materials to have its influence on entrepreneurial emergence.
4. **Market:** The potential of the market constitutes the major department of probable rewards from entrepreneurial function the size and composition of market monopoly in a particular product influence entrepreneurship. Practically, monopoly in a particular product in a market becomes more influential for entrepreneurship than a competitive market. However, the disadvantage of a competitive market can be cancelled to some extent by improvement in transportation system facilitating the movement of raw material and finished goods, and increasing the demand for producer goods.
5. **Infrastructure:** Expansion of entrepreneurship presupposes properly developed communication and transportation facilities. It not only helps to enlarge the market, but expand the horizons of business too. Take for instance, the establishment of post and telegraph system and construction of roads and highways in India. It helped considerable entrepreneurial activities which took place in the 1850s. Apart from the above factors, institutions like trade/ business associations, business schools, libraries, etc. also make valuable contribution towards promoting and sustaining entrepreneurship' in the economy

II. Non-economic Conditions: These conditions are social conditions, psychological conditions and political or governmental actions. Sociologists and psychologists view that the influence of economic factors on entrepreneurial emergence largely depends upon the existence of non-economic factors.

Social Conditions are as follows:

1. Socio-cultural norms and value.
2. Degree of approval or disapproval of entrepreneurial behavior.
3. Family back ground, standard of education, technical knowledge and information.
4. Financial stability, caste and religious affiliations.

Psychological Conditions are as follows.

1. David McClelland's Theory of Need Achievement. According to him a constellation of personality characteristics and high need achievement is the major determinant of entrepreneurship.
2. Individual works in the society but remains different.
3. Impact of achievement motivation and training programs influence development of entrepreneurship.

Political/Government Action

1. Government encourages entrepreneurship by creating basic facilities, utilities and services and by providing incentives and concessions.
2. Government provides the prospective entrepreneurship a facilitative socio-economic setting.
3. Entrepreneurship development is based on the Government interest in economic development of the society.

These factors are interlocking mutually dependent and mutually reinforcing.

Factors Affecting Entrepreneurship

The emergence and development of entrepreneurship is not a spontaneous one but a dependent phenomenon of economic, non-economic, environmental, social, political, psychological factors often nomenclature as supporting conditions to entrepreneurship development. These conditions may have both positive and negative influences on the emergence of entrepreneurship. Positive influences constitute facilitative and conducive conditions for the emergence of entrepreneurship, whereas negative influences create inhibiting milieu to the emergence of entrepreneurship.

Factor	*Examples, evidence*
CULTURE	Attitudes to wealth, elders, youth, experimentation, risk, work, professions, achievers, success etc. Family, extended family, collective ownership vs. individual, Treatment of women, castes, classes, minorities, etc. Religion and ethical attitudes to business.
INFRASTRUCTURE	Tangible, intangible, telecommunications, transport, distribution, health, public safety, law and courts, education system, etc.
SOCIAL	Demographic profile (*e.g.*, ageing population reduces entrepreneurship and start up rates). Immigration and migration patterns. Caste and class rigidities, and social homogeneity.
ECONOMIC	Growth opportunities, domestically and across borders. Cyclical opportunities and threats (unemployment may lead to entrepreneurship).Taxation treatment of capital gains, start up expenses, intangible asset expenditure, stock options, etc.
LEGAL AND REGULATORY	Administrative burden imposed on smaller firms and start ups. Regulatory barriers (licenses, etc.). Property rights (tangible, intangible) can be protected and marketed. Right to incorporate and costs of incorporation. Costs of defending or enforcing agreements or rights. Penalties imposed for "failure", treatment of bankrupts. Specific regulations and laws relating to specific markets or activities.

Factor	*Examples, evidence*
INFORMATION	Access to information about opportunities, technology, partners, laws and regulations etc. Freedom of press and ability to advertise or disseminate information (*e.g.,* about new products). Accessibility of information in different languages
FINANCE	Discrimination in finance (*e.g.,* age, gender, class discrimination). Sophistication and development of markets (*e.g.,* microfinance, start up and seed finance, angles, equity, religion [*e.g.,* Muslim finance], Venture Capital, second board and OTC markets, mezzanine, etc.). Continuity in finance markets (*i.e.,* are the gaps in the markets, or can an entrepreneur expand smoothly from seed to IPO). Competition in financial markets (*e.g.,* competitive finance markets reduce the margin above cost of finance to lenders, and increase range of services). Ability to use property rights as security (enables entrepreneurs to secure finance)
TECHNOLOGY	Access to large firms or universities and research labs for technology transfer. Access to supply chains. Access to incubators and technology support
EDUCATION and HUMAN RESOURCES	Levels of literacy, numeracy Computer and ICT literacy — Specific education in entrepreneurship at school, university - Access to training programs, mentoring, advice
MARKET STRUCTURES	Monopolistic behaviour, predatory pricing by large firms. Networks, clusters. Flexibility in labour markets. Industry or market specific incentives and subsidies
INDIVIDUAL	Individual personality and motivation traits *e.g.* locus of control, risk taking, innovativeness. Individual experience and knowledge.

Fig. 2.1: Factors Affecting Entrepreneurship

Causes of Slow Growth of Entrepreneurship in India

Entrepreneurship developed only in the beginning of the 19th century and through the base for industrialization had been laid a century ago. The following be the main reasons, which could be responsible for lack of initiatives and entrepreneurial spirit among the Indians.

1. Caste System: This decided occupation for members from each caste. The altitudes were restrictive and therefore there were no changes of accumulating wealth and promoting production.

2. Agriculture: Agriculture was the main occupation. Farmers and cultivators were always in the clutches of the money lenders. The zamindars, nawabs and rajahs exploited the laborers. They spent money on enjoyment and luxury and never risked money in industry. Banking and commercial system was also absent so even if there were savings, they could not be utilized for productive use.

3. Educational System: Talented young men were prepared to take white collared jobs or join government or professional services. Many were attracted towards politics. The result was that very few young men got attracted towards becoming efficient, industrialists, technicians, managers etc

4. Colonial Rules: The British rulers adopted discriminatory policy Rich Indian businessman had special connections with foreign rulers and both satisfied their self interests. Even the few insurance and banking service scattered to the needs of some rich Indian businessman, Britishers in India did it all not to encourage Industrialization.

5. Managing Agents: There were just a handful of people who were known to be having managerial skills. On common basis, these agents would lend their skills to some top industries. Industrialists could not manage their own units. They were always at the mercy of the managing agents who filled their pockets with big chunks of the companies' profits and took full advantage of Indian industrialists till the managing agency system was abolished in 1970.

6. Joint Family System: Younger members of the family always depended on the Head who never gave any kind of independence or encouraged units other than family business ones. A number of young men were discouraged from diversifying from family business and doing something new and different.

7. Religious Attitude: Indians were very religious minded. They gave more time to religion than to earning material wealth. Religion got priority over business. Some religions even condemned excess earnings and indulgence in comforts. Industrial activity was, therefore, given secondary consideration by the religious Indians.

8. Mindset: The mindset of the average Indian was never entrepreneurial. Our religious literature and epics told us to have patience and to keep on working without expecting the fruits of labor. This also killed the drive and desire to get into entrepreneurial activities.

9. Recognition by the Society: In earlier days, the heroes of India were the social reformers and the politicians. Now it is the era of sportsmen, models and film stars. It is sad that successful or the struggling entrepreneurs have never been recognized as heroes. Entrepreneurial activity did not get due importance in the Indian society.

10. Family Background: Empirical studies have shown that a good number of entrepreneurs come from families with industrial backgrounds. Unfortunately, only a few entrepreneurial communities in India made entrepreneurial contribution. These communities could also not make headway in the entrepreneurial field on account of the colonial rule, lack of infrastructure and other facilities. Entrepreneurship development could only take place after independence in India.

THE ENTREPRENEURIAL PROCESS

The process of starting a new venture is embodied in the entrepreneurial process, which involves more than just problem solving in a typical management position. An entrepreneur must find, evaluate, and develop an opportunity by overcoming the forces that resist the creation of something new. The process has four distinct phases:

(1) Identification and evaluation of the opportunity
(2) Development of the business plan
(3) Determination of the required resources,
(4) Management of the resulting enterprise.

Although these phases proceed progressively, no one stage is dealt with in isolation. For example, to successfully identify and evaluate an opportunity (phase 1), an entrepreneur must have in mind the type of business desired (phase 4).

Phase I: Identify and Evaluate the Opportunity

Opportunity identification and evaluation is a very difficult task. Most good business opportunities do not suddenly appear, but rather result from an entrepreneur's alertness to possibilities, or in some case, the establishment of mechanisms that identify potential opportunities. For example, one entrepreneur asks at every cocktail party whether anyone is using a product that does not adequately fulfill its intended purpose. This person is constantly looking for a need and an opportunity to creat a better product. Another entrepreneur always monitors the play habits and toys of her nieces and nephews. This is her way of looking for any unique toy product niche for a new venture.

Although most entrepreneurs do not have formal mechanisms or identifying business opportunities, some sources are often fruitful: consumers and business associates, members of the distribution system, and technical people. Often, consumers are the best source of ideas for a new venture. How many times have you heard someone comment, "If only there was a product that would..." This comment can result in the creation of new business. One entrepreneur's evaluation of why so many business executives were complaining about the lack of good technical writing and word-processing services resulted in the creation of her own business venture to fill this need.

Due to their close contact with the end user, channel members in the distribution system also see product needs. One entrepreneur started a college bookstore after hearing all the students complain about the high cost of books and the lack of service provided by the only bookstore on campus. Many other entrepreneurs have identified business opportunities through a discussion with a retailer, wholesaler, or manufacturer's representative.

Finally, technically oriented individuals often conceptualize business opportunities when working on other projects. One entrepreneur's business resulted from seeing the application of a plastic resin compound in developing and manufacturing a new type of pallet while developing the resin application in another totally unrelated area—casket moldings.

Whether the opportunity is identified by using input from consumers, business associates, channel members, or technical people, each opportunity must be carefully screened and evaluated. This evaluation of the opportunity is perhaps the most critical element of the entrepreneurial process, as it allows the entrepreneur to assess whether the specific product or service has the returns needed compared to the resources required. This evaluation process involves looking at the length of the opportunity, its real and perceived value, its risks and returns, its fit with the personal skills and goals of the entrepreneur, and its uniqueness or differential advantage in its competitive environment.

The market size and the length of the window of opportunity are the primary basis for determining the risks and rewards. These risks reflect the market, competition, technology, and amount of capital involved. The amount of capital needed provides the basis for the return and rewards. The methodology for evaluating risks and rewards frequently indicates that an opportunity offers neither a financial nor a personal reward commensurate with the risks involved. One company that delivered bark mulch to residential and commercial users for decoration around the base of trees and shrubs added loam and shells to its product line. These products were sold to the same customer base using the same distribution (delivery) system. Follow-on products are important for a company expanding or diversifying in a particular channel. A distribution channel member such as Kmart, Service Merchandise or Target prefers to do business with multi-product, rather than single-product, firms.

Finally, the opportunity must fit the personal skills and goals of the entrepreneur. It is particularly important that the entrepreneur be able to put forth the necessary time and effort required to make the venture succeed. Although many entrepreneurs feel that the desire can be developed along the venture, typically it does not materialize. An entrepreneur must believe in the opportunity so much that he or she will make the necessary sacrifices to develop the opportunity and manage the resulting organization.

Opportunity analysis, or what is frequently called an opportunity assessment plan, is one method for evaluating an opportunity. It is not a business plan. Compared to a business plan, it should be shorter; focus on the opportunity, not the entire venture; and provide the basis for making the decision of whether or not to act on the opportunity.

An opportunity assessment plan includes the following: a description of the product or service, an assessment of the opportunity, an assessment of the entrepreneur and the team, specifications of all the activities and resources needed to translate the opportunity into a viable business venture, and the source of capital to finance the initial venture as well as its growth. The assessment of the opportunity requires answering the following questions:

- What market need does it fill?
- What personal observations have you experienced or recorded with regard to that market need?
- What social condition underlies this market need?
- What market research data can be marshaled to describe this market need?
- What patents might be available to fulfill this need?

- What competition exists in this market? How would you describe the behavior of this competition?
- What does the international market look like?
- What does the international competition look like?
- Where is the money to be made in this activity?

Phase II: Developing a Business Plan

A good business plan must be developed in order to exploit the defined opportunity. This is a very time-consuming phase of the entrepreneurial process. An entrepreneur usually has not prepared a business plan before and does not have the resources available to do a good job. A good business plan is essential for developing the opportunity and determining the resources required, obtaining those resources, and successfully managing the resulting venture.

Phase III: Determine the Resources Required

The resources needed for addressing the opportunity must also be determined. This process starts with an appraisal of the entrepreneur's present resources. Any resources that are critical need to be differentiated from those that are just helpful. Care must be taken not to underestimate the amount of variety of resources needed. The downside risks associated with insufficient or inappropriate resources should also be assessed.

Acquiring the needed resources in a timely manner while giving up as little control as possible is the next step in the entrepreneurial process. An entrepreneur should strive to maintain as large an ownership position as possible, particularly in the start-up stage. As the business develops, more funds will probably be needed to finance the growth of the venture, requiring more ownership to be relinquished. Alternative suppliers of these resources, along with their needs and desires, need to be identified. By understanding resource supplier needs, the entrepreneur can structure a deal that enables the recources to be acquired at the lowest possible cost and the least loss of control.

Phase IV: Manage the Enterprise

After resources are acquired, the entrepreneur must use them to implement the business plan. The operational problems of the growing enterprise must also be examined. This involves implementing a management style and structure, as well as determining the key variables for success. A control system must be established, so that any problem areas can be quickly identified and resolved. Some entrepreneurs have difficulty managing and growing the venture they created.

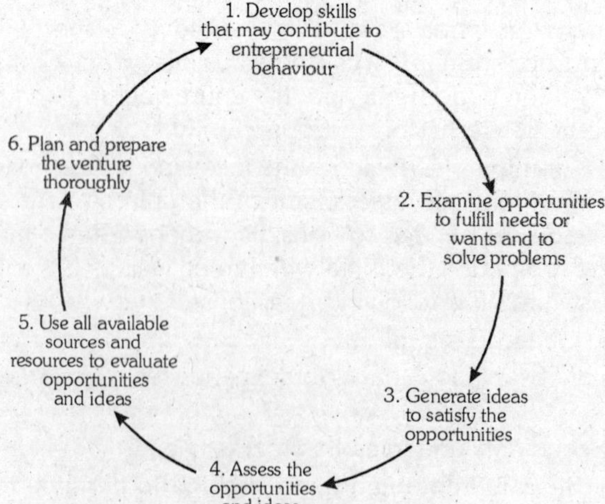

Fig. 2.2: Entrepreneurial Process

Entrepreneurial Motivation

The basic function of an entrepreneur is to secure maximum performance for the attainment of organizational objectives the performance of an entrepreneur depends mainly on their ability to perform and willingness to perform. Ability is a function of education and experience and skill. Willingness to perform depends upon the level of motivation.

In order to motivate entrepreneur, an entrepreneur must understand and satisfy their needs, aspiration and ambitions. Human behavior is governed by needs and desires. Entrepreneur feel motivated when their needs and expectation are satisfied as a result of working for the enterprise.

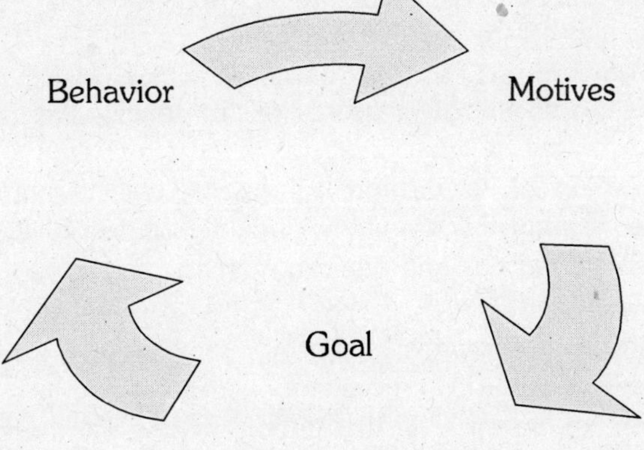

Fig. 2.3: Motives

Motivational Theories:

1. Maslow Theory of Hierarchical Need: Physiological need, Security needs Social need, Esteem need and Self actualization need.

(a) Level 1: Physiological needs: basis/primary survival needs for food, drink, clothes, shelter, sex and sleep.

(b) Level 2: Security needs: The need for self-preservation and the protection of others future assurance ex. Employment

(c) Level 3: Social needs: The desire to belong, need for affiliation, need to be part of a reference group.

(d) Level 4 : Esteem needs: The need for self esteem, need for self confidence, need for self image and need for recognition by one's peers.

(e) Level 5: Self Actualization: A need to stretch one's capabilities includes the need for achievement , self fulfillment, need to develop own skills and express self.

2. McClelland's Acquired Need Theory: As a result of one's life experience a person experiences three types of needs.

1. **Need for affiliation:** It refers to establish and maintain healthy, friendly and warm relations with others. Entrepreneurs are believed to be low on affiliation, as they are and expected to be, innovative, trendsetters and tradition breakers. However, it is not necessary that affiliation should only interfere with achievement. In certain cultures, family comprises the bedrock on which the successful careers are built. Desire to carry on the tradition of business in the family and the community to which one belongs, may be interpreted as reflecting need for affiliation as well. In the countries with the colonial past, the first generation of entrepreneurs in independent India was driven by patriotic fervor and the desire to rebuild the economy left stagnant by the alien rulers. One can certainly trace some elements of affiliation motivation in such instances.

2. **Need for power**: These means the one desire to dominate and influence other by physical action or objects. It is concern for influencing people or the behavior of others, for moving in the chosen direction and attaining the envisioned objectives. In common perception that politician, social religious leader CEOs, Civil Servant typify the need for power. In the same vein business ownership too may imply a need for power. Moreover, he/she would appreciated that in the process of founding a business, one as to win the commitment of capital providers, supplier of equipment and materials, the employees and that of the customers. Power may not be used to further one's self- interest alone, it may be also be used to touch the lives of others, to make a difference. Entrepreneurs driven by this socialized face of the need of power, found organization that are a source of sustenance and self-respect for many.
3. **Need for achievement:** Drive to do well, strive for excellence and overcome challenges and obstacles in the pursuit of goal. It also implies a desire to accomplish something difficult.
   - To master, manipulate, or organize physical objects, human beings or ideas.
   - To do this as rapidly and as independently as possible.
   - To overcome obstacles and attain a high standards.
   - To excel one's self.
   - To rival and surpass others
   - To increase self-regard by successful exercise of talent.

McClelland suggests an entrepreneur the importance of high need for achievement is found dominating one. People with high need of achievement are characterized as:

1. They decide moderate, realistic and attainable goals for them.
2. Prefer to situations in which they can find solutions for solving personal responsibility.
3. They need concrete feed back about their performance.
4. They have need for achievement for attaining personal accomplishment.
5. They look for challenging task.

Motivating Factors

Following are the motivating factors for an entrepreneur.

I. Internal factors.

1. Desire to do something new.
2. Educational qualification.
3. Technical background.
4. Number of years of experience.
5. Occupation back ground

II. External factors.

1. Government support and assistance.
2. Availability of factors of production.
3. Encouragement from already established business house.
4. Promising demand for the product.

Entrepreneurial Competencies

Competence motivation is a drive to do high quality work. Entrepreneurial competencies are refers to the key characteristics that should be possessed by successful entrepreneur in order to perform entrepreneurial functions effectively. It is an underlying characteristic of a person which leads to his/her effective or superior performance in job/business.

Competent entrepreneurs are

- ❖ Seek mastery in job or tasks that they are undertaking.
- ❖ Develop problem solving skills and
- ❖ Strive to be innovative.

In general they tend to perform good work because the inner satisfactions they feel and esteem them gain from others due to their competence.

McClelland and McBer have given some of the Characteristics of Entrepreneurial Competencies.

1. **Initiative:** The entrepreneur should be able to take actions that go beyond his job requirements and to act faster. He is always head of others and able to become a leader in the field of business. For example acts to extend the business into new areas, products or services.
2. **Sees and Acts on Opportunities:** An entrepreneur always looks for a takes action on opportunity.
3. **Persistence:** An entrepreneur is able to make repeated efforts or to take different actions to overcome on obstacle that get in the way of reaching goals.
4. **Information Seeking:** An entrepreneur is able to take action on how to seek information and to help achieve business objectives or classify business problem.
5. **Concern for High Quality of Work:** An entrepreneur acts to do things that meet certain standards of excellence which gives him greater satisfaction.
6. **Commitment to Work Contract:** An entrepreneur places the highest priority on getting a job completed.
7. **Efficiency Orientation:** A successful entrepreneur always finds way to do things faster or with fewer resources or at a lower cost.
8. **Systematic Planning:** An entrepreneur develops and uses logical step by step plan to reach goals.
9. **Problem Solving:** Successful entrepreneur identifies new and potentially unique ideas to achieve his goals.
10. **Self-confidence:** A successful entrepreneur has a strong belief in self and own abilities.
11. **Assertiveness:** An entrepreneur confronts problems and issues with other directly.
12. **Persuasion:** An entrepreneur can successfully persuade or influence others for mobilizing resources, obtaining inputs, organizing production and selling his products or services.
13. **Use of Influence Strategies**: An entrepreneur is able to make use of influential people to reach his business goals.

Some of the Entrepreneurial Competencies that would-be entrepreneur should possess:

1. Organizing ability: An entrepreneur should be wise enough in choosing the people with whom he will work. He must choose people who possess skills that are needed for the improvement and success of the business.

2. Problem-solving ability: An entrepreneur should be rational rather than emotional in handling obstacles. He is also firm enough when making decisions without hurting others.

3. Ability to absorb setbacks and recovery: Analysis in absorbing setbacks and recovery of the business are important competencies of the entrepreneur. Accepting and analyzing the difficulties encountered help in the improvement and success of the business.

4. Human relations ability: Personality factors such as emotional stability, personal relations, sociability, consideration, and tactfulness are important contributors to the entrepreneur manager's success in small business. One of the most important facets of human relations is one's ability to put him in someone else's place and know how the other person feels. This is the ability to practice empathy.

An entrepreneur must maintain good relations with his customers if he is to establish a relationship that will encourage them to continue to patronize his business. They can be given personal consideration to fit their specific needs. It is because of them that business is producing products continuously. An entrepreneur should be able to handle customer complaints directly. He must train his employees to maintain good customer relations. He must develop and maintain harmonious working relationships with his employees to make them perform their jobs at a high level of efficiency. This relationship will give him opportunity to gain greater understanding of their needs and wants. Problems can be worked out on a face to face basis. One problem is income that sometimes can not sustain employees' needs. If it is possible, give them benefits, allowances, and the facilities. In this way, employees will cooperate to form an effective work team.

5. Communications ability: An entrepreneur should have an ability to communicate effectively both orally and in writing. Communication also means that both the sender and the receiver understand and are understood.

The employee who tells his boss what he thinks his boss wants to hear rather than what he considers to be bad news is not really communicating. Lack of communication can result from different ways of doing things. To one person, belonging to a certain organization may mean social acceptance. To another person, it may mean conformity for the sake of conformity. Words also have different meanings for different individuals.

Effective written communication is much more difficult to achieve than effective oral communication. For example, the teacher might walk into his class and in a pleasant voice, with a smile, say, "This class can go jump in the lake." Very few students would be offended, although they might be puzzled. On the other hand, if the instructor wrote the same message on the blackboard and left it for the class to read, he would probably receive a wide range of reactions, from anger to amusement.

The small business manager who can effectively communicate with customers, employees, suppliers, and creditors will be more likely to succeed than the manager who can not. For example, a business firm may have a good customer who has forgotten to make a payment on time. It sends out a form letter that says, "We have not received your monthly payment; please remit at once." The business firm intends only to remind the customer, however, the customer may take it as a dun and an implication that he is not meeting his debts. Some individuals may be offended enough to stop trading with the business, and the firm would never know why.

6. Ability to make sound decisions and to take full responsibility for decisions made: An entrepreneur is the leader, the boss. All those under him are dependent on the decisions he makes. Thus, he should have a sound judgment which will be fair to all.

7. Persistence and patience to wait until the business really becomes successful: Failure in running a business is not an obstacle for entrepreneurs. It will instead be a challenge to their abilities to handle it. Searching for the best way to succeed is a necessary skill for them.

8. Technical knowledge on how to operate the business: A basic knowledge in handling a business is necessary for entrepreneurs in order to be able to organize and manage a business.

9. Sense of independence and self-confidence: An entrepreneur should have trust in him and in his work. His sound judgment, self-confidence, and independence in his job will enable him to succeed.

10. Good health and enthusiasm: An entrepreneur who is physically as well as mentally fit would have a good chance of success. He will be able to grapple with the problems in the business

Entrepreneurial Mobility

Location or geographical mobility of entrepreneurs represents the drive and initiative to move to other places in search of better opportunities for example, Marwaris and Sindhis in our country have moved to almost every corner of India to carry on business activities. Such a spirit helps to reduce regional imbalances in economic growth. Development of technological parts, competing hub centre at Bangalore, cluster growth schemes and Special Economic Zones are the important dimension of centralized entrepreneurial behavior at a particular place.

These are three stages of entrepreneurial mobility.

1. In the initial stage entrepreneurs are tied to their usual place of working.
2. With gradual growth, they are likely to become relatively mobile within a limited area.
3. When they become highly resourceful greater degree of mobility occurs.

This implied that in any country only a handful of entrepreneur tend to be mobile. If entrepreneurial class is limited and unevenly distributed, there will be strong regional imbalances in industrial development.

All entrepreneurs are not easily mobile from place to place and the degree of mobility increases as their resources expands, experience widens and information gathering process develops. Analyzing such mobility may be helpful to formulate policy making which reduces regional imbalances in the Indian context. The spatial mobility of the better entrepreneurial opportunities, it is adapting to the changing situation, like Marwaris, Sindhees have moved to almost every corner of the country to carry on their entrepreneurial activities. Such spirit of mobility and dynamism should be cultivated among more and more social groups to remove regional imbalances.

There are two types of mobility that is social and regional mobility.

Social Mobility

One of the important characteristic of the achievement oriented person is that he puts all his efforts to realize his goal. For achieving certain thing he does not mind to move geographically. He also attempts to move upward in the social ladder by breaking all the barriers- caste, community, profession or income, because the entrepreneurship offers tremendous opportunity for self advancement and social mobility.

Social mobility has been examined in terms of parental profession, the highest percentage of entrepreneurs that is 48.36% came from the family of traders and businessmen. Among other 33.6% came from the family depended on service and 9% were from the agriculture. However, it is interesting to note that a very large number of first generation entrepreneurs are from service background, where business and industry is controlled by the families of businessmen.

Regional Mobility

Inter and intra regional mobility is an important characteristic of achievement oriented people. Like social barriers, they can break the geographical barriers. If opportunity and potentiality exists this type of entrepreneurs will move from their home town to other place. People migrate to other place if sufficient opportunities are not prevalent at their own place and if the better opportunities are available at distance place. The major factor of mobility is the availability of incentives in backward districts.

Therefore , if potentiality and facilities are created to a certain level to help entrepreneur, there will be an automatic increase in supply of entrepreneurs. It is a fact that entrepreneurship is not only the product of motivation but also the favorable existence of social and economic factors, particularly the access to resources.

Entrepreneurship Development Program

The entrepreneurship development is a key to achieve overall economic development through higher level of industrial activity. Every individual has certain qualities of an entrepreneur. If such qualities are developed as an entrepreneur, such individuals can become successful entrepreneurs. Entrepreneurship development program plays very important role in this direction. The economic and industrial development of developing country like India are only due to rapid entrepreneurship development. In India, rapid growth of small-scale sector is mainly due to the entrepreneurship development. Entrepreneurship Development Program (EDP) focuses on identifying entrepreneurship qualities of an individual, providing training required for entrepreneurship development, preparing related project profiles, preparing entrepreneurs by providing and with regard to finance, production, technology, marketing, management, infrastructure facilities etc and trying to solve problems and difficulties to entrepreneurs by showing remedial measures. It is, therefore context that an increasingly important role has been assigned to Entrepreneurship Development Program for promotion of an entrepreneur.

Based on the belief that potential entrepreneurs can be identified and trained, the entrepreneurship development program (EDP) has been designed to promote small enterprises by tapping the latent talent. The programs uniqueness lies in its integrated approach, which provides instructions and counseling from selection through the actual operation of enterprises.

Meaning of EDP

A Program designed to help a person in strengthening and fulfilling his entrepreneurial motives and in acquiring skills and capabilities necessary for playing his entrepreneurial role effectively is called Entrepreneurship Development Program (EDP).

EDP is primarily meant for developing those first generation entrepreneurs, who on their own can not become successful entrepreneurs.

Objectives of Entrepreneurship Development Programs

1. Analyze, the environmental set up relating to small industry and small business.
2. Selection of product and project.
3. Develop and strengthen entrepreneurial qualities.
4. Understand procedure of small-scale industries.
5. Develop wide vision about the business.
6. Develop passion for integrity and honesty.
7. Understand the need of entrepreneurial discipline.
8. To accelerate the process of entrepreneurship development ensuring its impact throughout the country and among all strata of the society.
9. To help/support and affiliate institution/origin in carrying out training and other ED related activities with greater success.
10. To evolve standardized materials and processes of selection, training, support and sustenance to potential entrepreneurs.
11. To provide vital information support to trainers, promoters and entrepreneurs by organizing research and documentation relevant to ED.
12. To identify, train and assist potential entrepreneurs for setting up enterprise self employment ventures in small industries including services and small business mainly through sponsored EDPs.
13. To provide national and international forums for interaction and exchange of experiences helpful for policy formulation and modification at various levels.

Characteristics of Entrepreneurship Development Program

1. **Motivation and achievement motivation:** Motivation and achievement motivation are essential conditions of EDP.
2. **Provides opportunities:** Such programs provide opportunities for developing and strengthening skills of entrepreneurship of an individual.

3. **Objectives of developing first generation entrepreneurs:** EDP is aimed at developing the first generation entrepreneurs, who on their own cannot become successful entrepreneurs. Though for successful or failure entrepreneurs also. Such program are designed, in order to be more successful or to success from failure.
4. **Important tool for human resource development:** EDP is an important tool for human resources development. By such programs, surplus manpower can be directed towards self-employment.
5. **Main focus:** Main focus of EDP is on reducing unemployment, increasing industrial development, providing incentives to small-scale industries, optimum utilization of national resources and balanced economic development.
6. **Target for preparing entrepreneurs:** EDP is designed especially for preparing entrepreneurs. More over such programs are designed for specific time period, specific objectives and specific area or zone.
7. **It is a process:** EDP is a process. The process is designed into three stages namely- pre-training activity, training activity and post training activity.

Importance of Entrepreneurship Development Program

EDP has become extremely important in achieving goals of all round development in the country. With reference to India, the importance of EDP can be discussed as below.

1. For rapid industrial development

Entrepreneurs and entrepreneurship is base for industrial and economic development. EDP makes entrepreneurs for creation of entrepreneurship environment. In India, in every five year more and more amount is allotted for entrepreneurship development. After freedom, India has shown rapid industrial and economic development. This is only due to EDP. Because of EDP, now a days entrepreneur are on increasing in engineering, chemical, electrical, agriculture industries etc. i.e. to say that EDP plays a crucial role for industrial and economic development.

2. To remove or reduce regional industrial imbalance

In industrial backward zone, through EDP qualities of an entrepreneurship can be developed. Indian government has designed incentive plans in its industrial policy. In such industrial backward area, EDP arranges various training programs and makes the individual aware about the government rule and regulation regarding the industrial policy, incentives and entrepreneurial opportunities.

3. Creation of suitable industrial environment for rapid economic development

For creation of industrial and entrepreneurial environment, various institutions have to give their contribution, institutions like- CED, EDI, IDBI, IFCI, SFC, DIC, SISI etc. EDP 's are arranged in rural, semi-urban and urban areas, so that the awareness can be spread all over about the entrepreneurship environment, support system through various publication of EDP.

4. Optimum utilization of available local resources

In India, every state has specific types of resources available for production purpose. If such resources are utilized for production purpose, new opportunities for local entrepreneurship development and local employment can be created and which lead towards rapid industrial and economic development.

5. Helps in reducing unemployment and poverty problems

India is facing unemployment and poverty problems since independence. So government has designed various programs rural development program, Prime Minister Rozgar Yajana (PMRY)for the removal of this unemployment and poverty problem. By arranging EDP for educated and unemployed individual they can be trained for self-employment and entrepreneurs, self-employment can also create employment opportunities for other.

6. To protect entrepreneurs from industrial monopoly

Some large industrial units have created monopoly conditions in their area. So, government has been forced to reserve some goods and services for the small-scale industries. Thus due to such decentralization, small entrepreneurs can be protected from industrial monopoly of large-scale industries.

7. New sources of income for Government

For the arrangement of EDP, central and state government has to spent large amount. But government also gets income tax by medium of venture of new entrepreneurs. Some export-oriented industrial unit help government in earning of foreign exchange.

8. Progress and expansion of social wealth

Because of growth of industrialization in rural areas, living standards of rural areas have remarkaly changed. Government's special schemes for rural wealth have been reached to actual rural areas by EDP. EDP helps to divert unorganized and hidden youth of various areas towards planned industrialization.

9. EDP is a vehicle for social-economic revolution

EDP is designed for the various classes of the society. In rural, semi-urban and urban areas, with a view to direct woman towards self-employment and freedom, special EDPs are designed for SC, ST, Ex-Servicemen, Women, Physically handicapped etc.

10. To develop and upgrade managerial skill

EDP is designed and implemented to develop entrepreneurial opportunities for potential entrepreneurs as well as to upgrade managerial skills for the existing entrepreneurs.

Course Content of Entrepreneurship Development Program

1. **Selection of Potential Entrepreneurs:** Background information like skills, experience in the field, physical resources available, family occupation etc.
2. **Technical Knowledge and Skills:** Once the entrepreneur select a particular enterprise in-depth knowledge about the technical aspects of the trade is essential. He has to be well conversant with the process of manufacturing and trading for which a particular training for which a particular training based on sound theory is essential. He needs to know the economic aspects of the technology including costs and benefits field trips to a few industrial units and implant training can be very helpful.
3. **Achievement Motivation Training (AMT):** In order to develop human resources development achievement motive is essential. The purpose of AMT is to develop the need to achieve, risk taking, initiative and other such behavioral or psychological traits. A motivation development program creates self awareness and self confidence among the participants and enables them to think positively and realistically. Motivation training initiates people to business activity or helps them to expand their business ventures. They learn to strive for excellence to take calculated their risk, to use feedback for improvement, sense of efficacy etc.
4. **Support System and Procedure:** Training needs to include information about support system. The participants have to be explored to agencies like the local banks, and other financial institutions, industrial service corporation and other institutions dealing with supply or raw materials, equipments, etc. The session on support system needs to also include the procedures for approaching them, applying and obtaining assistance from them and availing of the services provided by them. A linkage between the training institute and the support system agencies can be established by participation of these agencies in sponsoring and financing the EDP.

EDP: A Conceptual Framework

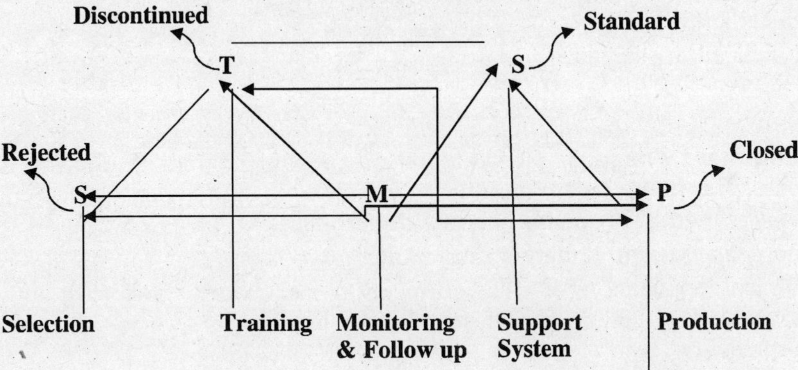

Fig. 2.3: A Conceptual Framework of EDP

1. Selection Procedure 2. Entrepreneurial Traits 3. Sustainability and Viability of Activity	1. Training Program 2. Training Infrastructure 3. Content 4. Methods 5. Project Preparation	1. Credit Institutions 2. Service Institution 3. Implementing Institution	1. Credit 2. Raw Materials 3. Services 4. Marketing 5. Repayment and Reinvestment

5. **Market Survey:** The participants should be given opportunity to actually conduct market surveys for their chosen project. This would help expose the candidate to the marketing avenues available and could be followed by sessions on methods of dealing in the markets.
6. **Managerial Skill:** Once a participant is able to start the enterprise, he requires managerial skills. A list of the agencies along with details of the formalities to be completed, specimen forms to be filled in would greatly facilitate the entrepreneurs. It should include all aspects of financial management. Managerial skills are particularly essential for small scale entrepreneurs who cannot afford to employ specialists in different areas of management. The aim should be to enable the participant to look at an enterprise in its totality and to develop overall managerial understanding.
7. **Project Preparation:** Lot of time is devoted in this process. Their active involvement in this task would provide them necessary understanding and also ensure their personal commitment.

PHASES OF ENTREPRENEURSHIP DEVELOPMENT PROGRAM

Broadly entrepreneurship development consists of three following phases.

I. Initial Phase: Creation of awareness about the entrepreneurial opportunities based on survey. In its developmental process an individual is the most important factor. An individual should possess certain qualities that are necessary to become successful entrepreneur. These qualities are

1. Basic ability mix.
2. Socio-economic history and background.
3. Family background brief history.
4. Educational, skill, aptitudes and motives.

5. Knowledge application of skills, motivation.
6. Technical know-how.
7. Communication abilities.
8. Pleasing personality.
9. Academic performance.

II. Development Phase: Implementation of training program to develop motivation and management skills. This phase is very crucial as it impart education to the selected entrepreneurs for his all-round development. This phase has two distinct parts.

1. General knowledge, understanding and comprehension.
2. Technical application of skills. Education framework must take into account the development of certain qualities and traits in a person who is to be groomed as an entrepreneur.
    - *(a)* Strong will power.
    - *(b)* Self-confidence.
    - *(c)* Sound and operative technical knowledge.
    - *(d)* Capacity to shoulder risks and work efficiently under acute uncertainties.
    - *(e)* Ever ready to accept the change at all possible costs.
    - *(f)* Ability to explore, expand and jump at new opportunity.
    - *(g)* Ability to initiate.
    - *(h)* Dynamic and dashing in decision making.
    - *(i)* Ability to generate and secure resources.
    - *(j)* Organizational and administrative ability.

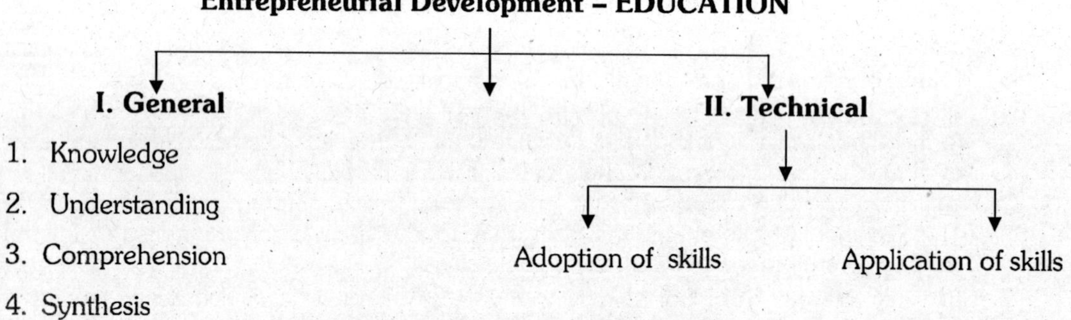

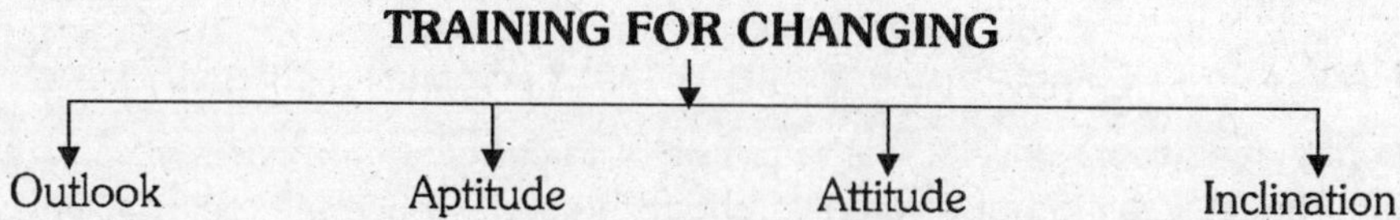

Fig. 2.4: Educational Developments for Entrepreneur

In all this process a candidate is gradually transformed from negative thinking to positive thinking. This steadily results into positive approach and constructive attitude from this.

Education and Training for entrepreneurial development must be active, meaningful and purposeful in all aspects.

III. Support Phase: Infrastructural support of counseling, assisting to establish new enterprise, and to develop existing units.

EVALUATION OF ENTREPRENEURIAL DEVELOPMENT PROGRAMS (EDP)

Entrepreneurial Development Programs can be evaluated in the following ways:

(1) Program Objective: Evaluation of an EDP may begin with an assessment of the philosophy or the central objectives of the program. The agency conducting the program must be clear about the purpose underlying entrepreneurial development. The objective may be to increase production, to generate employment to uplift certain people, etc. It becomes easier to assess the goals when they are clearly defined.

The agency starts EDP with certain assumptions, which may be based on experienced, research or pure hunch. These assumptions should be evaluated along with the objectives. The assumptions of EDP are:

1. Everyone cannot be an entrepreneur. An individual must have certain traits in order to be successful entrepreneur.
2. The traits required for successful entrepreneurship can be identified and measured through psychological test and certain social indices.
3. Person who possess these traits will be more successful than those not having.
4. Persons possessing such traits can be trained to further develop them on other dimensions of entrepreneurship too.

Evaluation of some of these assumption required data might be collected from the trained and rejected candidates.

(2) Selection Strategy and Procedures: It is impossible to train each and everyone intending to be an entrepreneur. It s desirable that only those candidates are selected for training who are likely to be successful in setting up and successfully summing their own enterprise. The success of an EDP depends largely on proper selection of trainees. Therefore, evaluation of selection strategy and procedure is necessary. The Behavioral Science Centre (India) New Delhi has been rating the selection of potential entrepreneurs, positive self concept, initiative, independence, problem solving, hope of success, searching environment and time bound planning.

A three stage selection procedure is followed in this case. It begins with screening through a carefully designed application blank which collect data on dimensioned mentioned above followed by psychological tests and behavioral exercises and games meant for assessing certain other qualities finally personal interviews are held.

Several test may be used to judge the effectiveness of selection procedures. The proportion of those setting up enterprise from the selected group as compared to those from the rejected group can be one such test.

(3) Training Program: It covers the contribution of the curriculum and its design, the content of the program the faculty, the sharing of practical experiences and even the follow up. Curriculum design deals with issues like nature (full/part time) and duration of the program classes' schedule, components of the program the type of preparation required for student and faculty.

Training can be assessed by:

(a) Comparison of a random sample of entrepreneur from the trained group with those of a random sample from untrained group.

(b) Comparison of a trained group with those from the rejected group.

(c) Interviewing the trained group to find out their opinion on the training.

(d) Surveying the expectations and experience of those under training.

(e) Examination of the curriculum content by a group of experts.

(f) Assessment of trained entrepreneur in their business operations.

(4) Organizational Policies and Structures: EDP are generally institutionalized a local, regional, national or international agency, often takes the initiative in starting, funding and executing the program. These are promotional agencies without the institutional supports EDP are not likely to be successful. So assessment of these programs begins with the evaluation of the effectiveness of the organisation or agencies concerned with the sponsoring, funding and execution of the program. It may cover evaluation of the agencies resources and development needs, which may relate to financial resources, faculty requirements, viable structure to attract entrepreneur and to provide them with continuous support, physical facilities, such as a workshop, a study cell etc.

The following criteria were used to assess the impact of training program.

1. Activity level of the respondents.
2. New business or activity started.
3. Fixed capital investment made.
4. Total investment made.
5. Number of people employed.
6. Number of jobs created.
7. Mean increase in profits.
8. Estimated tax flows.
9. Increase in sales.
10. Involvement in community affairs.
11. Diversification.
12. Risk taking.
13. Increased efficiency of operations.
14. Goal setting behavior.
15. Quicker repayment of loans.

A brief of important institutes engaged in entrepreneurial development training is given below:

***(i)* The National Institute for Entrepreneurship and Small Business Development (NIESBUD):** NIESBUD was established in 1983 by the Ministry of Industry (now Ministry of Small Scale Industries), Govt. of India, as an apex body for coordinating and overseeing the activities of various institutions/ agencies engaged in Entrepreneurship Development particularly in the area of small industry and small business. The Institute which is registered as a society under Govt. of India Societies Act (XXI of 1860) started functioning from 6th July, 1983.

Major activities of the Institute are:

- Evolving effective training strategies and methodology
- Standardizing model syllabi for training various target groups
- Formulating scientific selection procedure
- Developing training aids, manuals and tools
- Facilitating and supporting Central/State/Other agencies in organizing entrepreneurship development programs
- Conducting training programs for promoters, trainers and entrepreneurs.
- Undertaking research and exchange experiences globally in development and growth of entrepreneurship. The Institute is actively involved in creating a climate conducive to emergence of entrepreneurship.

The trainings conducted by the Institute include:

- Training of Trainers/ promoters
- Accreditation Programme for Entrepreneurial Motivation Trainers.

- Trainers' Training Programme for Enterprise Launching and Management.
- Trainers/Promoters Programme for support organisations such as SISIs, DICs, Development Corporations etc.
- Small Business Promotion Programme.
- Entrepreneurship Orientation Programme for HoDs and Senior Executives.
- Evolves Standardized Material and Research Publications

***(ii)* National Institute of Small Industry Extension Training (NISIET):** NISIET since its inception in 1960 by the Government of India, has taken gigantic strides to become the premier institution for the promotion, development and modernization of the SME sector. An autonomous arm of the Ministry of Small-scale Industries (SSI), the Institute strives to achieve its avowed objectives through a gamut of operations ranging from training, consultancy, research and education, to extension and information services. It has been renamed as National Institute of Micro, Small and Medium Enterprises (NIMSME) (www.nimsme.org) from April 2007. The primary objective of the Institute was to be the trainer of trainers. Today, with the technological development and ever-changing market scenario, their involvement has undergone changes too. From being merely trainers they have widened their scope of activities to consultancy, research, extension and information services.

***(iii)* Indian Institute of Entrepreneurship (IIE):** With an aim to undertake training, research and consultancy activities in the small industry sector focusing on entrepreneurship development, the Indian Institute of Entrepreneurship (IIE) was established in the year 1993 at Guwahati by the erstwhile Ministry of Industry (now Ministry of Small-scale Industry) , Government of India as an autonomous national institute. The institute started its operations from April 1994 with North-east Council (NEC), Govt. of Assam, Arunachal Pradesh and Nagaland and SIDBI as other stakeholders.

The activities of the Institute include identification of training needs, designing and organizing program both for development functionaries and entrepreneurs; evolving effective training strategies and methodologies for different target groups and locations; organize seminars, workshops and conferences for providing for interaction and exchange of views by various agencies and entrepreneurs; undertaking research on entrepreneurship development, documenting and disseminating information needed for policy formulation and implementation on self-employment and entrepreneurship.

The Institute acts as a catalyst for entrepreneurship development by creating an environment for entrepreneurship in the support system, developing new entrepreneurship, helping in the growth of existing entrepreneurs and propagation of entrepreneurial education.

***(iv)* Entrepreneurship Development Institute of India (EDII):** The Entrepreneurship Development Institute of India (EDI), an autonomous body and not-for-profit institution, set up in 1983, is sponsored by apex financial institutions, namely the Industrial Development Bank of India (IDBI), IFCI Ltd. ICICI and State Bank of India (SBI). The Institute is registered under the Societies Registration Act 1860 and the Public Trust Act 1950.

An acknowledged national resource institution, EDI is committed to entrepreneurship education, training and research. The institute strives to provide innovative training techniques, competent faculty support, consultancy and quality teaching and training material.EDI has been spearheading entrepreneurship movement throughout the nation with a belief that entrepreneurs need not necessarily be born, but can be developed through well-conceived and well-directed activities.

***(v)* The Institute of Small Enterprises and Development (ISED):** The Institute of Small Enterprises and Development (ISED) stand for 'Sustainable development through enterprise'. It is a multi-faceted center for advanced learning and practice in the area of development. For the past decade, the Institute for Small Enterprises and Development has focused on research, education, innovative program design and entrepreneurship development initiatives, advocacy and networking dedicated towards sustainable development through enterprise creation. Among the similar institutions

ISED's leading-edge is the identification of methodologies and processes that empower one to break out of existing 'mental models' in order to identify new opportunities, while exploiting the emerging niche. ISED's interest in linking research, policy, and action is realized through the programmes of its Activity Centers. The integration of the outcomes takes place at the Centre for Policy Integration. In realizing its vision and fulfilling its mission, the Institute also collaborates with like-minded institutions and individuals

ENTREPRENEURIAL BEHAVIOR

Entrepreneurship is a dynamic process of creating wealth whether in small organizations or large organizations. Entrepreneurship is a continuous search for change, responding to it and exploiting it as an opportunity. Most successful organizations are successful because of the entrepreneurial behavior of their leaders and the entrepreneurial culture prevalent in the organization. The key entrepreneurial behaviors include the following:

1. The desire to win and succeed coupled with vision

Entrepreneurs want to succeed. They are goal oriented and focus their attention and energy on the achievement of specific goals. Many business people go to business without clear goals and therefore they fail to succeed as entrepreneurs. Entrepreneurship therefore has been a leading factor in the success of many businesses both large and small. The small scale enterprises are much more numerous than the large ones and the tendency has been to believe that they are automatically entrepreneurial. However, this is not the case as the growth of these businesses would have been taken for granted. Small businesses are established for various reasons

2. A need for achievement

Related to the need to win is the need to achieve. McClelland (1961), argues that successful entrepreneurs are characterized by a strong need for achievement and this drives them to achieve. This drive makes them creative and enables them to take risks. What else does a business require? Goals to achieve, the desire to achieve them, the intensity of purpose, and the drive to do what it takes to achieve the goal.

3. They love change

Entrepreneurship is a continuous search for change and a continuous exploitation of the change as an opportunity. Entrepreneurs are thrilled by anything knew and frustrated by a slackness of things. In today's changing environment, with ups and downs that characterize the business environment, the only organization sure to survive is the one that is entrepreneurial. There is evidence that the success of Microsoft, Toyota, British Airways, is a result of their ability to cause change themselves. And the failure of many companies is a result of their inability to keep up with the change.

4. They are the creative type

Creativity is the generation of ideas and precedes innovation. Innovation is a specific function of an entrepreneur (Drucker, 1993). Innovation is something new or different. To be able to adjust to change or manage change, business must continuously come up with new ideas, new products, new processes. These can only come from creative people. Entrepreneurs come with ideas as a result of changing needs and changing environmental factors and translate these ideas to create wealth.

5. Risk taking

While entrepreneurs are not high risk takers, they do take risks. And risk is the source of reward (Business reward). Entrepreneurs take risks and succeed. Risk involves looking into the future and believing that there is a probability of the occurrence of certain events. And on this basis a decision is taken to do or not to do something.

Shah *et-al.*, has developed an index to measure entrepreneurial behavior on four dimensions.

(1) Planning Orientation: It is an extent to which entrepreneur makes rational decisions after considering alternative courses of action, how he collects and uses information from environment and the extent to which he is clear about the goals.

(2) Achievement Orientation: entrepreneur concern for excellence is reflected in his behavior.

(3) Expansion Orientation: It measures the extent to which the entrepreneur expanded his business since his first inception.

(4) Operations Management: It assesses the managerial effectiveness of the entrepreneur in running the enterprise. It deals with all the managerial functions.

REVIEW QUESTIONS

1. Explain the various factors affecting Entrepreneurial Growth.
2. Explain in brief the concept of Entrepreneurial Motivation.
3. Discuss about the Motivational Theories of Entrepreneurship.
4. What is the different motivational factors?
5. Explain Entrepreneurial Competencies.
6. Explain the Entrepreneurial Mobility.
7. Explain in brief about the Entrepreneurial Development Program (EDP). Write about its objectives.
8. Explain the course contents and curriculum of Entrepreneurship Development Program.
9. Discuss the various phases of Entrepreneurship Development Programs.
10. Explain about the Evaluation of Entrepreneurship Development Programs.

Fill in the blanks

1. ___________ refers to the key characteristic that successful entrepreneur should posses to perform the entrepreneurial activity
2. Who has given the characteristic of Entrepreneurial competencies
3. EDP stands for___________________
4. An entrepreneur confront problems and issues with other directly, this competency is called ________________
5. There are _________stages of entrepreneurial mobility
6. EDP is designed to promote____________________
7. EDP provides _________ and ___________ from selection through the actual operation of an enterprise
8. Once the entrepreneur select a particular enterprise in depth knowledge about the ___________ of the trade is essential
9. In order to develop _______________development of achievement motive is essential
10. The purpose of AMT is to develop______________, ______________, __________ and _____________
11. A linkage between the training institute and the _________________ can be established by participation and sponsoring of the EDP
12. The participant of the EDP should be given an opportunity to conduct _________ for their chosen projects
13. EDP consist of ___________ phases
14. In ___________ phase of EDP motivation and managerial skills are developed in an entrepreneur.
15. In ___________ phase of EDP infrastructural support, counseling and assistance is provided to the entrepreneurs
16. The traits required for successful entrepreneurship can be __________ and _________ through

psychological test.

17. TRYSEM stand for________________________________
18. TRYSEM was an ______________ program started by Government of India
19. Rural Entrepreneurship is subjected to these type of risks____________, ____________,____________ and ____________
20. Four dimensions of Shah et.al are __________,__________,__________ and ______
21. Maslow's Hierarchical are ______, _______, ____________,___________ and ___________
22. Entrepreneurs are ____________ who take risk to achieve goals.
23. An entrepreneur who combine their technological and entrepreneurial skills are called_____________
24. The _____________ between human needs and the available products and services lead to entrepreneurship.
25. Private entrepreneurship are absent in ____________ economic system
26. India has ____________ economic system
27. Small scale enterprises are more ________ than the large scale enterprise.

Answer:

1. Entrepreneurial Competencies
2. McClelland and Mc-Ber
3. Entrepreneurship Development Program
4. Assertiveness
5. Three
6. Small-scale enterprises
7. Instruction and Counseling
8. Technical aspects
9. Human resource
10. The need to achieve, risk taking, initiative and behavioral traits
11. Support system
12. Market Survey
13. Three
14. Development
15. Support
16. Identified and Measured
17. Training for Rural Youth for Self-employment
18. Anti-poverty
19. Technical, Economic, Social and Environmental
20. Planning, Achievement, Expansion and Operation Management
21. Physiological need, Safety, Social, Esteem and Self-actualization
22. Action-oriented
23. Techno-preneurs
24. Gap filling
25. Socialism
26. Mixed
27. Labor Intensive

◆ ◆ ◆

Small Enterprise

Chapter 3

CHAPTER OUTLINE

- Relationship of Small Enterprises with Large Units
- Characteristics of Small Enterprise
- Enterprise Development Strategy
- Objectives of Small Enterprise
- Scope of Small Enterprise
- Government Policy towards Small Enterprises
- Limitation of Small Enterprise
- Measure for Promotion, Development of MSME
- Impact of Globalization on Small-scale Industries in India

- **Choosing an Entrepreneurial Career**
- **Opportunities of Entrepreneurial Career**
- **Role of Small Enterprise in Economic Development**
- **Project Cycle**
- **Importance of Project Identification**
- **Ownership Structure of SSI**
- **Content of Project Report**
- **Need for Project Formulation**
- **Project Appraisal**
- **MSME ACT**

The contribution of small and medium-sized enterprises to employment, growth and sustainable development is now widely acknowledged. Their development can deepen the manufacturing sector and foster competitiveness. It can also help achieve a more equitable distribution of the benefits of economic growth and thereby help alleviate some of the problems associated with uneven income distribution.

The small medium sized enterprises have played a major role in the growth and development of all the leading economies in Asia. The Asian experience clearly shows that it is mainly the growth-oriented medium-sized enterprises among the small medium enterprises that have a high propensity to apply technology and training and serve specialized niche markets. Among the factors that have contributed to the success of such small medium enterprises is a high incidence of cooperative inter-firm relationships, which have rendered individual firms less susceptible to risks, fostered mutual exchanges of information and know-how between firms and created a rich pool of collective knowledge. A key factor has also been the provision by Governments to small medium enterprises of technological extension services (such as quality assurance, research support and information on sources of technology.

Small enterprises constitute a vibrant and dynamic sector of the industrial economy of India. This sector has shown consistently good growth in terms of production, creation of additional employment and spectacular performance in exports, year after year. Its contribution to industrial growth and economic development of the country has been very significant. It encompasses both traditional industries (includes some of the prominent export intensive segments such as handicrafts, handlooms, carpets and gems and jewellery) and the modern small industries which uses latest appliances, machinery and technologies, and includes electronics, computer software, cotton/leather garments and accessories, auto components, food processing and machine tools and scientific instrumentation. Small in India is more than beautiful — it is efficient, adaptable and adds value in economic and social spheres.

Small Enterprise: Small enterprises have played an important role in the economic development of India. It accounts for 40% of industrial production and 35% of total exports. In addition their role in providing equitable development has also been commendable. Small enterprise provide employment, production, export, ownership structure. The operational efficiency of Small Scale Industries would depend solely upon the entrepreneur's management's skill.

Small enterprises are those business enterprises characterized by size, as well as the way they are operated. They are considered small based on the size of their business volume, the value of assets, and the number of people working. They are usually operated and managed solely by an individual entrepreneur.

Unlike medium and large enterprises which usually have a management team to oversee various business functions such as marketing, finance, operation, HRD, technology management engineering and research and development etc., in small enterprise all these functions are done by one individual entrepreneur.

Small Enterprise Finance Centre

Definition: A small enterprise is a business that is privately owned and operated, with a small number of employees and relatively low volume of sales small businesses are normally privately owned corporations, partnerships, or sole proprietorships. The legal definition may vary with different countries.

Definition of SSI in India: The following requirements are to be complied with by an industrial undertaking to be graded as Small-scale Industrial undertaking, *w.e.f.*, 21st Dec., 1999.

"An industrial undertaking in which the investment in fixed assets in plant and machinery whether held on ownership terms on lease or on hire purchase does not exceed Rs. 10 million/10 lakhs (Subject to the condition that the unit is not owned, controlled or subsidiary of any other industrial undertaking).

Small businesses serve as engines of innovation, growth and employment, due to their flexibility and their potential for rapid growth. Successful small enterprises are not able to grow over time, their benefits are lost to the country. A crucial difference between developing countries and more advanced economies lies in the potential growth paths of small and medium enterprises. In developing countries, very few small enterprises grow to become medium and very few medium grow to large companies. This has a negative impact on innovation, employment and growth in developing countries. In addition to its impact on the overall economy. The business environment which Small medium enterprises face has important implications for equity, social mobility and poverty elimination.

(a) "owned" shall have the meaning as derived from the definition of the expression "owner" specified in clause (1) of section 3 of the said Act;

(b) "subsidiary" shall have the same meaning as in clause (47) of section 2, read with section 4, of the Companies Act, 1956 (1 of 1956);

(c) the expression "controlled by any other industrial undertaking" means as under:

(i) where two or more industrial undertakings are set up by the same person as a proprietor, each of such industrial undertakings shall be considered to be controlled by the other industrial undetaking or undertakings,

(ii) where two or more industrial undertakings are set up as partnership firms under the Indian Partnership Act, 1932 (1 of 1932) and one or more partners are common partner or partners in such firms, each such undertaking shall be considered to be controlled by other undertaking or undertakings,

(iii) where industrial undertakings are set up by companies under the Companies Act, 1956 (1 of 1956), an industrial undertaking shall be considered to be controlled by other industrial undertaking if:

(a) the equity holding by other industrial undertaking in it exceeds twenty four percent of its total equity; or

(b) the management control of an undertaking is passed on to the other industrial undertaking by way of the Managing Director of the first mentioned undertaking being also the Managing Director or Director in the other industrial undertaking or the majority of Directors on the Board of the first mentioned undertaking being the equity holders in the other industrial undertaking in terms of the provisions of the following items *(a)* and *(b)* of sub-clause *(iv)*;

(iv) the extent of equity participation by other industrial undertaking or undertakings in the undertaking as per sub-clause (iii) above shall be worked out as follows:

(a) the equity participation by other industrial undertaking shall include both foreign and domestic equity;

(b) equity participation by other industrial undertaking shall mean total equity held in an industrial undertaking by other industrial undertaking or undertakings, whether small scale or otherwise, put together as well as the equity held by persons who are Directors in any other industrial undertaking or undertakings even if the person concerned is a Director in other Industrial Undertaking or Undertakings;

(c) equity held by a person, having special technical qualification and experience, appointed as a Director in a small scale industrial undertaking, to the extent of qualification shares, if so provided in the Articles of Association, shall not be counted in computing the equity held by other industrial undertaking or undertakings even if the person concerned is a Director in other industrial undertakings or undertakings;

(v) where an industrial undertaking is a subsidiary of, or is owned or controlled by, any other industrial undertaking or undertakings in terms of sub-clauses *(i)*; *(ii)*; or *(iii)* and if the total investment in fixed assets in plant and machinery of the first mentioned industrial undertaking and the other industrial undertaking or undertakings clubbed together exceeds the limit of investment specified in paragraphs (1) or (2) of this notification as the case may be, none of these industrial undertakings shall be considered to be a small scale or ancillary industrial undertaking.

Note 2

(a) In calculating the value of plant and machinery for the purposes of paragraphs (1) and (2) of this notification, the original price thereof, irrespective of whether the plant and machinery are new or second hand, shall be taken into account.

(b) In calculating the value of plant and machinery, the following shall be excluded, namely:-

(i) the cost of equipments such as tools, jigs, dies, moulds and spare parts for maintenance and the cost of consumable stores;

(ii) the cost of installation of plant and machinery;

(iii) the cost of research and development equipment and pollution control equipment;

(iv) the cost of generation sets and extra transformer installed by the undertaking as per the regulations of the State Electricity Board;

(v) the bank charges and service charges paid to the National Small Industries Corporation or the State Small Industries Corporation;

(vi) the cost involved in procurement or installation of cables, wiring, bus bars, electrical control panels (not those mounted on individual machines), oil circuit breakers or miniature circuit breakers which are necessarily to be used for providing electrical power to the plant and machinery or for safety measures;

(vii) the cost of gas producer plants;

(viii) transportation charges (excluding of sales tax and excise) for indigenous machinery from the place of manufacturing to the site of the factory;

(ix) charges paid for technical know how for erection of plant and machinery;

(x) cost of such storage tanks which store raw materials, finished products only and are not linked with the manufacturing process; and

(xi) cost of fire fighting equipments.

(c) In the case of imported machinery, the following shall be included in calculating the value, namely:-

(i) import duty (excluding miscellaneous expenses as transportation from the port to the site of the factory, demurrage paid at the port);

(ii) the shipping charges;

(iii) customs clearance charges; and

(iv) sales tax.

Fig. 3.1: Explanation of Small-scale Industries

Ancillary Industrial Undertakings: The following requirements are to be complied with by an industrial undertaking for being regarded as ancillary industrial undertaking: An industrial undertaking which is engaged or is proposed to be engaged in the manufacture or production of parts, components, sub-assemblies, tooling or intermediates, or the rendering of services and the undertaking supplies or renders or proposes to supply or render not less than 50 per cent of its production or services, as the case may be, to one or more other industrial undertakings and whose investment in fixed assets in plant and machinery whether held on ownership terms or on lease or on hire-purchase, does not exceed ₹ 10 million.

Tiny Enterprises: Investment limit in plant and machinery in respect of tiny enterprises is ₹ 2.5 million irrespective of location of the unit.

Women Entrepreneurs: A Small-scale Industrial Unit/Industry related service or business enterprise, managed by one or more women entrepreneurs in proprietary concerns, or in which she/they individually or jointly have a share capital of not less than 51% as Partners/Shareholders/Directors of Private Limits Company/Members of Cooperative Society.

Relationship of Small Enterprises with Large Units

All industrial units with a capital investment of not more than ₹ one crore are, at present, treated as small-scale units. For ancillary units i.e., those supplying components etc., to large-scale industries and the export-oriented units, the limit of capital investment is also Rs. one crore. Industrial units with an investment of up to Rs. 25 lakhs belong to the tiny sector. It may be noted that capital investment covers only investment in plant and machinery, land and factory buildings are excluded. As per this classification all industries with capital investment higher than specified for small-scale units are large-scale industries.

The small-scale industries contribute a lot to the progress of the Indian economy. They have also a great potential for the future development of the economy. Let us discuss their role in detail.

Large Scope for Employment: The small-scale industries provide large scope for employment on a massive scale. In 2001, the employment generated in this sector was 19.2 million. This is of great significance for a country like India which is a labour-surplus economy, and where labour-force is increasing at a very rapid rate. Moreover, the small-scale industries being labour-intensive they employ more labour per unit of capital for a given output compared to the large-scale industries. This is evident from the fact that the small-scale sector accounts for as much as 80% of the total employment in the industrial sector.

The small-scale industries are also specially suited for overcoming various types of unemployment in the rural and semi-urban areas. With little capital and other resources, mostly available locally, these industries can be set-up everywhere in the country, even at the very door-step of the workers. For this reason the small farmer and agricultural worker can combine their work in agriculture with that in these industries. Further, these industries provide part-time as well as full time work to rural artisans, women, and poor of the backward classes.

Large Production: The small-scale industries also contribute a sizeable amount to the industrial output of the country. Out of the total output of the manufacturing sector, as much as 40% comes from these industries. And out of the total supplies of industrial consumer goods a major part originates in the small-scale sector. Almost all the products of this sector are in the nature of consumer goods, with a significant part consisting of luxury goods. The adequate availability of consumer goods plays an important role in stabilizing and developing the economy.

Large Exports: Many products of the small-scale industries like handloom cotton fabrics, silk fabrics, handicrafts, carpets, jewellery, etc. are exported to foreign countries. Their share in the total exports is as much as 40%. In this way the small-scale sector makes a very valuable contribution to the accumulation of foreign exchange resource of the country.

Use of Latent (domestic) Resources: The small-scale industries used resources which are available locally which would otherwise have remained unused. These resources are, the hoarded wealth, family-labour, artisan's skills, native entrepreneurship, etc. Being thinly spread throughout the country, these resources cannot be used by large-scale industries which need them in big amounts and at a few specified places.

Besides using these resources, the small-scale industries provide an environment for the development of forces of economic growth. Using the hoarded wealth, these industries put into circulation savings which propel investments in the economy. These industries also provide opportunities to the small entrepreneurs to learn, to take risks, to experiment, to innovate and to compete with others.

Promoting Welfare: The small-scale industries are also very important for welfare reasons. People of small means can organize these industries. This in turn increases their income-levels and quality of life. As such these industries help in reducing poverty in the country. Further, these industries tend to promote equitable distribution of income. Since income gets distributed among vast number of persons throughout the country, this help in the reduction of regional economic disparities.

Another advantage of great significance of these industries is the upgrading of the lives of the people in general. The freedom to work, self-reliance, self-confidence, enthusiasm to achieve and all such traits of a healthy nation can be built around the activities performed in these industries. It also becomes possible to preserve the inherited skill of our artisans which would otherwise disappear. Moreover, many ills of urbanization and concentration inherent in large-scale industries can be avoided by setting up of small industries. All these benefits flow from the fact that these industries are highly labour-intensive, and that these can be set up anywhere in the country with small resources.

Characteristics of Small Enterprise

The following are the characteristics of the small enterprises.

1. In large enterprises there is frequently separation between management and ownership where as small enterprises are more likely to operate as extension of their owner's manager.
2. Small enterprises may be faced with fewer investment and financing options.
3. Small enterprises often suffer from resource poverty, particularly of a financial nature.
4. Starting from a smaller fare, small enterprises are generally more likely to experience problems associated with the consequences of growth, such as liquidity pressure.
5. Small enterprise financial management is inevitably more dependent on the ability of a single individual or a small number of individuals than is the ease on large enterprises.
6. The absence of a well formed market for ownership stakes in small enterprises is likely to impact on this financial management.

Enterprise Development Strategy

Current Challenge: Most countries in the region are under going reforms that are opening their economies to greater international competition. However, domestic factor markets are not adequately developed to ensure the successful adaptation of small medium enterprises to this new competitive environment. Unlike larger frame which can more easily absorb the transaction costs small medium enterprises are at a disadvantage and require specific compensatory assistance.

Economic Role and Small Medium Enterprises: The importance of small medium enterprises to longer term economic stability, drives from their size and structure which, under adequate condition i.e., well developed factor markets allow them the flexibility and ability to weather adverse economic conditions. Small medium enterprises are more labor intensive than larger firm and therefore, have lower capital cost associated with the creation of jobs. Consequently, small medium enterprises play an important role in fostering income stability growth and employment. Modern economies operate as complex networks of firms in which a firm's competitive position depends, impart, on the efficiency of its suppliers. Therefore, Small Medium Enterprises' competitiveness affects the competitive position of the economy as a whole. In addition, Small Medium Enterprises improve the efficiency of domestic markets and make productive use of scarce resources, such as capital, facilitating long term economic growth.

Features of Small Medium Enterprises: Their characteristics distinguish Small Medium Enterprises from larger firms. Larger firms often have direct access to international and local capital markets while Small Medium Enterprises are often excluded because of the higher intermediation costs for smaller projects. Additionally, the fixed costs of complying with regulations a limited capacity to market products abroad, and limited access to policy makers against the SME more than the larger firm. Micro enterprises largely operate at a threshold which falls below the regulatory and institutional constraints that inhibits other Small Medium Enterprises and, in some cases, would expand if the barriers to their operations were removed. Because high transactions cost are one of the most important barrier their reduction will promote the creation and expansion of Small Medium Enterprises and in particulars, encourage micro enterprises to expand for the purpose of bank strategy, Small

Medium Enterprises will be taken to include the smallest business units with growth potential although it is recognized that micro enterprises have their own unique characteristics and have a social as well as economic role.

Constraints/Problems to Small Medium Enterprises (SME) face a variety of constraints owing to the difficulty of absorbing large fixed costs, the absence of economies of scale and scope is the key factors of production and the higher unit costs of providing services to smaller firms. A set of constraints which is not intended to be exhaustive, is are:

I Input Constraints:

1. **Debt and Equity:** Small Medium Enterprises have limited access to capital market, locally and internationally, in part because of the perception of higher risk, informational barriers, and the higher costs of intermediation for smaller firms. As a result Small Medium Enterprises often cannot obtain long term finance in the form of term debt and equity.
2. **Labor Market:** An insufficient supply of skilled workers can limited the specialization opportunities, raise costs, and reduce flexibility in managing operations.
3. **Information and Technology:** Small Medium Enterprises have difficulties in gaining access to appropriate technologies and information on available techniques. This limits innovation and SME competitiveness. At the same time, other constraints on capital and labor, as well as uncertainty surrounding new technologies, restrict incentives to innovations.
4. **Production Inputs:** Small Medium Enterprises face constraints in the availability of production inputs for instance , better quality raw material are generally exported or are available only to larger firms and their suppliers tend to be oligopolies. Inadequate infrastructure and weak provision of basic services such as transportation, energy, urban planning and production sites represent particular impediments for Small Medium Enterprises.

II Output Constraints:

1. **Domestic Markets:** The diminished role of the state in productive activity and renewed private investment has created new opportunities for Small Medium Enterprises. Nonetheless, limited access to public contract, and sub contracts, often because of cumbersome bidding procedures or lack of information, inhibits participation in the markets. Also inefficient distribution channels and their control by larger firms are important limitations to market access for Small Medium Enterprises.
2. **International Market:** Previously insulated from international competition, many Small Medium Enterprises are now faced with greater external competition and the need to expand market share. Limited international marketing experience, poor quality control and product standardization and little access to international partners, however, impede expansion into international markets.

III Regulatory Constraints: Although wide ranging structural reforms have improved, prospects for enterprise development many issues remain to be addressed at the firm level.

1. **Taxation and Tariffs:** Complicated and inefficient tax codes that include cascading sales taxes and stamp taxes are least favorable to Small Medium Enterprises and artificially promote large scale firms and micro enterprises. At the same time, the tariff and non-tariff barriers which favor larger firms that play a role in policy making are often biased against Small Medium Enterprises.
2. **Legal:** High start up costs for firms including licensing and registration requirement can impose excessive and unnecessary burdens on Small Medium Enterprises. The high cost of setting legal claims and exercise delays in court proceedings adversely affect SME operations. The absence of antitrust legislation favors larger firms, while the lack of protection property rights limits SME access to foreign technologies.

3. **Capital Movement:** Even though most countries have significantly relaxed restrictions to capital movement, bureaucratic complications and distortions in the foreign exchange markets which remain there, tend to affect Small Medium Enterprises most strongly because they lack the wherewithal of large firms.
4. **Labor Market:** Inflexible labor codes and other indirect labor costs bear most heavily on Small Medium Enterprises, raising their cost of doing business and depriving them of the flexibility to adapt.

IV Management Constraints: The lack of economies of scale and competition for one of the most scare resources, management know how, place significant constraints on SME development.

1. **Management Skills and Training:** Even though Small Medium Enterprises tend to attract motivated managers, they can hardly compete with larger firms. The scarcity of management talent, prevalent in most countries of the region, has a magnified impact on Small Medium Enterprises.
2. **Consulting Services:** The lack of support services or their relatively higher unit cost can hamper SME efforts to improve their management because consulting firms often are not equipped with appropriate cost effective management solutions for the scale of Small Medium Enterprises, further more, the rare awareness, absence of information or time to take advantage of existing services results in weak demand of time.

V. Institutional Constraints: The lack of cohesiveness and the wide range of SME interests limits their capacity to defend their collective interests and their effective participation in civil society.

Association and Collective Action: Associations providing a voice for interest of Small Medium Enterprises in the policy making process had a limited role compared to those of larger firms. Many of the entrepreneurs associations have yet to complete the transition of their goals from protectionism to competitiveness. Additionally, the potential economies of collaborative arrangements in production and sale among Small Medium Enterprises have not adequately explored.

The problems faced by the small enterprises particularly in accessing technology and maintaining competitiveness have been formidable. Lack of familiarity with new options, inability in accessing them, and organizing necessary finance for growth are a few which need to be addressed through institutional support. Absence of a platform where small enterprises can tap opportunities at the global level for acquisition of technology or establish business collaboration has been compounding the problem. Technology Bureau for Small Enterprises is an endeavor to bridge the technology gap. Resulting from the collaboration between the United Nations' Asian and Pacific Centre for Transfer of Technology (APCTT) and Small Industries Development Bank of India (SIDBI) it represents, under one roof, synergy of technology and finance. Its objectives, role and important features:

- Offers a professionally managed system for partner search
- Helps in building up confidence between prospective partners.
- Lends a friendly hand in the intricate task of negotiations and matching of perceptions.
- Provides a gateway to global technology market through Internet and other channels.
- Unique mechanism for arranging technology and finance.
- Renders customized service and wide ranging affiliations.
- Takes up project appraisal and preparation of business plan.

Objectives of Small Enterprise

Small enterpriser always represented the model of socio-economic policies of government of India which emphasized judicious use of foreign exchange for import of capital goods and inputs, labor intensive mode of production, employment generation, non-concentration of diffusion of economic power in the hands of few, discouraging monopolistic practices of production and marketing, and finally effective contribution to foreign exchange earning to the nation with low import –

intensive operations. It was also coupled with the policy of de-concentration of industrial activities in few geographical centers.

It can be observed that by and large, Small Medium Enterprises in India met the expectations of the government in this respects. Small Medium Enterprises developed in a manner, which made it possible for them to achieve the following objectives.

1. High concentration to domestic production.
2. Significant export earnings.
3. Low investment requirements.
4. Operational flexibility.
5. Location wise mobility.
6. Low intensive imports.
7. Capacities to develop appropriate indigenous technology.
8. Import substitution.
9. Contribution towards defense production.
10. Technology – Oriented industries.
11. Competitiveness in domestic and export markets.

Scope of Small Enterprise

The scope for small business is vast covering a wide variety of activities starting from retailing to manufacturing. There are some specific areas of economic activity which can be effectively and successfully managed by forming small business enterprises. Let us discuss about the scope for small business.

1. Trading which involves buying and selling of goods and services requires less capital and time to start. This area of economic activity is dominated by small-scale entrepreneurs.
2. The activities which require personalized service like motor repairing, tailoring, carpentry, beauty parlour etc. are run by establishing small business.
3. It is the best option for those who do not like to be an employee, but become self-employed. People can work independently by running a small enterprise of their own.
4. For products and services, which are of less demand or their demand is limited to any specific area; the small-scale business is most suitable for them.
5. A large industrial unit cannot run smoothly without the support of small units. These industrial units often depend upon the small units (ancillary industrial undertaking) to get some parts or spares, which cannot be profitably produced by them.
6. In the era of business process outsourcing (BPO), many new areas have opened up for small business enterprises.
7. The business enterprises, which require constant touch of the owners with customers as well as the employees, can only be successfully run in the form of small enterprises.

Government Policy towards Small Enterprises

The Government of India has given special importance to small business enterprises due their vast potentiality for development of social and economic condition of the country. Several assistance and support are announced from time to time keeping in view the changing economic conditions. The following are some of such steps taken by the Government for development of small business in India.

1. It provides liberalized credit policy like, fewer formalities to process the loans and advances, loans at concessional rate, etc.

2. To keep away from the competition with large scale industries, the Government of India has reserved about 800 items for exclusive production by small scale industries.
3. It provides concession and exemption in excise and sales tax to the small scale units. The excise exemption has risen from ₹ 50 lakh to ₹ One crore for small industries.
4. The Government also gives preference to the products of small enterprises while purchasing stationery and other item for its own consumption and use.
5. For promotion, financing and development of small-scale industrial enterprises several institutes like Small Industrial Development Bank of India (SIDBI), National Bank for Agriculture and Rural Development (NABARD), District Industries Centres (DICs) etc. have been set up by the Government.
6. The Government of India has set up separate Ministry of Micro, Small and Medium Enterprises for effective planning and monitoring of the development of small business enterprises in the country.
7. To provide benefits of its plans and policies to large number of industries, it has lowered the investment limit from ₹ 3 crore to ₹ One crore.
8. The Government provides capital subsidy of 12% for investment in technology in select sectors of small-scale business.
9. To encourage total quality management (TQM) the Government provides grant of ₹ 75,000 to each units that obtains ISO 9000 certification.
10. To provide finance, design and marketing support to handloom sector it has launched the Deendayal Hathkargha Protsahan Yojana.
11. The Government of India has permitted upto 24% of total shareholding of small-scale units by other industrial units.
12. The Government provides land, power and water, etc., at concessional rates to small business enterprises.
13. Special incentives are also provided for setting up of small enterprises in rural and backward areas.
14. The Government encourages establishing small-scale industry by providing developed land and industrial estates

Limitation of Small Medium Enterprises

1. Low capital base.
2. Concentration of function in one/two persons.
3. Inadequate exposure to international environment.
4. Inability to face impact of WTO regime.
5. Inadequate contribution towards research and development.
6. Lack of professionalism.

In spite of these limitations the Small Medium Enterprises have made significant contribution towards technological development and exports.

Small Medium Enterprises have been established in almost all major sectors in the Indian Industry such as:

1. Food processing.
2. Agricultural inputs.
3. Chemicals and Pharmaceuticals.
4. Engineering, Electrical, Electronics.
5. Electro Medical Equipment.

6. Textiles and Garments.
7. Leather and leather goods.
8. Meat products.
9. Bioengineering.
10. Sport goods.
11. Plastic products.
12. Computer Software etc.

Those Small Medium Enterprises who have strong technological base, international business outlook, competitive spirit and willingness to restructure themselves shall with stand the present challenges and come out with shinning colors to make their own contribution to the Indian Economy.

Importance of Small-scale Industries

1. Provide increased employment through labor intensive process.
2. Require lower gestation period.
3. Easy to set up in rural and backward areas.
4. Need small/local market.
5. Encourage growth of local entrepreneurship.
6. Create a decentralized pattern of ownership.
7. Foster diversification of economic activities.
8. Introduce new products particularly to cater to local needs.
9. Influence the standard of living of local people.
10. Provide equitable dispersal of industries throughout rural and backward areas.

Measures for Promotion, Development and Enhancement of Competitiveness of Micro, Small and Medium Enterprises

1. **Measures for promotion and development:** The Central Government may, change policies from time to time, for the purposes of facilitating the promotion and development and enhancing the competitiveness of micro, small and medium enterprises, particularly of the micro and small enterprises, by way of development of skill in the employees, management and entrepreneurs, provisioning for technological upgradation, providing marketing assistance or infrastructure facilities and cluster development of such enterprises with a view to strengthen backward and forward linkages, specify, by notification, such programs, guidelines or instructions, as it may deem fit.
2. **Credit facilities:** The policies and practices in respect of credit to the micro, small and medium enterprises shall be progressive and such as may be specified in the guidelines or instructions issued by the Reserve Bank, from time to time, to ensure timely and smooth flow of credit to such enterprises, minimize the incidence of sickness among and enhance the competitiveness of such enterprises.
3. **Procurement preference policy:** For facilitating promotion and development of micro and small enterprises, the Central Government or the State Government may, by order notify from time to time, preference policies in respect of procurement of goods and services, produced and provided by micro and small enterprises, by its Ministries or departments as the case may be, or its aided institutions and public sector enterprises.
4. **Funds:** These shall be constituted, by notification, one or more Funds to be called by such name as may be specified in the notification and shall be credited thereto any grants made by the Central Government under section 13.

5. **Grants by Central Government:** The Central Government may, after due appropriation made by Parliament by law in this behalf, credit to the Fund or Funds by way of grants for the purposes of this Act, such sums of money as that Government may consider necessary to provide.

IMPACT OF GLOBALIZATION ON SME/SSI IN INDIA

Effects of Globalization on Indian Industry

Effects of Globalization on Indian Industry started when the government opened the country's markets to foreign investments in the early 1990s. Globalization of the Indian Industry took place in its various sectors such as steel, pharmaceutical, petroleum, chemical, textile, cement, retail, and BPO.

Globalization means the dismantling of trade barriers between nations and the integration of the nations economies through financial flow, trade in goods and services, and corporate investments between nations. Globalization has increased across the world in recent years due to the fast progress that has been made in the field of technology especially in communications and transport. The government of India made changes in its economic policy in 1991, by which it allowed direct foreign investments in the country. As a result of this, globalization of the Indian Industry took place on a major scale.

The various beneficial effects of globalization in Indian Industry are that it brought in huge amounts of foreign investments into the industry especially in the BPO, pharmaceutical, petroleum, and manufacturing industries. As huge amounts of foreign direct investments were coming to the Indian Industry, they boosted the Indian economy quite significantly. The benefits of the effects of globalization in the Indian Industry are that many foreign companies set up industries in India, especially in the pharmaceutical, BPO, petroleum, manufacturing, and chemical sectors and this helped to provide employment to many people in the country. This helped reduce the level of unemployment and poverty in the country. Also the benefit of the Effects of Globalization on Indian Industry are that the foreign companies brought in highly advanced technology with them and this helped to make the Indian Industry more technologically advanced.

The various negative Effects of Globalization on Indian Industry are that it increased competition in the Indian market between the foreign companies and domestic companies. With the foreign goods being better than the Indian goods, the consumer preferred to buy the foreign goods. This reduced the amount of profit of the Indian Industry companies. This happened mainly in the pharmaceutical, manufacturing, chemical, and steel industries. The negative Effects of Globalization on Indian Industry are that with the coming of technology the number of labor required decreased and this resulted in many people being removed from their jobs. This happened mainly in the pharmaceutical, chemical, manufacturing, and cement industries.

The effects of globalization on Indian Industry have proved to be positive as well as negative. The government of India must try to make such economic policies with regard to Indian Industry's globalization that are beneficial and not harmful.

Globalization and Structural Changes in the Indian Industrial Sector

Globalization and Structural Changes in the Indian Industrial Sector took place in the early 1990s, when the government decided to open the markets to foreign investments by forming new economic polices. Structural Changes in the Indian Industrial Sector and Globalization were initiated because the government wanted to encourage growth by doing away with supply bottlenecks that stopped efficiency and competitiveness.

Globalization implies the dismantling of trade barriers between nations and the integration of the economies of the nations through financial flow, trade in services and goods, and corporate investments between nations. Globalization has increased in the recent years due to the rapid progress that has been made in the area of technology especially in communications and transport. The Indian policies with regard to the industrial sector before globalization had imposed many restrictions on the sector with regard to the use and procurement of capital and raw material, type and nature of industry where the entry of private sector was allowed, the operation scale, and the various markets where they could supply. The Indian industrial policies favored firms of small size that were labor intensive.

The Structural Changes in the Indian Industrial Sector was brought about by the New Economic Policy of 1991, which did away with many of the regulations and restrictions. The various advantages of Globalization and Structural Changes in the Indian Industrial Sector are that it brought in huge amounts of foreign investments and this gave a major boost to this sector. Many foreign companies entered the Indian market and they brought in highly technologically advanced machines into the country as a result of which the Indian Industrial Sector became technologically advanced. With new companies being set up in the Indian Industrial Sector it provides employment opportunities for many people in the country which in its turn helps to reduce the level of poverty in the country. The number of factories in India in 1990-1991 stood at 110,179 and in 2003-2004, the figure increased to 129,074.

The various disadvantages of Globalization and Structural Changes in the Indian Industrial Sector are that with many foreign companies entering the sector increased the competition for the domestic companies. With foreign goods being better then the Indian products, the consumer in the country preferred to buy the foreign goods. This reduced the profit levels of the Indian companies and they had to resort to lowering the prices of their products which in turn further lowered their levels of profit. With highly advanced technology entering the Indian Industrial Sector, the number of labor required in the sector reduced. The number of labor in the Indian Industrial Sector in 1990-1991, was 81,62,504 and in 2003-2004, the figure has decreased to 78,70,081. Thus, Globalization and Structural Changes in the Indian Industrial Sector poses advantages and disadvantages for the country. So the government of India must take steps in order to ensure that the changes in the structure of the Indian Industrial Sector are such that it facilitates globalization in a manner that is gainful and constructive for a country like India.

The small-scale sectors have, over the part six decades, acquired a prominent place in the socio-economic development in the country. SSI sector has demonstrated its strength the basic accent of small-scale industrial policy has been defensive aiming to insulate the sector from the dynamics of competitive growth.

The process of liberalization and economic reforms, since 1991, while creating tremendous opportunities for the growth of SSIs have, however thrown up new challenges for the sector. In the changing scenario, building competitive strengths, introducing technology up gradation and quality improvement are vital issues which need to be addressed. In order to build the capability to with stand emerging pressure and ensure sustainable growth.

The SSI never had a strong desire to grow the medium / large scale because of the benefits of protection given to it. Many of the policies also discouraged the growth of small scale units into large ones had a stunting effect on manufacturing, employment and output growth. With globalization, the SSI are more exposed to severe competition both from the large scale sector domestic and foreign and from MNC's.

The poor growth rate in the SSI during the post liberalization period can be attributed to various factors such as the new policies of the government towards liberalization and globalization without ensuring the interest or priority of the sector.

Problem of SSIs in the liberalized environment are multidimensional delay in implementation of projects, inadequate availability of finance and credit, expensive, mode of communication, marketing problems, cheap and low quality products, delay in payment, technological obsolescence, imperfect knowledge of market condition, lack of infrastructure facilities, and deficient managerial and technical skills, to name some.

Business environment is changing fast globalization, whether understood in a limited way in terms of multilateral trade liberalization or in the broader sense of increasing internationalization of production, distribution and so on, has resulted in the opening up of markets leading to intense competition in the domestic market has further intensified with the arrival of MNC as the restrictions are foreign direct investments have been removed.

SSI needs to integrate itself with the overall domestic economy and global markets by gearing itself to greater interdependence by networking and subcontracting. To meet the present as well as future requirement the policies / projects for the SSI should be effective and growth oriented so as to achieve competitiveness, collective approach, and capacity to upgrade.

In order to protect, support and promote small enterprises as also to help them, become self supporting a number of protective and promotional measures have been undertaken by the central government. The promotional measures cover.

1. Industrial extension services.
2. Institutional support in respect of credit facilities.
3. Provision of developed sites for construction of sheds.
4. Provision of training facilities.
5. Supply of machinery on hire purchase terms.
6. Assistance for domestic marketing as well as exports.
7. Technical consultancy and financial assistance for technological up gradation.
8. Special incentive for setting up enterprises in backward areas and else where.

The Merits of Globalization are as follows:

❖ There is an International market for companies and for consumers there is a wider range of products to choose from.

❖ Increase in flow of investments from developed countries to developing countries, which can be used for economic reconstruction.

❖ Greater and faster flow of information between countries and greater cultural interaction has helped to overcome cultural barriers.

❖ Technological development has resulted in reverse brain drain in developing countries.

The Demerits of Globalization are as follows:

❖ The outsourcing of jobs to developing countries has resulted in loss of jobs in developed countries.

❖ There is a greater threat of spread of communicable diseases.

❖ There is an underlying threat of multinational corporations with immense power ruling the globe.

❖ For smaller developing nations at the receiving end, it could indirectly lead to a subtle form of colonization.

Choosing an Entrepreneurial Career

Anyone who has ever worked for someone has had the following thought run through his or her mind: "I would be much better off being my own boss." Many people decide to take that thought and run with it, joining the ranks of many who become entrepreneurs. Many small start-up businesses see great success while others fail.

Today, entrepreneurship seems unambiguous. It is difficult to open a newspaper without being bombarded with stories about start up companies and the people who drive them. Simple as it may seem, entrepreneurship is a complex and interesting profession. But it's not all hunky dory and as an entrepreneur, you must be prepared to endure your share of anxiety, acidity and sleepless nights.

Entrepreneurs start new businesses and take on the risk and rewards of being an owner. This is the ultimate career in capitalism — putting their idea to work in a competitive economy. Some new ventures generate enormous wealth for the entrepreneur. However, the job of entrepreneur is not for everyone. He needs to be hard-working, smart, creative, willing to take risks and good with people. Entrepreneur need to have heart, have motivation and have drive.

Due to largely self-originating selection of potential entrepreneurs, their motivation plays a central role in the formation of new companies, based on the three distinct level of approach:

1. **Preference for an entrepreneurial career:** An eventual gulf between professional goals and their achievement in the current job situation leads to a deficit in job satisfaction; people with a high mobility may then develop a readiness to change the job, which in turn triggers the search for alternatives. Interactions for instance with people who used to be, or still are entrepreneurs may direct the search for alternatives in the direction of entrepreneurial career. Now, if an entrepreneurial career has more power of attraction than a change within the employee career, it will be given preference over competing alternatives and become the new professional goal.

   The feedback loop from the preference to the professional goals shows that deficits in job satisfaction are more likely to arise in goal dimensions which are especially unfavorable in terms of attractive job alternatives. It can be added that this preference anticipates a satisfaction potential as defined by the expectancy/valence theories (Vroom, Porter, Lawler). Preference is given to the job with alternative with the comparatively highest satisfaction potential i.e. the entrepreneurial career.

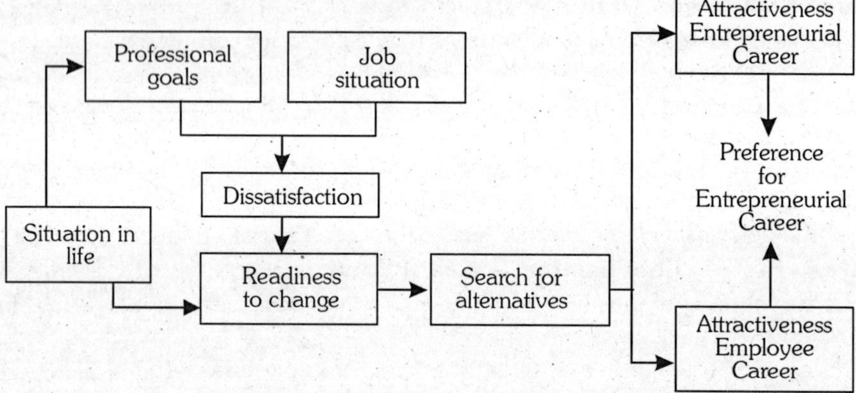

Fig. 3.2: Preference for an Entrepreneurial Career

2. **Motivation for new-venture creation:** If a person rates the chances of realizing the new-venture project as low, he will hardly start a new company, the search for alternatives start again and he chooses another professional activity and does not set up a company – or not before the chance a realization are perceived as better. The motivation to start a new company is clearly dependent upon the combination of strong preference with perceived reasonable chances of realization. The chances of realization for their part are determined by the subjective expectancy to be personally up to the standards of an entrepreneurial career and to be able to raise the necessary resources.
3. **The new company's entry into the market:** Individual motivation is translated into a new venture creation is in addition dependent upon the (objectives) environment-related circumstances, more concretely, upon the outcome of negotiations with the resource suppliers. Moneylenders in particular exercise something like an indirect selective function, to the effect that new venture projects come to naught if the necessary funds are not procurable.

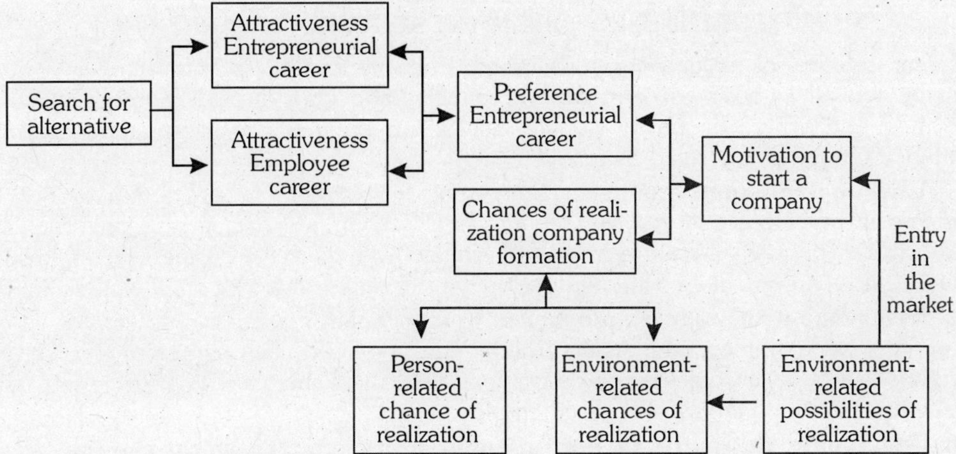

Fig. 3.3: Motivation to start a New Company

These are a number of factors that make an entrepreneurial career distinct from the more traditional career where one is employed by an organisation.

1. **Personal commitment:** Entrepreneurial careers are marked by a substantially higher degree of personal commitment to the success of the firm since the career and the business are intertwined.
2. **Lower degree of structure:** Entrepreneurial career is unique in its lower degree of structure, predictability and support as compared to what an employer would provide.
3. **Greater tendency towards action and innovations:** Entrepreneurial career must process greater tendency towards action and innovation. Specifically the nature of entrepreneurial firms is that decisive actions are required to respond to changing market conditions by extensions, the entrepreneur, as the person in charge, must show the ability to respond, quickly to environmental change.
4. **Perform different functions at a time:** Entrepreneur career is that the entrepreneur performs a number of functional roles simultaneously. More precisely the entrepreneurs can be involved with operation, marketing, accounting, human resources, and planning functions all at the same time.
5. **Autonomy and independence:** It imply that the individual experiences a substantial amount of freedom in his/her job freedom of choice in decision making, freedom of expression in work, freedom from close supervision and freedom from the bureaucratic process. With autonomy the individual can implement his/her self concept and live out important values. Entrepreneurship allows for self determination, financial independence, and acting on the belief that there is a "better way" of doing something".
6. **Tolerance for ambiguity:** The ability to accept and deal with conflicting and uncertain situation and to handle multiple ambiguous assignments does appear to the entrepreneurial personality.
7. **Risk taking propensity:** Willingness to take risks is a common element in describing the entrepreneur.
8. **Entrepreneurial self-concept:** Entrepreneur's primary concern is to create something new involving the motivation to overcome obstacles, the willingness to run risks and the desire for personal prominence in whatever is accomplished. Entrepreneur reflects a desire to have freedom and autonomy to build the organisation and create the business into own self image.

Opportunities of Entrepreneurial Career

Career is a way of making one's livelihood. Entrepreneurship is also a career because one may employ oneself in business or in service activities and earn one's livelihood. With growing unemployment and lack of adequate job opportunities, entrepreneurship has become very significant. Its importance can be enumerated as follows.

1. Advantage of small business: Small-scale business has several advantages over large-scale business. It can be easily started, and requires small amount of capital investment. The enterprise involving activities on a small-scale is a good alternative to large scale business which has brought various evils like environmental pollution, development of slums, exploitation of workers, and so on.

2. Preference over wage employment: In small enterprise there is no limit of earnings as is the case with wage employment. As an entrepreneur, one can use one's talent for own benefit. The decisions can be taken quickly and conveniently. All these factors act as strong motivators for self-employment to be preferred over wage employment.

3. Developing the spirit of entrepreneurship: Entrepreneurship involves taking risks because the entrepreneur tries to innovate new products, new methods of production and marketing. Self-employment, on the other hand, involves either no risk or very little risk. But, as soon as the self-employed person starts becoming innovative and takes steps to expand his business, he becomes an entrepreneur. Therefore, self-employment becomes a launching pad for entrepreneurship.

4. Promotion of individualized services: Entrepreneurial career may also take the form of providing individualized services like tailoring, repair work, dispensing of medicines etc. Such services are helpful in providing better consumer satisfaction. These can be easily started and run by individuals.

5. Scope for creativity: It provides opportunity for development of creativity and skills in art and crafts, leading to preservation of the cultural heritage of India. For example, we can see creative ideas reflected in handicrafts, handloom products, etc.

6. Reducing the problem of unemployment: Entrepreneurial career provides opportunities of gainful occupation to those who otherwise remain unemployed. Thus it reduces the problem of unemployment.

7. A boon to under-privileged in respect of higher education: Everyone may not be able to pursue higher education after Secondary or Senior Secondary examination due to one or the other reason. Such persons can start their career as entrepreneurship in occupations that do not require higher education. It may be noted that entrepreneur has been given high priority in government policies and programs. A number of schemes have been initiated all over the country to encourage entrepreneurship.

Role of Small Enterprise in Economic Development

Small and Medium scale industries can play an important role in the process of a country's industrial and economic development in particular, SME can make significant contribution to achieve social and economic objectives such as labor absorption, income distribution, rural development, poverty eradication and balanced economic growth. There are several important reasons why these small industries are contributing a lot to the progress of the Indian Economy.

1. Production: The small enterprise plays a vital role in the growth of the county. It contributes almost 40% of the gross industrial value added in the Indian economy. It has been estimated that a million rupees of investment in fixed assets in the small-scale sector produce 4.62 million worth of goods and services with an approximate value addition to 10% points.

The small scale sector has grown rapidly over the years. The growth rates during the various plan periods have been very impressive. The number of small-scale units has increased from an estimated 0.87 million units in the year 1980-81 to over 3 million in the years 2000.

When the performance of this sector is viewed against the growth in the manufacturing and the industry sector as a whole, it instills confidence in the resilience of the small-scale sector.

2. Employment: SSI sector in India creates largest employment opportunities for the Indian population, next only to agriculture. It has been estimated the 1,00,000 rupees of investment in fixed assets in the small-scale sector generates employment for four persons.

3. Export: SSI sector plays a major role in India's present export performance. It contributes 45% – 50% of the Indian Exports. Direct exports from the SSI account for nearly 35% of the total exports. Besides direct exports, it is estimated that SSI units contribute around 15% to export indirectly. This takes place through merchant exporters, trading houses and export houses. They may also be in the form of export orders from large units of the production of parts and components of use for furnished exportable goods.

It would surprise many to know that a non-traditional product accounts for more than 95% of the SSI exports. The exports from SSI sector have been clocking excellent growth rates in this decade. It has been fuelled by the performance of garments leather and gems and jewellery etc. The product groups where the SSI dominates in exports are sports goods, readymade garments, woolen garments, and knitwear, plastic products, processed food and leather products.

4. Opportunity

The opportunities in the SSI are enormous due to the following factors.

1. Less capital intensive.
2. Extensive promotion and support by government.
3. Reservation for exclusive manufacture by SSI.
4. Project profiles.
5. Funding – Finances and Subsidies.
6. Machinery procurement.
7. Raw material procurement.
8. Man power training.
9. Technical and Managerial skills.
10. Tooling and testing support.
11. Reservation for exclusive purchase by government.
12. Expert promotion.

Growth of demand in the domestic market size due to overall economic growth increasing export potential for Indian product growth which is requirements for ancillary units due to the increase in number of large scale sector. SSI has performed exceedingly well and enabled our country to achieve a wide measure of industrial growth and diversification.

Project Identification and Selection

Project identification is the first step of new venture. A right direction may enable an entrepreneur to scale new heights. Otherwise he has to undergo a number of hurdles in his way. It is therefore, very crucial to entrepreneurs to identify projects. An entrepreneur has an infinitely wide choice with respect to the project. The important dimensions of choice are; product / service market, technology, equipment, scale of production, location, incentives, and time phasing. The task of identifying a feasible and promising project is difficult. It is interrelated with the government policies, infrastructural development and skills of people.

Project identification is concerned with collection, compilation and analysis of economic data for the eventual purpose of locating possible opportunities for investment and with the development of such opportunities.

According to Drucker opportunities are of three kinds.

1. Additive: Additive opportunities are those opportunities which enable the decision maker to better utilize the existing resources without in any way involving a change in the character of business. These opportunities involve minimum disturbance to the existing state of affairs and hence the least risk.

2. Complementary: Opportunities involves the introduction of new ideas and as such do lead to a certain amount of change in the existing structure. The element of risk is greater here.

3. Breakthrough: Opportunities involve fundamental changes in both the structure and character of business. It involves minimum disturbance to the existing state of affairs and hence the least risk.

Project identification can be done through.

1. Observation: It is one of the most important sources of project ideas. The observant mind continuously come across situation which can be utilized to develop investment opportunities.

2. Trade and Professional Magazines: Provide a very fertile source of project ideas. The statistics and information given by these magazines and report and records of professional bodies often reveal opportunities which can be eventually developed into investment prepositions. It is very important for every person who is involved in the development of new investment opportunities to remain in touch with the latest developments in his own field of specialization.

3. Bulletins of Research Institutes: are also a very fertile source of information for new project ideas and opportunities. These bulletins generally give the broad outlines of the new processes or products developed by research institution.

4. Departmental Publications of various department of government also provide useful information which can help in the development of new project idea. These publications are either periodical in character or are issued on special occasion. The census document which is a periodical publication is a very useful source of information about the economic structure of the society and various trends in the growth of economy and purchasing power and can be used to develop new ideas.

Project Cycle

Although instinct might encourage business professionals to drive right into projects, successful leaders understand that effective project cycles contain seven distinct phases. Few projects actually move through all seven phases in order. Some projects may require retooling that causes more time for preparation and presentation. Longer projects may necessitate alternating phases for implementation, monitoring, and evaluation. In all cases, however, project managers should prepare for the distinct needs of each project phase.

1. Identification

Most projects enter the first phase of the project cycle with little or no structure. Ideas that start in the back of the mind start to bubble up into potential projects. As creative professionals include colleagues, supervisors, or investors, projects become more formalized and start to follow the traditional phases of a project cycle.

On the other hand, regular project cycles, such as grant competitions and workplace initiatives, often operate from a top-down level. Project leaders usually issue a request for proposals or a call for submissions, in order to discover the most effective solution to a particular problem. In this kind of project, judges must sift through different ideas before settling on the team that will take a project through the project cycle's six remaining stages.

2. Preparation

This phase of the project cycle requires leaders and managers to research both the needs and the impact of a project. The preparation phase often includes brainstorming sessions that result in "pie in the sky" estimates instead of true cost/benefit analysis. Effective preparation also includes laying the groundwork for the evaluation phase of the project cycle. Without agreeing on specific goals or outcomes, participants have no reliable way to measure the success of their project.

3. Appraisal

During the appraisal phase of a project cycle, project managers negotiate with stakeholders for resources while setting timelines. Depending on the scope of a project, leaders must determine whether hiring or outsourcing human resources will play a role during the implementation phase. Other resources, like technology and real estate, require budget estimates and impact statements during this phase. The appraisal phase of the project cycle ends once a clear plan with a timeline, budget, and expected outcome is ready for submission to decision makers.

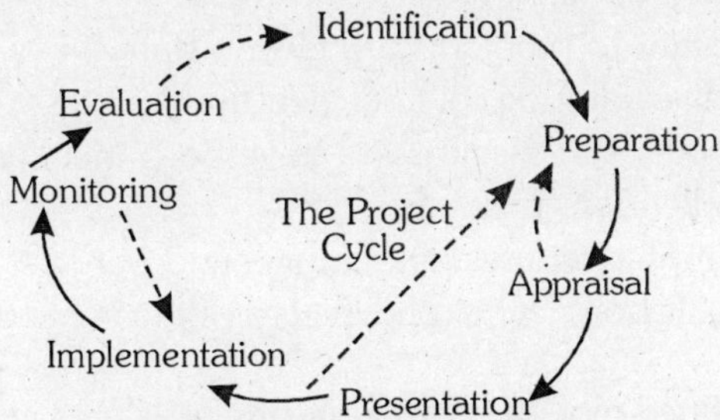

Fig. 3.4: Project Cycle

4. Presentation

Arguably the most crucial phase in any project cycle, the presentation often determines whether or not a project will reach its eventual conclusion. Depending on the nature of the project, decision makers could include board members, supervisors, investors, creditors, community members, customers, or other stakeholders. By the presentation phase, project managers and planners should be able to communicate: project need goals and expected outcomes budget timeline.

Although many project managers prepare for the presentation phase of the project cycle by building Gantt charts and PowerPoint decks, most veteran planners recommend that presenters prepare to debate and to defend the merits of their proposals. It's not uncommon for projects to move between the first three phases numerous times before receiving approval.

5. Implementation

While implementation represents just one phase of a seven-step project cycle, it frequently takes the longest amount of time. During this phase a project manager actually takes the steps to lead a team through the process developed during the previous four stages.

6. Monitoring

While some project management professionals prefer to view monitoring as a task that happens throughout the project cycle, many business schools now teach students to treat this important task as its own dedicated stage. Building a monitoring stage into a project cycle can involve measuring independent benchmarks or scheduling formal progress meetings. Unlike the evaluation stage of the project cycle, monitoring focuses more on individual tasks or personnel in order to make adjustments. Projects often shift between implementation and monitoring phases multiple times during a project cycle.

7. Evaluation

Highly functional organizations use the evaluation phase of the project cycle to answer three important questions:

- ❖ What went well during the project?
- ❖ What didn't go so well?
- ❖ What would project leaders and team members do differently during future projects?

A successful evaluation phase requires effective planning during the preparation phase. If project members succumb to office politics or fail to document the shifting scope of a project, the evaluation phase of a project cycle can easily shift to "blaming and shaming." However, when measurable goals are set and stakeholders agree on desired outcomes, all parties can make honest, insightful evaluations.

The stages of the project cycle provide a structure that ensures that:

- problem analysis is thorough
- stakeholders are clearly identified and monitored
- quality assurance is built in
- objectives are relevant to problems are clearly stated
- outputs and objectives are logical and measurable
- beneficiaries' strengths and weaknesses have been identified
- assumptions are taken into account
- monitoring concentrates on verifiable targets and outputs
- evaluations identify 'lessons learnt' and integrates them into the cycle for similar succeeding projects
- sustainability is defined, not essentially by 'organizational continuity', but primarily by the continuous 'flow of benefits'

Importance of Project Identification

Project identification is often of great importance for the following reasons.

1. They become the catalytic agents of economic development.
2. They initiate the process of development in terms of employment and income generation.
3. They have beneficial consequences which are long term in nature.
4. Projects provide the framework of the future pattern of activities and services of the enterprises.
5. Projects usually involve substantial financial outlays.
6. They also initiate development of basic infrastructure and environment.
7. Project commitments cannot be easily reversed.
8. Project identification brings the necessary changes in society in course of time.
9. Project accelerates the process of socio-cultural development.

There are many organizations that provide information on business opportunities such as:

1. District Industry Centers DIC.
2. Technical Consultancy Organization TCO.
3. Centers for Entrepreneurship Development CED.
4. Small Industry Service Institutes SISI.
5. Leading Banks.
6. Industrial Extension Bureaus. IEB.
7. National Institute of Small Industry Extension and Training, Hyd. NISIET.
8. National Industrial Development Corporation Delhi NIDC.
9. Khadi and Village Industries Commission New Delhi KVIC.
10. Entrepreneurship Development Institute of India Ahmedabad EDII.
11. Small Industries Development Bank of India Lucknow SIDBI.
12. National Institute of Entrepreneurship and small Business Development New Delhi. NIIESBD.

Criteria for Selecting a Particular Project

After gathering a large number of project profiles. The entrepreneur should consider the following criteria for selecting a particular project.

Investment Size: Professional manager, who have worked in MNC or large Indian Companies should think of starting medium-sized or large sized units only the investment size (project cost) should be at least ₹ 3-5 crores) for small enterprises require maximum ₹ 2 crores. In fact, under the present circumstances, it will be much easier to get project cleared by the all India Institution, requiring even lesser promoter's contribution.

Location: A new entrepreneur should locate his project to the extent possible, in and around the state head quarters. There are many background areas around such cities. It is necessary to have such a location so to attract competent managers. This will also facilitate liaison with State Electricity Board, State Industrial Development Corporation and various other agencies.

Technologies: The first project should not be for a product which requires high technology, necessitating foreign technical collaboration. It is better to go in for product with a proven technology that is indigenously available makes life easier to begin with.

Equipment: The entrepreneur should select the best equipment as per the advise of experienced technical consultants. He should not compromise on the quality of the equipment. Many entrepreneurs enter into some sort of a deal with the equipment manufactures for a "kick-back" and in the process sacrifice quality.

Marketing: It is not advisable to get into a project particularly the first, which would mean survival amidst cut-throat, competition involving direct selling to the ultimate consumers. One should go in for products with a limited number (say 10-20) of industrial customers.

Project Formulation and Selection

(a) Product or Service Selection:

The entrepreneur has to decide on a suitable product or a service based on which project can be started. He has to consider various factors before deciding on suitable projects the main factors are as follows:

- Background and experience of the entrepreneurs.
- Availability of technology and know-how for projects.
- Marketability of the product/services.
- Investment capacity.
- Availability of plant and machinery.
- Availability of raw material.
- Availability of proper infrastructure facilities (land, power, water, transport and soon).

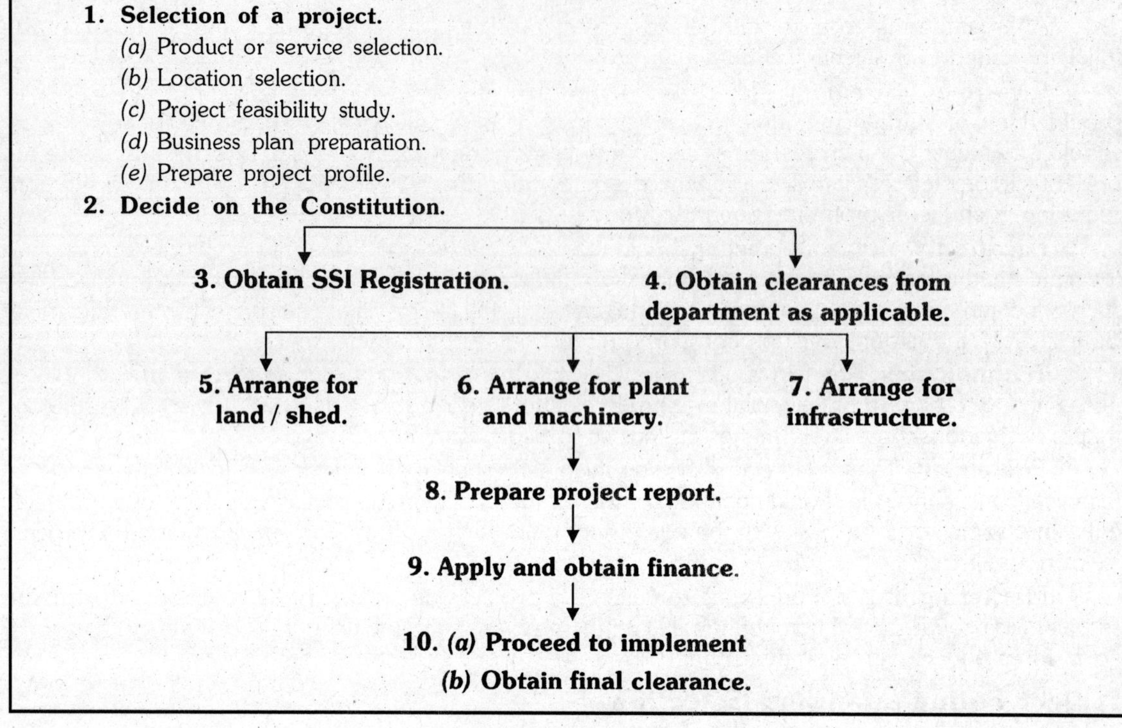

Fig. 3.5: Project Formulation

***(b)* Location Selection:** One of the major decision as entrepreneur has to make is about the location of the project, where is the unit. Some of the major aspects to be considered before deciding on the location of the project are.

- ❖ Proximity to market.
- ❖ Availability of raw material.
- ❖ Availability of transportation and communication facilities.
- ❖ Availability of incentives / concessions.
- ❖ Government policy.
- ❖ Availability of suitable infrastructure facilities.
- ❖ Convenience for the promoter.

***(c)* Project Feasibility Study:** The important facets of a project feasibility study are as follows;

***(i)* Market analysis:** The kind of information required.

- ❖ Consumption trends in the past and the present consumption level.
- ❖ Past and present supply position.
- ❖ Production possibilities and constraints.
- ❖ Import and export.
- ❖ Structure of competition.
- ❖ Cost structure.
- ❖ Elasticity of demand.
- ❖ Consumer behavior, intentions, motivation, attitudes, preferences and requirements.
- ❖ Distribution channels and marketing policies in use.

- ❖ Administrative, technical and legal constraints.
- ❖ Technical analysis:

1. Technical analysis: Analysis of the technical and engineering aspects of a project needs to be done continually when a project is formulated. Technical analysis seeks to determine the following:

- ❖ Have the preliminary tests and studies done?
- ❖ Has the availability of raw material, power established?
- ❖ Is the selected scale of operation is optimal?
- ❖ Is the production process chosen suitable?
- ❖ Are the equipment and machine chosen appropriate?
- ❖ Is the proposed layout of the site buildings and plant sound?

2. Economic Analysis: It referred to as social cost benefit analysis is concerned with judging a project from the larger, social point of view in such an evaluation the focus is on the social costs and benefits of a project, which may be often be different from its monetary costs and benefits.

- ❖ What are the direct economic benefits and costs of the project measured in term of price?
- ❖ What would be the impact of the project on the distribution of income in the society?
- ❖ What would be the impact of the project on the level of savings and investment in the society?
- ❖ What would be the contribution of the project towards the fulfillment of certain criteria like self-sufficiency, employment and social order?

3. Ecological Analysis: In recent years environmental concerns have assumed a great deal of significance Ecological analysis should be done, particularly for major projects which have significant ecological implications like power plants and irrigation schemes, and for environment polluting industries like drugs, chemicals and leather processing.

- ❖ Damage caused by the project to the environment.
- ❖ Cost of restoration measures required to ensure that the damage (acceptable limits)

4. Business Plan Preparation: A business plan is a document where you plan your business to have an organized and effective response to a situation which may arise in future. It can be used to establish realistic goals or targets to achieve and to determine the current position it is also used to help make crucial start up decision's to reassure lenders, inverter etc.

A workable business plan has the following features:

- ❖ Determines where the company needs to go.
- ❖ Foreworns of possible roadblocks along the way.
- ❖ Formulates responses to contingencies.
- ❖ Keeps the business on tract to reach its planned goals.

While making a business plan the following points are to be kept in mind.

1. **Keep target audience in view:** while writing business plan the intended audience should be kept in mind and why reason of writing the plan (to get debt financing the emphasis should not be on the huge profit potential but on the certainty that the debt can be repaid).
2. **Strategy core of a business plan:** Basically the first part of the business plan should be geared towards helping develop and support solid business strategy. The plan should explain the market, the industry, target customers and competitors. Write about customer need and the benefits of current product and services. Evaluate the strength, and weakness of each competing firm and draw out the opportunities for product service in the market plan.

The second half of the business plan should explain how to execute selected business strategy for product, services.

3. **Think Competitively Throughout:** As an entrepreneur you need to identify, where you will do things in a manner similar to your competitors and where will you do things differently, what will be your strength and real weaknesses, where will you create your niche focus differently on you business plan.
4. **Be Realistic:** Lots of business plans sound good on paper, but do not work in the real world market place. It is difficult to attract people to a new product / service just because it is better so forecast conservatively and try to have an extra cushion of cash tucked in reserve to handle unseen expenditure cost over runs expensive problems etc.
5. **Involve People:** Involve key employees or expert opinion to create a business plan. Then work with them until you are satisfied. The more input people have in creating the plan, the more responsibility they will feel towards it.
6. **Key Question:** A business plan is a document, which provides flesh and blood to your business idea. It focus on the following:
    1. Product features, capacity, uses.
    2. Market prospects, Selling Price and Cost of Selling.
    3. Production Process and Technical Assignments.
    4. Plant and Machinery, Supplies and Cost.
    5. Location.
    6. Infrastructure Facilities.
    7. Raw Material and other Requirement.
    8. Manpower.
    9. Working Capital.
    10. Project Cost.
    11. Means of Finance.
    12. Capacity Utilization and Income Estimation.
    13. Expenditure.
    14. Profit and Tax and
    15. Risk Analysis.

Project Profile: It gives a bird's eye view of the proposed project. It may be used to obtain the Provisional Registration Certificate (PRC) from District Industries Centre and for applying for Industrial Area Development Board for land and shed.

Project profile consists of the following:

1. Introduction
2. Promoter(s) Background: (experience, education etc).
3. Product(s) Description: (Specification, uses etc).
4. Market and Marketing
5. Details of infrastructure needed.
6. Plant and Machinery (description, capacity cost etc).
7. Process details
8. Raw Materials (Requirement, specification, cost etc).
9. Manpower required (type of personnel required and salaries / wages).
10. Cost of the project and means of finance.
11. Cost of production and profitability.

OWNERSHIP STRUCTURE OF SSI

Many first time entrepreneurs do not have a clear perspective of the issues, legal or otherwise, involved in choosing one of the other form of a business. This often results in avoidable mistakes, which later, cost time and money to rectify. In India setting up a private limited company is the most popular choice among the entrepreneur.

To start an industry the promoters have to decide on the constitution of the unit. The alternatives are:

***(a)* Sole proprietorship:** The sole proprietorship is the oldest, simplest, and most common form of business entity. It is a business owned by a single individual. For tax and legal liability purpose, the owner and the business are one and the same. The proprietorship is not taxed as separate entity. Note that the earnings of the business are taxed at the individual level, whether or not they are actually in cash. There is no vehicle for sheltering income. For liability purposes, the individual and the business are also one and the same. Thus, legal claimants can pursue the personal property of the proprietor and not simply the assets used in the business.

The important features of a sole proprietorship are:

1. Sole ownership
2. One man control
3. Unlimited risk
4. Undivided risk
5. No separate entity of the firm
6. No Government regulation

Advantages of Sole Proprietorship

1. **Easy and Simple Formation:** A Sole trading concern can be formed without any difficulty. Unlike other forms, no legal formalities are necessary for its formation. It can be started and can also be closed according to wishes and whims of the sole trader. Thus, there are no legal formalities for expansion, contraction or dissolution of business enterprise.
2. **Direct and Exclusive Control:** The proprietor has full authority to manage the business. He is not accountable to anyone and nobody interferes in his working. Thus, there is no problem of co-ordination; he is in a better position to maintain good relations with all his employees, if any.
3. **Promptness in Decision Making:** The sole trader is the sole dictator of the business and relatively free from outside interference. He is capable of taking prompt action which is necessary for business success.
4. **Direct Motivation and Incentive to Work:** The owner enjoys the entire profits of the concern alone. The existence of the direct relationship between the effort and the reward serves as a powerful incentive and makes the sole trader work very hard and manage his concern most efficiently.
5. **Maintenance of Secrecy:** In any business enterprise, maintenance of business secrecy is an important factor; and it is in this individual entrepreneurial organization that the sole trader will get this object fulfilled as there is no need to give publicity to accounts and affairs of his business.
6. **Personal Touch with Customers:** As the enterprise is generally small and most often the proprietor himself manages it, he can develop close personal relations with his customers. This promotes customer satisfaction which, subsequently, adds to goodwill of the concern.

7. **Economy in Management:** The business of sole proprietorship is mostly supervised, managed and controlled by the sole proprietor alone or with the help of his relatives and friends and sometimes by one or two paid assistant; hence the costs of management are comparatively low.
8. **Minimum Government Regulation:** The operations of a sole proprietor are regulated by Government and law to the minimum extent. He is of course, has to comply with tax and Labour laws, but otherwise he is free from interference. There are no legal formalities in formation, expansion or dissolution of the business enterprise.
9. **Socially Significant:** Sole proprietorship is important from social point of view also. It is a means for earning livelihood independently. The owner is his own master. It ensures diffusion of business ownership and, thus, concentration of wealth and power in a few hands is avoided. It further, helps in the development of entrepreneurial qualities such as self-reliance, self confidence, responsibility, tact and initiative etc. in the individual entrepreneurs.

Disadvantages of Sole Proprietorship

1. **Limited Financial Resources:** A single individual normally does not posses enough capital. His borrowing capacity is also limited. Therefore, a soil proprietorship firm suffers from lack of financial resources. Consequently, it has to confine its activities within a limited range.
2. **Limited Managerial Ability:** The limitation of managerial ability is a glaring as that of capital. An individual, howsoever, capable and qualified may be cannot manage all functions of the business. He is not supposed to posses' knowledge of all the functional areas of the business. Moreover, because of the small size of the business and limited financial resources available to him, he may not be in a position to appoint expert managers. Thus, in the modern competitive world of business where different aspects are managed by experts, sole proprietor's concern likely to suffer from stagnation in the absence of required managerial ability.
3. **Unlimited Liability:** The unlimited liability of the single proprietor is a great disadvantage to him; because business debts run against his entire property and not merely against the amount invested in the business. This discourages the risk-taking instinct of the entrepreneur.
4. **Uncertainty of Continuity:** Continuity of the sole proprietor's business is difficult to maintain. When the proprietor dies there is no guarantee for the continuity of the business; because there is no legal obligation to continue the same concern. The legal heir of the proprietor may lack requisite qualities or may not have any liking for the same business. With the result, the business may come to an end. There is also no legal obligation that once a business is started, it must be continued under any circumstances. Thus, the continuity of the business solely depends on the sole proprietor and his legal heir.
5. **Diseconomies of Small Size:** A small scale firm cannot economies in purchase, production and marketing. In a sole trader's concern, overhead cost is also more. Thus, a sole proprietorship firm suffers from diseconomies of small scale and is not in a position to compete with the large-scale organizations having economies of large-scale.
6. **Limited Growth:** Growth is a normal rule of life. A business firm is bound to grow in size; as it is a living organism. Practically, due to the limitations of capital and managerial ability as discussed above, the growth of the sole trader's business is affected adversely; it is never in a position to bloom fully.

Thus, sole proprietorship is a common form of organization in retail trade, professional firms, household and personal services. This form of organization is quite popular in our country. It accounts for the largest number of business establishments in India, in spite of its limitations.

***(b)* Partnership:** A type of unincorporated business organization in which multiple individuals, called general partners, manage the business and are equally liable for its debts; other individuals called limited partners may invest but not be directly involved in management and are liable only to the extent of their investments. Unlike a Limited Liability Company or a corporation, in a partnership each partner shares equal responsibility for the company's profits and losses, and its debts and liabilities. A financier may need a managerial expert as well as a technical expert and all of them may combine to set up a business with common ownership and management. Thus, partnership organization has grown out of necessity to arrange more capital; provide better management and control, to take advantage of high degree of specialization and division of labour, and to share the risks. The partnership itself does not pay income taxes, but each partner has to report their share of business profits or losses on their individual tax return.

The main features of partnership form of business ownership/organization in a more orderly manner as follows:

1. **More Persons:** As against sole proprietorship, there should be at least two persons subject to a maximum often persons for banking business and twenty for non-banking business to form a partnership firm.
2. **Profit and Loss Sharing:** There is an agreement among the partners to share the profits earned and losses incurred in partnership business.
3. **Contractual Relationship:** Partnership is formed by an agreement – oral or written – among the partners.
4. **Existence of Lawful Business:** Partnership is formed to carry on some lawful business and share its profits or losses. If the purpose is to carry some charitable works, for example, it is not regarded as partnership.
5. **Utmost Good Faith and Honesty:** A partnership business solely rests on utmost good faith and trust among the partners.
6. **Unlimited Liability:** Like sole proprietorship, each partner has unlimited liability in the firm. This means that if the assets of the partnership firm fall short to meet the firm's obligations, the partners private assets will also be used for the purpose.
7. **Restrictions on Transfer of Share**: No partner can transfer his share to any outside person without seeking the consent of all other partners.
8. **Principal-Agent Relationship:** The partnership firm may be carried on by all partners or any of them acting for all. While dealing with firm's transactions, each partner is entitled to represent the firm and other partners. In this way, a partner is an agent of the firm and of the other partners.

Advantages of Partnership

1. **Easy Formation:** Formation of partnership is easier and no legal formalities are to be observed to establish it. At the same time, unlike a company not much of expenses are incurred for its formation. However, as compared to sole trader's concern, it may involve certain difficulties, especially in selection and organization of partners, etc.
2. **Larger Financial Resources:** In a partnership, since several persons pool their financial resources into a common business, the amount of capital accumulation becomes much higher than what can be contributed by one person in sole trader's concern. The scale of operations can be enlarged to reap the economies of scale. There is always scope for the introduction of new partners to augment resources.
3. **Flexibility:** It's a highly flexible organization. Changes can be introduced easily. The necessary additional capital can be raised; new partners can be introduced, the place and

object of the firm can be changed. Business of the firm can also be expanded or contracted according the requirements of the business.

4. **Combined Abilities and Balanced Judgement:** In a partnership firm, better management of the business is ensured because capital and brain of two or more persons are pooled. Combined abilities and balanced Judgement produce appreciable results. Two heads are better than one is an old saying.
5. **Direct Motivation:** Since the partners themselves manage the business, they are likely to manage it with great care, caution and interest. Moreover, partnerships provide a fair correlation between rewards and efforts on the part of owners, and as such partners are motivated to apply the best of their energy and capacity for the success of the business.
6. **Division of Risks:** In sole proprietorship, the risks of business are to be shouldered by one person alone; but in partnership, the risks are to be shared by all the partners. Thus, partnership is more useful for risky business.
7. **Business Secrecy:** The annual accounts and reports of a partnership firm do not require circulation and publicity and, therefore, secrecy can be maintained about the business.
8. **Protection of Minority Interest:** The Partnership Act provides equal rights and powers for all the partners irrespective of their capital contributions. Every partner has a right to participate in the management of the business. All important decisions are to be taken by the consent of all the partners. If a majority decision is enforced on minority, affected partners can get the business dissolved.
9. **Encouragement of Mutual Trust and Interdependence:** Each partner is an agent for the others. Therefore, all the partners act with utmost mutual trust. They also develop a sense of interdependence and team spirit. At the same time each partner develops his individuality through his responsibility for others and the firm as a whole.
10. **Easy Dissolution:** A partnership firm can easily be .dissolved. It is a kind of voluntary association for carrying on business operations. Therefore, it can be dissolved by the partners merely by expressing to each other their intention to do so. In the case of a partnership-at-will, it can be dissolved by giving 14 days notice to other partners.

Disadvantages of Partnership

1. **Unlimited Liability:** The partners, like a sole proprietor but unlike shareholders of a joint stock company, may be personally held liable for the debts of the firm. Their private property also remains at stake. Due to the dangers associated with unlimited liability, partners are overcautious and play safe. This restricts the expansion and growth of the business.
2. **Limited resources:** There is an upper limit to the number of partners in a partnership firm - 20 in a general business and 10 in a baking business. Due to this, in spite of the pooling of the resources by all the partners, it becomes difficult for a partnership to manage the increasing requirements of capital and managerial skills of expanding business. This limitation limits the growth of business beyond a certain size.
3. **Instability:** A partnership firm suffers form the uncertainty of duration; because it can be dissolved at the time of death, or insolvency of a partner. Sometimes petty quarrels among the partners may also bring the partnership to an end. The discontinuity of the business is not only inconvenient to the consumers and workers but is also a social loss.
4. **Non-transferability of Interest:** Partners cannot transfer their interests in the partnership firm to outsiders without the consent of all other partners. This non-transferability is a drawback of the partnership firm and dissuades many persons from investment in such

a firm. On the other hand, shares of a joint stock company are easily transferable and, thus, provide liquidity to the investment.

5. **Lack of Public Confidence:** Since there is no publicity of the working of a partnership through its published periodical accounts and there is absence of legal control over it, the general public may not have full confidence in them.
6. **Risk of Implied Authority:** A partner, being an agent of the firm and his co-partners, can make deals and contracts that would be binding on other partners. Therefore, when a partner is negligent, or commits a wrong, or in guilty of a fraud, within the scope of his authority, other partners are equally liable financially without any limit. Thus, the honest and efficient partner may have to pay the penalty for follies and vices of other partners.
7. **Lack of Centralized Authority:** The power of management is vested in all the partners; there is absence of a supreme and central authority.

Consequently, many problems crop up, particularly when there is absence of mutual understanding and co-operation. Constant opposites and disagreements on the part of partners hamper the growth of the partnership business at every stage and, ultimately, may even put an end to the existence of the partnership, after a short span of life.

***(c)* Corporation/Limited Company: *(i)* Corporation:** An entity, usually a business, created by a legislative act or by individuals who have agreed upon and filed articles of incorporation with the state government. Ownership in the corporation is typically represented by shares of stock. Furthermore, a corporation is legally recognized as an artificial person whose existence is separate and distinct from that of its shareholders who are not personally responsible for the corporation's acts and debts. As an artificial person, a corporation has the power to acquire, own, and convey property, to sue and be sued, and such other powers of a natural person that the law may confer upon it.

***(ii)* A Limited Company:** A limited liability is more commonly called a limited liability company, or LLC. It is a fairly new business entity and it serves as an alternative to a partnership or other type of corporation. An LLC offers similar advantages to those offered through a partnership and other corporations, so opting for an LLC should be based upon what makes the most financial sense for your business. The owners of an LLC are referred to as members versus shareholder or partner; each member has a monetary interest in the company. At present, there is no limit as to how many members can make up a limited liability company.

***(iii)* Co-operative:** A cooperative is a business. In many ways it's like any other business; but in several important ways it's unique and different. A cooperative business belongs to the people who use it – people who have organized to provide themselves with the goods and services they need. These member-owners share equally in the control of their cooperative – they meet at regular intervals, hear detailed reports and elect directors from among themselves. The directors in turn hire management to manage the day-to-day affairs of the cooperative in a way that services the members' interests. Members invest in shares in the business to provide capital for a strong and efficient operation. All net savings (profits) left after bills are paid and money is set aside for operations and improvements, are returned to co-operative members.

Features of Co-operative Organization

1. **Voluntary Association:** A co-operative organization is a voluntary association of persons. Its voluntary character is one of the most guiding principles of co-operative organization. It implies principles of co-operative organization. It implies that every individual, irrespective of his caste, creed, religion, sex, etc. is free to become member of the co-operative and leave it any time, after giving proper notice. It also implies that none should be forced or coerced to join it.

2. **Equal Voting Rights:** In co-operative form of organization, each member has equal voting right. This means that every member irrespective of his holdings of shares or status is given one vote. A rich person cannot hold control of the cooperative organization on the basis of his wealth. All members have equal voice in the management of the organization.
3. **Democratic Management:** Democracy is the rule of co-operatives. In a co-operative society since each member has equal voting right, its management is essentially democratic. All the members of a society elect a body of persons to conduct and control the working of the society. The members frequently meet and give guidelines to its executive. Thus, a co-operative organization is an emblem of true democracy.
4. **Service Motive:** The primary objective of establishing co-operative form of organization is to render maximum service to its members. Here, the aim is not to earn profits. The cooperative societies do earn a nominal amount of profit to cover-up administrative expenses. Thus, co-operatives promote social justice.
5. **Limited Return of Capital:** The capital invested in a co-operative is not given an undue preference. A limited rate of interest is allowed; because capital appreciation is not the main motto of co-operation. Under the existing law in India, a maximum of 10 per annum can be given as return on capital contribution to the co-operative. This is a first charge on surpluses of the society.
6. **Separate Legal Entity:** A co-operative society must get itself registered under the Co-operative Societies Act, 1912 or under the Co-operative Societies Act of a State Government. Like a joint stock company, it is a separate legal person; it can own property, enter into contracts, sue and be sued in its own name.
7. **Equitable Distribution of Surplus:** Unlike other forms, of business organization, surplus earned by a co-operative society is distributed among its members equitably on basis other than capital contribution of the members. As per the law governing Co-operative organization, 25 per cent of its profits after meeting its trading expenses and paying a fixed rate of dividend on capital not exceeding 10 per cent is to be transferred to general reserves. In addition, a portion of the profit not exceeding 10 per cent may be utilized for the general welfare of the locality in which the co-operative society is functioning. The residual, if any, may be distributed among members on the basis to be decided by the members collectively. Normally, in case of consumers' co-operatives, this residual is distributed according to purchases made by the members from the Co-operative Society; and in case of producers co-operatives, this profit is distributed in proportion to the goods delivered to the Co-operative society for sale.
8. **State Control:** The activities of the co-operative societies are subject to certain rules and regulations framed by the Government. There are many formalities which are required to be completed for getting the society registered under the Co-operative Societies Act, 1912 or the State Co-operative Societies Act of the particular State. The audited accounts and affairs of the society are inspected by the Government periodically. Besides this, a co-operative society has to submit annual reports and accounts to the Registrar of Co-operative Societies.

Advantages of Co-operative Society

1. **Easy to Form:** As compared to a joint stock company, it is easy and simple to form a co-operative society. The legislative formalities required for its formation are not many. In addition to this, it is economical, as the expenses involved in its formation are comparatively less.

2. **Democratic Management:** A co-operative society is managed in a true democratic way. All the members have a say in its working. They elect a managing committee on the basis of "one-man-one-vote". This committee looks after the working of the organization in the general interest of all the -members. It is not controlled by vested interests only.
3. **Limited Liability:** The members' liability remains limited to the extent of capital contributed by them.
4. **Perpetual Succession:** Unlike sole proprietorship and partnership, it does not cease to exist on the death, lunacy, insolvency, permanent incapability etc. of, its members. Like a company it has perpetual succession; because it has separate legal entity which is not affected by the changes among its members.
5. **Economic Operation:** The working in a co-operative society is quite economical. Several expenses are reduced due to elimination of the middlemen, voluntary services provided by its members, or services provided at lower salary, and also because there is no need to maintain huge stocks.
6. **State Patronage:** The co-operatives have been adopted by the Government as an instrument of economic policy. Therefore, they are assisted in various ways by the Government so as to make them a success.
7. **Social Benefits:** Co-operation is a philosophy and a way of life. It helps to educate members to live together. It teaches them thrift, self help, mora1values and self-government. It promotes the spirit of cooperation in place of spirit of competition. It enables them to serve others rather than exploit others. Thus, it raises the standard of living of the members and also raises moral standards of the masses.
8. **Scope for Internal Financing:** Since a co-operative society has to create some compulsory reserves out of its profits, there is enough scope for ploughing back of profits in such organizations. This source of internal finance can be utilized for modernization and growth of the co-operatives.

Disadvantages of Co-operative Society

1. **Limited Resources:** The co-operatives are not able to raise huge amounts of capital; because their membership comprises persons of limited means and is limited to local areas. The principle of one-man one-vote and limit on divided also subdue the enthusiasm of their investing members.
2. **Limited Size:** Since the principle of co-operation cannot be extended beyond a certain limit, the co-operatives are likely to fail if they choose expansion of their organization like big joint stock companies. Large-scale production or distribution is not suitable for co-operative organizations
3. **Lack of Secrecy:** A co-operative society, being separate legal entity is required to disclose fuller information to its members. Thus, secrets of the business cannot be maintained.
4. **Lack of Motivation:** Since there are restrictions on the rate of dividend, the members of the managing committee do not feel motivated enough to put their best to make the organization a success.
5. **Inefficient Management:** A co-operative society is managed by a managing committee which is composed of elected members who are not necessarily experts in management. Moreover, they are not in a position to attract professional managers; because they are not in a position to pay high salaries to them. Thus, the co-operatives in general, suffer from inefficient management.
6. **Internal Quarrels and Rivalries:** The members of a co-operative are very enthusiastic in the beginning; but after the initial zeal is over they start showing indifference towards

their organization. Often, they quarrel on petty matters. The normal working of the co-operative is affected due to factionalism among the members. This further weakened by power politics and casteism, etc.

7. **Excessive Government Interference:** The co-operatives are exposed to a considerable degree of regulation by the co-operative department. A certain degree of control is welcome; but too much of it and unwanted interference acts as a deterrent to the - voluntary nature of co-operatives; it goes against the operational flexibility of the co-operatives and, thus, affects efficiency of management of the co-operatives.

(d) Franchising: Franchising can be described as a 'business marriage' between a 'franchisee' and a 'franchisor'. As the franchisee - the purchaser of the franchise - you pay an initial investment for the licensed rights to operate under an established brand, and to be trained and supported by a central franchisor. The 'marriage' is protected by a Franchise Agreement which provides you with an exclusive territory for a set period of time on a renewable basis.

Advantages of Franchising:

1. **Proven idea:** Entrepreneur is based on a proven idea. Businessmen can check how successful other franchises are before committing themselves.
2. **Brand Name/Trademark:** Entrepreneurs can use a recognized brand name and trade marks. They benefit from any advertising or promotion by the owner of the franchise - the 'franchisor'.
3. **Support:** The franchisor gives support to the entrepreneur - usually including training, help setting up the business, a manual telling you how to run the business and ongoing advice.
4. **Exclusive rights:** Entrepreneurs usually have exclusive rights in their territory. The franchisor would not sell any other franchises in the same territory.
5. **Financing** the business may be easier. Banks are sometimes more likely to lend money to buy a franchise with a good reputation. Entrepreneurs get benefit from communicating and sharing ideas with, and receiving support from, other franchisees in the network. Relationships with suppliers have already been established.

Disadvantages of Franchising:

1. **Cost:** Costs may be higher than expect. As well as the initial costs of buying the franchise, entrepreneurs have to pay continuing management service fees and they may have to agree to buy products from the franchisor.
2. **Restriction:** The franchise agreement usually includes restrictions on how entrepreneur can run the business. They might not be able to make changes to suit their local market.
3. **Bad Reputation:** Other franchisees could give the brand a bad reputation, so the recruitment process needs to be thorough
4. **Difficult to sell:** Entrepreneurs may find it difficult to sell their franchise - They can only sell it to someone approved by the franchisor.
5. **Sharing of Profits:** All profits (a percentage of sales) are usually shared with the franchisor.

Registration: **Obtain SSI Registration**. Small-scale and ancillary units that is undertakings with investment in plant and machinery of less than ₹. 1 crore should seek registration with the Directors of Industries of the concerned State Government. Entrepreneurs desiring to start a SSI have to initially obtain a Provisional Registration Certificate. Once the unit goes into production, the PRC has to be converted into a Permanent Registration Certificate (PMC).

Provisional Registration Certificate (PRC): A Provisional Registration for starting a small scale industry. It enables the entrepreneur to initiate necessary steps to bring the unit into existence.

The entrepreneurs should apply and obtain a PRC after selection of the project and deciding on the location of the unit. A PRC is necessary for applying for infrastructure facilities (such as land, shed etc).

Benefits of Registering

The registration scheme has no statutory basis. Units would normally get registered to avail some benefits, incentives or support given either by the Central or State Govt. The regime of incentives offered by the Centre generally contains the following:

- Credit prescription (Priority sector lending), differential rates of interest etc.
- Excise Exemption Scheme
- Exemption under Direct Tax Laws.
- Statutory support such as reservation and the Interest on Delayed Payments Act.

(It is to be noted that the Banking Laws, Excise Law and the Direct Taxes Law have incorporated the word SSI in their exemption notifications. Though in many cases they may define it differently. However, generally the registration certificate issued by the registering authority is seen as proof of being SSI).

States/Union Territories have their own package of facilities and incentives for small scale. They relate to development of industrial estates, tax subsidies, power tariff subsidies, capital investment subsidies and other support. Both the Centre and the State, whether under law or otherwise, target their incentives and support packages generally to units registered with them.

Objectives of the Registration Scheme

They are summarized as follows:

- To enumerate and maintain a roll of small industries to which the package of incentives and support are targeted.
- To provide a certificate enabling the units to avail statutory benefits mainly in terms of protection.
- To serve the purpose of collection of statistics.
- To create nodal centers at the Centre, State and District levels to promote SSI.

Features of the Scheme

Features of the scheme are as follows:

- DIC is the primary registering centre
- Registration is voluntary and not compulsory.
- Two types of registration is done in all States. First a provisional registration certificate is given. And after commencement of production, a permanent registration certificate is given.
- PRC is normally valid for 5 years and permanent registration is given in perpetuity.

Provisional Registration Certificate (PRC)

This is given for the pre-operative period and enables the units to obtain the term loans and working capital from financial institutions/banks under priority sector lending.

Obtain facilities for accommodation, land, other approvals etc. Obtain various necessary No-objection Certificates and clearances from regulatory bodies such as Pollution Control Board, Labour Regulations etc.

Permanent Registration Certificate

Enables the unit to get the following incentives/concessions:

- Income-Tax exemption and Sales Tax exemption as per State Govt. Policy.
- Incentives and concessions in power tariff etc.
- Price and purchase preference for goods produced.

- ❖ Availability of raw material depending on existing policy.
- ❖ Permanent registration of tiny units should be renewed after 5 years.

Procedure for Registration

Features of the present procedures are as follows:

- ❖ A unit can apply for PRC for any item that does not require industrial license which means items listed in Schedule-III and items not listed in Schedule-I or Schedule-II of the licensing Exemption Notification. Units employing less than 50/100 workers with/without power can apply for registration even for those items included in Schedule-II.
- ❖ Unit applies for PRC in prescribed application form. No field enquiry is done and PRC is issued.
- ❖ PRC is valid for five years. If the entrepreneur is unable to set up the unit in this period, he can apply afresh at the end of five years period.
- ❖ Once the unit commences production, it has to apply for permanent registration on the prescribed form.

The following form basis of evaluation:

- ❖ The unit has obtained all necessary clearances whether statutory or administrative. e.g. drug license under drug control order, NOC from Pollution Control Board, if required etc.
- ❖ Unit does not violate any location restrictions in force, at the time of evaluation.
- ❖ Value of plant and machinery is within prescribed limits.
- ❖ Unit is not owned, controlled or subsidiary of any other industrial undertaking as per notification.

Clearances from Specific Departments: Several clearances are required from different authorities depending on the type of industry and the location of the unit.

Examples:

Agricultural land conversion
Urban land ceiling clearance
Building Plan approval
Factories Act
Trade Licence
Pollution Control Board Clearances
Sales Tax Registration.
Central Excise Registration
Bureau of India Standards (BIS) Certificate
Fruit Products Order (FPO) licence
Food Adulteration Act licence
Power Loom Registration
Drugs and Cosmetics Licence
Approvals of Hotels
100% Export-oriented unit

Arrange for Land/Shed: for any industrial project, a suitable industrial site or a ready industrial shed is required. The promoter of the unit could consider taking an industrial site and constructing a shed as per their requirement. Alternatively they could consider taking ready industrial shed or on ownership basis.

Industrial Land: Once the location of the unit is decided, the land for the project could be conveniently taken from the State Industrial Areas Development Board. However, private land could also be purchased, but it has to be converted for industrial purpose and other necessary legal/ formalities will have to be completed.

Industrial Shed: For setting up an SSI unit, the promoters could consider using a ready industrial shed. This could be on rent or on ownership basis. Rental sheds have to be arranged from private owners. Purchase of industrial sheds has to be arranged from private owners. Purchase of industrial sheds is possible under outright purchase or hire purchase scheme.

Arrange for Plant and Machinery: The plant and machinery required for the project could be purchased from recognized manufacturer/dealers. The plant and machinery could also be taken on a hire purchase scheme operated by the National Industries Corporation (NSIC) which is a Government of India Corporation.

Arrange for Infrastructure: The main infrastructure facilities required for a SSI unit are land or shed for the project, power connection, water supply and telephone facilities.

Prepare Project Report: A detailed project report provides, plan for the project. The report is useful to the entrepreneur for planning and implementing the project. It is essential finance and other clearances for the project. The project reports a detailed insight of the project and indicates, the techno-economic viability of the project.

The project report is a document created through systematic recording of all the details about a project, with an analyze and validation of data/information. This is most important document of any project. It consists of following characteristics.

- Standard format
- Completeness of data
- Proper definitions of assumptions
- Imparting of data/information from reliable sources
- Emphasis on the main objectives of the project
- Scientific analysis of the data
- Preservation of confidential data/information
- Effective presentation and avoiding repetition
- Cost effectiveness
- Timeliness

Contents of a Project Report

1. **Executive Summary:** Introduction, financial performance Balance sheet analysis, proposed, project, project profitability and analysis and SWOT analysis.
2. **Company Details:** History, Manufacturing facilities, promoters, shareholders, pattern, Board of directors, Key executives, Major products, Major customers, Details of divisions and Group units.
3. **Operational Details:** Capacity and utilization, profit and loss account, Balance sheet, Term loans and advances, Working Capital loans, marketing and Distribution Network of the company, Marketing Strategy, Export Sales, trends in selling prices and Details of Sub contractors, out sourcing etc.
4. **Project Details:** Proposed projects, Order and enquiries Location, Manufacturing process, Technical feasibility Technical know-how, Inputs for production, Power Manpower, Water, Marketing.
5. **Project Cost:** Land, Building and Civil Works, plant and machinery, pre-operative expenses and Margin money for working capital.
6. **Means of Finance:** Equity share capital, Internal Accruals, Deposits, Debts and other sources.

7. **Project Status:** Implementation schedule PERT and CPM analysis, current status, and Government approval.
8. **Profitability and Risk Analysis:** Project financials of the company, analysis of break even point, return on investment, pay back period, internal rate of return and sensibility, Major risk factor.
9. **Company vs. Related Industry:** General analysis competing industries and advantages of the company.
10. **Employment Generation:** Direct/Indirect.
11. **Conclusions:**
12. **Annexure:** Promoter's bio-data, organisation chart, details of group units, statutory sanctions, arrangement of land/building, statement of cost of plant and machinery. Details of orders and enquiries, process chart, etc.

Apply and Obtain Finance: There are various sources of funds. They are as follows:

Share capital short-term borrowings.

Internal accruals (wages, salaries) Long-term loans

Deposits own/public, Bridge loans

Debentures, Working capital loan like cash credits.

Means of Finance:

- Own equity
- Banks
- Inter corporate deposits/investment.
- State financial institutions and other
- Other borrowing like, CED, FDI, etc
- State subsidy and seed capital
- Lease finance.

Small-scale units can obtain finance for their projects under two main categories.

(a) **Term Loan:** For starting a SSI unit term loan finance for fixed assets can be availed. Term loans can be availed from the State Finance Corporation or from commercial banks. The term loan is usually decided on the bass of the fixed assets required for the project the fixed assets of a project are land, building and plant and machinery. The extend of loan depends on the project, cost and the entrepreneur's background. The security margin money to be brought in by the entrepreneur depends on the location, scheme, and type of industry. The repayment of loan advanced is generally spread over a period of 5-8 yeas. The repayment period and size of installments are based on estimated cash generation and profitability of the project.

(b) **Working Capital Loan:** Such a loan is needed for the day-to-day operation of the unit. Working capital is required for raw material purchase, credit sales, for the products / goods in the process of manufacture, for the finished goods kept in stock and for working expenses, for such purposes commercial banks provide working capital loans. Usually, the security for such loans are the materials (raw materials goods), book debts and bills raised for sales for working capital loans, banks require the industries / SSI Units to bring in a certain amount of margin money. The margin money requirement varies for different types of securities offered or for assess the working capital needs of the individual industry while sanctioning it.

(c) **Arranging Finance:** To start and set up business, all SSI units need monetary support. Before seeking fund, estimate the cost including that of working capital required for a

minimum of 6-8 months and always keep a provision for buffer. They can take the help of a Chartered Accountant or the concerned officials in the Entrepreneurship Development Institutes, to work out the total financial costs of our project. Decide the form in which they are going to raise the capital equity finance, debt finance loans or a combination of these.

This need for finance can be classified into the following types.

Long and medium-term loans

Short-term or working capital requirements

Risk capital

Seed capital/marginal money

Bridge loan

SFC, SIDBI and SIDC provide long and medium term loans. Banks also finance term loans; this type of financing is needed to fund purchase of land, construction of factory building and for purchase of machinery and equipment. Term loans are secured against mortgage of assets such as land, building, machines and other stocks.

Short-term loans are required for working capital requirements which find the purchase of raw material and consumables, payment of wages and other immediate manufacturing and administrative expenses. Such loans are generally available from commercial banks.

Single Window Scheme for SSI units has one agency either the bank or the financial institutions fund both the term loan and working capital requirement. It applies to all SSI with project cost ₹ 50 lakhs. Working capital loan is generally secured against:

Pledging of stocks, raw material and finished goods.

Advances against work-in-progress and

Advance against bills.

Implement the Project and Obtain Final Clearances: The entrepreneurs will have to take necessary steps to physically implement the project after obtaining the various, licenses, clearances, infrastructure facilities and so on. The following are the major activities that the entrepreneurs have to undertake for implementing the project.

1. Construct shed/building.
2. Order for Machinery.
3. Recruit Personnel.
4. Arrange for Raw Materials.
5. Marketing.
6. Erection and Commissioning.
7. Obtain final clearances, ex: pollution related clearance etc.

Need for Project Formulation

The entrepreneur in a developing country has to encounter a number of problems while establishing a new project. These problems cause greater concern to many enthusiastic entrepreneurs. However, they could be saved to a greater extent by under taking a project formulation exercise at the appropriate time.

1. **Selection of Appropriate Technology:** The first problem faced by an entrepreneur is in the matter of selection of appropriate technology for his enterprise Modern technology developed in highly industrialized countries may not be suitable for adoption in the developing countries as the conditions prevalent differ from country to country.
2. **Influence of External Economies:** The second problem relates to the absence or non-availability of external economies. No project can function in isolation in any economy.

It has to depend on other industries for the supply of raw materials, power, tools, spare parts etc or on ancillary enterprises which can provide technical, financial and managerial services or on a complex network of communication and transport facilities. So, entrepreneur has to consider not only the basic cost of the project but also the ancillary cost.

3. **Dearth of Technically Qualified Personnel:** The third problem is the non availability of technically qualified and appropriate personnel. Modern technology calls for a certain minimum supply of various skills that are generally lacking in developing countries.
4. **Resource Mobilization:** In the content of present day development of the magnitude and size of project it would be very difficult for an entrepreneur to provide the entire development capital that a project may need.
5. **Knowledge about Government Regulations:** The entrepreneurs have to comprehend a number of government directives, important export policies, price control, etc. The difficulty is to be familiar with all these regulations, for they are not available in a consolidated and detailed form in most of the developing countries. However, in India a compendium entitled "Guidelines for Industries" has been published by the Ministry of Industrial Development. It provides information, regarding the industrial policy. Licensing procedure, guideline for foreign collaboration, import and export control order and foreign exchange order. It also provides future development information in various industrial fields.

PROJECT APPRAISAL

Project appraisal is the analysis of costs and benefits of a proposed project with the goal of assuring a rational allocation of limited funds among alternative investment opportunities in view of achieving certain specified goals. Project appraisal is necessary for the number of projects to satisfy the identified needs always exceeds the availability of resources and a choice among alternative projects is to be made.

Project appraisal is a process of transmitting information accumulated through feasibility studies into a comprehensive form in order to enable the decision-maker undertake a comparative appraisal of various projects and embark on a particular project or projects for allocating scarce resources. Keeping the overall objectives of the enterprise in view and all those of the project, appraisal is carried out employing certain decision criteria versus profitability or social profitability commonly suggested appraisal method are:

1. Payback period: The payback period is the length of time required to recover the initial cash outlay on the project. For example, of a project involves a cash outlay of ₹ 2,00,000 and the annual cash inflows are ₹ 50,000, ₹ 80,000, ₹ 60,000 and ₹ 40,000. During its economic life of four years, the payback period is 3,25 years. During 3 years and 3 months, the project cost can be recovered with the cash inflow. Hence it is the payback period if the above mentioned project returns constant annual cash inflows of ₹ 80,000 for four years. Then the payback period is 2.5 years (₹ 2,00,000/- ₹ 80,000/-).

Formula:

$$\text{Payback Period} = \frac{\text{Original cost of Investment}}{\text{Annual Cash Inflows or Savings}}$$

2. Average Rate of Return: The rate of return on an investment that is calculated by taking the total cash inflow over the life of the investment and dividing it by the number of years in the life of the investment. The average rate of return does not guarantee that the cash inflows are the same in a given year; it simply guarantees that the return averages out to the average rate of return.

$$ARR = \frac{\text{Average Earning or Return}}{\text{Average amount invested}} \quad ARR = \frac{\text{Average Earning or Return}}{\text{Average amount invested}} \times 100$$

(Calculate earnings over the entire economic life of project)

3. Net Present Value: The difference between the present value of cash inflows and the present value of cash outflows. NPV is used in capital budgeting to analyze the profitability of an investment or project. NPV analysis is sensitive to the reliability of future cash inflows that an investment or project will yield.

$$\sum \frac{pvcft}{(1+k)^t} - \text{Initial Investment}$$

NPV indicates the value added to the total assets of the firm by undertaking the proposed investment.

4. Cost Benefit Ratio: A ratio of whether or not and how much profit will result from an investment. It is calculated by taking the net present value of expected future cash flows from the investment and dividing by the investment's original cost. A ratio above one indicates that the investment will be profitable while a ratio below one means that it will not. A cost-benefit ratio is also called a profitability index.

$$B - \%_c \times 100$$

It is the ratio of gross discounted benefits to gross discounted cost (also called profitability index)

5. Internal Rate of Return: The discount rate often used in capital budgeting that makes the net present value of all cash flows from a particular project equal to zero. Generally speaking, the higher a project's internal rate of return, the more desirable it is to undertake the project. As such, IRR can be used to rank several prospective projects a firm is considering. Assuming all other factors are equal among the various projects, the project with the highest IRR would probably be considered the best and undertaken first. It is used when the cost of investment and the cash inflow are known. Usually a financial calculator has to be used to calculate this IRR, though it can also be mathematically calculated using the following formula:

$$CF_0 = \frac{CF_1}{(1+r)^1} + \frac{CF_2}{(1+r)^2} + \frac{CF_3}{(1+r)^3} + \frac{CF_n}{(1+r)^n} = 0$$

MSME ACT (MICRO, SMALL AND MEDIUM ENTERPRISES)

Worldwide, the micro, small and medium enterprises (MSMEs) have been accepted as the engine of economic growth and for promoting equitable development. The major advantage of the sector is its employment potential at low capital cost. The labour intensity of the MSME sector is much higher than that of the large enterprises. The MSMEs constitute over 90% of total enterprises in most of the economies and are credited with generating the highest rates of employment growth and account for a major share of industrial production and exports. In India too, the MSMEs play a pivotal role in the overall industrial economy of the country. In recent years the MSME sector has consistently registered higher growth rate compared to the overall industrial sector. With its agility and dynamism, the sector has shown admirable innovativeness and adaptability to survive the recent economic downturn and recession.

As per available statistics (4th Census of MSME Sector), this sector employs an estimated 59.7 million persons spread over 26.1 million enterprises. It is estimated that in terms of value, MSME sector accounts for about 45% of the manufacturing output and around 40% of the total export of the country.

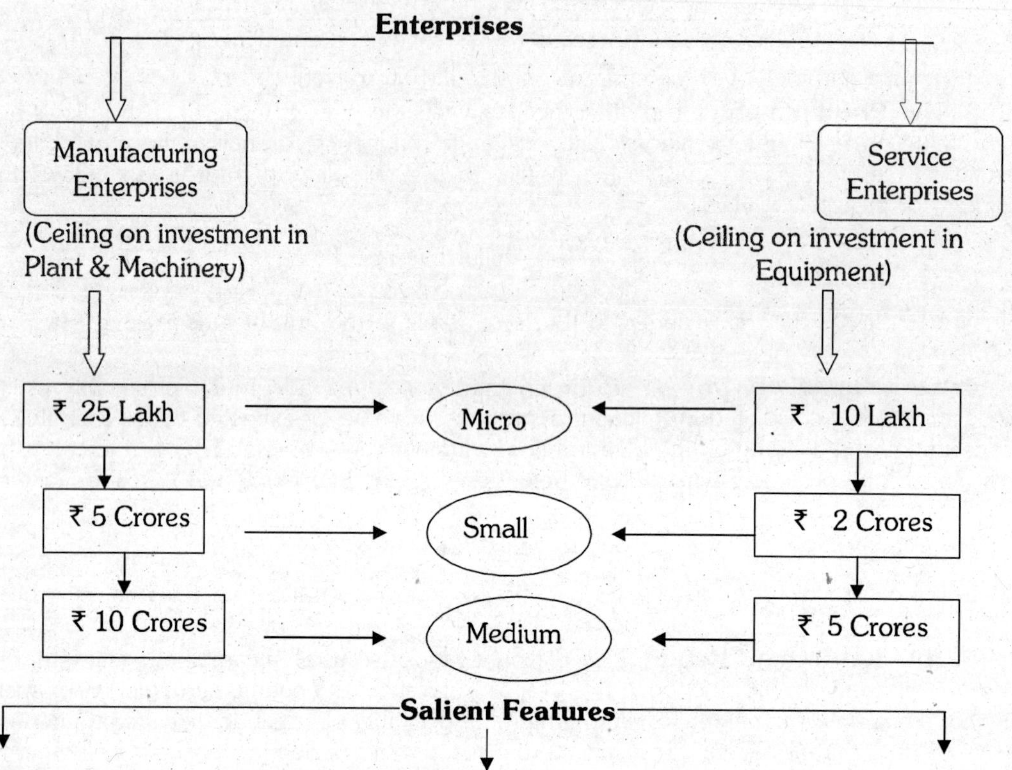

Definitions	Memorandum	Statutory Frame
❖ Defines " Enterprise" instead of "Industry" to give due recognition to the Service Sector. ❖ Pride of the place to Micro Enterprises. ❖ Investment ceiling for Manufacturing Small Enterprises raised to ₹ 5 crores. ❖ Defines "Medium Enterprises" to facilitate technology up-gradation and graduation	❖ Two. Stage registration process of SSI substituted with optional filing of memorandum with DICs by all micro and small enterprises ❖ Filing of memorandum by Medium enterprises rendering services also optional. ❖ Filing of memorandum by manufacturing medium enterprises with DIC instead of the Central Government	❖ Provides statutory basis (Legally enforceable) to Procurement Preference Policies of Central and State Govts. For goods and Services provided by micro and small enterprises. ❖ Representatives of enterprises Associations included in the MSE Facilitation Councils for adjudicating on cases of delayed payment. ❖ Provision for ensuring timely and smooth flow of credit to MSMEs. ❖ All Schemes/ Programs of assistance being notified under the Act. ❖ Provides for a statutory National Board for Micro, Small and Medium enterprises to advice the Central Government on matters under the Act.

Ministry of Small-scale Industries and Ministry of Agro and Rural Industries, Government of India

MSMED act was established to provide for facilitating the promotion and development and enhancing the competitiveness of micro, small and medium enterprises and for matters connected therewith or incidental thereto. The Act is operational from October 2,2006 The MSMED Act is superior as compared to the provisions for SSI under the IDRA in many ways. The scope of the promotion and protection measures under the IDRA was restricted only to SSI. However, during last 60 years of independence, the norms for the promotions and development have changed and the requirement to motivate the higher and different versions of SSI is felt. The MSMED Act not only addresses these issues but it also takes care of Micro, Small and Medium Scale enterprises ("MSM enterprises").

Another major highlight of the MSMED Act is that the MSM enterprises in the service sector are also covered under the Act. Separate investment limit for plant and machinery has been prescribed for MSM enterprises in the service sector.

The MSMED Act was framed with the following objects:

1. To facilitate the promotion and development of micro, small and medium scale enterprises (MSM enterprises);
2. To enhance the competitiveness of MSM enterprises;
3. To concentrate on the related matters of MSM enterprises;
4. To extend the scope of benefits from SSI undertaking and ancillary industries to MSM enterprises.

Review Questions

1. Define Small Enterprise. What are the characteristics of Small Enterprises?
2. State the Objectives of Small Enterprises
3. What are the advantages of Small Scale Industries?
4. Explain the Role of Small Scale Industries in Economic Development?
5. What are the problems faced by the Small Scale Industries?
6. Explain the career opportunities in Entrepreneurship?
7. Explain Project Cycle.
8. What are the various criteria for selecting a project? Explain.
9. Explain the importance of Project Identification.
10. What are the stages of Project feasibility analysis? Explain.
11. Explain the phases of Project Formulation. Explain the various sources of Project Finance
12. Explain in brief about project appraisal method?

Fill in the blanks

1. Small enterprises serve as an engine of innovation, growth and employment due to their ____________ and ________.
2. Small enterprises are more __________________ than larger firm
3. Small enterprise play an important role in fostering ___________, _________ and ___________
4. __________ limits the innovation and competitiveness of the small enterprises
5. Small enterprises always represent the model of ________________ of Government of India
6. Entrepreneurial careers are marked by a substantially higher degree of ________ to the success of the firm.
7. Small and medium scale industries play and important role in the process of country's __________ and _________ development.
8. SSI sectors in India creates largest ___________________ for the Indian population.
9. ______________ is the first step of a new venture.
10. Project identification is concerned with _________, __________ and ______ of economic data for the eventual purpose of locating possible opportunities for investment.
11. According to Drucker Opportunities are of three kinds________ , _________ and ________.

12. __________ referred to as social cost benefit analysis, is concerned with judging a project from the larger, social point of view
13. __________ gives a bird's eye view of the proposed project and may be used to obtain the provisional registration certificate.
14. A provisional certificate is the _____ for starting a small scale industry.
15. Once the unit goes into production the provisional certificate has to be converted into _______________
16. The loan that is given for fixed asset and can be availed from state financial institutions or any commercial bank is called as __________
17. The loan that is used for the day to day operation is called as __________
18. The analysis of cost and benefits of a proposed project is called as ___________
19. The length of time required to recover the initial cash out lay on the project can be understood through the ____________ method.
20. A_______________ is a document where you plan your business to have an original and effective response to a situation which may arise in future.
21. The first part of the business plan should be geared towards helping ,develop and support solid ____________
22. The _________________ is the oldest, simplest, and most common form of business entity. It is a business owned by a single individual
23. Due to largely ________________ selection of potential entrepreneurs, their motivation plays a central role in the formation of new companies.

Answer:

1. Flexibility and rapid growth
2. Labor intensive
3. Income stability, growth and employment
4. Appropriate technology
5. Socio-economic Policies
6. Personal commitment
7. Industrial and economic
8. Employment opportunities
9. Project identification
10. Collection, Compilation and Analysis
11. Additive, Complementary and Break through
12. Economic analysis
13. Project Profile
14. Initial registration
15. Permanent registration certificate
16. Term loan
17. Working capital loan
18. Project Appraisal
19. Payback period
20. Business plan preparation
21. Business strategy
22. Sole Proprietorship
23. Self-originating

◆◆◆

Marketing for Small and Medium Enterprises

4

Chapter

CHAPTER OUTLINE

- Introduction
- The Market
- Concept of Marketing
- Core Concept of Marketing
- Importance of Marketing for Small and Medium Enterprises
- Marketing Research
- Market Planning
- Marketing mix for the Small Enterprises
- Channels of Distribution
- Retail Marketing

- Retailer Marketing Decisions
- Importance of Retail Marketing
- Wholesale Marketing
- Wholesaler Marketing Decisions
- Importance of Wholesale Marketing
- Marketing Problems of Small Enterprises
- Managing of Small Enterprises
- Components of Small Enterprises
- Marketing Intermediaries and their Role
- Marketing Services Provided by the Indian Institutes
- Marketing Strategy for Small and Medium Enterprises (SMEs)

Introduction

What exactly is marketing and why is it important for an small and medium entrepreneur because marketing is doing everything to place the product or service in the hands of potential customers. It includes diverse disciplines like sales, public relations, pricing, packaging, and distribution. In order to distinguish marketing from other related professional services, S.H. Simmons, author and humorist, relates this anecdote.

"If a young man tells his date she's intelligent, looks lovely, and is a great conversationalist, he's saying the right things to the right person and that's marketing. If the young man tells his date how handsome, smart and successful he is — that's advertising. If someone else tells the young woman how handsome, smart and successful her date is — that's public relations."

The Market

In most cases, a market is characterized by a dynamic system of economic forces. The four most salient economic forces are supply, demand, competition, and government intervention. The terms buyer's market and seller's market describe different conditions of bargaining strength. We also use terms such a monopoly, oligopoly, and pure competition to reflect the competitive situation in a particular market. Finally, the extent of personal freedom and government control produces free market systems, socialistic systems, and other systems of trade and commerce.

Again, placing these labels on markets allows the marketer to design strategies that match a particular economic situation. For instance, that in a buyer's market, there is an abundance of product, prices are usually low, and customers dictate the terms of sale.

There is always the pressure of competition as new firms enter and old ones exit. Advertising and selling pressure, price and counter price, claim and counterclaim, service and extra service are all weapons of competitive pressure that marketers use to achieve and protect market positions. Market composition is constantly changing.

Types of Markets

Now that we have defined market in a general sense, it is useful to discuss the characteristics of the primary types of markets: (1) consumer markets, (2) industrial markets, (3) institutional markets, and (4) reseller markets. It should be noted that these categories are not always clear-cut. In some industries, a business may be in a different category altogether or may even encompass multiple categories. It is also possible that a product may be sold in all four markets. Consequently, it is important to know as much as possible about how these markets differ so that appropriate marketing activities can be developed.

1. Consumer Markets

When we talk about consumer markets, we are including those individuals and households who buy and consume goods and services for their own personal use. They are not interested in reselling the product or setting themselves up as a manufacturer. Considering the thousands of new products, services, and ideas being introduced each day and the increased capability of consumers to afford these products, the size, complexity, and future growth potential of the consumer market is staggering.

2. Industrial Markets

The industrial market consists of organizations and the people who work for them, those who buy products or services for their own businesses or to make other products. For example, steel mill might purchase computer software, pencils, and flooring as part of the operation and maintenance of their business. Likewise, a refrigerator manufacturer might purchase sheets of steel, wiring, shelving, and so forth, as part of its final product. These purchases occur in the industrial market. There is substantial evidence that industrial markets function differ from consumer markets and that the buying process in particular is different.

3. Institutional Markets

Another important market sector is made up of various types of profit and non-profit institutions, such as hospitals, schools, societies, and government agencies. Institutional markets differ from typical businesses in that they are not motivated primarily by profits or market share. Rather, institutions tend to satisfy somewhat esoteric, often intangible, needs. Also, whatever profits exist after all expenses are paid is normally put back into the institution. Because institutions operate under different restrictions and employ different goals, marketers must use different strategies to be successful.

4. Reseller Markets

All intermediaries that buy finished or semi-finished products and resell them for profit are part of the reseller market. With the exception of products obtained directly from the producer, all products are sold through resellers. Since resellers operate under unique business characteristics, they must be approached carefully. Producers are always cognizant of the fact that successful marketing to resellers is just as important as successful marketing to consumers

Concept of Marketing

Marketing is the social process by which individuals and groups obtain what they need and want through creating and exchanging products and value with others.(*Kotler*).

Marketing is essentially about marshalling the resources of an organization so that they meet the changing needs of the customer on whom the organization depends.(*Palmer*).

Marketing is the process whereby society, to supply its consumption needs, evolves distributive systems composed of participants, who, interact under constraints – technical (economic) and ethical (social) – create the transactions or flows which resolve market separations and result in exchange and consumption.(*Bartles*).

Marketing is not only much broader than selling, it is not a specialized activity at all It encompasses the entire business. It is the whole business seen from the point of view of the final result, that is, from the customer's point of view. Concern and responsibility for marketing must therefore permeate all areas of the enterprise.(*Drucker*).

This customer focused philosophy is known as the 'marketing concept'. The marketing concept is a philosophy, not a system of marketing or an organizational structure. It is founded on the belief that profitable sales and satisfactory returns on investment can only be achieved by identifying, anticipating and satisfying customer needs and desires.(*Barwell*).

Marketing holds that the key to achieve the organizational goals (goals of the selling products of the company) consists of the company being more effective than competitors in creating, delivering, and communicating customer value to its selected target customers. The marketing concept rests on four pillars:

- Target market
- Customer needs
- Integrated marketing and
- Profitability.

Target market

No company can operate in every market and satisfy every need nor can it always do a good job within one broad market. Target marketing is important because it help in analyzing a proportion of the population which is likely to purchase any products or service. By taking time pitch entrepreneur sales and marketing efforts to the correct niche market they will be more productive and not waste their efforts or time.

Target Marketing involves breaking a market into segments and then concentrating marketing efforts on one or a few key segments. Target marketing can be the key to a small business's success. The target marketing makes the promotion, pricing, and distribution of products and/or services easier and more cost-effective. Target marketing provides a focus to all of marketing activities. A well-defined target market is the first element to a marketing strategy. The target market and the marketing mix variables of product, place(distribution), promotion and price are the four elements of a marketing mix strategy that determine the success of a product in the marketplace. Two important factors are considered while selecting a target market segment is the attractiveness of the segment and the fit between the segment and the firm's objectives, resources and capabilities. While market segmentation can be done in many ways, depending on how you want to slice up the pie, some of the most common types are:

- Demographic bases (age, family size, life cycle, occupation)
- Geographic bases (states, regions, countries)
- Behavior bases (product knowledge, usage, attitudes, responses)
- Psychographic bases (lifestyle, values, personality)

A business must analyze the needs and wants of different market segments before determining their own niche. To be effective in market segmentation entrepreneurs has to keep the following things in mind:

- Segments or target markets should be accessible to the business.
- Each segmented group must be large enough to provide a solid customer base.
- Each segmented group requires a separate marketing plan.

Large companies segment their markets by conducting extensive market research projects. This research is often too expensive for small businesses to invest in, but there are alternative ways for a small business to segment their markets. A small business can do the following to gain knowledge and information on how to segment their markets:

Use secondary data resources and qualitative research., that can be available through, Trade and association publications and experts, basic research publications and external measurement services

Conduct informal factor and cluster analysis by, watching key competitors marketing efforts and copying them, by talking to key trade buyers about new product introduction or by conducting need analysis from qualitative research with individuals and groups.

There are many reasons for dividing market into smaller segments. Any time entrepreneur expect there are significant, measurable differences in their market and should consider market segmentation. By doing so entrepreneur will make marketing easier, discover niche markets, and become more efficient with their marketing resources.

There are several target market strategies that has to be followed by the entrepreneurs, which are categorized as:

1. **Single segment strategy:** One market segment (not the entire market) is served with one marketing mix. A single segment approach often is the strategy of choice for smaller companies with limited resources.
2. **Selective specialization:** This is a multiple-segment strategy, also known as differentiated strategy. Different marketing mix are offered to different segments. The products itself may or may not be different, in many cases only the promotional message or distribution channels vary.
3. **Product specialization:** The firm specializes in a particular product and tailors it to different market segments.
4. **Market specialization:** The firm specializes in serving a particular market segment and offers that segment an array of different products.

5. **Full market coverage:** The firm attempts to serve the entire market. This coverage can be achieved by means of either a mass market strategy in which a single undifferentiated marketing mix is offered to the entire market, or by a differentiated strategy in which a separate marketing mix is offered to each segment.

The following diagrams show examples of the five market selection patterns given three market segments, S_1, S_2, and S_3 and three products P_1, P_2 and P_3.

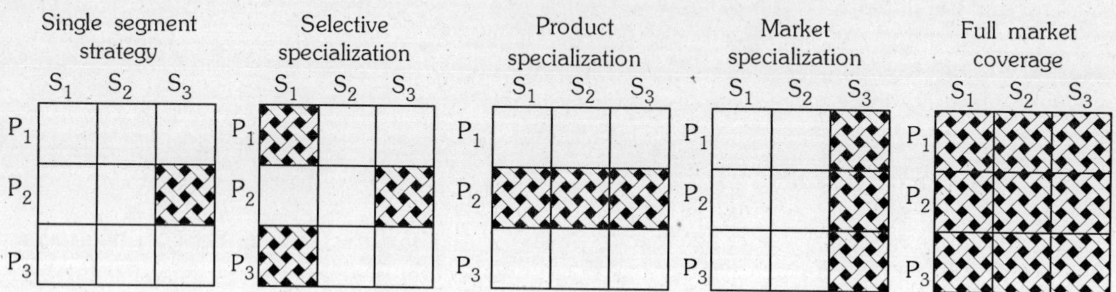

Fig. 4.1: Selection Pattern based on Market segment

A firm that is seeking to enter a market and grow should first target the most attractive segment that matches its capabilities. Once it gains a foothold, it can expand by pursuing specialization strategy, tailoring the product for different segments, or by pursuing a market specialization strategy and offer new products to its existing market segment. Another strategy that is increasing individual marketing, in which the marketing mix is tailoring on an individual consumer basis. While in the past it was impractical, now individual marketing is becoming more viable thanks to advances in technology.

Customer needs

Marketing is about meeting needs of target markets profitably. The key to professional marketing is to understand their customers' real needs and meet them better than any competitor can. Some marketers draw a distinction between responsive marketing and creative marketing. A responsive marketer finds a stated need and fulfills it. A creative marketer discovers and produces solutions that customer did not ask for but to which they enthusiastically respond.

"Entrepreneurs cannot manage a quality service organization unless they understand the nature of what they are providing; fully realize what their customers want from them and how they perceive them from the start". *(W. Martin)*

Once the entrepreneurs identified their customers, they need to assess what they need from their product and service. Most customer needs can be divided into four basic categories:

- The need to be understood: Customers need to feel that the message they are sending is being correctly received and interpreted
- The need to feel welcome: Customers need to feel that entrepreneurs are happy to see them
- The need to feel important: Customers like to feel important and special
- The need for comfort: Customers need physical and psychological comfort

Integrated Marketing

When all the company's department's work together to serve the customer's interests, the result is integrated marketing. Integrated marketing takes on two levels. First, the various marketing functions-sales force, advertising, product management, marketing research, and so on – must work together.

Second must be well coordinated with other company departments. The company is doing proper marketing only when all employees appreciate their impact on customer satisfaction. To foster teamwork among all departments, the company carries out internal marketing as well as external marketing. External marketing is marketing directed at people outside the company. Internal marketing is the task of successfully hiring, training, and motivating employees who want to serve the customers well. In fact internal marketing must precede external marketing. It makes no sense to promise excellent service before the company's staff is ready to provide excellent service.

1. **Assessing the Internal Environment:** Internal scan or assessment of the internal marketing of the organization involves identification of its strengths and weaknesses i.e., those aspects that help or hinder accomplishment of the organization's mission and fulfillment of its mandate with respect to the following Four Ps:
   - People (Human Resources)
   - Properties (Buildings, Equipments and other facilities)
   - Processes (Production, packaging etc.)
   - Products (Quality, etc.)
2. **Assessing the External Environment**: External scan refers to exploring the environment outside the organization in order to identify the opportunities and threats it faces. This involves considering the following:
   - Events, trends and forces in the Social, Technological, Economical, Environmental and Political areas.
   - Identifying the shifts in the needs of customers and potential clients and
   - Identification of competitors and collaborators

Profitability

The ultimate purpose of the marketing concept is to help organizations achieve their goals. In the case of private firms, the major goal is profit. Marketing managers have to provide value to the customer and profits to the organization. Marketing managers have to evaluate the profitability of all alternative marketing strategies and decisions and choose most profitable decisions for long-term survival and growth of the firm.

Core Concept of Marketing

There are many important aspects of marketing. Marketing can be defined as the process of creating, pricing, distributing, and promoting goods, services, or ideas to facilitate satisfying exchange relationships with customers. Basically, it involves creating the right product, at the right price, putting it in the right place with the right promotion in order to make customers happy.

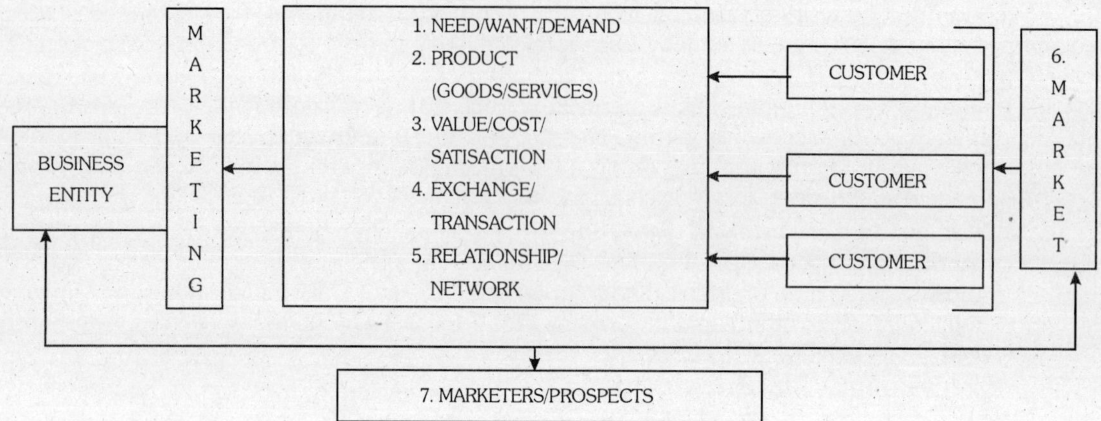

Figure: 4.2. Core concepts of Marketing

Needs are the basic human requirements. People need food, air, water, clothing, and shelter to survive. People also have strong needs for creation, education, and entertainment. The above needs become wants when they are directed to specific objects that might satisfy the need. Demands are wants for specific products backed by an ability to pay. Many people want a Mercedes; only a few are willing and able to buy one.

Companies must measure not only how many people want their product but also how many would actually be willing and able to buy it.

Understanding customer needs and wants is not always simple. Some customers have needs of which they are not fully conscious, or they cannot articulate these needs, or they use words that require some interpretation. Consider the customer who says he wants an "inexpensive car". The marketer must probe further. We can distinguish among five types of needs:

1. Stated needs (the customer wants an inexpensive car).
2. Real needs (the customer wants a car that operating cost, not its initial price, is low).
3. Unstated needs (the customer expects good service from the dealer).
4. Delight needs (the customer would like the dealer to include an onboard navigation system).
5. Secret needs (the customer wants to be seen by friends as a savvy consumer).

1. Need/Want/ Demand

Need: It is state of deprivation of some basic satisfaction. Ex: - food, clothing, safety, shelter.

Want: Desire for specific satisfier of need. Ex:- Indians *needs* food – *wants* paneer tikka/ tandoori chicken. Americans *needs* food- *wants* hamburger/ French fries.

Demand: Want for a specific product backed up by ability and willingness to buy. Ex:- Need – transportation. Want – car (say, Mercedes)……but able to buy only maruti. Therefore, *demand* is for maruti. Marketers cannot create needs. Needs preexists. Marketers can influence wants. This is done in combination with societal influencers.

2. Products-Goods/Services/Place

Product is anything that can satisfy need/ want. Product component are Physical Good, Service, and Idea. Ex.: Fast food: burger/ pizza. Physical Good is material eaten, Service is purchase of raw material / cooking, and Idea is speed of computer/ processing power. Hence, in marketing, focus is on providing/ satisfying service rather than providing products.

3. Value/Cost/Satisfaction

- ❖ Decision for purchase made based on value/ cost satisfaction delivered by product/ offering.
- ❖ Product fulfills/ satisfies Need/ Want.
- ❖ Value is products capacity to satisfy needs/ wants as per consumer's perception or estimation.
- ❖ Each product would have a cost/ price elements attached to it. Ex: Travel from city A to city B. Need – to reach B (from A) Method/ Products- Rail/ air/ road or train/ plane. Satisfaction – Estimated in terms of time lead and travel comfort. *Value:* Products capacity to satisfy. *Cost*: Price of each product.

4. Exchange/Transaction

To satisfy need/ want, people may obtain the product through, Self Production, by force or coercion, Begging and Exchange

Exchange: The act/ process of obtaining a desired product from someone by offering something in return. For exchange potential to exist, the following conditions must be fulfilled.

(i) There must be at least two parties.
(ii) Each party has something of value for other party.
(iii) Each party is capable of communication and delivery
(iv) Each party is free to accept/ reject the exchange offer.
(v) Each party believes it is appropriate to deal with the other party.

Transaction: Event that happens at the end of an exchange. Exchange is a process towards an agreement. When agreement is reached, we say a transaction has taken place. *(a)* Barter transaction. *(b)* Monetary Transaction. (1) At least two things of value. (2) Condition agreed upon. (3) Time of agreement. (4) Place of agreement. (5) May have legal system for compliance.

5. Relationship/Networking

Relationship marketing: It's a pattern of building long term satisfying relationship with customers, suppliers, distributors in order to retain their long term performances and business achieved through promise and delivery of high quality, good service, and fair pricing, over a period of time.

Marketing networking: It is made up of the company and its customers, employees, suppliers, distributors, advertisement agencies, retailers, research, and development with whom it has built mutually profitable business relationship. Competition is between whole network for market share and NOT between companies alone.

6. Market

A market consists of all potential customers sharing particular need/ want who may be willing and able to engage in exchange to satisfy need/ want.

7. Marketers/Prospects

Working with market to actualize potential exchange for the purpose of satisfying needs and wants. One party seeks the exchange more actively, called as "Marketer", and the other party is called "Prospect". Prospect is someone whom marketer identifies as potentially willing and able to engage in exchange. Marketer may be seller or buyer. Most of time, marketer is seller. A marketer is a company serving a market in the face of competition. Marketing Management takes place when at least one party to a potential exchange thinks about the means of achieving desired responses from other parties.

Importance of Marketing for Small and Medium Enterprises

If business is all about people and money and the art of persuading one to part from the other, then marketing is all about finding the right people to persuade. Marketing is the strategy for allocating resources (time and money) in order to achieve business objectives (a fair profit for supplying a good product or service). Marketing is the analysis, planning, implementation, and control of carefully formulated programs designed to bring about voluntary exchanges of values with target markets for the purpose of achieving organizational objectives. It relies heavily on designing the organization's offering in terms of the target markets' needs and desires, and on using effective pricing, communication, and distribution to inform, motivate, and service the markets. (Philip Kotler) Based on the above definition, we discuss each concept in detail, keeping small and medium enterprises in mind

Marketing Research: Market research helps entrepreneur to determine how their product or service will be accepted among different demographics. This information can help them in establishing which segment of consumers will have an interest in their product and services and ultimately end up purchasing from them. Small and medium entrepreneurs can use market research to gain specific information such as determining the age group, gender, location, and income level of potential customers that they should target using their marketing message. Market research enables them to create a marketing plan for their small business that is not only effective, but also cost efficient. Market research gives the information that need regarding the market. Marketing research is delving into the behavior and buying habits of a specific segment that entrepreneurs have decided to target and ultimately it saves their money by helping them avoid costly marketing mistakes.

Market Planning: A good marketing plan can help entrepreneurs to focus on their energy and resources. But a plan created in a vacuum, based solely on their perceptions, does not advance the agenda. That's why market research, however simple or sophisticated, is important. A marketing plan is more than the map for success. It's actually a map-making process that, when complete will reveal a clear route to enterprise prospective customers. A good map reveals specific items of information. Here are six things marketing plan should help entrepreneur accomplish.

- ❖ Prove that entrepreneur understand their industry. Knowing their product is not enough.
- ❖ Identify their target market. These are the people most likely to buy their product or use their services.
- ❖ Identify their competition. Who's out there and what are they doing?
- ❖ Establish their pricing, distribution, and product positioning. How much will it cost plus a fair profit? How will they get it there? And where do they fit into the marketplace?
- ❖ Focus on a single effective marketing concept. Define their strongest strength and lead with that. For example, Little Caesar's "pizza pizza" may not be the most innovative idea ever conceived — but it's certainly one of the more effective. Why? Because it's simple and consistent.

Market Positioning: Positioning of the product is a powerful tool that allows product to create an image. And image is the outward representation of being importance of the product that's why it is so important for entrepreneurs to transform their passion into a market position. If they don't define their product or service, a competitor will do it for them. The position in the market place evolves from the defining characteristics of their product. Positioning is the competitive strategy. What's the one thing they do best? What's unique about their product or service? Entrepreneurs have to identify strongest strength and use it to position their product. The primary elements of positioning are:

- **Pricing**. Is their product a luxury item, somewhere in the middle, or cheap,
- **Quality**. The product should be well produced, i.e. quality should be maintained. What controls are in place to assure consistency? Do they back their quality claim with customer-friendly guarantees, warranties, and return policies?
- **Service**. Do they offer the added value of customer service and support? Is their product customized and personalized?
- **Distribution**. How do customers obtain their product? The channel or distribution is part of positioning.
- **Packaging**. Packaging makes a strong statement. Make sure it's delivering the message they intend.

Market Segmentation: A market consists of large number of individual customers who differ in terms of their needs, preferences, and buying capacity. Therefore, it becomes necessary to divide the total market into different segments or homogeneous customer groups. Such division is called market segmentation. They may have uniformity in employment patterns, educational qualifications, economic status, preferences, etc.

Market segmentation enables the entrepreneur to match his marketing efforts to the requirements of the target market. Instead of wasting his efforts in trying to sell to all types of customers, a small scale unit can focus its efforts on the segment most appropriate to its market. A market can be segmented on the basis of the following variables:

- **Geographic Segmentation:** The characteristics of customers often differ across nations, states, regions cities, or neighbor hoods. The entrepreneur can decide to operate in one or a few or all the geographic areas, but pay attention to differences in geographic needs and preferences.
- **Demographic Segmentation:** Variables such as age, sex, family size, income, occupation, education, religion, race, and nationality are widely used for market segmentation.
- **Psychological variables:** Personality, life style, social class, etc. can also be used for market segmentation. For example, some products like pens, watches, cosmetics, and briefcases are designed differently for common men and status seekers.
- **Behavioral Segmentation:** Buyers are divided into groups on the basis of their knowledge, attitude, use, or response to a product.

Marketing Research

Marketing is the process of planning and executing the conception, pricing, promotion, and distribution of ideas, goods, and services to create exchanges that satisfy individual and organization objectives. The marketing concept requires that customer satisfaction rather than profit maximization is the goal of an organization. In other words, the organization should be consumer oriented and should try to understand consumers' requirements and satisfy them quickly and efficiently, in ways that are beneficial to both the consumer and the organization. This means that in any research organization should try to obtain information on consumer needs and gather marketing intelligence to help satisfy these needs efficiently.

A company faces many marketing problems. It faces problems about consumers, product, market competition, sales promotion, etc. Marketing research helps to solve these problems. Marketing research is a systematic process. It first collects data (Information) about the Marketing problem. Then it records this data, it analyzes data and then it draws conclusions about that data. After that, it gives suggestions (advice) for solving the marketing problem. So, marketing research helps to solve the marketing problems quickly, correctly and systematically.

"Marketing research is a systematic problem analysis, model building, and fact finding for the purpose of improved decision-making and control in the marketing of goods and services." (*Philips Kotler)*

Marketing research collects full information about the consumers. It finds out the needs and expectations of the consumers. So the company produces the goods according to the needs and expectations of the consumers. Marketing research helps the company to make its production and marketing policies. It helps the company to introduce new products in the market. It helps to identify new markets. Marketing research also collects full information about the competitors. The company uses this information to fight competition. It also helps the marketing manager to take decisions.

Marketing research is a critical part of such a marketing intelligence system, it helps to improve management decision making by providing relevant, accurate, and timely (RAT) information. Every decision poses unique needs for information, and relevant strategies can be developed based on the information gathered through marketing research in action. Too often, marketing research is considered narrowly as the gathering and analyzing of data for someone else to use. Firms can achieve and sustain a competitive advantage through the creative use of market information. Hence, marketing research is defined as information input to decisions, not simply the evaluation of decisions that have been made. Market research alone, however, does not guarantee success; the intelligent use of market research is the key to business achievement. A competitive edge is more than the result of how information is used than of who does or does not have the information.

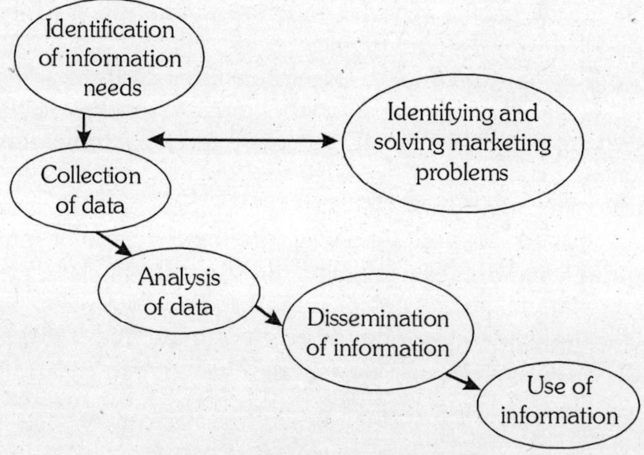

Fig. 4.3: Marketing Research

Marketing decisions involve issues that range from fundamental shifts in the positioning of a business or the decision to enter a new market to narrow tactical questions of how best to stock a grocery shelf. The context for these decisions is the market planning process, which proceeds sequentially through four stages; situation analysis, strategy development, marketing program development, and implementation. This is a never-ending process, so the evaluation of past strategic decisions serves as an input to the situation assessment. During each stage, marketing research makes a major contribution to clarifying and resolving issues and then choosing among decision alternatives.

Marketing research is not an immediate or an obvious path to finding solutions to all managerial problems. A manager who is faced with a particular problem should not instinctively resort to conduct a marketing research to find a solution to the problem. A manager should consider several factors before ordering marketing research. Sometimes it is best not to conduct marketing research. Hence, the primary decision to be made is whether or not market research is called for in a particular situation. Factors that influence this initial decision include the following.

- Relevance
- Type and Nature of Information Sought
- Timing
- Availability of Resources
- Cost-Benefit Analysis

Although research is conducted to generate information, managers do not readily use the information to solve their problems. The factors that influence a manager's decision to use research information are (1) research quality, (2) conformity to prior expectations, (3) clarity of presentation, (4) political acceptability within the firm, and (5) challenge to the status quo.

Researchers and managers agree that the technical quality of research is the primary determination of research use also; managers are less inclined to utilize research that does not conform to prior notions or is not politically acceptable. Some researchers argue that the use of information is a function of the direct and indirect effects of environmental, organizational, informational, and individual factors. However, a researcher should not alter the findings to match a manager's prior notions. Further, managers in consumer organizations are less likely to use research findings than their counterparts in industrial firms. This is due to a greater exploratory objective in information collection, a greater degree of formalization of organizational structure, and a lesser degree of surprise in the information collection.

Normally, three parties are involved in a marketing research project: (1) the client who sponsors the project, (2) the supplier who designs and executes the research, and (3) the respondent who provides the information. The issue of ethics in marketing research involves all three players in a research project. The increase in international trade and the emergence of global corporations resulting from increased globalization of business had a major impact on all facets of business, including marketing research. The need to collect information relating to international markets, and to monitor trends in these markets, as well also conduct research to determine the appropriate strategies that will be most effective in international markets, are expanding rapidly.

The marketing research industry in India is increasingly growing into an international industry, with more than one-third of its revenues coming from foreign operations. The increase in the importance of global business has caused an increase in awareness of the problems related to international research. As such, the basic functions of marketing research and the research process do not differ from domestic and multi-country research; however, the international marketing research process is much more complicated and the international marketing researcher faces problems that are different from those of a domestic researcher.

MARKET PLANNING

One of the main reasons for failure of small businesses is due to ineffective marketing. Small enterprise may have a great product or service, but they don't know how to tell those that would benefit from their product or service why customer should consider them.

Developing a marketing plan is the first step to ensuring small scale entrepreneurs don't become one of the failure statistics. Here is the simplified marketing plan for small businesses that removes the guesswork about what they absolutely need to know to market their business.

There are eight steps to developing a solid marketing strategy for their business as shown in the following diagram.

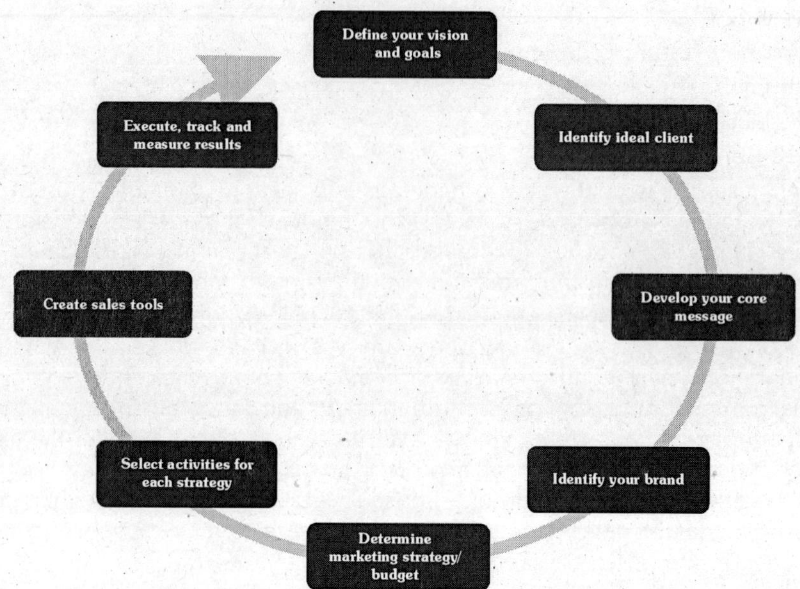

Fig. 4.4: Steps of Market Planning

- **Define vision and goals:** Start with a vision that describes what entrepreneur wants their business to be. The vision should inspire, energize, motivate and stimulate their creativity. Define goals they would like to accomplish in a 12 month period. These goals set the direction they want to take with their marketing activities. If they want to create visibility for their company, trying to generate demand for their services and want to establish themselves as the expert in their field, then their goals need to be SMART: specific, measurable, achievable, relevant and time-based.
- **Understand their ideal customer and competition:** Determine what motivates their ideal customer, what causes them pain, and why they would be interested in buying from entrepreneurs. Then determine how they are different from their competition and how they want to be viewed by their target. Highlight why they are different and what value they offer to their customers.
- **Develop their core message**: Small business core message is a short description of their business that enables prospective buyers to know what they work with and what value they bring to the relationship. It conveys this message in a manner that literally attracts the right customers to them. A good core message projects what makes entrepreneur unique and a benefit to their ideal client.
- **Identify their brand identity and apply it consistently across all of their marketing efforts:** Small entrepreneurs may need to define their personal brand and their corporate brand depending on their business. In either case, their brand should fit their personality and help get noticed.
- **Determine marketing strategy and budget:** Identify the strategy which will use to achieve their goals. Strategies will fall within the 7 marketing categories: Internet (including social media), advertising, direct marketing, public relations, events, word of mouth, and strategic alliances. The types of marketing helps in choosing within their own strategy will depend on their unique requirements. The budget will help them to determine their cash flow by mapping the budget needed for their sales tools and each area identified within their marketing strategy based on the tactics these entrepreneurs decide to use.

- **Identify activities for each strategy:** The entrepreneur should select such activities such that they accomplish their goals, reach their ideal customer, make sense for their business, can be executed regularly and effectively, and are affordable.
- **Create their sales tools to support the tactics:** These tools can include business cards, brochures, a web site or blog, white papers, testimonials, or promotional items.
- **Execute track and measure results:** Frequently these small entrepreneurs have to execute and measure their results, so that they can change their strategy according to their requirement.

MARKETING MIX FOR THE SMALL ENTERPRISES

The process of marketing or distribution of goods requires particular attention of management of business because production has no relevance unless products are sold. Marketing mix, simply stated, is the process of designing and integrating various elements of marketing in such a way to ensure the achievement of enterprise objectives. The elements of marketing mix have been classified under four heads - product, price, place, and promotion.

Decisions relating to the product include product designing, packaging and labeling and varieties of the product. Decision on 'Price' is very important because sales depend to a large extent on product pricing. Whether uniform price will be charged or different prices will be charged for the same product in different markets are examples of decision pertaining to the price of the product. The third important element is 'place', which refers to decision regarding the market where products will be offered for sale. 'Promotion' involves decisions bearing on the ways and means of increasing sales.

Different tools or methods may be adopted for this purpose. The relative importance to be attached to the various methods is decided while concentrating on the element of 'promotion' in marketing mix. Lastly, the marketing manager has to take into account the impact of external factors like consumer behavior, competitors' strategy, and Government policy on each element of marketing mix. In short, marketing mix involves decisions regarding products to make available, the price to be charged for the same, the incentives to be provided to the consumers in the markets where products would be made available for sale. These decisions are taken keeping in view the influence of marketing forces outside the organization. To create the right marketing mix, businesses have to meet the following conditions:

The Product: The product should have the right features - for example, it must look good and work well.

- The price must be right. Consumer will need to buy in large numbers to produce a healthy profit.
- The goods must be in the right place at the right time. Making sure that the goods arrive when and where they are wanted is an important operation.
- The target group needs to be made aware of the existence and availability of the product through promotion.

Successful promotion helps a firm to spread costs over a larger output, for example, a company like Kellogg's is constantly developing new breakfast cereals – the product element is the new product itself, getting the price right involves examining customer perceptions and rival products as well as costs of manufacture, promotion involves engaging in a range of promotional activities e.g. competitions, product tasting etc, and place involves using the best possible channels of distribution such as leading supermarket chains. The product is the central point on which marketing energy must focus. Finding out how to make the product, setting up the production line, providing the finance and manufacturing the product are not the responsibility of the marketing function. However, it is concerned with what the product means to the customer. Marketing therefore plays a key role in determining such aspects as:

- **The appearance of the product –** in line with the requirements of the market
- **The function of the product –** products must address the needs of customers as identified through market research.

The product range and how it is used is a function of the marketing mix. The range may be broadened or a brand may be extended for tactical reasons, such as matching competition or catering for seasonal fluctuations. Alternatively, a product may be repositioned to make it more acceptable for a new group of consumers as part of a long-term plan.

Fig. 4.5: Marketing Mix

The price: Of all the aspects of the marketing mix, price is the one, which creates sales revenue - all the others are costs. The price of an item is clearly an important determinant of the value of sales made. In theory, price is really determined by the discovery of what customers perceive is the value of the item on sale. Researching consumers' opinions about pricing is important as it indicates how they value what they are looking for as well as what they want to pay. An organization's pricing policy will vary according to time and circumstances

The place: Although figures vary widely from product to product, roughly a fifth of the cost of a product goes on getting it to the customer. 'Place' is concerned with various methods of transporting and storing goods, and then making them available for the customer. Getting the right product to the right place at the right time involves the distribution system. The choice of distribution method will depend on a variety of circumstances. It will be more convenient for some manufacturers to sell to wholesalers who then sell to retailers, while others will prefer to sell directly to retailers or customers.

The promotion: Promotion is the business of communicating with customers. It will provide information that will assist them in making a decision to purchase a product or service. The cost associated with promotion or advertising goods and services often represents a sizeable proportion of the overall cost of producing an item. However, successful promotion increases sales so that advertising and other costs are spread over a larger output. Though increased promotional activity is often a sign of a response to a problem such as competitive activity, it enables an organization to develop and build up a succession of messages and can be extremely cost-effective.

Channels of Distribution

Channel of distribution refers to how an organization will distribute the product or service they are offering to the end user. The organization must distribute the product to the user at the right place at the right time. Efficient and effective distribution is important if the organization is to meet its overall marketing objectives. If an organization underestimate a demand and customers cannot purchase products because of it, profitability will be affected.

Channel of distribution denotes the intermediaries involved in the process whereby a product passes from the manufacturer to consumers. It is very important for the producers to involve middlemen in order to reach consumers. Middlemen reduce the problems of both producers and consumers. Secondly, middlemen help in distributing the products over a large area. Middlemen also supply useful market information to the producer for improving the product. Involvement of middlemen adds to the convenience of consumers because they are able to lay many items from a single store. Some people feel that by involving more middlemen in the process of distribution, the final price of a products is considerably raised which is ultimately paid by the consumer.

Therefore the number of middlemen involved should be limited, if at all necessary: There can be various levels of channel. It is for the producer to decide which level would suit the sale of his product.

Number of Channel Levels

Distribution channel starts from the producer and ends with the consumer. Each layer of middleman that performs some work in bringing the product closer to the final layer is a channel level. The diagram given below shows the various channel levels.

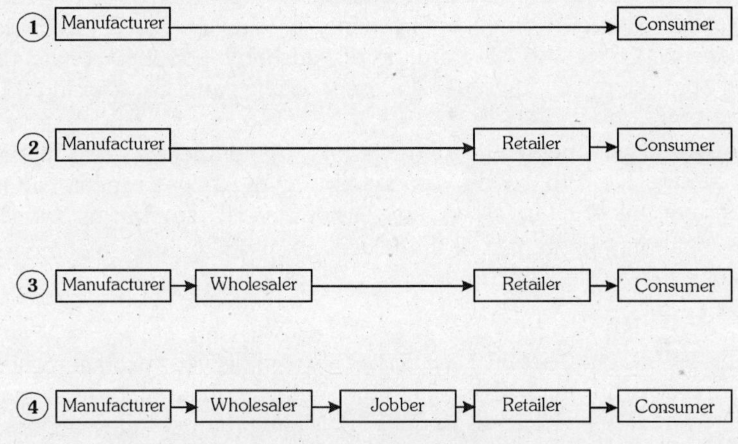

Examples of Customer Marketing Channels

Fig. 4.6: Channels of Distribution

Channel 1 is called a direct marketing channel. It has no intermediary level. Producers sell products directly to the consumers. Channel 2 includes one intermediary which is generally a retailer. Retailers buy products directly from the manufacturer and sell these to the consumers. Generally electronic goods like televisions, computers, are sold through this channel level. Channel 3 consists of two levels, typically a wholesaler and a retailer. This channel is often used by small manufacturers of food items, and other products. Channel 4 contains three middlemen levels come between wholesalers and retailers. They buy from wholesaler and sell to small retailers who generally are not served by wholesalers. There can be even more levels in distribution channel but from producer's point of view, greater number of levels means less control and greater complexity of channel.

Choice of channel of distribution

There are a number of factors which govern the choice regarding channel of distribution. These are listed below:-

1. Nature of product: For perishable goods, shorter channel is preferred whereas for durable goods channel 3 is more popular. If goods are made to order, direct selling may be effected. For technical products and costly products, manufacturers generally go for direct selling through agents specially hired for this purpose.

2. Nature of market: If the market is concentrated and not scattered, producers may go for direct selling but for scattered market, middlemen are involved. If there are more buyers, there may be a need to include more middleman. For consumer product market retailers are essential but in case of industrial products a shorter channel is preferred, hence middlemen may be eliminated.

3. Middlemen: Middlemen who can provide desired marketing services are given preference. The availability of middlemen also affects channel decision. The middlemen must be co-operative and honest. The channel which generates largest sales volume at lower unit cost will be given priority.

4. Size and Policy of the Company: There are many factors related to company which influence channel decision. A big size company with broader product line can afford to have shorter channel. New companies heavily rely on middlemen. A company with sufficient financial resources can spend heavily on advertisement and its own outlets. Hence need for middleman is reduced. Companies desiring efficient control over channel members will always prefer shorter channel.

5. Marketing Environment: During recession or depression shorter channels are preferred because of being less costly. In times of prosperity a wide choice is available. Technological inventions also have an impact e.g., distribution of perishable goods to distant places has become possible due to cold storage facilities in warehousing and transporting. Such facilities have expanded the role of intermediaries.

6. Competitors: Channels of distribution used by competitors also influence this decision. Some organization may like to follow the same chains as used by competitors. On the other hand, some organization may avoid channels already customary. They may have their own decisions.

Thus after visualizing the impact of the factors mentioned above a company adopts the best channel from among the available alternatives.

Physical Distribution

Physical distribution comprises all those activities which deliver customer satisfaction by supplying right type of products at right place and at right time regularly. Economical and satisfactory customer service is the primary goal of physical distribution. Providing the right type of goal at right place and at right time is the ultimate goal of any marketing department. These goals may be conflicting, sometimes, e.g., for meeting sudden and unforeseen demand for goods, maintenance of large inventory is suggested, but this involves cost as well as risk. This means that a proper balance between the cost and service should be achieved.

Components of physical distribution

1. Order Processing: Physical distribution begins with customers' order. Both the company and customer are benefitted if order processing is carried out quickly and accurately. These days computers are used which establish a link between retailers and producers. Producers keep a watch on the stock position at retailers' place retailers may also place orders through computer. This facility speeds up the process.

2. Warehousing: Every company must store goods to maintain a proper flow. Storage facilities are important because production and consumption cycles generally do not match. Companies need to decide the number, space and location of warehouses. The cost of these should be in balance with customer service. Companies may own warehouses or take them on rent.

3. Inventory: Inventory level also affects customer satisfaction. Marketers would like that company having enough stock to fulfill all customers' order immediately. But it involves heavy cost. Companies should, therefore, carefully plan when to order and how much to order

4. Transportation: Transportation has an impact, facilitated the physical distribution of goods and services over a larger area. Modes of transportation may include road, rail, water, air, etc. The choice of mode of transport affects the pricing and condition of goods. Hence this is an important decision and requires lot of thinking.

Distribution Strategies: Depending on the type of product being distributed there are three common distribution strategies available:

1. Intensive distribution: Used commonly to distribute low priced or impulse purchase products eg chocolates, soft drinks.

2. Exclusive distribution: Involves limiting distribution to a single outlet. The product is usually highly priced, and requires the intermediary to place much detail in its sell. An example would be the sale of vehicles through exclusive dealers.

3. Selective Distribution: A small number of retail outlets are chosen to distribute the product. Selective distribution is common with products such as computers, televisions household appliances, where consumers are willing to shop around and where manufacturers want a large geographical spread.

If a manufacturer decides to adopt an exclusive or selective strategy they should select a intermediary which has experience of handling similar products, credible and is known by the target audience.

Wholesalers and Retailers

Wholesalers and retailers are the two important types of middlemen forming a part of the distribution channels. They act as an intermediary link between the manufacturers and the consumers of goods. They specialize in providing a wide range of services for both the producers as well as the consumers. They reduce the amount of efforts required by the manufacturer in distributing his product to the final consumers and provide a vast market coverage to his products. They greatly increase the efficiency of exchange and lead to reduction in total cost of distribution of products. They provide ready delivery of goods to the consumers at places convenient and accessible to them. They also provide after sale services and handle consumer grievances. They also act as a communication channel by providing information about the products to the consumers, on one hand, and the consumer feedback to the producers on the other hand.

Retail Marketing

Retail market is now considered to be one of the most emerging and competitive markets in the entire economy. Almost every day you will get to see various new companies that are entering the market, thus in order to survive this highly competitive market one needs to have a strong hold upon it and this is only possible with the help of retail marketing. It is a systematic approach where marketing strategies are used to capture customers and to increase the overall profits. Whether it is a departmental store or a boutique, every retailer needs to adopt proper retail marketing strategies in order to earn huge profits and to set a strong impression in the minds of the customer.

Retail marketing even focuses on satisfying the customers, maintaining a proper profit margin for the owner of the goods. Customer needs are the basic key factors of retail. Retail marketing consists of 5 basic pillars, first is saving the precious time of the customers. Second is setting the right prices of the goods, third is creating a proper connection with the emotions of the customers, fourth pillar is paying the right respect to the customers and lastly solving the problems of the customer is another pillar of retail.

Retailing is all the activities involved in selling goods and services directly to final consumers for their personal, non business use. It consists of the sale of goods or merchandise from a fixed location, such as department store, or by post, in small or individual lots for direct consumption by the purchaser. Retailing may include subordinated services, such as delivery. Purchasers may be individuals or businesses. In commerce, a retailer buys goods or products in large quantities from manufacturers, either directly or through a wholesaler, and then they sells smaller quantities to the end user. Retailers are the end of the supply chain. Retail establishments are often called shops or stores. Manufacturing marketers see the process of retailing as a necessary part of their overall distribution strategy.

Most retailing is done in retail stores, in recent year's non- store retailing-selling by mail, telephone (telemarketing), door to door contact, vending machines, and numerous electronic means has grown tremendously.

Services provided by the retailers to the wholesalers and manufacturers:

- ❖ They provide selling outlets to wholesalers and manufacturers.
- ❖ They save the manufacturers from the inconvenience and expenses of selling the goods in small lots to a large number of consumers.
- ❖ They communicate the needs and desires of consumers to the manufacturers.
- ❖ They may also arrange for transportation of goods from the wholesalers' go downs to the ultimate consumers.
- ❖ They may also perform storage function by keeping stocks of goods.

Services provided by the retailers to the consumers:-

- ❖ They anticipate the needs of consumers and accordingly assemble goods of different varieties. Thus they satisfy their demands and provide them a wide choice of goods.
- ❖ They sort out goods supplied by the wholesalers and keep them in convenient packages for the benefit of the consumers.
- ❖ They even act as an advisor and guide to the consumers by bringing new products to their notice and educating them about its diverse uses.
- ❖ They keep the consumers informed about the changing trends in the market about the different varieties of products.
- ❖ They also provide other services to the consumers such as free home delivery, after-sale services, credit facility, etc.

Types of retailers

There are mainly two types of retailers, Store Retailers and Non-Store Retailers. Both types are classified as per the table below:

These types of retail store come in a variety of shapes and sizes, and new retails types keep emerging. They can be classified by one or more of several characteristics.

Amount of services: Different products require different amounts of services and customer service preferences vary,

Self-service retailers: Customers were willing to perform their own "locate-compare-select" process to save money. Today, self-service is the basis of all discount operations and typically is used by sellers of convenience goods (such as supermarkets) and nationally-branded, fast moving shopping goods (such as catalog showrooms).

Limited service retailers, provide more sales assistance because they carry more shopping goods about which consumers need information. Their increased operating costs result in higher prices.

Full service retailers, such as specialty stores and first-class department stores, have salespeople to assist customers in every phase of the shopping process. Full service stores usually carry more specialty goods for which customers like to be waited on. They provide more liberal return policies, various credit plans, free delivery, home servicing, and extras such as lounges and restaurants.

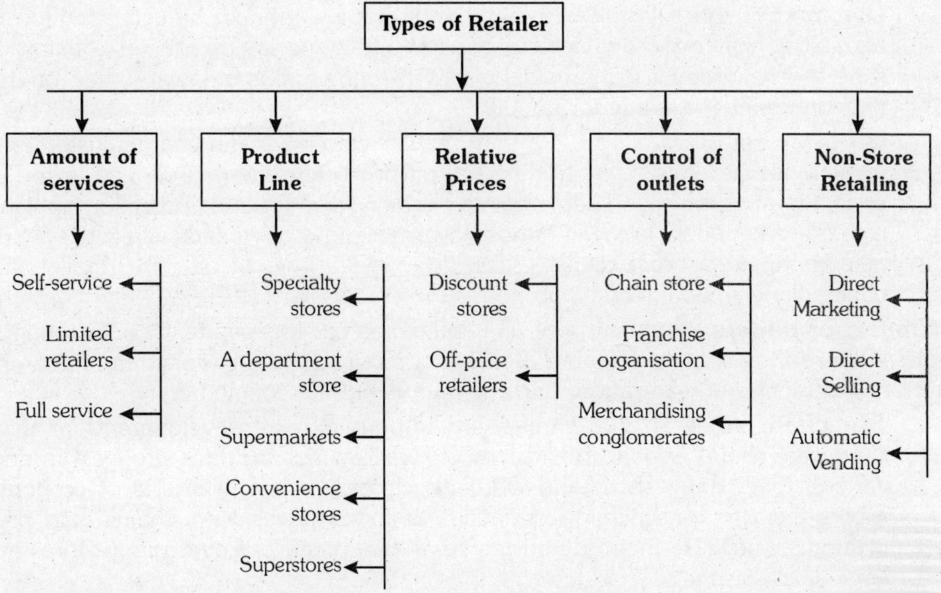

Fig. 4.7: Types of retailers

Product Line: retailers can also be classified by the depth and breadth of their product assortments:

Specialty stores carry a narrow product line with a deep assortment within that line. Examples include stores selling sporting goods, books, furniture, electronics, flowers, or toys. Today, specialty stores are flourishing, due to the increasing use of market segmentation, market targeting, and product specialization.

A department store carries a wide variety of product lines. Each line is operated as a separate department managed by specialist buyers and merchandisers.

Supermarkets are large, low-cost, low-margin, high-volume, self-service stores that carry a wide variety of food, laundry, and household products. Most US supermarket stores are owned by large chains such as Safeway, Kroger, Publix, Winn-Dixie, Jewel, and Tops. Chains account for almost 70% of all supermarket sales.

Convenience stores are small stores that carry a limited line of high-turnover convenience goods. These stores located near residential areas and remain open long hours, seven days a week. Convenience stores must charge high prices to make up for higher operating costs and lower sales volume, but they satisfy an important consumer need.

Superstores, combination stores, and hypermarkets are all larger than the conventional supermarket. Many leading chains are moving toward superstores because their wider assortment allows prices to be 5-6% higher than conventional supermarkets. Combination stores are combined food and drug stores. Hypermarkets combine discount, supermarket and warehouse retailing and operate like a warehouse. They usually give discounts to customers.

Relative Prices: retailers can be classified by the prices they charge. Most retailers charge regular prices and offer normal quality goods and customer service. Some offer higher quality goods and services at higher prices. Retailers that feature low prices include:

Discount stores sell standard merchandise at lower prices by accepting lower margins and selling higher volume. Occasional discounts or specials do not make a store a discount store. A true discount store regularly sells its merchandise at lower prices, offering mostly national brands, not inferior goods.

Off-price retailers buy at less than regular wholesale and charge customers less than retail. With the discounters trading up, off-price retailers have moved in to fill the low-price, high-volume gap. They obtain a changing and unstable collection of higher-quality merchandise, often leftover goods, overruns, and irregulars at reduced prices from manufacturers or other retailers. The three main types of off-price retailers are factory outlets, independents, and warehouse clubs.

Control of outlets: about 80% of all retail stores are independents, accounting for 2/3 of retail sales. Other forms of ownership include the corporate chain, the voluntary chain and retailer cooperative, the franchise organization, and the merchandising conglomerate.

The chain store is one of the most important retail developments of this century. Corporate chains appear in all types of retailing, but they are strongest in department, variety, food, drug, shoe, and women's clothing stores. The size of corporate chains allows them to buy in large quantities at lower prices, and chains gain promotional economies because their advertising costs are spread out over many stores and over a large sales volume.

A franchise is a contractual association between a manufacturer, wholesaler, or service organization (the franchiser) and independent business people (the franchisees) who buy the right to own and operate one or more units in the franchise system. Franchising has been prominent in fast-food companies, motels, gas stations, video stores, auto rentals, hair cutting salons, real estate, and dozens of other goods and services. The compensation received by the franchiser may include an initial fee, a royalty on sales, lease fees for equipment and a share of the profits.

Merchandising conglomerates are corporations that combine several different retailing forms under central ownership and share some distribution and management functions.

Types of store cluster: Most stores today cluster together to increase their customer pulling power and to give consumers the convenience of one-stop shopping.

- **Central business districts** were the main form of retail cluster until the 1950s. Every large city and town had a central business district with banks, department stores, speciality stores, and movie theatres. When people began to move to the suburbs, however, these central business districts (with their traffic, parking, and crime problems) began to lose business. In recent years, many cities have joined with merchants to try to revive downtown shopping areas by building malls and providing underground parking. Some central business districts have made a comeback; others remain in a slow, and possibly irreversible, decline.
- **A shopping center** is a group of retail businesses planned, developed, owned, and managed as a unit. All shopping centers combined account for about 1/3 of all retail sales.

Non-Store Retailing: Non-store retailing includes direct marketing, direct selling, and automatic vending. Although most goods and services are sold through stores, non-store retailing has been growing much faster than store retailing. Traditional store retailers are facing increasing sales competition from catalogs, direct mail, telephone, home TV shopping shows, and on-line computer shopping services, home and office parties, and other direct retailing approaches.

- **Direct Marketing** vehicles are used to obtain immediate orders directly from targeted consumers. Direct Marketing uses various advertising media that interact directly with consumers, generally calling for the consumer to make a direct response. Although direct marketing initially consisted mostly of direct mail and mail-order catalogs, it has taken on several additional forms, including telemarketing, direct radio and TV, and on-line computer shopping. Its growing use in consumer marketing is largely a response to the "de-massification" of mass markets, which has resulted in an increasing number of fragmented market segments with highly individualized needs. Trends that have increased the use of direct marketing include:

- Number of women in the workplace
- Higher costs of driving including traffic congestion and parking problems
- Shortage of retail help
- Longer checkout lines
- Toll-free telephone numbers
- Availability of credit through proliferation of credit cards
- Growth of computer power and communication technology and
- Increasing time pressures on consumers.

❖ **Direct Selling,** or door-to-door retailing, started centuries ago with roving peddlers. Direct Selling offers consumers the advantages of convenience and personal attention. But, the high costs of hiring, training, paying, and motivating the sales force usually results. Today, it has grown into a huge industry, with more than 600 companies selling their products door-to-door, office-to-office, or at home-sales parties. Although some direct selling companies are thriving, door-to-door selling has a somewhat uncertain future. Trends working against this form of selling includes:

- Increase in single- person and working-couple households decreases the chances of finding someone at home
- Home-party companies are having difficulty finding non working women who want to sell product part-time
- Increase in crimes against individuals has made consumers reluctant to invite strangers into their homes and
- Recent advances in interactive direct-marketing technology mean that the door-to-door salesperson may be replaced by the telephone, the television, and the home computer.

❖ **Automatic Vending:** Automatic Vending uses space-age and computer technology to sell a wide variety of convenience and impulse goods, including: beverages, cigarettes, candy, newspapers, foods and snacks, film, cosmetics, apparel, and fishing worms.

Retailer Marketing Decisions

Retailers always keep searching for new marketing strategies to attract and hold customers. Their marketing decisions include choices of target markets, positioning and the marketing mix-product assortments and services, price, promotion, and place.

❖ **Target market** a retailers most important decision concerns with target market. Until the target market is defined and profiled, the retailer cannot make consistent decisions on product assortments, store decor advertising messages and media, price and service levels.

❖ **Price** is the key positioning factors and must be decided in relation to target market, the product and service assortment mix, and competition.

❖ **Promotion** retailers use a very high range of promotion tools to generate traffic and purchases. They place advertisements, run special sales, issue money-saving coupons, and in store sampling. Each retailer must use promotion tools that support and reinforce its image positioning.

❖ **Place** retailers must select locations that are associable to the target market in areas that are consistent with the retailer positioning.

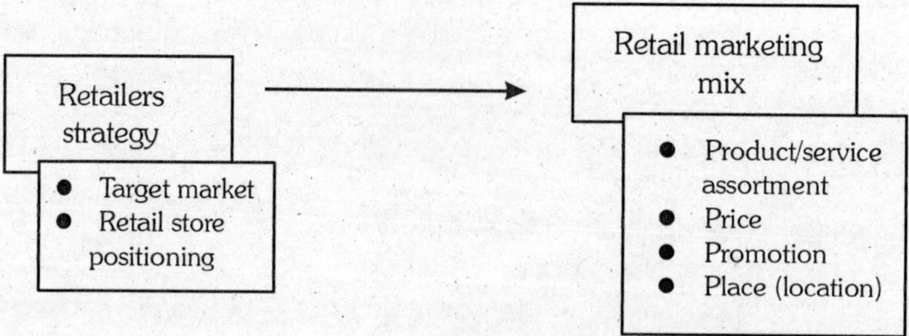

Fig. 4.8: Retailer Marketing Decision

IMPORTANCE OF RETAIL MARKETING

Through the years retailing has evolved, competition has gotten stiff and therefore marketing has become more integral in the direct selling of wares. From specialty mom-and-pop shop to mass-merchants, the methods by which stores are getting their products into the hands of customers are evolving. Because customers have more choices, stores have to reach them with advertising, entice them with promotions, and secure them with branding—hence the ever-growing need for marketing in retail outlets.

Advertising

There are two main functions of advertisements: to sell more products, and to inform the customer. Through newspaper, TV, radio and internet advertisements, retailers can inform their customers of the sales, promotions, and in-store events. Moreover, since the media is flooded with advertisements, the ability to create a more eye-catching or attention-grabbing advertisement directly influences sales. Stores that advertise—as opposed to those that don't—are kept at the top of their potential shoppers' mind, which can produce sales in the short and long term.

In-Store Promotions

Stores use promotions to prompt impulse buying behavior. A shopper may not intend to buy a product, but if there is a promotion, there is an incentive for immediate action. For example, a shopper may not need another dress shirt, but might still buy one if it is on sale. Additionally, promotions can prompt consumers to recall a product and thus instigate a purchase. Retailers also use promotional periods— corresponding with national holidays or well-know sales times—to sell off the previous season's merchandise. Promotional periods spike sales, and are a way retailers can reduce the loss of unsold inventory

In-Store Atmosphere and Customer Relations

Store design and consumer relationship marketing (CRM) directly affected the way customers purchase and retain goods. Things like the atmosphere, music, store layout, sales help, and post-purchase support can influence things like shopping time (the longer they shop, the more likely they are to buy), and how gratified they feel with their purchase. The more content a buyer is with their shopping experience, the more likely they are to buy merchandise, and the less likely they are to return it.

Branding Retail Outlets

It is necessary for retailers to develop their brand in order to stand out amongst the many other stores. With local boutiques, specialty stores, department stores, mass-merchants and internet stores, customers have more choices when it comes to buying. There is competition within each category, and competition between categories. For example, a local boutique selling dress shirts is competing with other local boutiques, and also with the mass-merchant who might be selling dress shirts at a cheaper price. It is therefore necessary for the boutique to create a brand position that a customer can identify with, to keep them loyal.

Private Labeling

Solidifying a retail brand's private label is the apex of the retail marketing evolution—and the most recent trend in high-end retailing. This is not a new concept for low- to mid-priced retail outlets, as everything from food to raincoats have been put under their brand's name. But what's new is stores that build their brand to the point where they can sell merchandise at a premium price. Doing so is more cost effective: they can reduce the costs associated with buying other brand names, source cheaper goods from private manufacturers and reap higher profits. As an added bonus, stores benefit from consumer loyalty to their stores and their products

WHOLESALE MARKETING

Wholesaling includes all activities involved in selling goods and services to those buying for resale or business use. Wholesaling is the sale of goods or merchandise to retailers, to industrial, commercial, institutional, or other professional business users, or to other wholesalers and related subordinated services. Wholesaler is those firms engaged primarily in wholesaling. Wholesalers are someone who buys large quantities of goods and resells to merchants rather than to the ultimate customers. Manufacturers use wholesalers rather than selling directly to retailers or consumers because, wholesalers are better at performing many channel functions.

Wholesalers frequently physically assemble sort and grade goods in large lots, break bulk, repack and redistribute in smaller lots. Business that buys goods from manufacturers and that sells goods, usually in large quantities to retailers, who in turn sell them to the end user. Virtually everything sold on a retail basis can be purchased from a wholesaler, who acts as middleman between the manufacturer (and owner, as in the case of list rentals) and the retailer. Wholesalers help manufacturers by absorbing some of the costs of sales and distribution, and allow manufacturers to concentrate their resources on manufacturing.

Functions of Wholesalers

- **Selling and promoting**: Wholesalers sales forces help manufacturers reach small customers at low cost. The wholesaler has more contacts and is often more trusted by the buyer than the distant manufacturer.
- **Buying and assortment building**: Wholesalers can select items and build assortments needed by their customers, thereby saving the consumers much work.
- **Bulk-breaking**: Wholesalers save their customers money by buying in carload lots and breaking these large lots into smaller quantities.
- **Warehousing:** Wholesalers hold inventory, thereby reducing the inventory costs and risks of suppliers and customers.
- **Transportation:** Wholesalers can provide quicker delivery to buyers because they are closer than the producers.
- **Financing:** Wholesalers finance their customers by giving credit, and they finance their suppliers by ordering early and paying bills on time.
- **Risk bearing:** Wholesalers absorb risk by taking title and bearing the cost of theft, damage, spoilage, and obsolescence.

- **Market information:** Wholesalers give information to suppliers and customers about competitors, new products, and price developments.
- **Management services and advice:** wholesalers often help retailers train their sales clerks, improve store layouts and displays, and set up accounting and inventory control systems.

Services provided by the wholesalers to the manufacturers:

- They place orders for the product in advance on the basis of expectations regarding the demand for the product. This enables the manufacturer to plan his production and secure the economies of scale.
- They may also provide transportation facility by carrying goods from producers to go downs and then to retailers.
- They perform advertising and sales promotion activities and also employ expert sales representatives for the purpose.
- They provide financial accommodation to manufacturers in the form of cash payments for goods purchased from them as well as provide credit to them.
- They keep the manufacturers updated on the changes in customers' habits, tastes, preferences, and fashion.
- They also play an important role in fixation of the final prices of the goods.

Services provided by the wholesalers to the retailers:

- They act as the retailers 'buying agent' and saves them from the trouble of searching out and assembling goods from several manufacturers.
- They inform the retailers about the new products, its uses and changes in their prices. They also assist the retailers in advertising and selling of the products.
- They provide financial assistance to retailers, sell goods on credit to retailers and thus help them to operate with small working capital.
- A wholesaler being the ware-house keeper of the market, they protect the retailers from the risk of loss arising from holding large stocks of the product.
- They may also sort out different grades of products according to quality and pack the goods into small lots for the retailers.

Types of Wholesalers

Wholesalers fall into three major groups: merchant wholesalers, brokers and agents, and manufacturers sales branches, and offices. They can be classified as shown below:

Independent Wholesaling Intermediaries:

Merchant wholesalers: They are independently owned businesses that title to the merchandise they handle. There are two types of such merchants. One is full service merchants who provide all the services relating to the marketing, carry stock and make deliveries. The other one is limited service wholesalers who provide limited services, examples electrical merchants, hardware merchants, pharmaceutical merchants that sell goods in particular category only. Full-service merchant wholesalers provide a full set of services, such as carrying stock, using a sales force, offering credit, making deliveries and providing management assistance. They are of two types:

- Wholesale merchants: Sell primarily to retailers and provide full range of services. Example, health foods wholesalers, and sea food wholesalers.
- Industrial distributors: Sell to manufacturers rather than retailers. Provide several services, such as carrying stock, offering credit and providing delivery

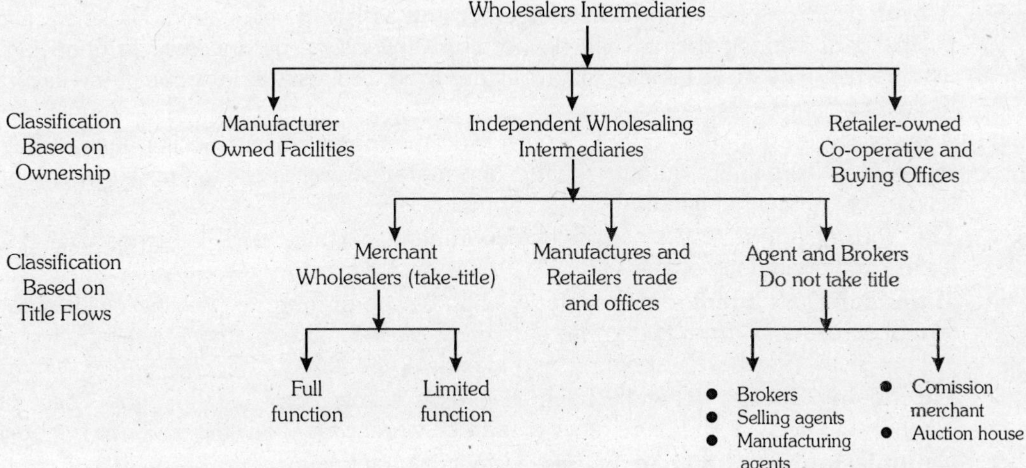

Fig. 4.9: Classification of Wholesalers Intermediaries

Limited service merchant wholesalers offer fewer services to their suppliers and customers, they are:

- **Cash and carry wholesalers:** Offer a limited line of fast-moving goods, sell to small retailers for cash, and generally do not deliver. A small fish store retailer, for example, normally drives at dawn to a cash-n-carry fish wholesaler and buys several crates of fish, pays on the spot, drives the merchandise back to the store, and unloads it.
- **Truck jobbers:** Perform a selling and delivery function. They carry a limited line of goods (such as milk, bread, eggs, or snack foods) that they sell for cash as they make their rounds of supermarkets, small grocery stores, hospitals, restaurants, factory cafeterias, and hotels.
- **Drop shippers:** Operate in bulk industries such as coal, lumber, and heavy equipment. They do not carry inventory or handle the product. Once an order is received, they find a producer who ships the goods directly to the customer. The drop shipper takes title and risk from the time the order is accepted to the time it is delivered to the customer.
- **Rack jobbers**: Serve grocery and drug retailers, mostly in the area of non-food items. Rack jobbers send delivery trucks to stores, and the delivery person sets ups racks of toys, paperback books, hardware items, pet supplies, health and beauty aids, and other items. They price the goods, keep them fresh, and maintain inventory records. Rack jobbers sell on consignment; they retain title to the goods and bill the retailers only for the goods sold to consumers
- **Mail order wholesalers:** Send catalogs to retail, industrial, and institutional customers, offering jewelry, cosmetics, specialty foods, and other small items. Their main customers are businesses in small, outlying areas
- **Producers' cooperatives:** Owned by farmer-members, they assemble farm product to sell in local markets. Profits are divided among members at the end of the year. They often try to improve product quality and promote a co-operative brand, such as Sun Maid Raisins, Sunkist Oranges, or Diamond Walnuts

Brokers and Agents: They differ from merchant wholesalers in two ways — (1) They do not take title to goods, and (2) They perform only a few functions. Their main function is to aid in buying and selling, and for these services they earn a commission on the selling price. Like merchant wholesalers, they generally specialize by product line or customer type.

- **A broker** brings buyers and sellers together and assists in negotiation. Brokers are paid by the parties hiring them. They do not carry inventory, get involved in financing, or assume risk. The most familiar examples are food, real estate, insurance, and securities brokers.
- **Agents** represent buyers or sellers on a more permanent basis. Selling agents contract to sell producers entire output — either the manufacturer is not interested in doing the selling, or feels unqualified.
- **The selling agent** serves as a sales department and has much influence over prices, terms, and conditions of sale.
- **Manufacturer's agent's** representatives handle two or more related lines, with separate formal agreements, from two or more different manufacturers. They are most often used in lines such as apparel, furniture, and electrical goods.
- **Purchasing agents** generally have long term relationships with buyers. They make purchases for buyers and often receive, inspect, warehouse, and ship goods to the buyers.
- **Commission merchants** (or houses) are agents that take physical possession of products and negotiate sales.

Manufacturers Sales Branches and Offices: Manufacturers set up their own sales branches and offices to improve inventory control, selling, and promotion. Sales branches carry inventory, and are found in industries such as lumber and automotive equipment and parts. Sales offices do not carry inventory, and are most often found in the dry goods and notion industries. Purchasing officers perform a role similar to that of brokers or agents but are part of the buyer organizations.

WHOLESALER MARKETING DECISIONS

Wholesalers now face growing competitive pressures, more demanding customers, new technologies, and more direct-buying programs on the part of large industrial, institution and retails buyers. As a result, they have taken a fresh look at their marketing strategies. As with retails, their marketing decisions include choices of target markets, positioning and the marketing mix- product assortments and services, price, promotion, and place.

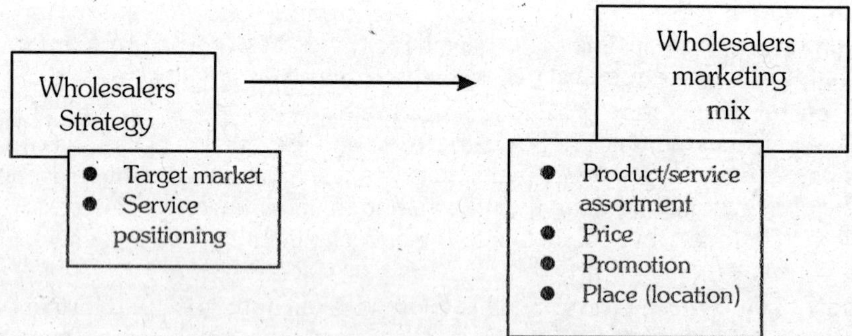

Fig. 4.10: Wholesaler Marketing Decision

Target Market and Positioning Decision

Like retails, wholesalers must define their target markets and position themselves effectively –they cannot serve everyone. They can choose a target group by size of customer large (only large retailers) types of customers, need for services or others factor. Within the large group, they can identify the more profitable customers, design stronger offers, and build better relationship with them.

- **Price** wholesalers usually mark up their cost of goods by conventional percentage to cover their expenses. They ask suppliers for a special price break when they can turn it into an opportunity to increase the supplier's sales.
- **Promotion** wholesalers rely primarily on their sales force to achieve promotional objectives. They need to develop an overall promotion strategy involving trade advertising, sales promotion, and publicity.
- **Place** wholesalers must choose the locations, facilities and web locations carefully.

Importance of Wholesale Marketing

- Wholesaling provides an expanded consumer market potential in terms of geographical locations and consumer purchasing power while at the same time providing a cash flow for the manufacturer. There are several major reasons for the importance of wholesaling. First, all goods, and necessary supplies for their production pass through some form of middle agent and wholesaling system. For this reason, the effective functioning of wholesale linkages contributes directly to the economic well-being of a society.
- Secondly, for most small producers, an immediate geographic location is typically insufficient to provide and maintain an on-going customer base for their operations. As a means to sell their goods, smaller producers must have avenues to develop market segments of potential customers and must make sure their goods are of the quality customers want at prices they are willing to pay. The role of wholesalers is to provide links to an expanded market base, i.e., to discover where customers are located and how best to reach them. In this sense, wholesaling uses time and place as it relates to information and availability. Wholesalers create utility through holding goods that can be drawn upon by buyers at a cost lower than direct exchange.
- Finally, wholesalers act as distribution channels and interface with markets and producers within markets. Whereas wholesaling and retailing provide similar functions in that they receive, store, and distribute goods, the importance of wholesaling is in its ability to moderate supply and demand fluctuations and cope with larger transactions with less emphasis on selling techniques and services and product promotion. Wholesaling has the capability to adjust the distribution of goods from surplus to deficit areas.

Wholesalers are successful only if they are able to serve the needs of their customers, who may be retailers or other wholesalers. Some of the marketing functions provided by wholesalers to their buyers are:

- Providing producer's goods in an appropriate quantity for resale by buyers
- Providing wider geographical access and diversity in obtaining goods
- Ensuring and maintaining a quality dimension with the goods that are being obtained and resold
- Providing cost-effectiveness by reducing the number of producer contacts needed
- Providing ready access to a supply of goods
- Assembling and arranging goods of a compatible nature from a number of producers for resale
- Minimizing buyer transportation costs by buying goods in larger quantities and distributing them in smaller amounts for resale
- Working with producers to understand and appreciate consumerism in their production process.

Marketing Problems of Small Enterprises

One of the major marketing problems faced by small business enterprises in India is lack of understanding and the application of marketing concept. Most Indian small business owners equate 'marketing' to 'selling' and this is reflected in their various dysfunctional business behaviors against customer satisfaction and good business orientation. They lack the knowledge and skills of basic marketing ingredients – marketing research, market segmentation and marketing planning and control. The outcome of this is poor quality products, unawareness of competition, poor promotion, poor distribution, and poor pricing methods. They are not marketing oriented and market-focused if a marketer is defined as someone who understands and applies marketing in order to create, build, and maintain beneficial relationships with target markets. Baker (1979) and Doyle (1985) identified lack of marketing orientation as the major factor for business failure. Some of the marketing problems commonly faced by the small scale entrepreneurs in India are:

1. **Competition from large scale sector:** Because of scarcity of resources, small entrepreneurs usually use inferior technology. As a result their products are not standardized. The obsolete technology used by them gets translated into inferior quality of products.
2. **Lack of marketing knowledge**: Most of the small scale entrepreneurs are not highly educated or professionally qualified to have knowledge of marketing concept and strategy. Their lack of expertise further inhibits their understanding of the prevailing trends in the market.
3. **Lack of sales promotion:** Small units lack the resources and knowledge for effective sales promotion. Large scale units mostly have well-known branded names. They also have huge amount of resources to spend on advertisement and other sales promotion tools. Small scale units, on the other hand, have to pay a heavy commission to dealers for their selling efforts, which reduce profits margins.
4. **Weak bargaining power:** At the time of purchase of inputs, large scale entrepreneurs manage to get huge discounts and credit. Such facilities are not available to small units.
5. **Product quality:** It is costly and difficult for a small unit to have quality testing and evaluating equipment.
6. **Credit sales:** The small scale enterprise is invariably called upon to sell on credit. However, when it comes to purchasing inputs, they are denied liberal credit facilities. As a result, they have to borrow excessive working capital than actually needed. This increases the general cost of production and prices, making it non-competitive

Marketing for the Small Enterprise

The essence of marketing is to understand customers' needs and develop a plan that surrounds those needs. Suppose if a businessman has a desire to grow their business, the most effective way to grow and expand their business is by focusing on organic growth. Increase in organic growth can be possible by four different ways and all of these will increase revenue and profit

- Acquiring more customers by increasing customer base and product should satisfy the customer
- Persuading each customer to buy more products by spend time for researching and create a strategic marketing plan.
- Persuading each customer to buy more expensive products or up selling each customer by develop their message and materials based on solution marketing and satisfying customer.
- Persuading each customer to buy more profitable products, by price products and services competitively.

The majority of small business owners marketing budget is limited. The most effective way to market a small business is to create a well rounded program that combines sales activities with marketing tactics. Sales activities will not only decrease their out-of-pocket marketing expense but it also adds the value of interacting with prospective customers and clients. This interaction will provide research that is priceless. Small businesses typically have a limited marketing budget if any at all. It just means they have to think a little more creatively. How about launching their marketing campaign by doing one of the following:

- ❖ Call vendors or associates and ask them to participate with them in co-operative advertising.
- ❖ Take some time to send their existing customers' referrals and buying incentives.
- ❖ Introducing themselves to the media, free publicity has the potential to boost their business. By doing this they position themselves as an expert in their field.
- ❖ Invite people into place of business by piggybacking onto an event. Is there a concert coming to town. It could mean free radio publicity. why not be a public outreach and distribute their material

When entrepreneur spend money on marketing, do not forget to create a way to track those marketing efforts. They can do this by coding their advertisement, using multiple toll-free telephone numbers, and asking prospects where they heard about their product. This enables entrepreneurs to notice when a marketing tactic stops working, entrepreneurs can then quickly replace it with a better choice or method.

Managing of Small Enterprises

Small business entrepreneur is the manager himself, the planner, the organizer, the goal, setter, the fund raiser, the fund allocator, the fund utilizer, the researcher, the evaluator, the accountant. He first contemplates the idea of starting the business which may come from his earlier experiences, or from the felt need for such in the area etc. He then sets the research regarding the feasibility of starting the new business, then he moves on to the planning and goal setting, setting the technology rightly, does the budgeting and moves on to arrange for the equity funding and the external funding. He does the cost arrangement and subsequently the price setting keeping in view his profit requirements and planning. Before this, obviously he sets right his mandatory paper requirements conforming to his area of operation from the right authorities. He also keeps his heels on the risk management as well as the inventory management, indulging himself on the whole record keeping. He sets the marketing goals and does the marketing of his products in the best way applicable to him.

This successfully managing his business he also reaps in the profit. Starting and managing a small business is an irresistible challenge. Creating and running own business can be immensely rewarding in various ways, personal fulfillment, self discovery, financial independence, a way to make a mark in life and also to make a positive contribution to the local community or the chosen business area.

The objective of all business enterprises is to satisfy the needs and wants of the society. Marketing is, therefore, a basic function of all business firms. It has been established that access to profitable markets is a key factor which determines the long term success for all businesses. For small and micro enterprises, however, various constraints limit this access, such as inadequate technology, geographic isolation, lack of raw material and inefficient production.

Small firms virtually have no sources of information on other markets or opportunities outside their immediate surroundings. The lack of knowledge and limited access to information on market opportunities have used small sector enterprises to depend on judgment and speculation.

In a competitive business environment, this is very costly and limits their ability to expand the market. Existing arrangements to supply such information to SMEs are gross inadequate and the lack of access to modern information technology (IT) has further aggravated the situation. Most SMEs service regional or local markets. Their market information is often limited to their specific market segments. Quite often, information relating to developments in market demand and innovation is received through word of mouth. The information requirements of SMEs depend on the size of the enterprise, stage of growth and type of business.

In addition to lack of information, the absence of marketing skills at enterprise level has led to SMEs being more production oriented rather than becoming more market oriented. Many of the SMEs especially small scale enterprises lack skills on product design, packaging and sales promotion which are vital for being attractive and competitive in the market. The typical selling method of SMEs especially small scale enterprises is to operate through their own outlets. Many of them are also not in a position to promote their products and services through advertising and sales promotion mainly due to lack of skills and high cost. In fact, the absence of marketing skills has resulted in the early demise of business enterprises. By providing ways to overcome these constraints, marketing service providers plays an essential role in developing the business of small and micro producers. Marketing service providers are specialized intermediaries that facilitate access to profitable markets, whether through direct sales or via brokering or sub contracting. In addition these intermediaries offer a variety of ancillary services, and although the demand for these services may vary depending on the targeted sector and market.

Components of Small Enterprises

Small Scale Industries may sound small but actually plays a very important part in the overall growth of an economy. Small Scale Industries can be characterized by the unique feature of labor intensiveness. The total number of people employed in this industry has been calculated to be near about one crore and ninety lakhs in India, the main proponents of Small scale industries.

The importance of this industry increases manifold due to the immense employment generating potential. The countries which are characterized by acute unemployment problem especially put emphasis on the model of Small Scale Industries. It has been observed that India along with the countries in the Indian continent have gone long strides in this field.

Small business is made up of the following components are Organizational components. Technical component, financial component, marketing component, Managerial component, Risk and fluctuations component.

Organizational component: Small business needs to have a strong organizational component before setting up. Before setting up a small business it is important to know exactly what the organizational set up would suit perfectly i.e. Single ownership, partnership, cooperative etc. The selection of the organizational component would depend upon the entrepreneur, his needs, confidences, manpower strength, his strength, and weaknesses etc.

Technical component: The technique of production/business is largely important when setting/starting up a new business. It affects the size of the business. The optimum use of technical factor is crucially important. This can be achieved through diversion of labour and integration of processes.

Financial component: Financial considerations directly have a bearing on the size of the business. The finances are required firstly for establishing a unit/business and then for expanding it. The financial need will be fixed and working capital. Fixed capital is required for the acquisition of fixed assets and working capital is needed for day to day working of the business. The financial component comes from personal sources and borrowing sources.

Marketing component: The extent of market influences the scale of production/business and also raises certain marketing problems. Marketing component exercises great influence in the successful running of a business venture. Marketing component includes different marketing strategies formulated well ahead for buying as well as selling. The strategies should be well adapted to the varying local conditions keeping in mind about the fluctuating needs of the consumer market.

Managerial component: This is a very vital component for forming and running successfully a business venture. This component includes basically the human resource/personal component. The successful running of already launched business depends upon the organizing/managing capability of the entrepreneur.

Risk and fluctuating component: The frequent changes of demand should be considered while planning the size of the business. There are always fluctuations in demand. The demand for goods may be influenced by a number of factors. The fluctuation in demand may be both for a short period and a long period. The business has to withstand fluctuating demand. The size of a unit should be such that it should be able to adjust its production/sales according to market requirements. Demand changes may be due to permanent causes, pricing effect, cyclic changes, seasonal changes and erratic changes.

Marketing Intermediaries and their Role

The producers wishing to penetrate new markets or improve their position in the current market, the use of an intermediary may significantly reduce marketing costs, provide important consumer feedback, and open up access to a larger client base. The time-consuming tasks assumed by marketing service providers include identifying new clients or markets, consolidating existing ones, sourcing good raw materials, or figuring out how to ship various kinds of goods to different destinations by various means of transportation. From working in specific sectors, marketing service providers often become experts on relevant issues, such as consumer preferences, new trends and designs. This expertise translates into important feedback for the producers in terms of what to produce and how. Greater value is added to a product with each transaction that takes the product further from the source, and with each process that transforms or alters the form of the product. When carrying out a number of functions, marketing service providers can shorten this value-added chain considerably by limiting the number of actors. Both producers and consumers are interested in keeping the chain short and reducing the costs of bringing the goods to market.

Marketing Services

Marketing services are characterized as services related to different stages of production and sale, when offered as a package by the same service provider. The various services may be offered separately, and then may not necessarily be characterized as marketing. The variety of marketing services can be divided into an input phase, or the phase prior to production, and an output phase, which is the phase after production.

Marketing Services in the Input Phase

1. The input phase includes activities such as technical assistance or training, product development and design, provision of raw materials, or credit for production.
2. Training and technical assistance are services for which it is perceived that there is a large necessity, and consequently many institutions providing business development services offer technical assistance or training in some form. Whether provided to groups or to individuals, training for which there is a demand, and which help the entrepreneurs develop their skills or their businesses, may be provided for a fee. A number of demand-driven training programs claim high levels of cost-recovery.
3. Product development and design are services that are especially important where products or markets are constantly changing, such as in the case of handicrafts. These services may be provided through advice or suggestions for change or development of a product, which makes it difficult to measure the exact cost or benefit. In other cases, outside consultants may be brought in for shorter periods of time, and thus the exact cost may be calculated.

4. Access to raw materials is limited for many small producers. By grouping together, or by developing special arrangements with buyers or marketing service providers, purchases can be made in bulk at lower prices. Some marketing service providers provide raw materials instead of credit, with a surcharge or added interest at the time of payment.

Marketing Services in the Output Phase

The output phase includes activities such as quality control, packaging, transportation, and market information.

1. Quality control can be performed at different stages of production and delivery. Marketing intermediaries exercise quality control independently of production and may thus enforce consistent quality standards. Depending on the product, performing quality control objectively and critically can be a very time-consuming and expensive task, and could be priced accordingly. One example is the time involved when examining handicrafts from different producers that must comply with certain pre-set standards.
2. The need for packaging and transportation very much depends on the nature of the product, and the final destination. When required, both services are costly. These are functions that could be separated into isolated cost-effective functions (one of the case studies will show how one organization is attempting to let producers take over the separate function of packaging).
3. By making available to the producers information on prices, consumer preferences, competition, new raw materials, and potential markets, the marketing service provider adds transparency to the market, and gives the producers the opportunity to make intelligent decisions about future production.

Marketing Services Provided by the Indian Institutes

I. Integration Technology Up-gradation and Management Program: The Office of the Development Commissioner (Small Scale Industries) has launched a scheme namely the 'Integrated Technology Up-gradation and Management Program (UPTECH) in 1998, now renamed as 'Small Industry Cluster Development Program'. The scheme applies to any cluster of industries where there is a commonality in the method of production, quality control and testing, energy conservation, pollution control etc. among the units of the cluster. The scheme aims to take care of the modernization and the technological needs of the cluster. It covers a comprehensive range of issues related to technology up-gradation, improvement of productivity, energy conservation, pollution control, product diversification and their marketing, training needs etc. Scope of the Scheme are:

The scheme is exclusively for a cluster of industries. To carry out the technology status and needs studies of identified clusters.

1. To scout for and identify appropriate technologies and their providers on the basis of these status and needs studies.
2. To facilitate contract/need based research, if any required, adapting the available technology to the specific needs of the end users.
3. To facilitate and promote the demonstration of technologies to the target groups of small enterprises.
4. To promote and facilitate the delivery of the technology from its producer to the recipient user
5. To promote the assimilation and diffusion of the identified technology across the cluster of small enterprises.

II. Sub-Contracting Exchange: Under the programme of ancillary development, sub-contracting Exchanges (SCEs) have been set up. A Sub-contracting Exchange is a Store House of

Data with regard to the capacities of the small- scale units in terms of products manufactured/services rendered idle capacities available on particular processes/machines on one hand and storing data with regard to the requirements of the buyers, which could be product/components/sub assemblies/ services. The exchange also stores data about the specifications, class of accuracy, quantities, etc. The main objectives of these Sub-contracting Exchanges are:

1. To register capacities of manufacturing or services available with the small scale and tiny units.
2. To obtain details of items required regularly by other large units which can be manufactured in the small scale sector?
3. To arrange Buyer-Seller Meet/Vendor Development Programmes so as to display the products required by large undertakings and to discuss the specifications and other requirements with the small scale units' participants in such meets.

The Exchange is, therefore, in a position to a great extent to provide sufficient information to vendees to have access to the details of facilities available with the Sub- Contractors who could meet their requirements. On the other hand it also helps to provide information to Sub-contractors/ Vendors about the Vendees who are looking for outsourcing. Following the announcement of the liberalized policy package in 1991, a Scheme for the setting up of SCEs backed by Industry Association/ -NGOs was also launched. Under this particular Scheme, SCEs are sanctioned for various parts of the country by providing financial assistance up to Rs. 4.7 lakhs to set up Sub- Contracting Exchanges to provide impetus to outsourcing.

NSIC provides diversified marketing support to small-scale units through various marketing assistance schemes for reaching multidimensional and multi-location markets in India and abroad. NSIC acts as a nodal agency to bring SSI units closer to various Government purchasing agencies, the largest buyer of various types of products and services, with the intention of creating confidence in the purchasing agencies about SMEs and their capability to supply goods and services of requisite quality, competitive prices and adherence to agreed delivery schedules.

Ancillary industries development is an outstanding facet of small-scale industries development in India. Mutual dependence of small-scale industries strengthens the industrial structure of the country, besides procurement of parts and components most economically from the small-scale units. The country's resources are best utilized by a balanced distribution of capital investment in large and small-scale industries. Decentralized production pattern has inherent advantages; it generates more job opportunities per rupee of investment. Sub-contracting Exchange is a novel concept announced under the liberalized policy package in 1991. The Exchange is an information centre where machine capacities of small scale industries are registered and enquiries from large industries for the manufacture of different components and sub-assemblies are passed on to the appropriate registered small scale units.

Identifying suitable vendors/sub-contractors by vendees for outsourcing is not an easy task. It may be difficult time consuming and sometime frustrating too. The same is equally applicable for vendors/sub-contractors to locate a suitable vendee, which can provide them long-term linkages. Another effort lies in promoting Sub-contracting Exchanges or Sub-contracting Partnership Exchanges. Such an Exchange is a Store House of Data with regard to the capacities of the small scale units in term of products manufactured services rendered on one hand while maintaining data with regard to the requirement of the buyers, which could be products /components/ subassemblies/ services on the other hand. The Exchange also stores data about the specifications and quantities etc. of the various facilities available with the sellers/required by the buyers in the above cases. The main objective of storing such a data is to arrange matchmaking through appropriate software between a buyer and a seller that may result in increased business opportunities.

The Exchange is, therefore, in a position to a great extent to provide sufficient information to vendees to have access to the details of facilities available with the Sub- Contractors who could meet their requirements. On the other hand it also helps to provide information to Sub-contractors/Vendors about the Vendees who are looking for outsourcing.

III. Tender Marketing: The Corporation participates in bulk global tender enquiries and local tenders of Central and State Government and Public Sector Enterprises on behalf of small-scale units. It is aimed to assist small units with ability to manufacture quality products but which lack brand equity and credibility or have limited financial capabilities. Under this scheme, the Corporation has identified large number of items for which it actively participates in tenders of these Departments and Enterprises. On receipt of the orders, Corporation farms out these orders to the units on whose behalf it has quoted. This assistance has enabled a large number of small units to compete for the orders, which are normally out of reach of the individual units because of the bulk requirement. The main benefits of the scheme are:

- Small scale units are provided with all requisite financial support depending upon the units' individual requirements like purchase of raw material and financing of sale bill.
- Enhanced business volume helps small units achieve maximum capacity utilization.
- They are exempted from depositing earnest money.
- Small units are helped to participate in large and global tenders up to its capacity and capability.
- They are also assisted technically for quality up-gradation and new product development in addition to testing facility.
- Ensures fair margin to small units for their production.
- Publicity to small industries products.
- Production of quality products from the small scale sector.

IV. Consortia Marketing: A small unit in its individual capacity faces problem very often to procure and execute large orders, which inhibits and restricts the growth of small scale units. National Small Industries Corporation Limited (NSIC) accordingly adopted Consortia Approach and built groups/consortia of units manufacturing same products, thereby easing out marketing problem of SSI units. The Corporation explores market and secures orders for bulk quantities. These orders are then farmed out to small units in tune with their production capacity. Testing facilities are also provided to enable units to improve and maintain the quality of their products conforming to the standard specifications. The main benefits of the scheme are:

(a) Participation and Procurement of Orders for bulk quantities.
(b) SSIs capacity of participating in large tenders enhanced.
(c) Support testing facility provided by NSIC.
(d) Financial assistance for Raw Material, Bill discounting etc. provided by NSIC.
(e) Wherever required, equipment is also financed to the SSI on priority.
(f) Help in developing /designing of new products and quality enhancement of SSI products.

V. NSIC and Government Stores Purchase Programme: The Government is the largest single buyer of a variety of goods, and with a view to increase the share of purchases from small scale sector, the Government Stores Purchase Programme was launched in 1955-56.

The rationale of launching this programme is to direct Government purchases in favor of small industries which will give tremendous boost to the marketing of their quality products and in the process, they will be oriented to produce goods in conformity with the standards laid down by the buying agencies. Initially, the Programme was started with Directorate General of Supplies and Disposals. The Ministry of Supply laid down a procedure for purchase of stores from small scale industries. The role of National Small Industries Corporation (NSIC), in securing for them a large share of Government orders, was also spelt out. The items of stores other than textile items reserved for purchase from the Handloom Sector required by the Central Government departments are categorized under 2 broad heads, namely.

(a) Those reserved for exclusive purchase from KVIC/Women's Development Corporations/ Small scale sector units and

(b) Other not so reserved.

The first category would comprise items in respect of which the demand can be fully met by the KVIC/Women's Development Corporations/Small Scale Sector units or any combination of these sectors and such items of stores would be reserved for exclusive purchase from them. 409 items reserved for exclusive purchase from the Small Scale Sector continue to be so reserved for KVIC/ Women's Development Corporations/Small Scale Sector units

The eligible small scale units are registered under the Single Point Registration Scheme of NSIC as competent to execute Government Orders. A provision has also been made for extension of preferential purchase policy in respect of small scale industries to all Central and State Government Departments and Public Sector Enterprises,

1. In terms of purchases from small scale sector as per reservation
2. Identification of new products made in the small scale sector for purchase and enlarging the number of suppliers
3. Effective recognition of the Single Point Registration Scheme of NSIC
4. Exempting units enlisted under the Scheme from payment of earnest money, fee for tender documents and security deposits
5. Prompt payment to small scale units.

VI. Symbiotic Marketing: Symbiotic marketing occurs when two or more independent organizations combine in a joint venture that provides benefits to the parties involved. This arrangement is becoming increasingly prevalent, though it is not always easily recognizable.

While many different types of marketing agreements are possible, they generally fall into two categories: a company brokers its product through another company on either a long or short-term basis without making any major organizational changes or two companies create a third organization, which may be temporary group or a separate corporation. Most symbiotic marketing ventures involve the creation of new entities, even though many brokering relationships are quite sophisticated operations.

One interesting symbiotic venture involved Pillsbury and its line of refrigerated dough that had received wide acceptance in stores. Pillsbury's marketing problem centered around the fact that the items required special refrigerated display cases. Since Kraft Foods had extensive experience in this area with its cheese products, a symbiotic arrangement was established whereby Kraft initially sold and distributed these Pillsbury products.

Another beneficial opportunity for a symbiotic organizational structure occurs when an existing sales force is unavailable or inappropriate. When this occurs, several noncompeting companies can establish a sales staff that is independent but jointly owned. For example, five newspapers- the St. Louis Post Dispatch, the Washington Star, the Boston Globe, the Philadelphia Bulletin, and the Milwaukee Journal-Sentinel- established and jointly owned Million Market Newspaper, Inc., a sales/ advertising company. The symbiotic arrangement gave each of the newspaper marketing impact far beyond its individual capability.

In these and other instances, symbiotic marketing allowed companies to take advantage of new opportunities. As costs soar and competition intensifies, more symbiotic arrangements will be established.

How Marketing Services should be provided

Given wide differences in products, producers, and economic sectors, it is difficult to develop generally applicable guidelines for providing marketing services. A set of principles for good practice has been established for how best to deliver non-financial or business development services to micro, small and medium enterprises. These principles are in general applicable to marketing services, and include:

1. Providing the service in a business-like and demand-led manner;
2. Aiming at long-term sustainability;
3. Specializing in a service or related set of services; and
4. Providing sub-sector specific services (tailoring programs to specific needs).

The first two principles are related to the issue of sustainability and the last two to the development of a strategy.

Sustainability

The long-term sustainability of the services provided depends on the level of cost-recovery. The service of buying and selling, or brokering, can generally be provided in a sustainable manner, using a simple mark-up mechanism. But some of the ancillary services may be less viable, such as training or the provision of market information. These activities are often subsidized, for a number of reasons: clients may be unwilling to pay because they do not foresee any short-term benefits; clients may have limited ability to pay, or past practices by service providers may have created a situation where these services are expected to be provided for free. The combination of services, or an integrated service package, may therefore prove less profitable, and may narrow the margins of the marketing service provider. By charging fees, service providers can enhance cost-recovery as well as obtaining important feedback about the demand for the service - the client's willingness to pay is an indicator of the relevancy of the service. In the short term, full cost-recovery for additional services may be difficult to obtain, at least in the short-term. Business interests can be compatible and complementary with development needs on a long-term basis, however, and as markets develop, higher levels of cost-recovery can usually be reached. As will be seen from the case studies presented, a mix of services may be provided, of which some are profitable and others not. Providers may choose to provide unprofitable services to their clients and then cross-subsidize with revenues from more profitable services. Unless the provider calculates costs and revenues for each service, the level of cost-recovery or profitability of these activities can only be estimated.

Marketing Strategy

Even if financial profitability is not readily obtained in the short-term, marketing services must be provided in a manner that guarantees long-term access to markets on the part of small producers. This implies developing a strategy based on the particular demands of a specific market, whether local, regional, or international, which then determines which services are necessary to assist producers in meeting that demand. Such demands may be identified by the marketing service providers through an exercise such as a sub-sector analysis. A sub-sector analysis is used to map out various players in the chain of events from producers to consumers within a sub-sector, and identify where the constraints to meeting market demands exist. The marketing provider may then try to seek possible solutions to specific problems, such as shortage of raw materials, lack of storage facilities or market information, through the provision of integrated marketing services. This approach also seeks to find ways to capture more links in the value chain of the economic activities in which small producers are engaged, to the producers' benefit.

Which services to provide, how, and for whom, are questions the marketing service provider addresses when defining their own strategy. Strategies serve to reach certain goals, such as profitability or social development. Successful providers of marketing services, like successful businesses, aim to develop unique strategies, which allow them to reach these goals. Aiming to assist small and micro producers in increasing their production and sales, service providers may choose to provide services at all levels, from the provision of raw materials to quality control to transportation of the goods, and meet all needs of the targeted clients. Institutions aiming for higher levels of cost-recovery may adopt a minimalist strategy, in which a limited number of clients are provided with a small number of critical services, for which cost-covering fees are charged.

Marketing Strategy for Small and Medium Enterprises (SMEs)

Pressures of brand and budget have somewhat marred the marketing success of Small and Medium Enterprises (SMEs). However, implementation of strategic planning, creative decisions, and strong analysis on time, information, imagination, and energy can help the small budget companies to embark on successful process-driven marketing. A huge marketing budget does not assure the SMEs to enjoy the success in the market as the market is full of unorganized competitors, each having the same.

The very core of marketing lies in the brand building, for which a huge sum is eventually not enough. In essence, with effective planning, Small and Medium Enterprises can easy tackle the catastrophes of brand building and budget.

Budget is a primary constraint for SMEs and for brand building, a widespread reach among customers is required, which again leads to investment on Advertising and Promotion. Focus is the key here. An SME has to first focus on identifying its customer base, and then imply strategic planning keeping customers in view, to come up with a marketing technique on which it can have strong control. Small companies, small budgets, and big dreams are the mixture of great success.

Rapidly changing technology has broaden the province of marketing of which, Advertising and Promotion is a small part. There are other aspects as well that are cheaper and proves to be effective to connect with clients. Thus, rather than focusing on advertising as a marketing channel, an SME should focus on the quality and innovation on quality. With this, it can always introduce to clients an advance range that is globally different or difficult to access.

SMEs enjoy another benefit, which a large scale companies probably miss out, and even if they get the opportunity, they have to face the criticism and enormous loss both of money and goodwill. This benefit is of being small; an advantage through which they can easily re-implement a process in every aspect of marketing, in case a strategy does not works out well. The fact here is SMEs entertain a small market base clients, thus they have the opportunity to access to their clients on a short notice.

The load that slows down the process of planning and implementation can be easily shed out or re-shaped to make things work. Devising new strategies for marketing is the key to the success of SMEs since it gets difficult to stand against the deep pockets of big companies and MNCs.

Review Questions

1. Define market? What are the types of market?
2. Briefly explain the concept of marketing?
3. Explain the market segmentation?
4. What are the core concepts of marketing?
5. Describe the importance of marketing for small and medium enterprises?
6. What is marketing research? Explain the process of market research.
7. Explain the steps of market planning?
8. What is marketing mix? Explain its main components.

9. What is distribution channel? Explain the factors that govern the distribution channels.
10. What is the difference between wholesaler and retailer?
11. Explain the types of retailer.
12. Discuss the importance retail marketing.
13. What are the different types of wholesalers?
14. Briefly explain the problems of marketing for small enterprises?
15. What are the functions of wholesalers?
16. What are market intermediaries and its role in marketing?
17. Explain the marketing services provided by:
    (a) UPTECH
    (b) NSIC
    (c) State Government

◆ ◆ ◆

Institutional Finance to Entrepreneurs

5

Chapter

CHAPTER OUTLINE

- Need for Institutional Support to Entrepreneurs
- Commercial Banks
- The Industrial Credit and Investment Corporation of India – ICICI
- Unit Trust of India – UTI
- Development Banks
- Industrial Development Bank of India – IDBI
- Industrial Finance Corporation of India – IFCI
- Industrial Investment Bank of India – IIBI
- Life Insurance Corporation of India – LIC
- State Financial Corporation – SFC

- State Industrial Development Corporations – SIDC
- Small Industries Development Bank of India – SIDBI
- The Export Import Bank of India – EXIM BANK
- Role of NSIC – National Small Industries Corporation Limited
- Small Industries Development Organization – SIDCO
- Small Industries Service Institutes – SISI
- The Micro, Small and Medium Enterprises Development institute – MSMEDI
- District Industries Center's – DIC
- Centre for Financial Markets and Institutions – CFMI
- Industrial Estates
- Technical Consultancy Organization – TCO:
- Small-scale Industries Board – SSIB
- State Small Industries Corporations – SSIC
- Microfinance Institutions
- Specialized Institutions

NEED FOR INSTITUTIONAL SUPPORT TO ENTREPRENEURS

Meaning of Institutional Support: The term institutional support refers to the part of economic environment of industry and business. It consist of authorities and institutions whose decisions and active support in form of laws, regulation, financial and non-financial help brings a lot of changes in the functioning of any business.

Formation of the Institution: The institutions could be government owned, statutory, semi autonomous or autonomous. It is the government or government supported institutions authorized to take up certain activities-financing, marketing, project preparation, training to promote industrial activities in the state.

Stages of Institutional Support: There are three stages of promotion - inception stage, operational stage and expansion or diversification stage. The Government through its plans and policies assisted the business houses in facilitating in the above stages through various specialized institutions set up as per the law.

An entrepreneur who needs to set up a business unit of his own or with his friends and relatives is supposed to know the various institutions or organizations working as per the law for the purpose. Dissemination of information in this regard can only help them in achieving the very dream of becoming a successful entrepreneur.

Formation of the Institutions at different levels in India: With the launching of the five-year plans, in the absence of a sufficiently broad domestic capital market, there was need for adopting and enlarging the institutional structure to meet the medium and long term credit requirements of the industrial sector. It was in this content that the RBI took the initiative in setting up statutory corporations at the all India and regional levels to function as specialized financial agencies providing term credit.

Institutional finance for large, medium, small and tiny industries by commercial banks the SBI group, nationalized banks private sector banks and development corporations which have been especially established to provide, industrial finance. In addition, the RBI gives credit guarantee and the ECGC gives export guarantees to the SSI sector. By its refinance operations, the IDBI too plays a significant role in the promotion of the small scale sector, for it has enabled the SFCs, SSIDC/SSIACS and commercial banks to extend a large quantum of financial assistance to this sector. The NSIC offers financial assistance in the form of its hire- purchase schemes.

In India, long-term loans are provided for a host of financial institutions of IDBI and SIDBI are apex banks providing refinance facilities to other institutions. Like wise NABARD is an apex bank for agricultural finances and EXIM Bank for Export-import trade. Then industrial development banks special institutions, saving and investment institutions, financial service institutions and regulatory institutions. RBI, SEBI and NSEIL are three regulatory bodies.

1. The Reserve Bank of India (RBI): The RBI is the supreme monetary and banking authority in the country and has the responsibility to control the banking system in the country. It keeps the reserves of all scheduled banks and hence is known as the "Reserve Bank".

2. Public Sector Banks:

- State Bank of India and its Associates
- Nationalized Banks
- Regional Rural Banks Sponsored by Public Sector Banks

3. Private Sector Banks:

- Old Generation Private Banks
- Foreign New Generation Private Banks
- Banks in India

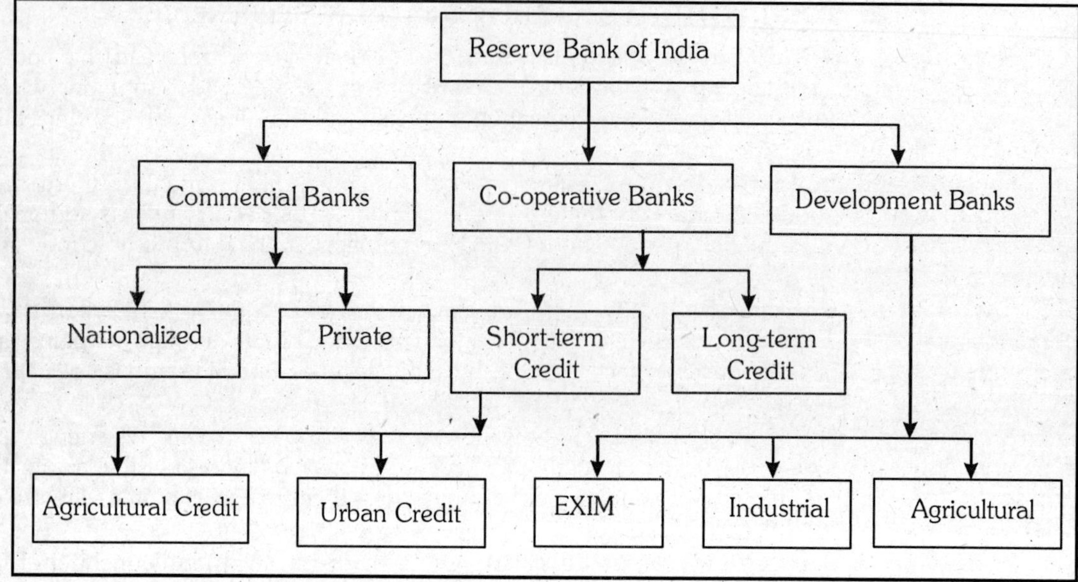

Fig. 5.1: Formation of the Institutions at different levels in India

4. Co-operative Sector Banks:

- State Co-operative Banks
- Central Co-operative Banks
- Primary Agricultural Credit Societies
- Land Development Banks
- State Land Development Banks

5. Development Banks: Development Banks mostly provide long term finance for setting up industries. They also provide short-term finance (for export and import activities)

- Industrial Finance Co-operation of India (IFCI)
- Industrial Development of India (IDBI)
- Industrial Investment Bank of India (IIBI)
- Small Industries Development Bank of India (SIDBI)
- National Bank for Agriculture and Rural Development (NABARD)
- Export-Import Bank of India (EXIM)

Role of Banks in Economic Development

Banks play a positive role in economic development of a country as repositories of community's savings and as purveyors of credit. Indian Banking has aided the economic development during the last fifty years in an effective way. The banking sector has shown a remarkable responsiveness to the needs of planned economy. It has brought about a considerable progress in its efforts at deposit mobilization and has taken a number of measures in the recent past for accelerating the rate of growth of deposits. As recourse to this, the commercial banks opened branches in urban, semi-urban and rural areas and have introduced a number of attractive schemes to foster economic development.

The activities of commercial banking have growth in multi-directional ways as well as multi-dimensional manner. Banks have been playing a catalytic role in area development, backward area development, extended assistance to rural development all along helping agriculture, industry, international trade in a significant manner. In a way, commercial banks have emerged as key financial agencies for rapid economic development.

By pooling the savings together, banks can make available funds to specialized institutions which finance different sectors of the economy, needing capital for various purposes, risks and durations. By contributing to government securities, bonds and debentures of term-lending institutions in the fields of agriculture, industries and now housing, banks are also providing these institutions with an access to the common pool of savings mobilized by them, to that extent relieving them of the responsibility of directly approaching the saver. This intermediation role of banks is particularly important in the early stages of economic development and financial specification. A country like India, with different regions at different stages of development, presents an interesting spectrum of the evolving role of banks, in the matter of inter-mediation and beyond.

Mobilization of resources forms an integral part of the development process in India. In this process of mobilization, banks are at a great advantage, chiefly because of their network of branches in the country. And banks have to place considerable reliance on the mobilization of deposits from the public to finance development programmes. Further, deposit mobalization by banks in India acquired greater significance in their new role in economic development.

Commercial banks provide short-term and medium-term financial assistance. The short-term credit facilities are granted for working capital requirements. The medium-term loans are for the acquisition of land, construction of factory premises and purchase of machinery and equipment. These loans are generally granted for periods ranging from five to seven years. They also establish letters of credit on behalf of their clients favouring suppliers of raw materials/machinery (both Indian and foreign) which extend the banker's assurance for payment and thus help their delivery. Certain transaction, particularly those in contracts of sale of Government Departments, may require guarantees being issued in lieu of security earnest money deposits for release of advance money, supply of raw materials for processing, full payment of bills on the assurance of the performance etc. Commercial banks issue such guarantees also.

COMMERCIAL BANKS

Commercial Banks in India are broadly categorized into Scheduled Commercial Banks and Unscheduled Commercial Banks. The Scheduled Commercial Banks have been listed under the Second Schedule of the Reserve Bank of India Act, 1934. The selection measure for listing a bank under the Second Schedule was provided in section 42 (60 of the Reserve Bank of India Act, 1934).

Activities of Commercial Banks

The modern Commercial Banks in India cater to the financial needs of different sectors. The main functions of the commercial banks comprise:

- Transfer of funds
- Acceptance of deposits
- Offering those deposits as loans for the establishment of industries, purchase of houses, equipments, capital investment purposes etc.

The banks are allowed to act as trustees. On account of the knowledge of the financial market of India the financial companies are attracted towards them to act as trustees to take the responsibility of the security for the financial instrument like a debenture.

The Indian Government presently hires the commercial banks for various purposes like tax collection and refunds, payment of pensions etc.

Functions of Commercial Banks

The functions of commercial banks are divided into two categories:

(i) Primary functions, and

(ii) Secondary functions including agency functions.

***(i)* Primary functions:** The primary functions of a commercial bank include:

***(a)* Accepting deposits**

The most important activity of a commercial bank is to mobilize deposits from the public. People who have surplus income and savings find it convenient to deposit the amounts with banks. Depending upon the nature of deposits, funds deposited with bank also earn interest. Thus, deposits with the bank grow along with the interest earned. If the rate of interest is higher, public are motivated to deposit more funds with the bank. There is also safety of funds deposited with the bank.

***(b)* Grant of loans and advances**

The second important function of a commercial bank is to grant loans and advances. Such loans and advances are given to members of the public and to the business community at a higher rate of interest than allowed by banks on various deposit accounts. The rate of interest charged on loans and advances varies depending upon the purpose, period and the mode of repayment. The difference between the rate of interest allowed on deposits and the rate charged on the Loans is the main source of a bank's income.

***(i)* Loans**

A loan is granted for a specific time period. Generally, commercial banks grant short-term loans. But term loans, that is, loan for more than a year, may also be granted. The borrower may withdraw the entire amount in lump-sum or in installments. However, interest is charged on the full amount of loan. Loans are generally granted against the security of certain assets. A loan may be repaid either in lump-sum or in installments.

***(ii)* Advances**

An advance is a credit facility provided by the bank to its customers. It differs from loan in the sense that loans may be granted for longer period, but advances are normally granted for a short period of time. Further the purpose of granting advances is to meet the day to day requirements of business. The rate of interest charged on advances varies from bank to bank. Interest is charged only on the amount withdrawn and not on the sanctioned amount.

Modes of short-term financial assistance

Banks grant short-term financial assistance by way of cash credit, overdraft and bill discounting.

***(a)* Cash Credit**

Cash credit is an arrangement whereby the bank allows the borrower to draw amounts up-to a specified limit. The amount is credited to the account of the customer. The customer can withdraw this amount as and when he requires. Interest is charged on the amount actually withdrawn. Cash Credit is granted as per agreed terms and conditions with the customers.

***(b)* Overdraft**

Overdraft is also a credit facility granted by bank. A customer who has a current account with the bank is allowed to withdraw more than the amount of credit balance in his account. It is a temporary arrangement. Overdraft facility with a specified limit is allowed either on the security of assets, or on personal security, or both.

***(c)* Discounting of Bills**

Banks provide short-term finance by discounting bills that is, making payment of the amount before the due date of the bills after deducting a certain rate of discount. The party gets the funds without waiting for the date of maturity of the bills. In case any bill is dishonored on the due date, the bank can recover the amount from the customer.

(ii) Secondary functions

Besides the primary functions of accepting deposits and lending money, banks perform a number of other functions which are called secondary functions. These are as follows:

(a) Issuing letters of credit, traveler's cheques, circular notes etc.

(b) Undertaking safe custody of valuables, important documents, and securities by providing safe deposit vaults or lockers;

(c) Providing customers with facilities of foreign exchange.

(d) Transferring money from one place to another; and from one branch to another branch of the bank.

(e) Standing guarantee on behalf of its customers, for making payments for purchase of goods, machinery, vehicles etc.

(f) Collecting and supplying business information;

(g) Issuing demand drafts and pay orders;

(h) Providing reports on the credit worthiness of customers.

ICICI: The Industrial Credit and Investment Corporation of India

The ICICI was set up in 1955 to encourage and assist investment and industrial development in India. The idea of establishing the ICICI was first crystallized s a result of certain deliberations among the government of India. The World Bank and certain American financiers combined and form this bank for the industrial development. Unlike other development banks the ICICI was organized as a wholly owned private institution.

Objectives: The major objective of the ICICI was to meet the needs of the industry for permanent and long term funds in the private sector. Its objectives are:

(a) To assist in the creation, expansion and modernization of industrial enterprises in the private sector.

(b) To encourage and promote the participation of private capital both internal and external, in such enterprises and

(c) To encourage and promote private ownership of industrial investment and expansion of markets.

(d) To assist in the development of the capital market through its underwriting activities

Forms of Financial Assistance: In pursuit of its objectives of promoting industrial development, ICICI provides financial assistance to enterprises in various forms such as:

(a) Underwriting of public and private issues and offers of sale of industrial securities ordinary shares, preference shares, bonds and debenture stock.

(b) Direct subscription to such securities.

(c) Providing loans in rupees, repayable over periods up to 15 years.

(d) Providing similar loans in foreign currencies for payment for imported capital equipment and technical services.

(e) Guaranteeing payments for credit given by Indian and foreign sources.

(f) Providing credit facilities to indigenous manufactures for promoting sales of industrial equipment on deferred payment terms.

(g) Leasing of equipment.

(h) It provides project consultancy services to industrial units for new projects

Promotional Activities: ICICI has set up a Project Promotion Department in order to provide promotional services and assistance to individual project on selective basis. It also participates in the co-coordinated efforts of the All India Financial Institutions, State level finance and promotion agencies and nationalized bank in identifying and developing projects and entrepreneurs in backward regions, in preparing techno-economic surveys for backward States, conducting, feasibility studies and implementing identified projects.

The corporation is empowered to provide any amount of financial assistance to any business unit in the private sector, public sector, joint sector or co-operative sector. Any company with limited liability, any sole proprietary concern, partnership concern and any co-operative society may approach the corporation for assistance in financing a sound project.

Normally it provides such assistance within the range of self imposed limits. Accordingly, ₹ 5 lakhs is the minimum amount sanctioned by it to a single concern and normally it does not go beyond the maximum limit of Rupees one crore. However no project is too large for ICICI to handle. In promoting industrial investment, ICICI seeks to encourage other financial institutions, both Indian and foreign, to collaborate in its lending operations.

Financial assistance granted and disbursed by ICICI over the years has grown steadily. ICICI has disbursed a total financial assistance of ₹ 4225 crores during the three months period from Ist April 1998 to 30th June 1998. The total amount sanctioned during this period is ₹ 9135 crore. ICICI has promoted the following institutions in recent years, showing widening scope of activities of ICICI:

1. ICICI Securities and Finance Co. Ltd.
2. ICICI Asset Management Co. Ltd.
3. ICICI Investors Services Ltd.
4. ICICI Banking Corporations Ltd.
5. Credit Rating Information Services of India Ltd. (CRISIL)
6. Technology Development and Information Company of India Ltd. (TDICI)
7. Program for the Advancement of Commercial Technology.
8. Program for Acceleration of Commercial Energy Research (PACER)

UTI: Unit Trust of India

The unit trust of India is a statutory public sector investment institution established under the UTI Act, 1963. It began functioning on 1st July, 1964. It commenced its operations with an initial capital of ₹ 5 Crores contributed as follows:

RBI – ₹ 2.5 Crore; SBI – ₹ 75 Lakh; LIC – ₹ 75 Lakh.

Scheduled Bond and other financial institution ₹ 1 Crores with the amendment of the public financial institutions laws, the contribution made by RBI to the initial capital and the control exercised by it are vested in the IDBI with effect from 16th February, 1976.

The total investment made by UTI in industrial securities (shares, debentures, and bonds) is divided into smaller parts called 'unit', the UTI sell units under different schemes and also buys back its own units at the purchase price fixed by its from time to time. Units have a face value of ₹ 10 each.

Objectives:

(i) To encourage savings of people belongings to middle and low income groups.

(ii) To mobilize savings from the small savers.

(iii) To channelize savings to industrial growth.

(iv) To investors to participate in the prosperity of the industries.

Functions:

1. To mobilize the savings of the community through sale of units.
2. To invest the savings so mobilized in corporate securities such as shares and debentures.
3. To serve unit holders along with the length and breadth of the country.
4. To underwrite the issues of shares and debentures.

Development Banks

A Development Bank is a polygonal development finance institution devoted for improving the social and monetary development of its associate nations. Its main emphasis is the welfare of the people. For example the Asian Development Bank's overarching goal is to decrease poverty in Asia and the Pacific. It helps improve the value of people's lives by providing loans and scientific support for a broad variety of development activities.

A development bank's policies or programs center on the following priorities:

(a) Economic Growth
(b) Human Development
(c) Gender Development
(d) Good Governance
(e) Environmental Protection
(f) Private Sector Development
(g) Regional cooperation

The main functions of a Development Bank:

1. Increase loans and equity investments to its developing associate countries (DMCs) for their monetary and social development.
2. Provides technical help for the planning and implementation of development projects and programs and for advisory services.
3. Promotes and facilitates speculation of public and private capital for growth and development.
4. Responds to requests for assistance in coordinating growth policies and plans of its increasing member countries.

Formation of Development Banks In India

Development banks were set up in India at various points of time starting from the late 1940s to cater to the medium to long term financing requirements of industry as the capital market in India had not developed sufficiently. The endorsement of planned industrialization at the national level provided the critical enticement for organization of Development banks at both all-India and state levels.

In order to perform their role, Development Banks were extended funds in the shape of Long-term Operations (LTO) Fund of the Reserve bank of India and government guaranteed bonds, which constituted main sources of their funds. Funds from these sources were not only available at concessional rates, but also on a long term basis with their maturity period ranging from 10-15 years.

On the asset side, their operations were marked by near absence of competition. A large variety of economic institutions have come into existence over the years to perform a type of financial actions While some of them operate at all-India level, others are state level institutions.

Besides providing direct loans, financial institutions also extend economic assistance by way of underwriting and direct contribution and by issuing guarantees. Recently, some Development Banks have started extending short-term/working capital finance, although long-term lending continues to be their major activity.

IDBI: Industrial Development Bank of India

It was set up in July 1964 as an apex term lending financial institution in India. However, it was restructured and designed as the principal financial institution of the country in 1975, for coordinating the activities of other institutions including banks, engaged in financing, promoting or developing industry in conformity with the national priorities.

IDBI has played a pioneering role, particularly in the pre-reform era (1964–91), in catalyzing broad based industrial development in the country in keeping with its Government-ordained 'development banking' charter. In pursuance of this mandate, IDBI's activities transcended the confines of pure long-term lending to industry and encompassed, among others, balanced industrial growth through development of backward areas, modernization of specific industries, employment generation, entrepreneurship development along with support services for creating a deep and vibrant domestic capital market, including development of other institutional framework. Thus the role of IDBI may be stated as under:

(1) As an apex financial institution, it coordinates the working of other financial institutions.

(2) It assists in the development of other financial institutions.

(3) It provides credit to large industrial concerns directly.

(4) It undertakes other activities for the development of industry

Objectives:

The main objectives of IDBI are to serve as the apex institution for term finance for industry in India. Its objectives include:

- Co-ordination, regulation and supervision of the working of other financial institutions such as IFCI, ICICI, UTI, LIC, Commercial Banks and SFCs.
- Supplementing the resources of other financial institutions and thereby widening the scope of their assistance.
- Planning, promotion and development of key industries and diversifications of industrial growth.
- Devising and enforcing a system of industrial growth that conforms to national priorities.

Schemes of Assistance:

(a) IDBI provides direct assistance to industrial concerns in the form of loans, under writing of and subscribing to shares and debentures and guarantees.

(b) It provides soft loans for modernization, replacement and renovation.

(c) It refinances industrial loans granted by banks and other financial institutions.

(d) It rediscounts bill arising out of sales of indigenous machinery on deferred payment basis.

(e) It finances export in the form of direct loans and guarantees to exporters in participation with commercial banks and refinances medium term export credit provided by commercial banks and overseas creditors.

(f) It assists other financial institutions by way of subscription to their shares and bonds.

(g) It engages in promotional activities for bringing about industrial development and

(h) It co-ordinates the activities of other financial institutions set up to provide assistance to industries.

IFCI: Industrial Finance Corporation of India

It was set up as a statutory corporation in 1948 with the objective of providing medium and long term credit to eligible industrial concerns. It has now been converted into a joint stock company.

Financial Activities:

(i) Providing rupee loans and foreign currency loans.

(ii) Guaranteeing such loans.

(iii) Underwriting and subscribing to shares and debentures of public limited companies.

Promotional Activities: The objectives of IFCI has been

(a) To fill in gaps in the institutional infrastructure for promotion and growth of industries.

(b) To provide much needed guidance in project identification, formulation, implementation, operation etc. to the new, tiny, small scale or medium scale enterprise.

(c) To improve the productivity of human and material resources, giving at the same time a better deal to the weaker and under privileged sections of the society in consonance with the socio-economic objectives, laid down by the Government of India.

(d) Undertaking research and surveys for evaluating or dealing with marketing of investments and carrying on techno-economic studies in connection with the development of industries.

(e) Providing technical and administrative assistance to any industrial concern for the promotion management or expansion of any industry.

(f) Undertaking merchant banking operations.

Corporate Advisory and Infrastructural Services

At a time, when India is throwing up investment avenues in newer sectors and projects, there is a critical need to provide specialized advisory services to the Indian Corporate Sector in their efforts towards Industrial Advancement. IFCI with its team of seasoned professionals and rich experience of over six decades in the financial sector is uniquely positioned to fulfill this need. As a catalyst of Industrial growth, IFCI provides the following Advisory Services:

- Investment appraisal of Navratna (most valued public sector companies) Companies.
- Project Conceptualization and related services, including Guidance in relation to Selection of Projects, Preparation of feasibility studies, DPR, Capital Structuring, Techno-economic Feasibility, Financial Engineering, Project Management Design etc.
- Credit Syndication including preparation of Information Memorandum, Syndication of domestic/foreign loans, Post Sanction follow-up, Assistance in legal documentation etc.

Infrastructure Advice

IFCI offers a range of services to the infrastructure Sector, with specific emphasis on roads, port, power and urban infrastructure. Total solution catering to the specific needs of clients, starting from the stages of investment. Identification to financial closure are provided.

The Services Provided in the Infrastructure Sector Includes:

- Facilitation of Credit Documentation.
- Due Diligence.
- Agreements and Document Review/Advice.
- Pre-Investment Review.
- Project Conceptualization and Feasibility Studies.
- Risk Allocation, Assessment and Reasonableness of Cost.
- Advise on Financing Options – Sources, Cost and Risk.
- Financial Analysis and Modeling – Scenario Analysis.
- Potential Joint Venture Partner Profiling.
- Negotiating Support for Equity Buy In.
- Project Evaluation.
- Credit Syndication – Domestic and Overseas.
- Arranging Deferred Payment Guarantee, ECB.
- Placement of debt and equity.
- Capital Market Advisory Services

IFCI provides assistance both for setting up new units as well as for modernization and expansions of existing units. IFCI offers a wide range of products to the target customer segments to satisfy their specific financial needs. The product range includes following credit products:

Short-term Loans (up to two years) for different short term requirements including bridge loan, Corporate Loan etc Medium-term Loans (more than two years to eight years) for business expansion, technology up-gradation, Research and Development expenditure, implementing early retirement scheme, Corporate Loan, supplementing working capital and repaying high cost debt Long-term Loans (more than eight years to up to 15 years) - Project Finance for new industrial/ infrastructure projects Takeout Finance, acquisition financing (as per extant RBI guidelines / Board approved policy), Corporate Loan, Securitization of debt Structured Products: acquisition finance, pre-IPO investment, IPO finance, promoter funding, etc.

Lease Financing Takeover of accounts from Banks / Financial Institutions / NBFCs

Financing promoters contribution (private equity participation)/subscription to convertible warrants Purchase of Standard Assets and NPAs The product mix offering varies from one business/ industry segment to another. IFCI customizes the product-mix to maximize customer satisfaction. It's domain knowledge and innovativeness make the product-mix a key differentiator for building enduring and sustaining relationship with the borrowers.

IIBI: Industrial Investment Bank of India

IIBI was initially set up as Industrial Reconstruction Corporation Limited during 1971 when it was renamed Industrial Reconstruction bank of India with effect from March 20, 1985 under IRBI Act 1984 to take over the function of IRC. During 1997 the bank was converted to a joint stock company by naming it Industrial Investment Bank of India.

Its earlier functions were to provide finance for industrial rehabilitation and revival of sick industrial units by way of rationalization, expansion, diversification and modernization and also to co-ordinate the work of other institutions for these purpose agricultural and rural requirements.

It has been set up with a view to enabling it to function as the principal credit and reconstruction agency for industrial revival by undertaking modernization expansion, reorganization, diversification or rationalization of industry and to co-ordinate similar work of the other institutions engaged there in and to assist and rehabilitate industrial concerns. It provides financial assistance in the form of term loans, subscription to debenture equity shares and deferred payment guarantees.

Functions:

The IIBI is empowered to grant, loans and advances to industrial concerns; underwrite stock, shares, bonds and debentures, guarantee loan/deferred payments and performance obligations of any contract undertaken by industrial concerns and act as an agent of central and State Government, Reserve Bank, State Bank, Scheduled Commercial and State Co-Operative Banks, Public Financial institutions, State Financial Corporation and such other Government and person as Central Government may authorize. Its broad ranging functions also include such developmental activities as providing infrastructural facilities, raw materials, consultancy, managerial and merchant banking services for reconstruction and development of industrial concerns and providing machinery and other equipment on lease or hire-purchase basis, etc. IIBI is now also active in merchant banking and its services includes *inter-alia*, structuring suitable instrument for public rights issues preparation of prospective offer documents and working as a lead manager it also offers its services for debt syndication and package of services for merger and acquisition.

LIC: Life Insurance Corporation of India

LIC was established in 1956 as a wholly owned corporation of the Government of India. It was formed by the LIC Act, 1956, with the objectives of spreading life insurance much more widely and in particular to the rural areas. It also extends assistance for development of infrastructure facilities like housings rural electrification, water supply, sewerage etc. In addition, it extend resources, support to other financial institution through subscription of their share and bond etc.

Functions:

- LIC took over the life insurance business from private companies to carry on the business and deploy the funds in accordance with the plan priorities.
- LIC operates a variety of schemes so as to extend social security to various segments of society and for the benefits of individuals and groups from the urban and rural areas.
- The committee on reforms in the insurance sector set up by the government has recommended privatizations and restructuring of LIC with government retaining 50% stake.
- The committee has also suggested that foreign companies be allowed to conduct life insurance business in the country through joint ventures with Indian partners.

SFCs: State Financial Corporations

The State Financial Corporations set up under the State Financial Corporations Act, 1951, render assistance in their respective states. There are at present 18 State Financial Corporations including the Tamilnadu Industries Investment Corporation Limited (TIIC) which was set up in 1949 before the passage of the State Financial Corporations Act.

Forms of Assistance: Financial assistance from SFC takes the following forms:

(a) Granting of loans and subscribing to the debentures of industrial concerns, repayable within a period of not exceeding 20 years.

(b) Guaranteeing loans raised by the industrial undertaking in the capital market or from scheduled banks or state co-operative banks.

(c) Guaranteeing deferred payments due from any industrial concern in connection with its purchase of capital goods within India.

(d) Subscribing to the stocks, bonds or debentures of an industrial concern out of the funds representing the special class of share capital subscribed by the State Government and the Reserve Bank in accordance with the provisions of section 4A of the State Financial Corporations Act, 1951.

If the technically qualified people find it difficult to bring in enough funds as their contribution, State Financial Corporations assist them with a unique scheme known as the seed capital / soft loan scheme. Under this scheme, assistance up ₹ 2 lakhs will be given at an incredibly normal interest rate of 1% per annum. Higher quantum of assistance will also be considered in deserving cases under this scheme.

State Financial Corporations also assume the role of promotional agency rather than being a financing institution only by diversifying their activities to fill in the role of full fledged development banks, few State Financial Corporations have already set up entrepreneurial guidance-cum-assistance Bureau to help entrepreneurs particularly the first generation enterprises.

SIDCs: State Industrial Development Corporations

SIDCs, wholly owned by State Government, have been set up under the Companies Act, to promote and provide facilities for rapid industrialization in the respective states.

Functions: The major functions are:

(i) Providing risk capital to entrepreneur by way of equity participation and seed capital assistance.

(ii) Granting financial assistance to industrial units by way of loans, guarantees and, of late, lease finance by some corporations.

(iii) Administering incentive schemes of Central / State Government.

(iv) Promotional activities such as identification of project ideas through industrial potential surveys, preparation of feasibility reports, selection and training of entrepreneurs.

(v) Developing industrial areas/estates by providing infrastructure facilities.

Since the actual range of activities being undertaken by an individual SIDC depends upon the specific responsibilities entrusted by the respective State/Union Territory, there is considerable diversity in activities among different SIDCs.

SIDBI: Small Industries Development Bank of India

SIDBI (small industrial development bank of India) was started with the motto of refinancing as the sole business. RBI considers SIDBI and NABARD as two refinancing institutions. As the main focus always has been this rather than direct financing, the brand image of SIDBI has not changed in so many years. In the banking sector as a whole, there are too many middle level banks that come in direct contact with the customer and this has been the main reason SIDBI is considered as the last resort for financing. SIDBI almost had a monopoly in refinancing the small scale units but now there have been competition form other commercial banks as well, that have started initializing the SME finance like ICICI and SBI. SIDBI has also started tying up with other nationalized and commercial banks in this regard that can help it gain some more visibility and selling the products that need aggressive marketing.

SIDBI has a special corporate status because it has got an expertise since 1964 and has been an agent in government schemes and finance is provided considering all expenses related to the project from conceptualization of the project to the successful execution of the project. They target the SME as they are serving the niche market. It is also synonym to developmental banking as they have soft corner for the small and medium enterprises and for this section of industry they have liberal policies, promote and develop small scale industries. Helping entrepreneur is also one of the functions and duties of SIDBI.

The SDBI was set up as a subsidiary of the IDBI by a special Act, 1989 to function as the principal financial institution for the promotion, development and financing of industry in the small scale sector, and for coordinating the functions of institutions, engaged in similar activities. It has taken over the responsibility for administering Small Industries Development fund and National Equity fund which were earlier administered by the IDBI. However, it started functioning from April 21, 1990. The initial authorized capital of SIDBI is ₹ 250 Crores which can be increased by IDBI up to ₹ 1,000 Crores.

The business domain of SIDBI consists of small scale industrial units, which contribute significantly to the national economy in terms of production, employment and exports. Small scale industries are the industrial units in which the investment in plant and machinery does not exceed ₹ 10 million. About 3.1 million such units, employing 17.2 million persons account for a share of 36 per cent of India's exports and 40 per cent of industrial manufacture. In addition, SIDBI's assistance flows to the transport, health care and tourism sectors and also to the professional and self-employed persons setting up small-sized professional ventures.

State-owned SIDBI provides financial assistance to units in the small-scale sector. SIDBI provides refinance against term loans granted by banks to small scale industries, equity assistance, bills financing, project financing and resource support to institutions that are engaged in the development of small scale industries. It provides assistance to wide-range of industrial sectors including transport, health care, hotel and tourism and infrastructure. It also provides funds to the professional and self-employed persons setting up small-sized professional ventures.

Functions:

The SIDBI has outlined seven activities as its functions and three areas as immediate thrust areas. The seven activities are:

1. Refinancing of loans and advances extended by primary lending institutions.
2. Discounting and rediscounting of bills.

3. Extension of seed capital/soft loan assistance under National Equity Fund Seed Capital under Mahila Udayam Nidhi Scheme.
4. Granting direct assistance and refinance for financing exports of SSI sector.
5. Providing of factoring and leasing services.
6. Extending financial support to State Small Industries Development Corporation (SSIDC).
7. Extending financial support to National Small Industries Corporation (NSIC).

The important thrust area of SIDBI is technological up gradation, modernization, extending the channels for marketing the products of SSI units and promotion of employment oriented industries in semi-urban areas.

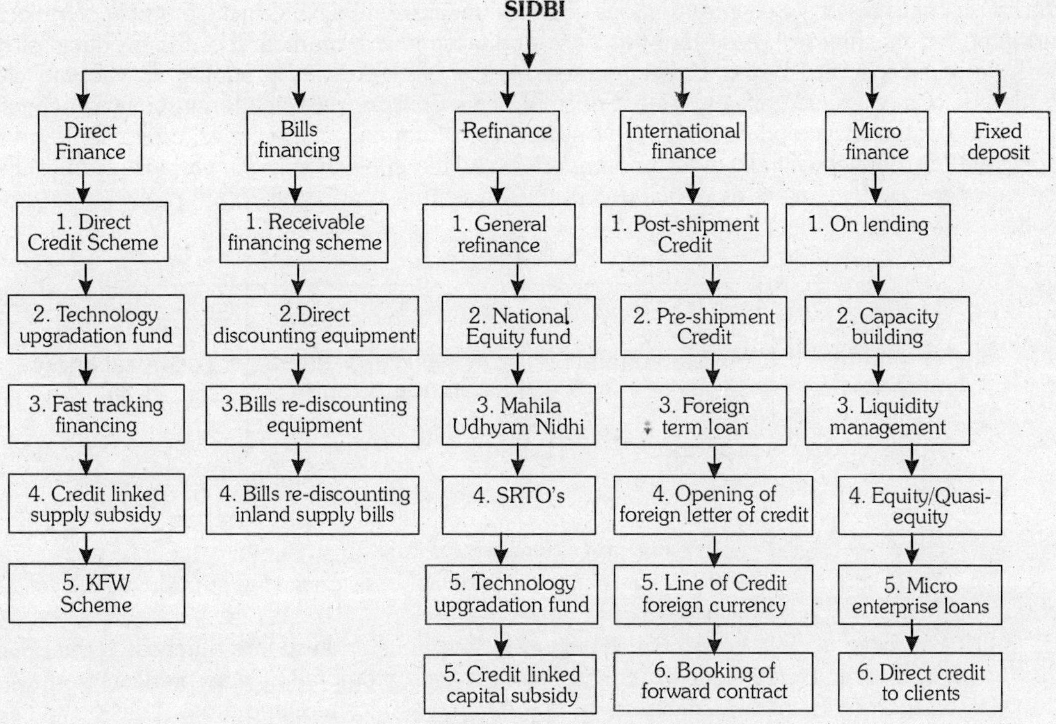

Fig. 5.2: Services of SIDBI

EXIM BANK: THE EXPORT IMPORT BANK OF INDIA

It was set up on Jan 1 1982, by an Act of Parliament as the principal financial institution for promotion and financing of India's international trade. EXIM Bank finances exporters and importers, co-ordinates the working of institutions engaged in financing export and import of goods and services, finances export-oriented units and undertakes promotional activities necessary for international trades.

- ❖ It has a menu of 23 major programs to meet the needs of different customer groups, viz., Indian Exporters, Overseas entities and commercial banks.
- ❖ Exporter's can avail of pre-shipment credit supplier's credit, overseas investment finance export product development loans, loans for export marketing, bulk import finance and investment vendors development finance.
- ❖ Foreign Governments and agencies are offered buyer's credit and lines of credit.

- To commercial banks in India, EXIM Bank offers export bills rediscounting facilities refinance of supplier's credit and refinance of term loans in respect of export-oriented units. It also participates in guarantee issued by commercial banks on behalf of Indian Project Exporters.
- Besides providing finance, EXIM Bank promotes exports through advisory and information services to exporters on procurement practices and bidding procedures of multilateral institutions, country risk analysis, merchant banking and marketing focused on catalyzing exports of non-traditional products to developed countries.

ROLE OF NSIC: NATIONAL SMALL INDUSTRIES CORPORATION LTD

It was set up by Government of India in 1955 with the objective of promoting and developing small scale industries in the country. Various activities undertaken by NSIC include supply of indigenous and imported machines on easy hire-purchase and lease terms, marketing of the products of small industries on consortia, basis, export marketing of small industries products, developing export worthiness of small scale units enlistment of small scale units for participation in Government stores purchase program development and modernization of prototypes of machines, equipment and tools supply and distribution of indigenous and imported raw materials, training in various technical trades and co-operation with other developing countries in setting up of small scale projects on turn-key basis.

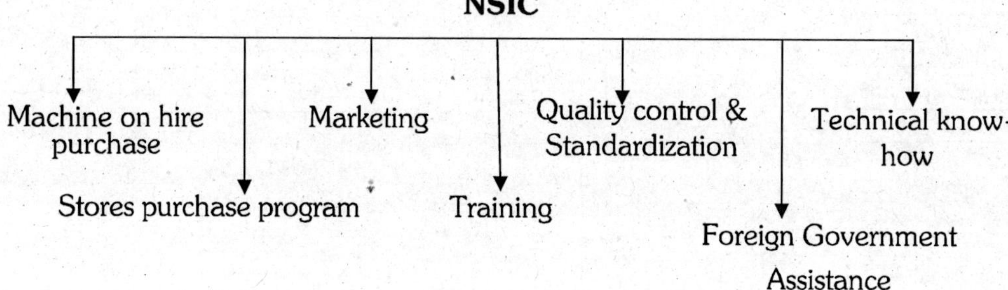

Fig. 5.3: Services of NSIC

The NSIC provides a complete package of financial assistance and support in the following areas:

1. Supply of both indigenous and imported machines on easy hire purchase terms. Special concessional terms have been introduced for units promoted by entrepreneurs from weaker section of the society, women entrepreneur ex-servicemen and those units located in the backward areas.
2. Marketing of small industries product within the country.
3. Export of small industries products and developing export worthiness of small scale units.
4. Enlisting competent units and facilitating their participating in Government stores purchase program.
5. Developing prototypes of machines, equipment and tools which are then passed on the small scale units for commercial production.
6. Technical training in several industrial trades with a view to create technical culture in the young entrepreneur.
7. Development and upgradation of technology and implementation of modernization programs.
8. Supply and distribution of indigenous and improved raw materials.
9. Supply of both indigenous and imported machines on easy lease terms to existing units for diversification and modernization.

10. Providing of common facilities through prototype Development and Training Centres.
11. Setting up small scale industries in other developing countries on turnkey basis.

Performance and Achievement of NSIC

National Small Industries Corporation Ltd (NSIC), a Government of India enterprise under the aegis of Ministry of SME, achieved record operational and financial performance in terms of gross volume of business and profitability in the recently concluded financial year 2009-10. The year witnessed the Corporation achieved new heights on all parameters. There was substantial improvement in enhancing the company's outreach and its volume of operations. With the opening of new offices the Corporation expanded its reach to serve larger number of SME, making the total number of NSIC offices 123. The Business Turnover of the Corporation for the year jumped to ₹ 4336 crore (pre-audited) over the previous year's turnover of ₹ 3508 crore.

NSIC continued with its efforts to provide various raw materials like steel, aluminum, zinc, copper, paraffin wax etc to SME through arrangements made with bulk manufacturers of these materials. In addition, the Corporation also started distribution of Coal to SME in West Bengal. Total raw material facilitation to SME increased from 302164 MTs in the year 2008-09 to 354725 MTs in the year 2009-10.

The Corporation during the year provided credit support of ₹ 1094 crore to SME as against ₹ 688 crore provided during the previous financial year, registering a growth of 59%.

In the year 2009-10, total 3327 new units were registered under Single Point Registration Scheme, while in the previous year 2677 units were registered. Under B2B portal, total 3802 members were added during the year 2009-10, as against 2808 members made under Info-mediary Services in the year 2008-09.

The Corporation's revenue from its above mentioned two membership schemes during the year 2009-10, increased to ₹ 5.52 crore from ₹ 4.12 Crore in the year 2008-09, registering the growth of 34%. The performance of NSIC's Technical Centers also showed remarkable improvement in the year 2009-10. The aggregate income of the technical centers rose from ₹ 12.54 crore in the year 2008-09 to ₹ 17.15 crore in the year 2009-10, registering a growth of 37%.

Under the Performance and Credit Rating Scheme, total 7505 micro and small enterprises were rated during the year, as against 5011units rated in the previous year.

NSIC organized 963 Marketing Promotion events including participation / organization / co-sponsoring of exhibitions, buyer-sellers meets and marketing campaigns as compared to 874 events in the previous year 2009-10. NSIC's 'Tech-mart 2009' organized at the India International Trade Fair during November, 2009 was awarded 'Gold Medal' for outstanding display of the SME technology and products.

During the year, NSIC continued its initiative to set up new Training-cum Incubation centers under Public-Private Partnership (PPP) mode for the purpose of inculcating entrepreneurial skills in the youth by way of skill development through which they become employable or create their own enterprises. So far, 45 such centers have been established at various locations in the country. These are in addition to three incubation centers opened at our technical centers. During the year, 8364 candidates were trained at these centers.

The overall improved performance resulted in achievement of higher profit. The Corporation, during the year achieved operating profit of ₹ 17.17 crore (pre-audited), showing a jump of 86% over the operating profit of ₹ 9.21 crore in the previous financial year. After amortization of VRS expenditure of ₹ 2.12 crore, the Corporation has earned a net profit (before tax) of ₹ 15.05 crore, as compared to ₹ 6.92 crore earned during the previous year.

The major highlights of the achievements of the Corporation for the financial year 2009-10 are briefly summed up here-below:

Under the Performance and Credit Rating Scheme, total 7505 micro and small enterprises were rated during the year, as against 5011 units rated in the previous year.

NSIC organized 963 Marketing Promotion events including participation/organization/co-sponsoring of exhibitions, buyer-sellers meets and marketing campaigns as compared to 874 events in the previous year 2009-10. NSIC 'Tech-mart 2009', organized at the India International Trade Fair during November, 2009, was awarded 'Gold Medal' for outstanding display of the SME technology and products.

During the year, NSIC continued its initiative to set up new Training-cum Incubation centers under Public-Private Partnership (PPP) mode for the purpose of inculcating entrepreneurial skills in the youth by way of skill development through which they become employable or create their own enterprises. So far, 45 such centers have been established at various locations in the country. These are in addition to three incubation centers opened at our technical centers. During the year, 8364 candidates were trained at these centers.

These pre-audited results are indicative of the continuous improvements in the performance of the Corporation. The MOU rating of the Corporation for the year 2009-10, based on the pre-audited data is 'Excellent'.

SIDCO: Small Industries Development Organization

It was established in 1954, on the recommendation of the ford foundation over the years, it has seen its role evolve into an agency for advocacy, handholding and facilitation for the small industries sector. SIDCO is policy making co-coordinating and monitoring agency for the development of small scale entrepreneurs. It maintains a close liaison with government financial institutions and other agencies which are involved in the promotion and development of small scale units. It provides comprehensive range of consultancy service and technical, managerial, economic and marketing assistance to SSI units.

Functions: The main functions of SIDCO are co-ordination, industrial development, industrial development and industrial extension service. Some important functions are:

(1) To assess the requirements of indigenous and imported raw materials and components for the small scale sector and to arrange their supplies.

(2) To collect data on consumer items which are imported, and encourage the setting up of new units by giving them coordinated assistance.

(3) To prepare model schemes, project reports and other technical literature for prospective entrepreneurs.

(4) To assist and advise the controller of import and exports in regard to the issue of import licenses and the imposition of import restriction on various products whose manufacture has already been undertaken indigenously by the existing or new units.

(5) To secure reservations of certain products for the SSIs.

SISI: Small Industries Service Institutes

Established in 1956, one in each state has been rendering very useful service to small scale industries the assistance rendered by the institute and its extension centres in Tamil Nadu may be listed as follow:

1. **Technical Consultancy and Advisory Service:** This relates to selection of profitable small enterprises, choice of appropriate machinery and equipment, appraisal of the technique of manufacture, processing of raw materials, adoption of recognized standards of testing quality performance of the small industry products and encouraging small units to participate in government stores purchase program. The institute explores the possibility of setting up small scale units to supply parts/components to large scale industries.

2. **Common Facility Service:** This includes supply of designs and drawings and provision of workshop facilities for the manufacture of dies, tools, jigs and fixtures and components.
3. **Training Facilities:** Training is provided to workers in basic trades in the workshops attached to this institute and its extension centers to increase their productivity and this helps to encourage development of SSI in rural areas.

   Training in various aspects of industrial and business management is also provided for the benefit of small industrialists.
4. **Testing Facilities:** Basic testing facilities (both physical and chemical) are provided in the laboratories and workshops attached to this institute at concessional rates.
5. **Marketing Assistance:** Economic information on the nature and extent of the market for specific products is collected and furnished to small industrialists at their request. The institute offers export promotion and trends in foreign markets.

MSMEDI: The Micro, Small and Medium Enterprises Development Institute

In accordance with the provision of Micro, Small and Medium Enterprises Development (MSMED) Act, 2006 the Micro, Small and Medium Enterprises (MSME) are classified in two Classes:

(a) **Manufacturing Enterprises:** The enterprises engaged in the manufacture or production of goods pertaining to any industry specified in the first schedule to the industries (Development and Regulation Act, 1951). The Manufacturing Enterprise are defined in terms of investment in Plant and Machinery.

(b) **Service Enterprises:** The enterprises engaged in providing or rendering of services and are defined in terms of investment in equipment. The limit for investment in plant and machinery/equipment for manufacturing/service enterprises, as notified, *vide S.O. 1642(E) dtd.29-09-2006,* are as under:

Manufacturing Sector

Enterprises	*Investment in plant and machinery*
Micro Enterprises	Does not exceed twenty five lakh rupees
Small Enterprises	More than twenty five lakh rupees but does not exceed five crore rupees
Medium Enterprises	More than five crore rupees but does not exceed ten crore rupees

Service Sector

Enterprises	*Investment in equipment*
Micro Enterprises	Does not exceed ten lakh rupees
Small Enterprises	More than 10 lakh rupees but does not exceed ₹ 2 crore
Medium Enterprises	More than 2 crore rupees but does not exceed ₹ 5 core rupees

Promotional Schemes

The small scale industry sector output contributes almost 40% of the gross Industrial value-added 45% of the total exports from India (direct as well as indirect exports) and is the second largest employer of human resources after agriculture. The development of Small-scale Sector has therefore been assigned an important role in India's national plans.

In order to protect, support and promote small enterprises and also to help them become self-supporting, a number of protective and promotional measures have been undertaken by the Government.

The promotional measures cover

- Industrial extension services
- Institutional support in respect of credit facilities,
- Provision of developed sites for construction of sheds,
- Provision of training facilities,
- Supply of machinery on hire-purchase terms,
- Assistance for domestic marketing as well as exports,
- Special incentive for setting up enterprises in backward areas etc.
- Technical consultancy and financial assistance for technological up-gradation.

While most of the institutional support services and some incentives are provided by the Central Government, others are offered by the state governments in varying degrees to attract investments and promote small industries in varying degrees to attract investments and promote small industries with a view to enhance industrial production and to generate employment in their respective States.

DICs: District Industries Centers

Governments both central and state, have in the part taken a number of measures for the development of small and village industries but the actual achievements have been far below the expectation. It was felt necessary to establish a development agency which could provide all services and facilities to village and small industries under one roof. Accordingly, the DICs were established in May 1978, in order to cater to the needs of small units.

Each district has a DIC at its headquarters. The main responsibility of DIC is to act as the chief coordinator or multifunctional agency in respect of various government departments and other agencies. The prospective small entrepreneur would get all assistance from DIC for setting up and running an industry in rural areas.

Organizational Setup: Each DIC have one general manages in the rank of Joint Director of Industries as the lead and seven managers each looking after a separate functional areas as follows;

1. Manager (Economic Investigation)
2. Manager (Machinery and Equipment)
3. Manager (Research, Extension and Training)
4. Manager (Raw Materials)
5. Manager (Credit)
6. Manager (Marketing)
7. Manager (KVIC and RAP)
   (Khadi Village Industries)

The GM has to provide an effective leadership and coordination. Hence the success of the centre largely depends upon the functioning of GM and his team of manager and other

Functions of DIC

1. **Identifications of Entrepreneurs:** DIC develops new entrepreneurs by conducting entrepreneurial motivation programs throughout the district especially in Panchayat Union Headquarter and small towns.
2. **Selection of Projects:** DIC offers technical advice to new entrepreneur for the selection of project suitable to them.

3. **Provisional Registration under SSI:** After the selection of projects, entrepreneurs are issued with provisional SSI Registration which is essential for obtaining assistance from the financial institutions.
4. **Purchase of Fixed Assets:** DIC sponsors the loan application to TIIC, SIDCO and banks for the purchase of land and buildings and sanctions margin money under Rural Industries Project Loan Scheme payable to other financial agencies for the purchase of plant and machinery.
5. **Clearance from Various Departments:** It takes the initiative to get clearances from various departments and takes follow up measures to get speedy power connection.
6. **Assistance to Raw Material Supply:** It makes necessary recommendations to the concerned raw material suppliers and issues the required certificated for the import of raw materials and machinery wherever necessary.
7. **Assistance to Village Artisans and Handicrafts:** DIC arranges for the financial assistance with the lead bank or nationalized banks of respective areas.
8. **Interest Free Sales Tax Loan:** SSI units set up in rural areas can get HST Loan up to a maximum limit of 8% of the total fixed assets from SIDCO. But the sanction order from the same is being issued by DIC. The DIC also recommends the SSI units to NSIC for registration fro government purchase program.
9. **Subsidy Scheme:** DIC assists SSI units and rural artisans to get subsidies such as power subsidy interest subsidy for engineers, subsidy under IRDP, etc. from various institutions.
10. **Training Programs:** DIC gives training to rural entrepreneurs and also assists other units giving training to small entrepreneurs.
11. **Self-employment for Unemployed Educated Youth:** This scheme was introduced in 1983-84, for youths between 18-25 years with SSLC, technocrats and women are given preference.

DIC are supposed to provide pre-investment, investment and post investment assistance to entrepreneur under one roof.

CFMI: Centre for Financial Markets and Institutions

Financial Markets and sectors associated with financial markets have seen significant growth and change in every parts of the world including India. The Finance and Economics Areas of Indian Institute of Management Bangalore (IIMB) contribute significantly in the form of research, training and courses covering various segments of financial markets. They are also rated best among business schools in India. Many faculty members of finance and economics are closely associated with regulators, stock exchanges, financial intermediary institutions and institutions providing technology and software to financial markets and institutions. IIMB contributes large managerial pool for the financial sectors and several IIMB students occupy important positions in various institutions connected with financial markets. In order to leverage the strength of the faculty members and their association with financial markets, the Institute has set up Centre for Financial Markets and Institutions (CFMI) with an objective to carry out cutting-edge research and offer specialized programs and training to meet the increasingly sophisticated demands of the financial sector.

The activities of the centre include:

- Conducting high-quality research on both technical and non-technical topics of financial markets and institutions addressing both immediate and long-term needs of the industry
- Close and active association and interaction with various agencies and organizations connected with financial markets and institutions.
- Disseminating the knowledge through new courses, case studies, executive training, conferences and workshops.

- Offering a forum for exchange of views between the practitioners and academics by inviting eminent scholars and experts from the industry and regulating agencies to discuss, debate and direct future policies relating to financial markets and institutions.
- Encouraging and sponsoring academic and industry exchange programs in which faculty members can spend a short period with some organizations and similarly practitioners can spend a short period in IIMB.
- Launching newer long-term programs in various areas of finance.
- Organizing national and international seminar where leading academics and practitioners from all across the globe meet and exchange their views on the fast changing scenario of the financial world.

INDUSTRIAL ESTATES

An industrial estate has been defined as a method of "Organizing housing and servicing industry, a planned clustering of industrial enterprises offering standard factory buildings erected in advance of demand and a variety of services and facilities to the occupants.

The main features of industrial estates are:

(i) It is a tract of land subdivided and developed into factory plot or sheds.

(ii) It provides several common facilities or infrastructural amenities such as, water, power, transport, tool-room, training, bank, port office, repairs and maintenance, etc, to the occupants.

(iii) It is planned clustering of industrial units.

(iv) It is designed as a tool of industrialization and balanced regional development.

(v) It may be developed in Urban, semi-urban or rural areas.

(vi) It may be large, medium and small.

(vii) It may be set up the Government, or by co-operative or by private agencies.

Types of Industrial Estates: Industrial estates may be classified into:

1. **General Purpose or Composite Industrial Estate:** Such an industrial estates provides accommodation to all types of SSI. Most of IE in India are of this type.
2. **Special Purpose Industrial Estate:** It particularly constructed for specified groups of entrepreneur e.g. technically qualified person, craftsmen artisans set up at Hyderabad.
3. **Functional Industrial Estates:** It consists of lower manufacturing units, which produce parts and components for a large industrial units. It is generally set up near the parent unit.
4. **Flatted Factory Estates:** There are multi-storey buildings constructed in big cities, to provide space to industrial units manufacturing light weights goods with the help of simple machine tools. They help to conserve space.

Advantages of Industrial Estates: Industrial estates offer the following benefits:

1. **Economies of Scale:** It arises because all the industrial units enjoy common infrastructural facilities. As the size of an industrial estate increases the costs of estate development and administration per unit of each facility decline.
2. **Economies of Agglomeration:** In an industrial estate, several industrial units are clustered together. They become interrelated and interdependent. This enables them to enjoy the benefits of agglomeration and external economies, like transportation facilities, availability of trained labor, regular supply of power and water etc.
3. **Low Investment:** A small scale entrepreneur can obtain an industrial plot or shed on rent or hire purchase basis. This reduces fixed capital requirements as well as fixed costs.

4. **Less Risk:** Industrial estates serve as risk absorbing device because of low capital investment and provision of common facilities and services.
5. **Saving of Time and Effort:** An individual entrepreneur is relieved of the trouble of searching for a suitable space. He need not waste his time and effort in formalities involved in acquiring land, obtaining the approval of local authorities, securing power connection etc.
6. **Nursery for New Entrepreneurs:** Industrial estates reduce risks and increase profitability through internal and external economies, this induces new entrepreneur to set up industrial unit.
7. **Mutual Cooperation:** Industrial estates promote the spirit of cooperation and joint efforts. All industrial units located in an industrial estate face common problems and seek common objectives.
8. **Balanced Regional Development:** By developing estates, in relatively background regions, the government can ensure the balanced industrialization of different part of the country. This will also lead to decentralization of industries.

Technical Consultancy Organization

Technical Consultancy Organizations were set up by the all India financial institutions during the 1970s and 1980s to cater to the consultancy needs of small medium industries and new entrepreneur.

Technical Consultancy Organizations provide a total package of consultancy services to small and medium scale enterprises, individual entrepreneur government departments and agencies various state level institutions, commercial banks, and other institutions for activities relating to industrial development and financing.

Services of Technical Consultancy Organizations are:

1. Preparing project profiles and feasibility studies.
2. Undertaking industrial potential surveys.
3. Identifying of potential entrepreneurs and provision of technical and management assistance to them.
4. Undertaking market research and surveys for specific products.
5. Carrying out energy audit and energy conservation assignments.
6. Project supervision and, where ever necessary, rendering technical and administrative assistance.
7. Taking up assignments on a turnkey basis.
8. Under taking export consultancy for export oriented projects based on modern technology.
9. Offering management consultancy services especially for diagnostic study of sick units or for improvement in existing units and their rehabilitation programs.
10. Conducting entrepreneurship development program and skill up-gradation programs.

SSIB: Small-scale Industries Board

The government of India constituted a board, named SSIB in 1954 to advice on development of SSI in the country. It is also known as central small industries board. SSIB helps in facilitating coordination and inter-institution linkages, the SSIB is an apex advisory body constituted to render advice to government on all issues pertaining to the development of SSI unit.

The industries minister of the government of India is the chairman of SSIB. It comprises of so members including state industry minister, some MPs and secretaries of various departments of government of India, financial institution and experts in the field.

SSICs: State Small Industries Corporations

Many state governments have set up small industries corporations in order to undertake a number of commercial activities. The most important of these are distribution of scarce raw materials, supply of machinery on hire-purchase basis, constitution and management of industrial estates, procurement of orders from government department assistance in export marketing and in certain cases provision of financial technical and managerial assistance to small enterprises.

Microfinance Institutions

Microfinance began as a financial system to provide poor families with very small loans (micro-credit) to help members begin or sustain income-generating activities. Micro-credit arose in the 1970s, through the efforts of Mohammad Yunus, a microfinance pioneer and founder of the Grameen Bank of Bangladesh.Microfinance refers to a variety of financial services that target low-income clients, particularly women. Since the clients of microfinance institutions (MFIs) have lower incomes and often have limited access to other financial services, microfinance products tend to be for smaller monetary amounts than traditional financial services. These services include loans, savings, insurance, and remittances. Micro-loans are given for a variety of purposes, frequently for micro-enterprise development. The diversity of products and services offered reflects the fact that the financial needs of individuals, households, and enterprises can change significantly over time, especially for those who live in poverty. Because of these varied needs, and because of the industry's focus on the poor, microfinance institutions often use non-traditional methodologies, such as group lending or other forms of collateral not employed by the formal financial sector.

A microfinance institution is an organization that offers financial services to low income populations. Almost all give loans to their members, and many offer insurance, deposit and other services. Various types of institutions offer microfinance: NBFCs, NGOs, cooperatives, private commercial banks and sectors of government banks.

Microfinance plays an important role in fighting the multi-dimensional aspects of poverty. Microfinance increases household income, which leads to attendant benefits: increased food security, the building of assets, and an increased likelihood of educating one and their children. Microfinance is also a means for self-empowerment. It enables the poor, especially women, to become economic agents of change - they increase income, become business-owners and reduce their vulnerability to external shocks (illness, weather, etc).

Micro Finance Institutions use two basic methods in delivering financial services to their clients:

1. Group Method

This is one of the most common methodologies for providing micro-finance. Group method primarily involves a group of individuals, which becomes the basic unit of operation for the MFIs. As we have discussed earlier, MFIs have to provide collateral free loans, group methodologies help in creating social collateral (peer pressure) that can effectively substitute physical collateral. Group becomes a basic unit with which MFIs deal. The advantage of group methodology is that

- Groups are trained to own joint responsibility for loans that are taken by individuals in the group.
- Groups ensure repayments from all individuals in that group and incase of a default
- Groups functions as the forum where the credit discipline and other related issues are discussed.
- Group may have to jointly own the responsibility of defaults and pay on behalf of defaulting client.

- ❖ Group also help credit appraisal and provide opinion on credit worthiness of each individual in the group.
- ❖ Groups methodology also helps in controlling cost.

This ensures that even without taking any physical collateral, the MFI is able to manage its credit risk (loan related risk). MFIs actually deliver the financial service at the client's location which could be a village in rural areas or a colony/slum in urban area. Having a group helps the MFIs in getting all clients at one spot rather than visiting each individual's house. This helps the MFI in increasing the efficiency of staff and controlling the cost. Group methodology creates a forum where individuals come and discuss, can provide opinion, and exert social pressure.

The advantage of Group methodology can easily be appreciated by the fact if the MFI employee has to visit each individual house in isolation, it would be very difficult. Also in the absence of a group, if a client refuses to pay there is no forum where such a case can be discussed or there is no method through which the MFI can expert pressure on the client.

Group methodology is also important because in case of larger loan defaults a financial institutions can take recourse to legal action but in small loans legal recourse is not an economically sound option. An MFI who may have an outstanding or ₹ 3,000 at default cannot apply legal pressure as the cost of recovery through that method can be higher than the amount to be recovered itself.

Moreover, the clients that the MFIs are dealing with are generally poor and may face genuine problems at times. Rather than taking an aggressive/legal approach, which such vulnerable clients it is always better to have more constructive and collective approach, which is provided by the Groups.

Due to the various advantages, as indicated above provided by groups, this methodology is widely accepted and used in micro-finance across the world.

Self-help Group and Joint Liability Groups (Grameen model and its variants) are two common credit delivery models in India.

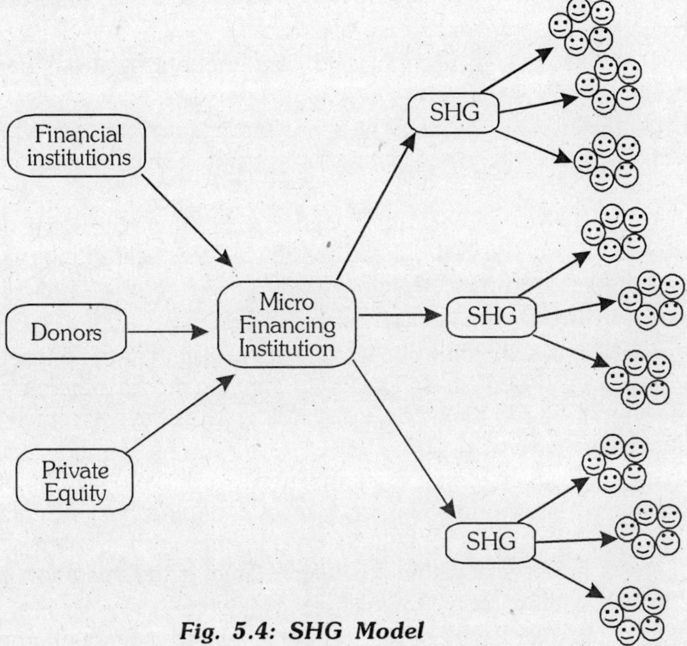

Fig. 5.4: SHG Model

Self-help Groups (SHGs)

Self-help Group concept has its origin in India. SHGs are now considered to be very important bodies in rural development and are therefore found in almost all parts of the country and their number is still rapidly growing. SHGs are formed by Non-Government Organisations as well as Government agencies are used as channels for various development programmes.

A Self-help Group is an association of generally up to 20 members (not exceeding 20 members), preferably from the same socio-economic background. SHGs are facilitated by Government agencies or NGOs for members to come together for discussing and solving their common problems either financial or social through mutual help. An SHG can be all-women group, all-men group, or even a mixed Group. However, it has been the experience that women's groups perform better in all the important activities of SHGs. Mixed group is not preferred in many of the places, due to the presence of conflicting interests.

Some of the distinct features of SHGs are

(i) Recognized by government: SHGs are well recognized and accepted by government, SHGs can open bank accounts in the name of SHG. They can also receive government grants and funds for development activities.

(ii) SHGs are social intermediaries: SHGs do not restrict their functions only to financial transactions. SHGs are often involved in many social activities. There are example where SHGs have taken up social issues and fought against social evils like alcoholism, violence, against women, dowry, getting into village politics and being elected as Sarpanch.

(iii) Books of accounts: SHGs maintain their own books of accounts. These are simple books to keep records of their savings, loans income and expenditures. Strong SHGs also make their Balance sheets and Income statements.

(iv) Have office bearers: SHGs gave a structure where there is a Group President, Secretary and Treasure. They are elected by the group.

(v) SHGs are more autonomous as they decide their own rules and regulations.

(vi) SHGs mobilize thrift and rotate it internally.

(vii) SHGs can hold bank account and can also borrow from banks and other financial institutions.

We see that SHGs are groups, which are more autonomous. While they are involved in financial transactions, their role is not just restricted to it. SHGs are also involved in various social issues.

As more SHGs are formed they have started federating themselves into clusters and clusters in turn as SHG Federations. The Federations are able to channelise funds to the SHGs and also help in improving, managing and financial skills of SHGs.

2. Joint Liability Group – Grameen Model

Grameen model is based on the concept of joint liability. It is the brainchild of Prof.. Muhammad Yunus, founder of Grameen Bank in Bangladesh. Grameen model is the most accepted and prevalent micro-finance delivery model in the world today. Many MFIs have accepted the model as it has high focus on standardization and discipline

Grameen model, as mentioned, is a joint liability group model. Here five-member groups are formed and eight such groups form a Center. Hence, in a full-capacity Center there are 40 members (8 × 5). However, over the years people have experimented with Centers of different sizes and now there are variations of 5-8 groups within a Center. Center is the operational unit for the MFI, which means that MFI deals with a Center as a whole.

Meetings also take place only at the Central level and individual groups do not meet. Group meetings take place only in front of the Field staff of the MFI. A Grameen model is focused on financial transactions and other social issues are generally not discussed. The Group and Center are

Joint liability Groups, which means that all members are jointly responsible ('liable') for the repayment. MFI recovers full money from Center, if any member has defaulted: the group members have to pool in money to repay to the MFI. If Group members are unable to do it, Center as whole has to contribute and share the responsibility

Despite the expansion of banks into rural areas of India, many poverty-stricken people still lack access to financial credit. Commercial financial institutions often require that borrowers have a stable source of income and collateral to ensure repayment of loans, both of which are often lacking. Moreover, commercial banks view the poor as high risk and find it costly to administer a large number of small loans. Without the option of borrowing from formal financial institutions, the poor are often forced to borrow from local moneylenders at extremely high interest rates of 36-60%, or else to do without.

An essential ingredient of the Grameen Banks approach involves group lending. To qualify for loans, borrowers must organize themselves into groups of five, who convene on a weekly basis. Seven groups are then organized into centers that convene on a weekly matter to discuss loan approval and repayment structures. Loans are granted on an increasing scale, with a maximum of 4000 rupees given as a first loan to a maximum of 8000 rupees in the fifth year. Borrowers also have access to additional loans, such as a housing loan after the second year. Clients are required to save 5 rupees per week in order to qualify as a member.

The groups enforce the high loan recovery rate. There is considerable group pressure to repay the loans on time, since default by any borrower jeopardizes the other group member ability to receive future loans. If a person does not attend the weekly meetings or misses or defaults on repayment, s/he may be fined or suspended by the other group members. The responsibility for repayment falls upon the group, whether or not individual members enter or leave the group. In the unlikely event that the entire group defaulted on a loan, the responsibility would still fall upon the center to which the group belonged. About 75% of the loans received by females were used for income-generating activities such as poultry raising, processing, and manufacturing activity, while about 50% of the loans received by males were used for trading and shop keeping.

One of the major differences between the microfinance approach versus the direct credit approach is that the microfinance institutions strive to attain long-run sustainability. The MFIs goal is to be self-sufficient in such a way that they can continue to provide financial services even when they no longer have government or donor funding.

Examples of Microfinance Institutions in India

Swayam Krishi Sangam (SKS) is a microfinance institution that operates in rural India, designed based on the Grameen Bank model. This organization was founded in 1998, with the establishment of a woman's banking center in the Medak District in the State of Andhra Pradesh, a region considered to be one of the poorest in India.

An example of a success story is the experience of Gangapur Beeramma, a blanket maker of Gangapur. Having lost her husband, she is the sole head of her household. Her family's one acre of land is infertile, and does not yield crops nor income for the family. As a result, the family depended on the minimal income earned from making blankets from the wool of their five sheep. A year ago, Beeramma applied to SKS for a loan of 2000 rupees, and used the funds to purchase extra sheep wool. As a result, her family was able to produce more blankets than they could have otherwise, and this significantly boosted their income as well as their ability to repay the loan. This success led her to pursue a second loan of 6000 rupees to generate further income.

Benefits of Micro Financing in India

The microfinance industry in India is growing by the day. According to one recent study by Intellecap, the 60 largest microfinance institutions in India have 10 million clients. That's 10 million of the working poor who have been given small loans that allow them to pull themselves and their family out of poverty. Microfinance loans are aimed at empowering the impoverished, mostly women, to start their own businesses and to grow their money so they can achieve long-term financial independence. That's why this concept carries many advantages over typical philanthropic endeavors.

The benefits are:

1. It is not a hand out-As mentioned earlier, microfinance is not about just giving out money to the poor. On the contrary, these are small loans that are paid back with interest. Of course, many people are skeptical when it comes to giving the poor financial loans. However, they are surprised to learn that of the over 100 million microfinance loans that have been given out, 97% of them have been repaid. That's why you cannot consider microfinance a hand out, but rather, it is a hand up.
2. It allows the poor to receive a loan — Traditionally, the poor have been unable to receive loans. That's because they don't have anything to offer as collateral. As a result, they get stuck in a vicious cycle of poverty, living and working in poor, rural areas. Should adversity strike, they simply don't have the means to combat it. Microfinance allows the poor to get the loans they need to save, invest, and create a sustainable lifestyle of financial independence and growth. These loans are used productively by the poor to create their own businesses, grow their assets, and get out of poverty once and for all.
3. It empowers women — Many efforts of the microfinance industry are aimed at empowering women to create their own businesses. From microfinance India to microfinance in other developing countries, small loans are given to those women who live on less than $1 per day. By giving these poor women loans, the microfinance industry not only helps them pull themselves out of poverty, but it also promotes gender equality throughout the world.
4. It creates long-term financial independence — The most important benefit of microfinance in India is that it helps create long-term financial independence in these poverty-stricken areas. See, it's one thing to send money, clothes, and other goods to the poor. It's a great gesture, but the results of this traditional style of charity are short-lived. Microfinance loans help create sustained impact by educating recipients on how to create their own businesses and how to properly manage and grow their money.

SPECIALIZED INSTITUTIONS

(1) KVIC Khadi and Village Industries Commission: It was established in 1953 with the primary objective of developing. Khadi and village industries and improving rural employment opportunities. Its wide range of activities include training of artisans, extension of assistance for procurement of raw material, marketing of finished products and arrangement for manufacturing and distribution of improved tools, equipment and machinery to producers on concessional terms.

(2) EGB: Entrepreneurial Guidance Bureau: The II C (Indian Investment Centre) has set up EGB in orders to guide entrepreneur in identifying investment opportunities, assisting them in selecting locations for the projects, preparing project profiles, assisting them to get financial assistance. It has been supplying information pertaining to the products that offer scope for manufacture, statistical details, relating to demand, capacity production, sources of raw materials types of equipments required, investment involved, source of finance etc.

(3) IIC Indian Investment Centre: It is an autonomous, non profit service organization financed and supported by the government of India. It is concerned with the important task of promoting mutually rewarding joint ventures between Indian and foreign entrepreneurs.

The centre acts as a clearing house for information on economic conditions, laws, procedures, government regulations, and specific opportunities for investment in India.

REVIEW QUESTIONS

1. What is the framework of Institutional Finance?
2. Explain Industrial Development Bank of India.
3. Explain Industrial Corporation of India
4. What are the Entrepreneurial Development schemes of IFCI?
5. Explain in brief about the IRBI
6. Write in detail about LIC.
7. Discuss about the Unit Trust of India
8. Write a brief on ICICI and how it provide finance for various industries?
9. Discuss the role of State Financial Corporation in entrepreneurship?
10. What are the functions and objectives of SFC?
11. Write a note on SIDBI
12. Discuss about the EXIM bank
13. What is Industrial Estate? Explain different type of Industrial Estates and its objectives?

Fill in the blanks

1. IDBI serves as the ____________ institution for term finance to industries.
2. One of the functions of IDBI is to assist other financial institutions by ____________ of loans granted for exports.
3. The primary objective of IDBI is to __________, _________and __________ the working of other financial institutions like IFCI SFCs, UTI.
4. The IDBI can grant a ____________ or loans and advances to other financial institutions.
5. IDBI was set up in the years___________.
6. The main objective of Industrial Financial Corporation of India is to _______.
7. IFCI is a _______________ company
8. The ICICI was set up in __________ to encourage and assist ________ and ________ development in India
9. ICICI has set up a _________ in order to provide promotional services and assistance to individual project on selective basis.
10. This is a primary agency for the rehabilitation of the sick industrial units ______
11. LIC was form with the objectives of __________ much more widely and in particular to the rural areas.
12. The Unit Trust of India is a ___________ investment institutions established in 1963.
13. The main aim of the UTI is to encourage _________________
14. State Financial Corporation assist the entrepreneurs with a unique scheme known as ______________
15. State Industrial Development Corporation Promote and provide facilities for rapid _________________ in the respective states.
16. The function of _______ is as the principal financial institution for the promotion, development and financing of industries in the Small scale sectors.
17. The important thrust area of SIDBI are _________, _________ and _____ of the product of SSI.
18. _________ Bank act as the principal financial institution for promotion and financing of India's international trade.
19. Besides providing finance _______ promotes exports through advisory and information services to exporters.
20. The ________ provides a complete package of financial assistance and support of the small scale industries.

21. _____ is the apex bank for agricultural finance.
22. SIDO stand for _______ and the main function of SIDO are ______, _______ and ________
23. The main responsibility of ___________ is to act as the chief coordinator or multi functional agency in respect of various Government department and other agencies.
24. Under ________ provisional registration certificate are issued
25. ___________ is a method of organizing, housing and servicing industry a planned clustering of industrial enterprises offering standard factory building erected in advance of demand and variety of services to the occupants.
26. _____ provides total package of the consultancy services to the small scale industries
27. This ________________ is the important institute which reserves the scarce raw material for the small scale industries.
28. KVIC was established in ________ and the primary objectives are to developing _____ and ___
29. _____________ is concerned with the important task of promoting mutually rewarding joint ventures between Indian and foreign entrepreneurs.

Answer:

1. Apex
2. Refinancing
3. Co-ordinate, regulate, supervise
4. Line of credit
5. 1st July 1964
6. Provide medium and long term credit to industries.
7. Joint Stock
8. 1955, Investment and industrial
9. Project Promotion Department
10. Industrial Reconstruction Bank of India
11. Spreading life insurance
12. Statutory public sector
13. Saving of the people
14. Seed capital or Soft loan scheme
15. Industrialization
16. Small Industries Development Bank of India
17. Technology up-gradation, Modernization and Extending channels of marketing
18. EXIM Bank
19. EXIM Bank
20. National Small Industries Corporation Ltd.
21. NABARD
22. Small Industries Development Organization. Coordination, Industrial development and Industrial extension services.
23. District Industries centers
24. DIC
25. Industrial Estate
26. Technical Consultancy Organization
27. State Small Industries Corporation
28. 1953, Khadi and Village industries and Improving rural employment opportunities.
29. Indian Investment Centers

◆ ◆ ◆

Venture Capital

6

Chapter

CHAPTER OUTLINE

- Concept of Venture Capital Financing VCF
- Venture Capital in India
- Types of Venture Capital Fund
- Features of Venture Capital Financing
- Private Equity
- Private Equity – Current scenario in India
- Types of Private Equity Investments
- Role of Private Equity in India
- The Regulatory Environment of the Private Equity Industry in India
- Stages of Financing
- Financial Analysis of Venture Capital

- Important Venture Capital Financing Institutions and their Schemes in India
- Investment Nurturing/After Care
- Valuation of Venture Capital Portfolio
- Exit Strategies of Venture Capital Financing
- Policy Imperative of VCF Development in India

CONCEPT OF VENTURE CAPITAL FINANCING VCF

Venture capital institutions which emerged the world over to fill gaps in the conventional financial mechanism focused on new entrepreneurs, commercialization of new technologies and support to small and medium enterprises in the manufacturing and the service sectors. Over the years the concept of venture capital has undergone significant changes. The modus operandi has shifted from technology-oriented manufacturing organization to being very close to "private equity class" for unlisted new companies in all sectors of the economy, irrespective of the nature of their projects. They also maintain a close rapport and a hands-on approach in nurturing investment during their association with the assisted companies as active partner rather than as passive investors.

Although the development of the venture capital started in USA in the mid fifties, venture capital institutions are fairly recent origin India. Before their emergence, the development finance institutions partially played the role of venture capitalists by providing assistance for direct equity participation to venture in the pre-public issues stage and by selectively supporting new technologies. The initial steps for the institutionalization of venture capital in India were taken by the Government in November, 1988, when guidelines were issued for setting up of venture capital funds/venture capital companies for investing in unlisted companies and to avail of a concessional facility of capital gains tax.

Venture capital refers to funds provided by investors to new companies with growth potential. As new ventures involve high risk, investors expect high returns from their funds. The rewards for these risk takers in new businesses are usually in the form of capital gains when these new ventures are finally fails, investors my loose all their money.

Since the early 1900s, a new generation of venture capitalists has emerged these financiers provide start up funds to young companies with growth potential. They will also fund the expansion of companies with good record but without access to stock markets. Some provide funds to revitalize ailing ventures.

A special feature in the VC industry is that these financiers continue to be involved in their investee companies after making the investment. They monitor the growth and assist in developing the business. Participants in the VC industry include fund management companies with whom institution and individuals invest their funds to be managed by professional fund managers.

VENTURE CAPITAL IN INDIA

In India, Venture Capital plays a vital role in the development and growth of innovative entrepreneurships. Venture Capital activity in the past was possibly done by the developmental financial institutions like IDBI, ICICI and State Financial Corporations. These institutions promoted entities in the private sector with debt as an instrument of funding. For a long time funds raised from public were used as a source of Venture Capital. This source however depended a lot on the market vagaries. And with the minimum paid up capital requirements being raised for listing at the stock exchanges, it became difficult for smaller firms with viable projects to raise funds from public. In India, the need for Venture Capital was recognized in the 7th Five Year Plan and long-term fiscal policy of Govt. of India in 1973, a committee on development of small and medium enterprises highlighted the need to foster VC as a source of funding new entrepreneurs and technology. VC financing really started in India in 1988, with the formation of Technology Development and Information Company of India Ltd. (TDICI) — promoted by ICICI and UTI. The first private VC fund was sponsored by Credit Capital Finance Corporation (CFC) and promoted by Bank of India, Asian Development Bank and the Commonwealth Development Corporation, viz., Credit Capital Venture Fund. At the same time Gujarat Venture Finance Ltd. and APIDC Venture Capital Ltd. were started by state level financial institutions. Sources of these funds were the financial institutions, foreign institutional investors or pension funds and high net-worth individuals.

Performance of VCF in India: The venture capital industry in India is a relatively recent origin. Before its emergence, the DFIS had partially been playing the role of venture capitalists by providing assistance for direct equity participation to ventures in the pre-public stage by selectively supporting new technologies. The concept of VC was institutionalized/operationalized in November, 1988 when the CCI issued guidelines for setting up of VCFs for investing in unlisted companies and to avail of a concessional facility of capital gains tax. These guidelines, however, construed VC rather narrowly as a vehicle for equity oriented finance for technological up-gradation and commercialization of technology promoted by relatively new entrepreneurs. There were repealed on July 25 1995. Recognizing the growing importance of VC, the government announced a policy for governing the establishment of domestic VCFs. They were exempted from tax on Income by way of dividends and long term capital gains from equity investments in the specified manner and in conformity with stipulations in unlisted companies in the manufacturing sector, including software units, but excluding other service industries. To augment the availability of VC, guidelines were issued in September 1995, to overseas VC investments in the country. After empowerment to register and regulate VCF, SEBI issued VCF Regulations 1996.

The VCFs in the country have been sponsored by five groups of financial institutions namely, central and state level development financial institutions , banks, private sector and overseas financial institutions.

Some important Venture Capital Funds in India

1. APIDC Venture Capital Limited ,1102, Babukhan Estate, Hyderabad 500 001.
2. Canbank Venture Capital Fund Limited, IInd Floor, Kareem Towers, Bangaluru.
3. Gujarat Venture Capital Fund 1997, Ashram Road, Ahmedabad 380 009.
4. Industrial Venture Capital Limited, Thyagaraya Road, Chennai 600 017.
5. Auto Ancillary Fund Opp. Signals Enclave, New Delhi 110 010.
6. Gujarat Venture Capital Fund 1995 Ashram Road Ahmedabad 380 009.
7. Karnataka Information Technology Venture Capital Fund Cunningham Rd Bangaluru.
8. India Auto Ancillary Fund Nariman Point, Mumbai 400 021.
9. Information Technology Fund, Nariman Point, Mumbai 400 021.
10. Tamilnadu Infotech Fund Nariman Point, Mumbai 400 021.
11. Orissa Venture Capital Fund Nariman Point Mumbai 400 021.
12. Uttar Pradesh Venture Capital Fund Nariman Point, Mumbai 400 021.
13. SICOM Venture Capital Fund Nariman Point Mumbai 400 021.
14. Punjab Infotech Venture Fund 18 Himalaya Marg, Chandigarh 160 017.
15. National Venture Fund for Software and Information Technology Industry, Nariman Point, Mumbai 400 021.

Types of Venture Capital Fund

1. **Institution fund:** Funds that come from subsidiaries of financial institutions, such as bank and insurance companies. Through, these subsidiaries, bank provide alternative financing for high risk, high potential investment which do not meet their regular loan requirements. These funds are mostly open ended and don't have pre-determined size or duration. They may invest some of the funds in debt financing (long term) rather than pure equity capital. This is partly to fulfill the requirement from their parent companies to show some continual return on investment in addition to the return from capital growth.
2. **Independent Fund:** That comes from sources such, wealthy individual's family groups, partnerships and corporations.

3. **Government Funds:** These funds may come from the government directly or through its development agencies. They are used to encourage expansion in specific industries identified in the government development plan.
4. **Corporate Funds**: Some of companies may set aside a special venture capital fund to take a minority equity stake in small firms in order to encourage product development and innovation. Some may use this fund to develop "Intrapreneurs" within the company.
5. **Nature of Venture Capital**: A venture capital firm serves as an intermediary between investors looking for high returns and entrepreneurs in need of capital. Several features distinguish venture capital financing from other types of capital investment.
   - Long-term finance (2-5 years) for entrepreneurs.
   - The venture capitalist providing and technical assistance when necessary.
   - Equity investment that generates long term capital gains.

Advantages of VCF: Companies (Seeking VCF)

- They provide funds which are not available from other sources.
- They help investee companies to seek listing on the stock exchange, either locally or abroad.
- Many have experience with investee companies in the same industry and are able to help in the company's growth.
- Many have experience in specific countries and are able to help entrepreneurs to set up a joint venture or explore markets in a foreign country.

Features of Venture Capital Financing

Venture capital has some how come to acquire various connotations. It is defined as equity/ equity related investment in a growth-oriented small/medium business to enable investee to accomplish corporate objectives, in return for minority shareholding right to acquire it.

Venture capital is a way in which investors support entrepreneurial talents with finance and business skills to exploit market opportunities and thus to obtain long-term capital gains. It is the provision of risk bearing capital, usually in the form of participation in equity, to companies with high-growth potential.

In addition, it provides some value addition in the form of management advice and contribution to over-all strategy. The relatively high risks are compensated by the possibility of high return, usually through substantial capital gains in the medium-term.

Some of the features of Ventures Capital are:

1. **Venture Capital is basically equity finance in relatively new companies when it is too early to go to the capital market to raise funds:** However, such investment is not exclusively equity investment. It can also be made in the form of loan finance/convertible debt to ensure a running yield on the portfolio of venture capitalists. Nonetheless the basic objective of venture capital financing is to earn capital gain on equity investment at the time of exit and debt financing is only supplementary.
2. **Venture Capital is long-term investment in growth oriented small/medium firms:** The acquisition of outstanding shares from other shareholder cannot be considered as venture capital investment. It is new, long term capital that is injected to enable business to grow rapidly.
3. **There is a substantial degree to active involvement of the venture capital institutions with the promoters of venture capital undertakings:** It means such finance also provides business skills to the investee firm which is termed as "hand on" approach management. Objective is to provide business managerial skill only and not interfere in management.

4. **Venture capital financing involve high risk return spectrum:** Some of the ventures field very high returns to more than compensate for heavy losses on others, which also may had potential of profitable returns. The returns in such financing are essential through capital against the time of exits from disinvestments in the capital market.
5. **Venture capital is not technology finance though technology finance may form a sub-set of venture capital financing**. The concept of venture capital embraces much more than financing new, high technology-oriented companies. It essentially involves the financing of small medium-sized firms through early stages of their development until they are established and are able to raise finance from the conventional, industrial finance market. The scope of venture capital activity is fairly wide.

PRIVATE EQUITY

The Private Equity sector is broadly defined as investing in a company through a negotiated process. Investments typically involve a transformational, value-added, active management strategy. Typical forms of private equity include venture capital, growth and mezzanine capital, investing and private equity funds. Private equity investors seek to obtain a substantial interest in a company in order to have an active role in firms' strategic decisions. Their goal is to boost the value of a company and walk away with substantially more money at the time of liquidating their investment.

Private equity consists of investors and funds that make investments directly into private companies or conduct buyouts of public companies. Capital for private equity is raised from institutional investors and can be used to fund new technologies, expand working capital within an owned company, make acquisitions, or to strengthen a balance sheet.

The term "private equity" encompasses a range of techniques used to finance commercial ventures in ways that do not involve the use of publicly tradable assets such as corporate stock or bonds.

Private Equity Funds: Private equity funds are investment companies that, as a rule, do not trade in publicly-traded securities. Instead, they normally seek equity stakes (that is, partial ownership) in private companies. They may also invest in so-called private placements of securities from public companies. Private equity buyers are extremely focused on cash-flow and have a reputation as cost-cutters.

PRIVATE EQUITY – CURRENT SCENARIO IN INDIA

India has a very vibrant Venture Capital (VC)/Private Equity (PE) industry with USD32.5 billion invested across more than 1500 VC/PE deals from January 2006, March 2010. Economists estimate that India needs about USD 1 trillion of investment over the next five years to sustain a GDP growth of above 9 per cent. This translates to USD 60-100 billion of VC/PE investments requirement over three years, against which industry estimates that PE investments would be in the range of USD 9-10 billion in the year ending December 31, 2010.

After a turbulent 2009, private equity investments in India displayed steady signs of recovery in the first quarter of 2010. The latest quarter registered the highest value of deals since 2009.

For the quarter ended March 2010, total announced deal value was $1,943 million, a jump of more than 185% from $675 million in Q1 2009. Total deal count in Q1 2010 also increased by35% to 88 deals, up from 65 in Q1 2009. Interestingly, despite the enormous growth in deal value on a quarter-on-quarter basis, the deal count decreased by 11% to 88, down from 99 in Q4 2009.

Private Equity Investment in India

Real estate, IT/IT Services and Energy were the most targeted sectors for investment with deals worth $0.65 billion, $0.62 billion and $0.54 billion respectively. Together, they accounted for more than 40% of total private equity deal value during the year 2009. The major PE investments influencing the deal values of these sectors were investments in Aricent Inc., Indiabulls Real Estate Ltd., Mohtisham Estates and Ind Barath Power Infra Pvt. Ltd. The other sectors, which have significantly contributed to private equity deal value in the year 2009, are Logistics and Telecom accounting for 15% of total deal value. Top Sectors by Deal Volume for the year 2009.

The most active sectors in terms of deal volume were IT/IT Services and Manufacturing which lead with 17% and 11% of deal volume respectively in 2009. Other sectors contributing significantly to deal volume were Banking, Finance and Insurance and Real estate accounting for 11% and 7% of deal volumes respectively. As seen in the year 2008, 2009, too large number of deals in IT/IT Services, Manufacturing, Banking, Finance and Insurance and Real estate.

Top Sector deals in 2009

Sector	Volume	Deal Value ($million)	Average Deal Size
Real Estate	20	657	43.8
IT/IT Services	47	621	15.9
Energy	16	538	41.4
Logistics	15	354	23.6
Telecom	5	336	84
Banking, Finance and Insurance	32	244	8.4
Manufacturing	34	242	9.3

Source: VCC Edge

TYPES OF PRIVATE EQUITY INVESTMENTS

Private Equity investments can be divided into the following categories:

1. Leveraged Buyout: Leveraged buyouts involve a financial sponsor agreeing to an acquisition without itself committing all the capital required for the acquisition. To do this, the financial sponsor will raise acquisition debt which ultimately looks to the cash flows of the acquisition target to make interest and principal payments. Acquisition debt in an LBO is often non-recourse to the financial sponsor and has no claim on other investment managed by the financial sponsor. Therefore, an LBO transaction's financial structure is particularly attractive to a fund's limited partners, allowing them the benefits of leverage but greatly limiting the degree of recourse of that leverage.

2. Venture capital: Venture capital is a broad subcategory of private equity that refers to equity investments made, typically in less mature companies, for the launch, early development, or expansion of a business. Venture investment is most often found in the application of new technology, new marketing concepts and new products that have yet to be proven.

Venture capital is often sub-divided by the stage of development of the company ranging from early stage capital used for the launch of start-up companies to late stage and growth capital that is often used to fund expansion of existing business that are generating revenue but may not yet be profitable or generating cash flow to fund future growth.

Entrepreneurs often develop products and ideas that require substantial capital during the formative stages of their companies' life cycles. Many entrepreneurs do not have sufficient funds to finance projects themselves, and they prefer outside financing. To compensate the risk of failure, venture capitalist's seeks higher return from these investments. Venture Capital is often most closely associated with fast-growing technology and biotechnology fields.

3. Growth capital: Growth capital refers to equity investments, most often significant minority investments, in relatively mature companies that are looking for capital to expand or restructure operations, enter new markets or finance a major acquisition without a change of control of the business.

Companies that seek growth capital will often do so in order to finance a transformational event in their life cycle. These companies are likely to be more mature than venture capital funded companies, able to generate revenue and operating profits but unable to generate sufficient cash to fund major expansions, acquisitions or other investments. The primary owner of the company may not be willing to take the financial risk alone. By selling part of the company to private equity, the owner can takeout some value and share the risk of growth with partners.

4. Distressed and Special Situations: Distressed or Special Situations are a broad category referring to investments in equity or debt securities of financially stressed companies. The "distressed" category encompasses two broad sub-strategies including:

- "Distressed-to-Control" or "Loan-to-Own" strategies where the investor acquires debt securities in the hopes of emerging from a corporate restructuring in control of the company's equity;
- "Special Situations" or "Turnaround" strategies where an investor will provide debt and equity investments, often "rescue financing" to companies undergoing operational or financial challenges.

5. Mezzanine Capital: Mezzanine capital refers to subordinated debt or preferred equity securities that often represent the most junior portion of a company's capital structure that is senior to the company's common equity. This form of financing is often used by private equity investors to reduce the amount of equity capital required to finance a leveraged buyout or major expansion. Mezzanine capital, which is often used by smaller companies that are unable to access the high yield market, allows such companies to borrow additional capital beyond the levels that traditional lenders are willing to provide through bank loans. In compensation for the increased risk, mezzanine debt holders require a higher return for their investment than secured or other more senior lenders.

6. Secondary: Secondary investments refer to investments made in existing private equity assets. These transactions can involve the sale of private equity fund interests or portfolios of direct investments in privately held companies through the purchase of these investments from existing institutional investors. By its nature, the private equity asset class is illiquid, intended to be a long-term investment for buy-and-hold investors. Secondary investments provide institutional investors with the ability to improve vintage diversification, particularly for investors that are new to the asset class. Secondary also typically experience a different cash flow profile, diminishing the effect of investing in new private equity funds. Often investments in secondary are made through third party fund vehicle, structured similar to a fund of funds although many large institutional investors have purchased private equity fund interests through secondary transactions. Sellers of private equity fund investments sell not only the investments in the fund but also their remaining unfunded commitments to the funds.

The Stages of Private Equity: Private Equity investments can be classified into:

- Seed stage financing provided to research, assess and develop an initial concept before a business has reached the start-up phase
- Start-up stage financing for product development and initial marketing.
- Expansion stage financing for growth and expansion of a company which is breaking even or trading profitably.

- Replacement capital purchase of shares from another investor or to reduce gearing via the refinancing of debt.

The above stages can be explained by the diagram which is shown below

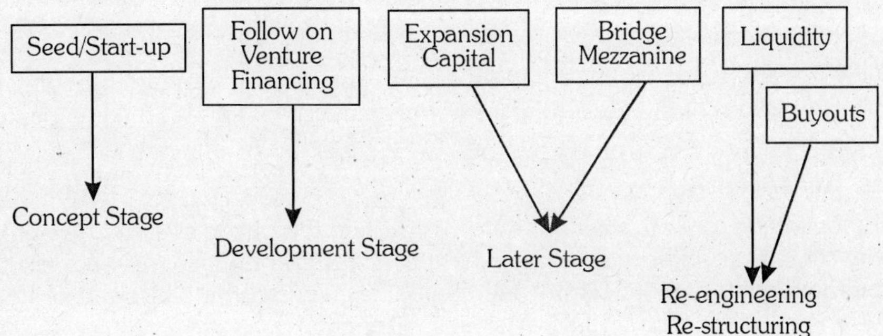

Fig. 6.1: Stage of Private Equity

Process of Private Equity Funds: The Private Equity Process has 6 Steps:

1. Deal Origination (Deal Sourcing): Deal Origination or as some call it 'Deal Sourcing' is how Deal Makers get their deals, a potential deal can either come through a company owner approaching them or from an intermediary who will try to bring both parties (Company and Deal Maker) to make the deal. In some cases, they may just approach companies who are expanding fast and wish to grow further. In a year, Deal Makers come across hundreds of potential deals -but only a few are selected.

2. Due Diligence: Due Diligence is what you could call 'doing your homework'. Before starting detailed negotiations, investor try to make sure everything is fair and secure. Although Auditors and Consultants are appointed to conduct the Financial, Tax, Legal and Technical Due Diligence - they also work side by side to understand the target company and its industry better. All the information collected at this time, is then used during negotiation.

3. Deal Negotiation: At the Deal Negotiation phase, investor set out the terms and conditions (covenants, representations and warranties) and other deal terms that defines (or makes the deal).Contracts such as Investment Agreement, Share Purchase Agreement, Management Agreement, Advisory Agreement, etc., are drafted to include all items that put the deal together.

4. Deal Closing (Acquisition): Deal Closing is probably the easiest part but also contains an element of risk. It's the conclusion of the deal, the signing of all Agreements and transferring funds from the buyer to seller, conducting other administrative functions (usually done by a separate entity) like updating any articles of association etc.

5. Post Acquisition Monitoring: Post Acquisition Monitoring requires the Deal Team (those who have worked on putting the deal together) to closely monitor the company, both from an operational and financial point of view against the expansion plan and budgets that were setup earlier by the company. Improvements to business, from Corporate Governance, Financial Reporting, and Information Flow to Strategy are made at each level through either the company's management or its board

6. Exit (IPO, Trade Sale or Buy back): As the company matures (usually after 2 - 4 years) with the presence of the Deal Team, investor prepare it for an Exit - either an IPO or a Trade Sale (sale to a larger party, multi-national or conglomerate) or in rare cases a Buy Back by the owners. By this time, the company will have grown quite a bit with still plenty of room to grow further. (There's a saying, in a deal - always leave something extra for the person buying – it makes everyone happy.) And once investor have exited the company, they return their money with the profit they gained for company after taking their fees for all the effort put in the above process. Although this may seem like a linear process - it isn't exactly so, primarily because investors deal with a number of companies and each one is at a different stage in the private equity process.

Advantages of Private Equity

Investing in a private equity fund has a lot of advantages compared to other investment areas; here are some advantages of private equity for not only investors but also the companies that private equity firms acquire.

Advantages for Investors

- By definition, private equity firms work outside the public eye and do not have to follow the same transparency standards that public firms and funds must adhere to. This allows private equity firms to reform the companies without the constraint of having to report quarterly to the SEBI, ROC or similar distractions.
- Private equity firms generally perform very rigorous due diligence on potential investments. By utilizing a team of researchers the private equity firm is able to identify most risks that would not otherwise be found.
- The management receives carried interest, a portion of the profits, so managers and their staff are motivated to produce good results to investors. Although carried interest is often criticized for taking money from the investors, it is a very big incentive for managers.
- Economic Scenario — India is one of the fastest growing economies in the world, with enormous growth potential in many industries. This means that capital requirements are high, translating into an ideal hunting ground for PE funds.
- Abundance of skilled labor — India offers a huge advantage in the form of its highly talented and skilled labor pool, which can lead to the success of the firms in which investment is made through the private equity route. The funds are not just bullish about the businesses in India but have also grabbed a fair share of highly rated managers like Vivek Paul, Rajeev Gupta, Avnish Bajaj, Akhil Gupta, and Nikhil Khattau. Private equity funds are invariably on the lookout for high profile managers, not only to manage their own funds but also as their representative on the board of companies in which they have invested.
- Success of several sectors — India has firmly established itself as the world's IT superpower with almost all major software development companies having an Indian development centre. It is also becoming the hub of back office operations, and a leading provider of BPO and KPO services. This has led to greater confidence in the future growth potential of Indian companies Mature Financial markets - Capital markets have stabilized in the recent past with regulators like SEBI keeping a firm watch on the market development. This means both increased opportunities as well as an easier and painless exit route for PE funds. The emergence of entrepreneurs in India who consider private equity their fulltime occupation is also a positive sign. Besides, there are well established corporate houses diversifying their surplus investment, as a strategy for their assets allocation, through PE funds without involving themselves directly in the operations of target companies.
- Successful Mergers and Acquisitions — A recent spate of mergers and acquisitions has given rise to yet another way of exiting from Indian companies for private equity investors.
- Successful track, record — The first generation of private equity players have realized significant success in the last several years. For instance, Warburg Pincus earned huge returns out from its investments in Indian companies like Bharti Telecom.

Advantages for Company

- Private equity managers are paid very well and so it is easy to attract high caliber, experienced managers that tend to perform very well. The same goes for lower level employees at private equity firms, they tend to be the top young business school graduates. This helps the company to utilize best talent in the industry without shelling out even a single penny from its pocket.
- Private equity helps a company to prepare for stock market listing (IPO) as the exit route of investment. It opens up enormous opportunities for companies to raise funds. The continuous scrutiny by stock market participants, SEBI and ROC facilitates efficiency improvement and proper strategic decisions.
- Private equity helps those companies which cannot raise money from the market. By private equity company get money from the investors, which help in the growth of the company.

Disadvantages of Private Equity

Disadvantages for Investors

- Difficulty to access for small and medium investors — Private equity limited partnership funds may only be marketed to institutions and very wealthy individuals; in addition the minimum investment accepted is usually more than £1 mn.
- Relative illiquidity — Private Equity funds normally invest in a unlisted space and they find it difficult to exit the investment at their wish, since it require concentrated efforts to find a suitable investor for unlisted company. Even in the listed space, the impact cost remains very high due to sheer magnitude of scale.
- A long-term investment perspective is necessary to achieve gains for a private equity investment program because the investment program depends on the company growth. It depends on the gap between entry and exit of the investor.
- Political condition – India, being divided into a number of states, causes an investment decision to be affected by politics. Changes in regulation and infrastructure development are often sidelined due to friction and conflict between the state and the federal government.
- Competition from China – China is a direct competitor of India and most of the private equity investors, eyeing the Asian region, draw a comparison across both the countries to decide where their money should be parked. The new state-of-the-art airports in China bear a stark contrast to the abysmal conditions of the terminals in India's main cities.
- High costs – private equity managers charge relatively high fees for managing capital committed by external investors (generally around 2%) and, if the fund performs well, take a sizeable proportion (generally 20%) of realized returns in excess of investment hurdle rates.

Disadvantages for Company

- It is a lengthy process since private equity managers conduct detailed market, financial, legal, environmental and management due diligence, which could take several months before they make final decisions on investing.
- Entrepreneurs have to give up some of their company's shares to a private equity investor, i.e., control. Because investor has some control over the company, so it is not easy for the entrepreneur to take decision independently. He has to take advice of the investor to take decision and it causes delay in the process.

- The private equity managers have control over the timing of a sale of (a part of) the business.
- Lack of promotion in investment across sectors — PE funds are being channelized into only a few sectors like IT, infrastructure and real estate and telecommunications, to the exclusion of the remaining industries, desperately in need of funds for growth.

ROLE OF PRIVATE EQUITY IN INDIA

Growth in India's private equity market has been a short but bumpy ride

The Indian private equity market has grown by leaps and bounds since its humble inception in the late 80s, becoming the second largest Asian Private Equity capital recipient after Japan less than two decades later. Despite a relatively young age, the industry has already seen its fair share of ups and downs. In the late 90s, the dot-com boom in Bangalore fuelled a rapid growth of Venture Capital/Private Equity companies, with the bubble bust ending up wiping most of these players from the market. Demonstrating its resilience, the industry recovered from a deal-value low point of $470 million in 2003, to a peak of $19.03 billion in 2007. In line with the increasing needs to improve India's facilities, the two biggest sectors for Private Equity investment are Real Estate and Infrastructure Management and Telecom. Overall Private Equity deal distribution, however, indicates large investments across varied sectors such as Power, Banking, Pharmaceutical and Media.

The current hot sectors for Private Equity are

- **Education:** Highly attractive with an estimated $40 billion market for private institutions. Over $300 million has been invested in Education ventures since 2006, and more than $800 million investment is being planned over the next 12 months.
- **Health care:** Significant capabilities in India for clinical research. Low average number of hospital beds will bring in massive investment to build more hospitals throughout the country. Over $686 million investment has taken place during the last 18 months.
- **Clean tech or renewable energy:** Dire need for a more reliable power supply throughout the country. Supportive regulations are providing a boost to clean tech/renewable energy. About $3.5 billion Private Equity investment is expected over the next few years.

The Indian Private Equity market is dominated by non-India GPs, even though many large domestic GPs already exist in the market. A key explanation for this phenomenon is the tax regulations, which make it more conducive for GPs to be incorporated outside India. LPs consist of foreign players due to nonexistent Indian endowment funds; Indian pension funds are not permitted to invest in private equity. Indian high net worth investors, on the other hand, prefer to invest in their own businesses or real estate. The Private Equity market in India has revealed a lot of potential but also in India, the economic downturn has caused a sharp fall in total Private Equity activities. 2008 saw a decrease of 44% in Private Equity deal value compared to 2007, while the first half figures for 2009 have not been encouraging as it shows less than 10% deal value of the whole of 2007. Nonetheless, with slowdown in funding from banks and IPOs, Private Equity is expected to remain a primary source of raising capitals in India

In general, drivers of private equity industry growth in India can be identified:

(1) Sustained rapid economic growth averaging 7% - 8% annually since 2000.

(2) Burgeoning domestic customer market with the middle class projected to grow from 50 million currently to 500 million in 2025.

(3) Well-established public equity market consisting of over 6,000 companies listed on Mumbai Stock Exchange with reasonable levels of liquidity and trading volume.

(4) Human capital and competitiveness in high-growth sectors, with one of the best higher education systems in the emerging market and widespread knowledge of English.

(5) Stable democratic government and credible legal framework as its common-law legal origin has provided the foundation for a well-established, credible legal system.

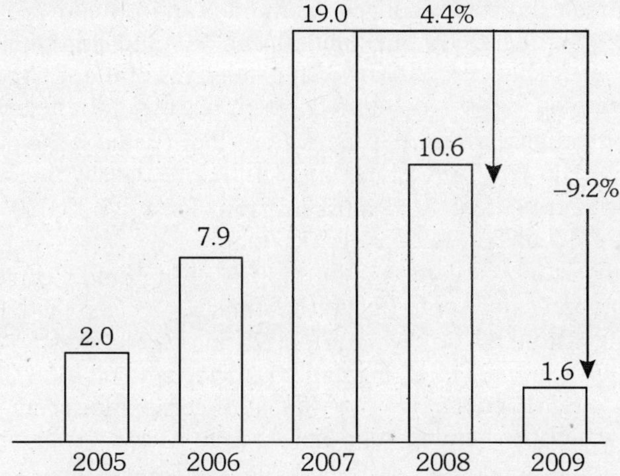

Fig. 6.2: Private equity deal value in India (US$ billion)

THE REGULATORY ENVIRONMENT OF THE PRIVATE EQUITY INDUSTRY IN INDIA

1. The Securities and Exchange Board of India (SEBI) issued its Regulations for Venture Capital in 1996, thus establishing the agency's authority over the funds, the limits on their activities, and incentives for them to finance and rescue troubled companies. There are no legal or regulatory differences between venture capital and private equity firms. The Government first permitted financial institutions (Industrial Development Bank of India, ICICI, and IFCI), commercial banks (including foreign banks), and subsidiaries of commercial banks to establish venture capital companies under guidelines issued in 1988. In addition, under current central bank regulations, banks' investments in mutual funds catering to venture capital funding are considered to be outside the ceilings applicable to banks' investments in corporate equity and debt.

2. Foreign venture capital funds have been permitted to operate in India since 1995. They may either hold the shares of unlisted Indian companies directly (up to a maximum of 25% of equity) or route their investments through domestic venture capital funds and companies. Before guidelines were issued in September 2000, direct exposure by offshore private equity funds in shares of unlisted companies was treated as a foreign direct investment and had to be approved in line with the Government's general policy on foreign investments. Indocean Venture Fund (now Indocean Chase), originally set up by George Soros and Chemical Bank in October 1994, was the first such overseas private equity fund.

3. The regulatory environment for the private equity industry was simplified in 1995–2000. Foreign institutional investors participated in the growth of the private equity industry through the foreign direct investment regulations of the Government and the simplified tax administration procedures under the Indo-Mauritius Double Taxation Avoidance Treaty. While the foreign direct investment route offered minimum investment restrictions for private equity funds, exit pricing and repatriation of capital were regulated by the Reserve Bank of India (RBI). To bring these capital flows under the regulation of the venture capital industry, new SEBI regulations were issued with simplified exit pricing and repatriation procedures for foreign investors.

4. Following amendments to the 2000 budget, the Government has allowed private equity funds "pass-through" status, meaning that the distributed or undistributed income of the funds is not

taxed. To avoid double taxation, the income of a private equity fund is taxed only in the hands of the investor.

5. SEBI was also made the sole regulatory authority, and private equity funds must submit quarterly reports to it. In September 2000 SEBI announced the guidelines that now govern venture capital investment, based on the January 2000 recommendations of the Chandrashekhar committee on venture capital. After another set of amendments in April 2004, the following rules now apply:

(i) Foreign venture capital investors can invest in India without the need for approval from the Foreign Investment Promotion Board if they register with SEBI.

(ii) Each investor in a venture fund must invest at least ₹ 500,000, and each fund must have at least ₹ 50 million in capitals.

(iii) A fund may invest in one company up to 25% of the fund's capital. It cannot invest in associated companies of ventures that it finances.

(iv) A fund must invest 66.67% (lowered from 75% in April 2004) of its investable funds in unlisted equity or equity-linked instruments. The remaining 33.3% can be invested in subscriptions to initial public offerings (IPOs) of companies or in debt instruments of a company in which the venture fund has already made an equity investment.

(v) The April 2004 amendments removed the previous 1-year lockup period for IPO subscriptions. They also allowed investments within the 33.3% category in preferential allotments of equity shares of a listed company, subject to a 1-year lock-in, and in equity shares or equity-linked instruments of a listed company that is financially weak.

(vi) The removal of the profitability criterion as a listing requirement had an important effect on the private equity industry as it provided an exit mechanism for investors. To replace the profitability requirement, a firm would be de-listed if it did not earn a profit within 3 years of listing.

(vii) The acquisition of shares in a venture fund by the investee company or its promoters is exempt from the provisions of the takeover code and will therefore not mandate an open offer.

(viii) Mutual funds may invest 5% of the capital of an open-ended scheme and 10% of the capital of a closed-ended scheme in a venture fund.

(ix) In April 2004 the SEBI also removed some previous restrictions and allowed venture funds to invest in real estate companies, gold financing companies, and equipment leasing and hire-purchase companies registered with the RBI.

6. These regulations have significantly improved the regulatory environment for private equity funds operating in India, such as BTS India Private Equity Fund. In addition, they reflect the strong commitment of the Indian Government to support the provision of long-term equity finance to domestic entrepreneurial companies.

Selection of Investment: The first step in VCF decision is the selection of investment. The starting point of the evaluation process by the VCI (Institution) in the business plan of the VC undertaking (promotes). The appraisal is a kin to the feasibility studies of the development finance institutions for grant of term loans and other financial assistance.

The selection of the investment proposal includes inter-alia stages of financing method to evaluate deals and the financial instrument of structures a deal.

Stages of Financing

The selection of investments by a venture capital institutions is closely related to the stages and type of investment from analytical, the different stages of investments are recognized and vary as regards. The time scales risk perceptions, and other related characteristics of the investment decision process of the venture capital institutions. The stages of financing as differentiated in the venture capital industry, broadly fall into two categories.

I. Early State Financing: This states includes *(i)* Seed capital pre start-up. *(ii)* Start-up and *(iii)* Second round financing.

(a) **Seed Capital:** This stage is essentially an applied research' phase where the concepts and ideas of the promoters constitute the basis of a pre-commercialization research project usually expected to end in a prototype which may or may not lead to a business launch. This phase gradually move towards the development phase leading to a prototype product testing and then to commercialization. The evaluation of the project by the Venture Capital Institutions has to ensure that the technology skills of the entrepreneurs match with market opportunities.

The main risk at this stage is marketing related. The commercial acumen of the promoter to take advantage of the market opportunity, awareness of competitions, the timing of launching the product and so on, is important elements of the appraisal. The risk perception of investment at this stage is extremely high. However, very few Venture Capital Institutions in this pre-commercialization/ seed stage of product development.

(b) **Start–Up:** This is the stage when commercial manufacturing has to commence. Venture capital financing here is provided for product development and initial marketing. The essence of this stage is that the product/service is being commercialized for the first time in association with the venture capital institutions. It includes several types of new projects such as *(i)* Greenfield based on a relatively new or high technology *(ii)* New business in which the entrepreneurs has good knowledge and working experience *(iii)* New projects by established companies and *(iv)* A new company promoted by an existing company with limited finance to commercialize new technology.

At this stage some indication of the potential market for the new product/services is available. Partly because of the equity dilution syndrome, in the sense of resistance from the promoters to the dilution of control of the business, and partly due to the unavailability of the small amount of equity investment, the involvement of the Venture Capital Institutions in start up project is generally and relatively low. The risk perception is very high.

(c) **Second Round Financing:** This represents the stage at which the product has already been launched in the market but the business has not, yet, become profitable enough for public offering to attract new investors. The promoters have invested their own funds but further infusion of funds by the Venture Capital Institutions is necessary. The time scale for the investment is shorter than in the case of start up. The Venture Capital Institutions provide larger funds at this stage than at other early stage. This financing is partly in the form of debt it also provide some income to them

II. Later Stage Financing: This stage of venture capital financing involves established business which requires additional financial support but cannot take recourse to public issues of capital. It includes:

(a) **Mezzanine/Development Capital:** This is financing the established businesses which have overcome the extremely high risk early stage, have recorded profits for a few years but are yet to reach a stage when they can go public to raise money from the capital market/conventional sources.

Among the uses of such types of VCI are purchases of new equipment/plant, expansion of marketing and distribution facilities, refinance of existing debt, penetration into new region, induction of new management and so on. The development finance stage has a time frame of one to three years and falls in the medium risk category. It constitutes a significant part of the activities of many Venture Capital Investors.

(*b*) **Bridge/Expansion:** This finance by Venture Capital Investors involves low risk perception and a time frame of 1-3 years. Venture capital undertakings use such finance to expand business by way of growth of their own productive asset or by the acquisition of other firms/assets of other firms. In a way, it represents the last round of financing before a planned exit.

(*c*) **Buy Outs:** These refers to the transfer of management control. They fall into two categories.

(*i*) **Management Buy outs:** In management buy outs venture capital institutions provide funds to enable the current operating management/investors to acquire on existing product line/business. They represent on important part of the activity of venture capital institutions.

(*ii*) **Management Buy Ins:** Management buy ins are funds provided to enable an outside group (of manager) to buy an ongoing company. They usually bring three elements together, a management teams, a target company and an investor (VCI) management buy ins are less popular than management buy outs. An MBI is inherently more risky because the management comes from outside and find it difficult to assess the actual potential of the target company. Generally management buy ins are able to target only the weaker/under performing companies.

Buyouts involve a time frame from investment to public offering of one to three years with low risk perceptions.

(*d*) **Turn around:** These area sub-set of buyouts and involve buying the control of a risk company. Two kinds of inputs are required in a turnaround. Money and management. The Venture Capital Investors have to identify good management and operations leadership. Such form of VCI involves medium to high risk and a time frame of 3-5 years. It is gaining widespread acceptance and increasingly becoming the focus of attention of venture capital institutions.

To conclude venture capital firms finances both early and later stage investments to maintain a trade off between risk and profitability. In early stage investment, particularly startups in high technology industries the technology is often untried at the commercial level of operations market is underdeveloped and potential competition, is unknown as the product itself is new. Apart from the evaluation of the technology and the likely market the most important factor to be considered by Venture Capital Institutions is the capability of the promoter/entrepreneurs implement the project with reasonable channels of success.

In later stage investment, the technology has already been tried out commercially, the products have been introduced in the market and the business entrepreneur has a track record which is closely examined by the venture capital institutions.

Financial Analysis of Venture Capital

Venture capital investments are generally **idea-based** and **growth-based** which are **asset-based**. While the later type are generally valued on the basis of tangible assets/future earnings stream, the former have to lie in the nature of things valued differently in order to decide the required venture capital percentage ownership of the Venture Capital Investors in venture capital undertaking. Some of the valuation methods of VCI are:

1. **Conventional Venture Capitalist Valuation Method:** This method of valuation of venture capital understanding (VCUs) investee companies (ICs) takes into account only two points of time in the life of the VCI, namely the starting time of investment and the exit time when the investments would be liquidated through sale of public/third party and so on. The sequence of steps in the valuation of the VCUs and the determination of the % share ownership of the Venture Capital Investors in ICS are

(a) To compute the annual revenue at the time of liquidation of the investments, the present annual revenue in the beginning is compounded by an expected annual growth rate for the holding period say 7 years.

(b) Compute the expected earning level that is equal to future earnings level multiplied by after tax margin percentage at the time of liquidation.

(c) Compute the future market valuation of the VCU that is equal to earnings level multiplied by expected P/E ratio on the date of liquidation.

(d) Obtain the present value of the ICs using suitable discount factor and

(e) If the present value of the VCU is ₹ 50 lakh and the entrepreneur want ₹ 20 lakh as the VC from the Venture Capital Investors minimum 20% of ownership required is two fifth 2/5 (40%).

The weakness of this method is that it ignores the stream of earning (losses) during the entire period and over-emphasizes the one exit date.

2. The First Chicago Method: This method is an improvement over the conventional method of valuation to the extent it gives allowance the nature of the path between the starting point and the exit point/date and considers the entire earnings stream. The steps involved in the valuation program.

(i) Three alternative scenarios, are perceived/considered, namely "**Success, 'sideways survival and failure'**. Each one of these is assigned a probability rating.

(ii) Using a discount rate the discounted present value of the VCU is computed. The discount rate is substantially higher to reflect risk dimension.

(iii) The discounted present value is multiplied by the respective probabilities. The expected present value of the VCU is equal to the total of these in the three alternative scenarios.

(iv) Assuming expected present value of the VCU at ₹ 5 crore and the fund requirement from the Venture Capital Investors as ₹ 2.5 Crore the minimum ownership required is 50% (half).

3. Revenue Multiplies Method: A revenue multiplies is a factor that can be used to estimate the value of a VCU. By multiplying that factor the annual revenue of the company is estimated by Venture Capital Investors symbolically.

$$M_t = \frac{V}{R} = \frac{(1+r)^n\,(a)\,(p)}{(1+d)^n}$$

V = Present value of the VCU.

R = Annual Revenue Level.

R = Expected annual rate of growth of revenue.

N = Expected no. of years from starting date to exit date (holding period).

A = After tax profit margin % at the time of exit.

P = Expected price/earning (P/E) ratio at exit time.

D = Appropriate discount rate for a venture investment at this stage risk and other.

This method an be used in the case of early stage/start up VCI when earning based on after tax profit.

Need and Relevance of VCF: Venture capital fund is usually used to denote institutional investors that provide equity finance or risk capital to little known, unregistered, highly risky, young and small private business, especially in technology oriented and knowledge intensive businesses or industries which have long development cycles and which usually do not have access to conventional sources of capital because of the absence of suitable collateral and the presence of high risk. The venture capital funds lay an important role in supplying management and marketing expertise also to such units.

Need: The venture capital funds provide seed capital and development capital for new enterprise and development capital to established enterprises. Broadly venture capital funds activities included.

(a) Seed capital for industrial start ups.
(b) Additional capital to new businesses at various stages of their growth.
(c) Bridge finance,
(d) Equity financing or leverage buy out financing to management groups for taking over other companies.
(e) Capital to new entrepreneur in foreign operation.
(f) Capital to mature enterprises for expansion, diversification and restructuring.

IMPORTANT VENTURE CAPITAL FINANCING INSTITUTIONS AND THEIR SCHEMES IN INDIA

Industrial Development Bank of India's Venture Capital Fund: IDBI's Technology Division Venture Capital Fund was set up in 1986. Under this scheme, assistance is available to all industrial concerns, both existing and new units. The assistance is generally was started with an initial capital of ₹ 10 crore and is a part of the technology department of the IDBI. It is meant primarily to assist projects which promote commercial application of indigenously developed technology or which adapt imported technology for wider applications. It assists high technology, small and medium styled projects with a maximum total cost or ₹ 2.5 crore. Such projects must employ technology that is new and untested in Indian conditions, financial assistance is provided right from the pilot state and covers up to 90% of the total cost, mostly in the form of equity and for conditional loans, where the return is in the form of royalty on sales, after commercial success. In specific terms, the assistance to the project may vary between ₹ 5 lakhs and ₹ 250 lakhs and may cover both capital and operating expenditure.

VCF of UTI: In 1988-89, the UTI set up a VCF of ₹ 20 crores in collaboration with the ICICI for fostering industrial development. Technology Development and Information Company of India. Ltd (TDICI) established by the UTI jointly, with the ICICI acts as an advises and manager of the fund. The UTI launched VC unit scheme to raise resources for this fund. It set up a second VC fund in March 1990 with a capital of ₹ 100 crore, with the objective of financing green field ventures and starting industrial development.

IFCI Venture Capital Funds Ltd. (IVCF)

IFCI Venture Capital Funds Ltd. (IFCI Venture) was originally set up by IFCI as a Society by the name of Risk Capital Foundation (RCF) in 1975, to provide institutional support to first generation professionals and technocrats setting up their own ventures in the medium scale sector through soft loans, under the Risk Capital Scheme. In 1988, RCF was converted into a company, Risk Capital and Technology Finance Corporation Ltd. (RCTC), when it also introduced the Technology Finance and Development Scheme for financing development and commercialization of indigenous technology. Based on IFCI Venture's credentials and strengths, UTI entrusted it with the management of a new venture capital fund named **Venture Capital Unit Scheme** in 1991. The size of VECAUS-III was Rs.80 crores, contributed by UTI and IFCI. To reflect the shift in the company's activities, the name of RCTC was changed to IFCI Venture Capital Funds Ltd. (IFCI Venture) in February 2000.

Over the years, IFCI Venture acquired expertise and experience of investing in technology-oriented and innovative projects. Since its inception, it has provided finance to over 350 ventures and supported commercialization of over 50 new technologies. It has pioneered effort for widening entrepreneurial base in the country and catalysed the introduction of Venture Capital activity in India.

IFCI Venture Capital Funds Limited (IFCI Venture) has launched three new funds in emerging sectors of the economy namely:

(i) India Automotive Component Manufacturers Private Equity Fund –1-Domestic (IACM-1-D) with a target corpus of Euro 60 million equivalent to ₹ 396 crores. This Fund will be dedicated for investment mainly in Indian Automotive Component companies and in other related/emerging sectors.

(ii) India Enterprise Development Fund (IEDF), a Venture Capital fund set up with target corpus of ₹ 250 crores to invest in knowledge based projects in key sectors of Indian economy with outstanding growth prospects.

(iii) Green India Venture Fund (GIVF), a Venture Capital fund setup with a target corpus of Euro 50 million (approx. ₹ 330 crores) with the objective to invest in commercially viable Clean Development Mechanism (CDM), energy efficient and other commercially viable projects with an aim to reduce negative ecological impact, efficient usage of resources such as energy, power etc and other related sectors/projects.

IFCI Venture has already received in principle approval from SEBI for the three funds. IFCI Venture with its background and experience is confident of generating good returns out of these funds.

SIDBI Venture Capital Funds

SVCL is a wholly owned subsidiary of State Industrial Bank of India (SIDBI), incorporated in 1999. SVCL's main aim/mission is to work upon the entrepreneurship idea by providing adequate capital and strategic inputs at various stages of the business for all round growth opportunities and also maximize the returns on investment. SVCL being a venture capital fund is regulated by SEBI (Venture Capital Fund) Regulations, 1996. Presently SVCL has two portfolios/funds with them, *viz.*, National Venture Fund for Software and IT Industry (NSFIT) The National Venture Fund for Software and Information Technology Industry has been set up by Small Industries Development Bank of India (SIDBI) in association with Ministry of Information Technology (MIT), Govt. of India during 1999-2000 and The SME Growth Fund (SGF) has been set up by Small Industries Development Bank of India (SIDBI) in association with other leading commercial banks such as Punjab National Bank, State Bank of India, Bank of Baroda, Bank of India, Central Bank of India, Union Bank of India, Oriental Bank of Commerce and Corporation Bank. Investments cover various diversified sectors such as engineering, information/communication technology, biotech, pharma etc.

National Venture Fund for Software and IT Industry (NSFIT): The National Venture Fund for Software and IT Industry (NSFIT) has been set up by SIDBI and managed by SVCL. The total value of the fund is ₹ 1000 million (US $ 22.22 million). Out of this half or ₹ 500 million has been contributed by SIDBI, a third portion, i.e., ₹ 300 million by Ministry of Information Technology, GOI and the rest ₹ 200 million by IDBI.

The fund primarily focuses on small scale units in information and communication technology like data centers, value added telecommunication service, networking, etc., which have the potential to grow with adequate provisioning of capital and expertise.

A part of the fund has also been earmarked for incubation projects which are high risk in nature and development of products, for whose evaluation a certain degree of expertise is required and also international exposure. This would in turn help the IT units to achieve success and growth at a rapid pace. SVCL may invest in the project various stages like startup, expansion and diversification, product developments etc.

The portfolio of the fund includes investments in Compulink, E-Cube India Solutions Ltd (it provides Smart Card Solutions), IndiaIdeas.com Ltd (an e-bill presentment and payment service in India, Indus Teqsite Pvt Ltd (manufacturer of Advanced test equipment, and rud-degised application in defense, aviation and space) etc.

Some of the other companies which were part of the fund are Axiom Consulting, Karrox Technologies, MutualFundsIndia.com, Parsec Technologies etc.

SME Growth Fund (SGF)

SVCL's SME Growth Fund was initiated to meet the venture capital requirements of SME units and enable them achieve success and growth along with the emerging sectors. The fund has a total value of ₹ 500 crore. It is registered with SEBI as a VCF (Venture Capital Fund) and it makes equity or equity related investments in growth oriented businesses which have significant market activity in India. The fund is aimed to gain capital appreciation over a long term horizon for its investors.

The fund's main focus or thrust area is to invest in unlisted entities in MSME in both manufacturing and service sector. It also provides infrastructure and allied services to these companies. Investment by SGF is mainly done during start up and second round of financing. The sectors in focus of the fund are engineering, life sciences, IT, food processing, healthcare etc.The fund for making an investment in a particular company first looks at its management, i.e., how committed and strong they are; long term capital appreciation, growth potential of business along with long term competitive advantage; sound and practical business plan; and most importantly a clear exit route available to the fund. If all these conditions are satisfied the fund makes investment in the company.

The major portfolio of the fund is comprised of engineering, service and supply chain and logistics companies. At present SIDBI plans to launch a ₹ 1,000 crore venture capital (VC) fund aiming at the high growth industries.

The SVCL strategy to provide funds for SME's will help to increase its returns this is because SME's has high potential to grow which will help SVCL to increase its investments for e.g. in last fiscal it was able to disbursements ₹ 32,000 crore and now the current target disbursements during the current financial year is ₹ 41,000 crore. This shows that the investments made by the SVCL are able to fetch higher returns.

SVCL focuses mainly on meeting growth risk capital needs of MSMEs operating in emerging sectors. However it has also been found that SVCL does not invest in Real Estate. If it starts its investments in Real Estate it may be able to increase returns because similar to SME's even Real Estate have high potentials. However, at present it should just keep the strategy ready to enter into real estate and enter when the Real Estate market is down.

SME growth funds

Venture Funds are recognized globally as the most suitable form of providing risk capital to innovative and high technology businesses. In order to meet the venture capital needs of SME units and enable them to achieve rapid growth by taking advantage of opportunities in the emerging sectors, SIDBI Venture Capital Ltd. has set up. The fund has a targeted corpus of ₹ 500 crore with a life of 8 years.

SME growth funds is registered with Securities and Exchange Board of India (SEBI) as a Venture Capital Fund and has been structured as a unit scheme to make primarily equity or equity-related investments in the growth oriented businesses having significant business activity in India. The Fund seeks to achieve attractive risk-adjusted returns for its contributors through long-term capital appreciation.

Investment Funds

SME growth fund's focus is to invest in unlisted entities in the small and medium enterprises in manufacturing as well as services sector and also businesses providing infrastructure or other support to small and medium enterprises. The Fund may also invest very selectively in listed entities, to take advantage of attractive opportunities in growing companies.

The Fund will typically invest in companies at early stage as well as in second round financing for those with a track record of proven technology or business model and opportunities for growth and earnings.

SME growth fund will focus at wide range of growth sectors, such as life sciences, retailing, light engineering, food processing, information technology, infrastructure related services, health care, logistics and distribution, etc.

Mode of Investment

SME growth fund provides financial assistance primarily by way of equity or equity-linked capital investment. It shall also endeavor to provide mentoring support and other value addition to enable the funded companies to achieve rapid growth and achieve/maintain their competitive edge in domestic and international markets.

The Fund will seek a strategic stake in the funded companies with broad representation and other rights as venture capital investor.

Investment criteria

SME growth funds is looking for investment in projects offering potential for attractive growth and earnings. Key criteria for project selection are –

- *Strong and committed core team:* The Fund will look for businesses managed by a team with a demonstrated performance track record, commitment and energy.
- *Growth potential:* The Fund will like to invest in promising businesses having potential for sustainable high growth.
- *Long-term competitive advantage:* The Fund will prefer to invest in innovative business operations with a sustainable competitive advantage.
- *Viable business plan:* The venture should have a viable business plan which offers above average profitability leading to attractive return on investment.
- *A Clear exit plan:* The Fund, being of limited life, will seek to invest in ventures offering a strategy for clear exit within a reasonable time period. The exit could be by way of IPO, offer for sale, merger and acquisition or sale to a strategic or a financial investor.

Technology Development and Information Company TDICI: It provides assistance to industries directly or through venture funds, which are managed by it for other institutions and venture funds out of its own resources. It was incorporated under companies Act by ICICI and UTI in July 1988 with a view to promoting technological development through transfer and up gradation of technology and through providing technology information it aims are (a) to develop indigenous technology (b) to develop technologists entrepreneurship (c) to support (commercial) Research and Development activities and technological innovations (d) to spread technology information. It provides assistance in the form of grants, conditional loans, Venture Capital equipment support, techno, managerial guidance equipment support, techno, managerial guidance. It has also launched a Technology Information Service (TIS), to develop value added technology and techno consultancy commercial support various industries and institutions in India.

Risk Capital and Technology Finance Corporations Ltd (RCTFC): The IFCI sponsored in 1985, the RCF Risk Capital Foundation to give positive encouragement to new entrepreneur. The RCF was converted into RCIFC on 12 January 1988. It provides both risk capital and technology finance under one roof to innovative entrepreneurs and technocrats for their technology oriented ventures. Most of the projects it has assisted have been forced either on new technology as on new usages of existing technology. They included business manufacture of antibiotic, drugs, radio paging system pay phones etc.

Credit Capital Venture Fund(India Ltd) (CCVF): It was launched in 1989 and it is the second VCF in the private sector in India. It is a joint venture of credit capital finances corporation (a private sector merchant bank in India). It initial capital of ₹ 10 crore was subscribed by Public and other financial institutions. Its thrust area are small export, oriented units and ancillary units. Apart from capital, it provides 'hand-on' management support to the projects.

VCFs of Commercial Banks: ANZ Grindlays Bank has set up India's first private sector VC funds, namely India Investment Fund with an initial capital of ₹ 10 crore subscribed by NRIs the fund provide start up share capital to new ventures and also to their promoters. It also invests in fresh issues of established companies with a good performance record. The objective of the fund is to achieve high capital growth for its investors by participating in fast growing companies or high technology companies with potential for high growth.

Among the Indian banks the subsidiaries of SBI and Canara bank has floated VCFs. They provide either equity capital or conditional loans. The projects assisted by them belong to industries like watches, seamless metal, cement and ceramics.

Structuring VCF: The structuring of VCF refers to the financial instruments through which VC investment is made. The availability of a wide variety of financial instruments provide considerable flexibility in structuring a VCF. The financial instruments of VCI can choose from, can be broadly divided into equity and debt instruments.

Equity Instruments:

(1) Ordinary equity shares
(2) Non-voting equity shares which are entitled to a higher dividend but carry no voting rights.
(3) Deferred ordinary shares on which the ordinary share rights are deferred for a specified period until the happening of a certain event such as listing of shares on the stock exchange or sale of the company.
(4) Preferred ordinary shares. In addition to the voting rights such shares also carry rights to a modest fixed dividend.
(5) Equity warrants entitle investors in debenture/bonds to acquire ordinary shares at a future date.
(6) Preference shares.
(7) Cumulative convertible preference share which are converted into equity shares after a specified time.
(8) Participating preference shares which, in addition to the preference dividend, are entitled to an extra dividend after the payment of dividend to the equity shareholders.
(9) Cumulative convertible participatory preferred ordinary shares combines the benefits of preferred dividend and cumulative as well as participative features.
(10) Convertible cumulative redeemable preferences shares have elements, convertibility into equity at specified point of time and redeem-ability on the expiry of a certain period. The redeemable part carries a fixed coupon rate by way of preference dividend.

Debt Instruments: To ensure that the entrepreneur retains managerial control and the VCI receives a running yield during the early years when the equity portion is unlikely to yield any return, debt instruments are also used by VCIs. They includes.

(a) **Conditional Loan:** This is a form of finance without any pre-determined repayment schedule or interest rate the supplier of such loans recover a specified percentage of sales towards the recovery of the principal as well as revenue in a pre-determined ratio, usually 50:50 the changes on sales is known as **Royalty**. The investor stands to gain/lose depending on whether the actual sales are higher/lower than the projected sales. Conditional loan, in a sense is quasi equity instrument.

(b) **Conventional Loan:** These are modified to the requirement of VCF. They carries lower interest initially which increases after commercial production commences. A small royalty is additionally charged to cover the interest foregone during the initial years. Although the repayments of the principal is based on a pre-stipulated schedule, Venture Capital Investors usually do not insist upon mortgage other security.

(c) **Income Notes:** These fall between the conventional and the conditional loans and carry a uniform low rate of interest plus a royalty on sales. The principal is repaid according to stipulated schedule.

(d) **Non-Convertible Debentures (NCDs):** These carry a fixed/variable rate of interest, are redeemable at part/premium are secured, and can be cumulative/non – cumulative.

(e) **Party Convertible Debentures (PCPs):** These have two components. (i) a convertible portion and (ii) a non-convertible portion. The convertible portion is converted into equity shares at par/premium. The non-convertible portion earns interest till redemption generally at part. Such instruments are best suited to second round venture capital financing.

(f) **Zero Interest/Coupon Bonds Debentures:** These can be either convertible or non-convertible with zero/no interest rate. The non-convertible bonds are sold at a discount from their maturity value while the convertible ones are converted into equity shares at a stipulated price and time. They offer considerable flexibility and are an appropriate instrument for later stage venture capital financing.

(g) **Secured Premium Notes:** These are secured, redeemable at premium in lump-sum/installments, have zero interest and carry a warrant which equity shares can be acquired. This instruments is also useful for later stage financing.

(h) **Deep Discount Bonds:** These are issued at a large discount to their maturity value. As a long-term instrument there are not suited to venture capital investment.

INVESTMENT NURTURING/AFTER CARE

Unlike the conventional financial institutions, which normally keep aloof from the management and operation of the assisted concerned, Venture Capital Investors have an active, intimate and constant ongoing involvement during the entire life of the investment in VCUs. The enduring relationship between the Venture Capital Investors and VCUs and the active role by the former in the management which is termed as **investment nurturing/after care**. The main elements are:

(1) After the stage of investment decisions, provision of continuing guidance and support to optimize the benefits of investment to both Venture Capital Investors and VCUs.

(2) Building of joint relationship to tackle operational and other problems of business.

(3) Protection of the investment / interest of the VCIs.

Investment nurturing differs from the investment monitoring by the conventional financial institutions which collect and use specific information about the operation of the assisted project, where as the former is wider in coverage to include the provision of guidance and skills of the management of the ventures.

Nurturing Methodologies

1. Hands on Nurturing: It refers to continuous and constant involvement in the operations of the investee company which is institutionalized in the form of representation on the board of directors. With wider exposure and experience, Venture Capital Investors can provide useful guidance on aspects of long term business planning, technology developments financial planning, marketing strategy. The hands on case is useful in early stage financing, i.e., seed capital and start up investments. This type of care is provided either by the in-house expertise or by a core group of external advisors/ experts in specific areas if the former is not available in all types of projects.

2. Hands of Nurturing: Venture Capital Investors play a relatively passive role in the hands of nurturing. Although they usually reserve the right, they rarely have nominee directors on the boards of the VCUs. Normally, they do not actively participate in formulating strategies/policy matters in spite of the right to do so. This type of nurturing is appropriate in case of syndicate joint venture financing in which some financiers may follow the hands-on approach while others may follow the hands-off approach. The hands-off may be appropriate after the initial plan of the venture is over and the business is running smoothly.

3. Hands Holding Nurturing: This is mid-way between hands-on and hands-off nurturing. It is, essentially a reactive approach. Like the hands-on style, the VCI has the right to have a nominee on the board of directors of the VCU, but actively participates in the decision making process. Only on being approached by the latter. If the VCU experiences any difficulty, the VCI provides either in house assistance or assistance from outside experts.

Objectives of Nurturing: *(i)* To ensure the proper utilization of assistance provided, any deviation from the program/appraisal should be within the prior approval of the VCI. *(ii)* To ensure the implementation of the venture within the time and cost envisages, *(iii)* In case of time and costs over runs beyond the control of the VCU, to assist in finding additional finance. *(iv)* To provide strategic inputs in technology production, finance, marketing, personnel and so on. *(v)* To anticipate likely problems and advice preventive/remedial actions. *(vi)* To ensure that the venture does not default in any statutory obligations *(vii)* To evaluate the performance of the projects and suggest measures for improvement. *(viii)* To use the feedback received during the course of nurturing the investment for studying the problems and finding suitable solution. *(ix)* To utilize the experience gained for a better appraisal of new ventures.

Techniques

(1) ***Personal Discussion:*** Obtaining information from a VCU is personal/informal discussion with entrepreneurs. It is useful when the venture is facing operational problems.

(2) ***Periodic Reports:*** Venture Capital Investors receive periods reports about the operation of project and analyzed if the projected and actual performance should be compared to follow up.

(3) ***Plant Visits:*** It refers to the collection of information from on the spot visit of the plant site at the implementation stage. The purpose is to review the progress of the project it involves the following aspects.

- The staffing pattern of the production, marketing, finances and personal department.
- Operational performance of the projects.
- Marketing aspects product acceptance, penetration, distribution, pricing, product awareness, advertising competition etc.
- Management of accounts with special reference to over dues of receivables.
- Proper costing of products and efficient control of inventory.
- Positions regarding statutory liabilities and
- Labor relations.

(4) ***Feedback through Nominee Directors:*** The nominee directors, not only protect the interest of the VCIs, but they are also expected of effectively contribute to the management and provide requisite guidance. They should also ensure that the business is run on a several basis. They should be able to anticipate problem and suggest solutions. The nominee directors should have a good exposure to industry, have adequate knowledge about technological development, change in government policies, financial management, laws and regulations.

(5) ***Commissioned Studies:*** If VCUs are not performing well/experiencing difficulties which cannot be solved by Venture Capital Investors themselves special studies may be commissioned to identify problem and offer solutions so that preventive action can be taken.

Valuation of Venture Capital Portfolio

The venture capital portfolio has to be valued from time to time to monitor and evaluate the performance of the venture capital investment that is, whether, there has been an appreciation in the value of the investment or otherwise. The portfolio, valuation techniques depend on the type of investments, namely, equity and debt instruments. These in turn, depend on the stage of investment, seed, start up, early and later stages of the venture.

(1) **Equity Investment:** The value of equity holding is recorded at the historical cost of acquisition until it is disposed of. Although simple, objective and easy to understand it does not indicate a fair value of investment does not reflect management performance and may result in two values for equity acquired at two different points in time. It does not provide a satisfactory basis of valuation of venture capital investment.

(2) **Market Value-based Methods:** Such method can be divided into

(a) **Quoted Market Value:** This is based on market quotation of securities. It is, therefore, relevant only to organisations, listed on stock exchanges. Moreover, market values may not be available for infrequently traded shares. In addition, if the holdings of Venture Capital Investors are substantially large, the realizable value on the market may be considerably lower than the quoted valued. In the foregoing situations, the market value may not reflect the real valuation. Therefore an appropriate discount should be applied to the quoted price while valuing the portfolio. This approach is better than the cost based approach for evaluation of a venture portfolio.

(b) **Fair Market Value Method:** This considers the fair price as the basis of portfolio valuation and is used where the quoted market value does not reflect the correct value of the venture capital investment. It refers to the price that would be agreed upon in an open and unrestricted market between fully informed knowledgeable and willing parties at an arms length without constraints.

It is based on the assumption that "assets are worth what they can earn". In operational terms a representative rate level of earnings is selected and capitalized by an appropriate multi-policy/capitalization rate which provides a reasonable return on the basis of the estimated future earnings and degree of risk.

Stages of Investments: The methods of portfolio valuation of shares depend on the stage of venture capital investment. From the view point of stages of investment, the equity investments falls into 3 broad categories.

(a) **Unquoted Venture Investments**: It can be defined as investments in immature companies, namely, seed, start up and early stage, until the companies stabilize and grow. They should generally be valued at cost as their market value is not available.

They may, however, have to be written up (valued at higher than cost) or written down in (assigned a lower value than cost).

(b) **Unquoted Development Investments:** These are investments in companies with a profit record and where an exit can be reasonably foreseen. They also do not have a market value. The basis of valuation is cost and bared on suitable P/E ratio applied to earnings of the venture, suitability discounted to take care of the limited marketability of the unquoted nature of investment.

(c) **Quoted Investments:** Quoted investments in companies which have achieved a possible exit by floatation of issues. They are valued at market quotation. In case of restriction limitations on the sale of shares a suitable discount should be applied to the market value of the shares. The rate of discount depend on the size and depth of the market, period of applicability etc.

(3) **Debt Instruments:** Venture Capital Investors provide in addition to equity capital, debt finance, from the point of view of their valuation as a part of the overall portfolio (fund) they are divided into.

(a) **Convertible Debit:** Debt instruments are generally valued at cost. But convertible debts are converted into equity at a specified price and time. They should, therefore be valued in the case of Venture Capital Investors on the same basis as equity investment. There are two appropriate methods for valuing them, that is,

(i) **Market Value Method:** This is appropriate for quoted convertible debt investments on the basis of the same principles as are applicable to quoted investments. A modified/refined version of this approach is the use of the moving average/weighted average of the market values of the investments at the end of pre-determined number of periods as the basis of valuation of convertibles. The use of this methods retains the benefit of the market value method and also the effects of temporary fluctuations re minimized as the average value represents the long term value of investments.

(ii) **Fair Value Method:** Under this method investment are originally recorded at cost and are reported at fair value. Dividends are reported as other revenues and gains. Under the equity method, investments are originally recorded at cost. Subsequently, the investment account is adjusted for the investor's share of the investee's net income or loss and this amount is recognized in the income of the investor. Dividents received from the investee are reductions in the investment account.

(b) **Non-Convertible Debt:** This debt supplied by Venture Capital Investors can be of two types.

(i) **Fixed Interest:** Bearing such as bonds debentures and mortgages; this should be valued by relating the nominal yield of the investment to an appropriate current yield which depends upon a number of factors such as interest yield on the date of valuation, maturity, date of the issue, safety of the principal, debt service coverage stability and growth of the earnings of the venture.

(ii) **Non Interest:** Bearing zero interest bonds and secured premium notes. A factor of critical importance in this case is the solvency of the venture. If it is doubtful an appropriate discount rate may be used to the value computed according to the method used for valuating fixed interest non convertible debt.

Exit Strategies of Venture Capital Financing

The last stage in VCF is the exit to realize the investment so as to make a profit/minimize losses. In fact, the potential exit in terms of the realization horizon (exit timing) has to be planned at the time of the initial investment itself. The precise timing of exit depends on several factors such as maturity of the venture. The extent and type of financial stake, the state of actual and potential competition, market conditions, the style of functioning as well as perception of Venture Capital Investors and so on for ex: early stage financing typically takes a long term view of eventual realization/exit from 5-7 years. In case of TATA stage financing, the realization horizon could be shorter in the range of 3-5 years.

The important aspect of the exit stage of VCF is the decision regarding the disinvestments/ realization alternatives which are related to the type of investment, namely equity/quasi equity and debt instruments.

Disinvestments of Equity/Quasi Equity Investments: There are five disinvestment channels for realization of such investments.

(i) **Going Public/Initial Public Offering/Flotation:** The most common channel of disinvestment by a VCI is through public issue of capital of the VCU, including its own holdings. The merits of public issues are liquidity of investments through listing on stock exchanges, higher price of securities compared to private placement, better image and credibility with public managers customers, financial institution and so on.

(ii) **Sales of Shares to Entrepreneurs/Employees/Earn-out:** The sales/stakes of Venture Capital Investors may be sold to the entrepreneur/companies themselves who are allows to buy their own equity. Alternatively the entrepreneur can acquire the shares from Venture Capital Investors through employees by forming an employees stock ownership trust. The sources of the trust to acquire the share holding of the Venture Capital Investors are contribution by the employees/company and borrowing from financial institutions and banks.

(iii) **Trade Sales:** The entire company is sold to another company/third party. Highly popular method, at times the trade sales may be through a management buy-in or buyout. The most appropriate method for sale would vary from one case to another, keeping in view taxation and other consideration. The alternative modalities for trade sales as.

(a) Cash sales of equity ownership of both the parties which would attract heavy tax burden.

(b) Against issue of notes secured by the assets of the buyer company and receive cash in pre-determined installments in order to ensure proper tax planning.

(c) In consideration for the shares of the buying company with no tax liability.

(iv) **Sales to a New Investor/Take out:** The equity stake of Venture Capital Investors can be sold to a new investor who may be a corporate body or even another venture capital organization. The corporate investor may acquire the stake to develop a business relationship due to consideration of synergy of operations. The purchase of the equity holdings of a VCI by another VCI may be related to the nature.

(v) **Liquidation:** This in an involuntary exit forced on the VCI as a result of a totally failed investment. The Venture Capital Investors can use this exit method when the venture is not performing well and has reached a stage beyond recovery due to stiff competition, technology failure/obsolescence of technology, poor management etc.

(vi) **Exit of Debt Instruments:** Exit in case of debt component of VCF in contrast with equity/quasi equity component, has to normally follow the pre-determined route. In case of a normal loan, the exit is possible only at the end of the period of loan. If the loan agreement permits, whole or part can be converted into equity prior to that. For conditional loans, exit, earlier than projected at the time of initial investment is possible on the basis of lump-sum repayment consistent with the expectations of the VCI of the likely return on the loan.

Policy Imperative of VCF Development in India

The need for VCF in the country was felt around 1985. Recognizing the acute need for higher investment in venture capital activities to promote technology and knowledge based enterprises, SEBI appointed, the Chandrasekhar Committee to identify the impediments in the growth of venture capital industry in the country and suggest suitable measure for its rapid growth.

Recommendations: The recommendations pertain to (1) harmonization of multiplicity of regulations (2) VCF structures (3) Resource raising (4) Investments (5) Exit, (6) SEBI regulations (7) Company law related issues and (8) other related issues.

(1) Multiplicity of Regulations and Need for Harmonization:

(a) Since SEBI is responsible for overall regulations and registration of VCFs the need is to harmonize and consolidate multiple regulatory requirements within the framework of SEBI regulations to provide for uniform, hassle free single window clearance.

(b) The existing section 10 (23fA) of Income Tax Act needs to be enacted to provide for automatic income tax exemption to VCFs registered with SEBI.

(2) VCF Structures:

(a) The necessary legislative provision for incorporation of entities such as limited liability partnership (LLP) Limited Liability Company (LLC) may be made by way of enactment of separate Act or by way of amending the existing Indian partnership Act and the Indian Company Act.

(b) SEBI regulations should be amended to include

(i) The eligibility for registration of other entities such as LLP, LLC as soon as when permitted to be incorporated under the respective statues.

(ii) A provision for registration of funds set up by or a scheme floated by a trust company, body corporate or any other entity.

(iii) Provisions for registration and regulation of foreign venture capital investor (FVCI).

(c) FVCI, registered with SEBI, would be eligible to make venture capital investments under automatic route without any ceiling and any requirement of RBI approval.

(d) Venture Capital Investors should be permitted to take part their foreign remittances in foreign exchange in a bank in India or outside till actually invested in VCUs and they should be permitted to obtain forward cover as permitted to.

(3) Resource Raising: It is recommended that mutual funds banks and insurance companies should be permitted to invest in SEBI registered VCFs.

(4) Investment Related Issues:

(a) Investment by VCFs in VCUs should not be subject to any sectoral restrictions except those to be specified as a negative list by SEBI in consultation with the government. These may include areas like real estate, finance companies and activities prohibited by law. This will also be a measure for investor protection as the quality of IPOs would be improved by the venture capitalist. Besides it would result in high industrial growth.

(b) The investment ceiling of 40% of the paid up capital of an investee company under CBDT and government of India guidelines needs to be removed. However, by way of prudential requirement of risk diversification, investment in one single undertaking by VCF should not exceed 20% of its investible fund.

(c) The investment criteria needs to be redefined to permit investments by a VCF, primarily in equity or equity related instruments or securities convertible into equity

of VCUs and also by way of subscription to an IFO and preferential offer in case of companies to be listed or already listed.

(5) Exit Related Issues:

(a) The provisions under the Companies Act for a buy back of securities need to be amended as:

(i) 24 months prohibition period for fresh issue of capital to be reduced to six months in the case of unlisted companies where the buy back of shares from VC investors.

(ii) Permit VCC/VCU to redeem its equity/preference shares to an extent of 100% of their paid up capital out of the sale proceeds of investment and assets and not necessarily out of free reserves securities, premium amount or the proceeds of fresh issue should apply to them.

(b) The VCF/joint promoters should be eligible as qualified investors to participate in the unlisted equity segment of the OTCEI or any other stock exchange permitted by SEBI.

(6) SEBI Regulations:

(a) A broad based definition of a VCU may be included in the regulations.

(b) The definition of a VCF should be amended to include the funds set up, scheme floated by a trust company, body corporate or other legal entities.

(c) The investment criteria needs to be redefined to permit investment by a VCF, primarily in equity or equity related instruments or securities convertible into equity of VCUs and also by way of subscription to an IPO and preferential offer in case of companies to be listed or already listed.

(d) The provisions for investment is listed securities of sick companies may be dispensed with

(7) Company Law Related Issues: In India, most VCFs are organized by trusts, mainly due to the lack of an alternative asset through structure for taxation in the hands of the contributors / investors in the funds. Moreover, there is the problem of extent of liability on the trustees who manage the funds.

(8) Other Related Issues:

(a) **Employer Stock Option Plan:** (ESOP) currently, the RBI permits resident employees investments up to US $ 10,000 in a period of 5 years under an employee stock option, scheme of a foreign company.

(b) **Exchange of shares of an Indian Company with Shares of foreign company:** Currently, Indian employees desirous of swapping the shares of an Indian Company with that of foreign company under an ESOP scheme, are not permitted by the RBI. The RBI should permit such a swap on an automatic basic.

(c) **Tax Incentives:** In order to create a sufficiently large pool of VC through domestic investment, the government may consider providing tax incentives to the investors contributing to the VCFs for a period of three years.

Review Questions

1. Explain in brief the concept of Venture Capital.
2. State the features of Venture Capital.
3. Explain the importance of Venture Capital in entrepreneurship.
4. State the advantages of Venture Capital Financing.
5. Explain in brief about the structuring of financing in Venture Capital.

6. Explain in details about the stages of financing in Venture Capital.
7. Explain in brief about the First Chicago Method.
8. Discuss in detail about the type of Exit Strategies in Venture Capital.
9. What are the different types of Venture Capital firms in India?
10. What is Investment Nurturing? What are the different methodologies of nurturing?
11. Explain the performance of TDICI in Venture Capital Financing.
12. Explain the role of SEBI in Implementing Venture Capital Financing.

Fill in the blanks

1. __________ refers to the funds provided by investors to new companies with growth potentials.
2. Venture capital funds are highly__________
3. Some large companies may set aside venture capital funds to take a minority equity stake in small firms in order to encourage product development is called __________ fund
4. Venture capital fund is a __________ investment in the growth oriented small/medium business.
5. A venture capital firm serves as an __________ between investors looking for high returns and entrepreneurs in need of capital
6. There is substantial degree to active __________ of the venture capital institutions with the parameters of venture capital undertaking.
7. __________ stage of investment is very high-risk oriented as it is essentially applied research phase.
8. It refers to the transfer of management control to other __________
9. The involvement of venture capital institution in buying the control of the sick company is called________
10. Venture capital investments are generally ________ and __________ based.
11. __________ method gives allowance to the nature of the path between the starting point and the exit point of the venture
12. The structuring of venture capital refers to the __________ through which venture capital investment is made.
13. The enduring relationship between venture capital institutions and the venture capital units and the active role by the former in the management of the later is termed as __________

Answer:

1. Venture Capital
2. Risky
3. Corporate fund
4. Equity
5. Intermediary
6. Involvement
7. Seed capital
8. Management buy outs
9. Turn around
10. Idea and growth based
11. First Chicago Method
12. Financial instrument
13. Nurturing

◆◆◆

Annexure 1: Case Studies

CASE 1: Entrepreneurship

When Deepak Joshi was 17 years old, he sampled ice cream at a store and thought that he could make it better. He made his own recipe and began selling ice cream bars, cones and cups in his home town Belgaum. People began asking him for more. Deepak got himself trained at Mysore and developed skills to prepare ice creams of different flavors and compositions. Using meager profits and his mother's kitchen, Deepak Joshi began making large batches of ice creams. He then designed his own wrappers and developed a commission system for friends who sold ice creams at several schools.

Business was so good that it became an obsession. Deepak worked after college, weekends and holidays and aside from a brief period when the health department suspended his operations until he obtained proper permits to make ice creams, he made different types of ice creams by trying his own methods until he graduated from college At first, he could meet the demand without purchasing special equipment or sacrificing other activities, but when he began providing ice creams for college fund raising events and fun fairs, demand exceeded capacity, and Deepak found himself buying professional equipment, hiring helpers, and purchasing bulk supplies.

Looking back Deepak recalled has obsession, the long hours, and the drive to learn about business. Deepak set about placing orders with local stores and developing contracts with dozens of schools, colleges, caterers, hotels and civic organizations. His business soon consumed his entire family and closest friends; he registered the company and set up an ice cream parlor. During the first month, he had 18,000 orders and by the time he graduated, Deepak was distributing specialty ice creams to rattails stores in three States.

At the age of 26, Deepak repositioned his company as a major distributor of specialty ice creams and began planning a chain of upscale ice cream parlors which complement his current ice cream manufacturing and distribution system. When he paused to think about his plans, he realized that to launch a regional or national chain would mean major changes in his organization. He and his family could not handle all the responsibilities and the nature of Deepak's ice cream business would change. Although the idea of pursuing a major business was exciting, Deepak would not help feeling apprehensive.

Reflecting upon his business, Deepak realized that many people considered his success to be no more than luck of a personable young man who made good ice creams and had accidentally stumbled upon a few good markets. In fact, he had worked extremely hard to attract clients. Most of the customers had not been comfortable buying from a young college student and customers seldom took him seriously until they have dealt with him for a long time. Winning over customers had always been a challenge to Deepak, not a roadblock and creating unusual ice creams had been exciting.

He was not anxious to become a corporate manager, and although he had always worked well with others, Deepak liked being independent. Running a company would mean sacrificing his autonomy, yet the idea of a chain of stores selling his specialty ice creams had been a dream for years. At the same time, expansion would mean financial risk, and Deepak had always avoided debt, he dealt in cash and had always carefully calculated his expenses to avoid even the slightest loss. He realized that he was at a major crossroad in his young career. The choice seemed to be whether to follow his dream and expand or to be content with his existing business.

Case Questions

1. Identify the entrepreneurial characteristic of Deepak Joshi. How do they match the characteristics described for successful entrepreneurs?
2. Take a position regarding the decision facing Deepak on whether to expand into a chain of ice cream parlors.
3. Based on what you know about Deepak and what you believe his characteristics to be, would you say his success was due to luck or persistence? Explain. How does luck play a role in any new venture?

CASE 2: Shahnaz Husain — A Successful Indian Woman Entrepreneur

She uses natural ingredients – fruits, flowers, herbs, vegetables, honey, — as the base for most of her products. More complicated and exclusive treatments using gold and pearls have also been developed. Shahnaz has recently launched the Oxygen Range with an Oxygen cream, an Oxygen mask and facials using ingredients which breathe life into the skin and revitalize it. The Shahnaz Husain Group has two R&D units and a herb and flower farm near Delhi. A degree of quality control is exercised at every stage of the product development, right from the raw material stage to the end product. Various methods of soil culture and cultivation are followed to improve the quality of the final product. The extraction of essential oils and decoctions, infusions, powders and tinctures, is carried out using the latest technology.

All the procedures are carried out in accordance with the Ayurvedic system. Shahnaz believes that high quality is ensured only by the rigid exercise of control at every stage of production. In spite of the huge size of her business and the wide variety of products she deals in, Shahnaz Husain has never advertised. She has relied entirely on word-of-mouth publicity to make her products known to customers.

She believes that a satisfied customer is the best form of advertisement. Before Shahnaz Husain entered the retail market, her clinics were the only outlets for her products. By the 1990s, the range and popularity of Shahnaz products had increased so much that her products were carried by most of the big retail stores in India and abroad

She has been able to achieve growth due to the quality of her products and the result-oriented treatments she offers. She commented, "I have relied only on clientele feedback, based on clinical treatments and this is what has made the ranges truly unique and result oriented." In 1977, when she returned to India, she set up a parlor at her home in New Delhi. She had then put up a banner with her qualifications on it.

Within days she was booked for the next 6 months. She said, "I removed the banner and since then I have never advertised. I have let my products speak for themselves." Shahnaz was disturbed by the fact that India was not represented in any of the Global beauty forums of the world beauty congresses. Deciding to change this situation, she represented the country for the first time in the CIDESCO beauty congress in the late 1970s.

"It was my aim to get India on the world beauty map as I felt terrible about the fact that India was never represented at any world beauty congress," said Shahnaz. She was appointed President for the day's proceedings at the congress and she used this opportunity to focus the world's attention on Ayurveda.

The Turning Point

The turning point in her business came when she represented India at the Festival of India in 1980. Her team was given a counter in the perfumery section of Selfridges in London. She managed to sell her entire consignment in 3 days and also broke the store's record for cosmetics sales for the year. As a result, she was offered a permanent counter in Selfridges. Shahnaz was the first Asian whose goods were retailed by the the Galeries Lafayette in Paris. Although it was not easy to enter the highly competitive western markets and especially difficult to attract attention to the Indian system of Ayurveda, she was able to gain a firm foothold in the markets. Shahnaz Husain products are sold at many prestigious stores around the world such as Harrods and Selfridges in London, the Galeries Lafayette in Paris, Bloomingdales in New York, the Seibu chain in Japan and Sultan Stores in the Middle East. Her products are also carried by other exclusive outlets in the Middle East, Asia and Africa. Shahnaz Husain has used the franchising mode to expand her business in India and abroad.

She has a large network of over 600 franchises and associate clinics around the world. All the franchisees are required to undergo training in specialized treatments at Shahnaz Husain's school of beauty therapy. All franchisees obtain the right to use the Shahnaz Husain name and her specialized treatments and are allowed a 30% profit margin on the sale of Shahnaz Husain products. In 2002, the Shahnaz Husain Group obtained distributor rights for Australia, New Zealand and the Fiji Islands.

Distribution channels were first set up in the major cities of Australia, and later in New Zealand and Fiji. This was followed by the setting up of herbal clinics, first in Sydney and later in other Australian cities, New Zealand and Fiji by the first half of 2003.The Shahnaz Husain Group has about 40 distributors and more than 600 sub distributors all over India. The Group sells not only in the cities but also in the small towns. In addition, the Group owns about 20 clinics and outlets in New Delhi. All other outlets are run on the franchise system. The Group does not make any financial investment in its franchises, nor does it have any share in their profits.

Diversification

The Group has diversified into Ayurvedic centers for *Panchkarma, Dhara and Kerala massage*. It has also set up two Shahnaz Husain Ayurvedic Health Resorts, one near Delhi and another in collaboration with the Hyakumata group of Japan in the US island of Saipan. These resorts which can accommodate about 200 people at a time, aim at providing urbanites treatments and programs designed to counteract the stress of modern life. The Group has also been holding discussions with major five star hotels in New Delhi and New York to set up health spas. Shahnaz Husain products normally cater to the premium end of the market and are rather expensive. Shahnaz justifies the price citing quality, purity and high excise duties as the reasons. In 2002, however, she developed a product for the mass market, a Fairness Dream Cream, priced at Rs 68 for 50gms.

This product will not only be advertised (unlike her other products), it will also be made widely available through all sorts of retail shops and even at railway stations. She claims that she has always wanted to create a product for the masses and the R&D deparment had been on the job since 1995, to create such a product

The group has also launched a line of herbal drinks under the brand name Fitness Fiesta Shadrink. These drinks are low calorie, cooling drinks to be consumed in the summer. The drinks are based on rose and khus (poppy seeds) extracts and contain essential nutrients, vitamins and minerals which nourish the body and help purify the blood. Shahnaz's love for animals prompted her to introduce a special range of ayurvedic products for pets – Shapet

This range includes hair care balms, anti-tick hair cleansers, talcum powder, anti-scabies skin oil, antiseptic balm, and anti parasitic lotions Shahnaz believes that chemical products and pesticides destroy the natural luster and health of the animal's coat. Natural products not only prevent this but also help soothe and cure infections.

Training Future Entrepreneurs

Seeing the need for internationally recognized institutes that offered professional training in beauty, Shahnaz Husain set up Woman's World International. This was started at a time when people who wanted to train in beauty treatments and therapy could only get apprenticeship training. The institute which is affiliated to ITEC, U.K offers training in cosmetic therapy and combines theoretical knowledge with practical training. Students study physiology and the human anatomy to understand the scientific principles of beauty and become familiar with the major systems of the human body. They are taught the practical skills of massage and make-up under the expert guidance of a qualified therapist. They also learn the use of various skin and hair gadgets. In addition, they study nutrition, weight control and exercise. Students are also given basic training on setting up and running salons and maintaining hygiene.

Case Question

1. Examine the true qualities involved in Mrs. Shehnaz Husain as a successful Women Entrepreneurs.

CASE 3: Tessera Enterprise Systems

Tessera Enterprise Systems, a custom software developer, was founded in Boston in 1995, by an executive team that had previously worked together for three years. Tessera's target market included some of the largest American retail and financial companies, such as Eddie Bauer and Charles Schwab. The founders provided initial funding for the venture, but after one year it was decided that venture capital was required to expand the company. Tessera, however, secured an investment offer from Greylock Management, a prominent Boston-based IVC. Greylock's status added legitimacy to the fledgling venture, permitting it to obtain contracts with target companies such as Charles Schwab, Eddie Bauer, and other prominent clients. Subsequent expansion and third-stage funding from two other prominent IVCs solidified Tessera in the market and led to a corporate expansion to San Francisco. At the same time, Tessera considered establishing an office in Switzerland to serve potential European clients. One of the VC providers likened internationalization to loading an airplane with stacks of cash and opening the doors while flying over the Atlantic.

Tessera nevertheless pursued its foreign market entry strategy and, while it slowly obtained some European contracts, it did so without the involvement or aid of its IVC investors. Had Tessera sought investment from a technology corporation such as Oracle (on whose products its offerings were often based), it might have been better able to leverage its investor's networks and knowledge to the benefit of its foreign business. A modest capital round was provided by IVCs and a private investors in preparation for an exit. Tessera, originally planning on a public offering and broad foreign expansion, was acquired in 2001 by iXL, an Atlanta-based internet services provider company with offices in San Francisco and London.

Making It Happen

- ❖ Since VC has the potential to change the nature of resources in an SME so dramatically, entrepreneurs must approach it with a strategic view of how it may best add value, and source it accordingly. At the same time as they assess their financial capital needs, SME managers should do the following:
- ❖ Carefully consider the type of advice, information, and network access you want from an investor in the light of current needs and strategic direction.
- ❖ Identify VC providers that have great reputations for providing value in a manner consistent with your willingness to cede some control.
- ❖ Ask others who have undertaken VC-backed ventures about their experience with investors — both IVC and CVC — and the success and problems they encountered.
- ❖ Identify companies that had exits — IPOs and acquisitions — most consistent with your goals and ask about their investors.

Conclusion

SMEs and young ventures that receive capital investments can often choose their source. The boundary-spanning role of investors, as both advisers and links to external networks, places VCs in a unique position to add value to a venture. The potential for investors to aid in the growth and development of such ventures demands that entrepreneurs and SME managers make their choice in a considered manner that is consistent with their overall strategy. Careful consideration of investor types can lead to an efficient selection process that provides value throughout the life of the venture.

Case Question

1. Examine the role of venture capital investment in entrepreneurship development.

CASE 4: Bowzo: a Case Study in Engineering Entrepreneurship

Jim Oswald, joint inventor of a product which, it is anticipated, will dramatically change the way the violin is learnt. Jim is a career inventor and design engineer who, having left Rolls Royce after 25 years in the world of engine components specialising in heat exchangers was ready for something new. It is fair to say that Jim found the first few months after his "release" uncomfortable. He had spent years working on major projects involving teams, many of which he had led himself. He missed teams, and he missed the challenge of project management. Fortunately, Bowzo arrived out of nowhere and provided what he needed.

Both Larry and Jim were attached to Coventry University's Vision Works in order to get help in developing some new business ideas. The Vision Works provides accommodation, telecommunications and computer facilities, plus, perhaps most importantly, mentoring and coaching services for start-up businesses. When Larry and Jim met, Larry was planning the launch of a multi-media design business but he had also been a professional musician and violin teacher. During a discussion about product ideas Larry revealed his thoughts about a device for helping novice violin players to learn faster and play more accurately by 'bowing' straight from the moment of the first lesson. The device fixed to the neck of the violin and offers precise control to students developing their bowing technique.

The Idea

Larry understood precisely the problems many students have in 'bowing' straight. The idea was to design and manufacture a simple device that controls the bowing technique by helping the student keep the bow straight at all times. Given Jim's background in product development and Larry's specialist knowledge both could see the potential of collaboration. It worked and one year later the first prototypes were finished and market testing was underway.

The Market

To help explore the initial reactions of violin teaching professionals across the world, to what appeared to be a brilliant solution to a longstanding problem; both Larry and Jim felt that independent marketing expertise was needed at an early stage. Some staggering facts emerged, not least that more than half a million new violins are brought throughout theworldeach year. This probably means that almost another half a million second hand violins are bought too, leading to lots of lessons for many students keen to learn fast. The most likely route to market was identified as via the traditional wholesaler/distributor to retailer network.

Initial research indicated that there was a market for a low cost, easy to use device and thus the design engineering and manufacturing priorities were set. University support mechanisms The market research was supplemented by further inputs from the University's Design Institute which provided a specialist support program for small to medium sized enterprises. This included a comprehensive range of services featuring marketing advice, product design and innovation processes as well as financial management and technology transfer. Jim was impressed." The range of services available from the Design Institute is fantastic; we were able to put the engineering issues on the table and deal with them in a wider team context with inputs from experts as required".

The issues were clear:

- Styling and design values. The first handmade prototype was certainly functional but needed more work. Soon a more aesthetic shape was created that added a great deal to the presentation and packaging of the product
- Durability. New materials were tested and the best of a number of options selected, we will have to wait until the launch to know more on this point.

- Manufacturing options. Low volumes could be laser cut but high volumes needed a more appropriate technique for cutting and forming. Which would be best at launch?
- Production costs. How fast would sales grow and what would be an acceptable pricing structure for customer and distribution chain alike?

Progress to date

The excellent teamwork involving the inventor, musicians, design engineers and marketers has resulted in pre-production prototypes that are working well in field testing. Seed capital has been secured on the back of this positive market research findings and the formal product launch is scheduled for early in 2006. The team are determined to bring a product to market that offers excellent design, practicality and the highest quality. To this end attention to detail is critical as are methodical engineering processes. Enter the entrepreneur, then exit.

The 'collision' between entrepreneur and inventor/engineer was brought about by the realisation of the existence of a market need. They met by accident and the inventor in Larry awakened the entrepreneur in Jim, and a new position for Jim, the inventor/engineer. He admits that he was feeling more open to other people's ideas at the time of meeting Larry and since then has probably reverted to type as he waits for "the next awakening'.

Conclusion:

1. Stay awake for new opportunities by not always being yourself.
2. Build a wider team to bring in new thinking on product development issues - you might be too close to the opportunity to see its full potential.
3. Engineers and entrepreneurs are interchangeable when they each see the market need clearly.

CASE 5: Analysis of a Successful Venture Capital Fund Raising Exercise

Introduction to the Company: The Company in this case is a Delhi based small logistic services provider. The company's business is to provide third-party logistics (3PL) service like warehousing, packing, unpacking etc for a number of large FMCG, Auto, Electronics companies.

Things that were working for the Company:

Team: The owner of the Company is a first generation entrepreneur who has built a good team by hiring two senior industry professionals to manage the future proposed growth of the company. Along with the promoter, these two provided enough expertise and credentials to the team. The team was a good combination of entrepreneurship skills of the promoter and professional experience of the other team members.

Clients: The Company had some of the best names in their industry as its clients to boast of though the revenue from each client was quite small. The company was providing its services to large and reputed clients in FMCG, Auto, Electronics and Beverages industry. This proved to the investor that the company has the ability to acquire, deliver and retain the best clients in their field.

Hot Growing Industry: Logistics has been a huge area of interest in the venture capital community in India for quite some time now. There have been a number of transactions in this industry already and most investors are still looking for good projects. Unfortunately, most Indian players who call themselves logistics companies are essentially transport companies but this Company was a good mix of warehousing, cold storage and transport business.

Things that were NOT working for the company:

Small size of operations: Though the company had some of the blue chip clients however the Company's profits were very low. At the time of fund-raising process, the company was making net profits of close to Rs. 10 lacs. The proposed investment was quite large in comparison to the Company's current scale of operations and it took some skill on the promoter's part to convince the investors that the company can manage a comparatively large operations.

No experience of some proposed businesses like Cold Storage: Some of the businesses proposed by the Company were completely new. No member of company's current team had any expertise in those businesses. However, inclusion of those businesses made tremendous strategic sense and that's why they were able to convince investors about inclusion of new businesses.

Valuation: Since the required investment was significantly large in comparison to the Company's current operations, the valuation became quite a challenge. Any standard valuation technique was leading to a very small stake for the promoters. The problem was solved by a performance linked valuation structure where promoters were rewarded by equity every time they met a performance benchmark.

Case Question:

1. Discuss the strength and weakness of the company.

CASE 6: A Successful Entrepreneur

Mr Aarish Rathi is a person who follows the above quote in true sense. Freedom was the chief reason for him to try the less traveled path of entrepreneurship. His story is highly inspirational, especially, for all the enterprising young Indian men who desire to be successful entrepreneurs. Aarish's journey started at Bilaspur in Madhya Pradesh where he was born, moving on to Bhilai where he spent his early years, and from where he did his school and college education, and finally to Raipur. It was at Raipur that he struck gold, that too in a big way. It is the classic, modern-day story of a middle class young man-turned-multi-millionaire. Aarish describes himself as "a serial entrepreneur and risk-taker who empowers others to accomplish their dream."This is his story

The Early Years

I come from a classic middle-class family: my grandfather, grandmother, father, and mother all living together in a joint family. Family values were strongly embedded into me as a result of this. I was born in Bilaspur and did my schooling at Shri Shankracharya School in Bhilai and then joined the Vivekananda College to do my graduation in civil engineering. I worked with TCS at Mumbai centre but left it after 2 yrs. During this time I realized that working under someone else was not my cup of tea. I was not exposed to business of any sort, but my father, dabbled in shares. He encouraged me to have freewheeling discussions on various aspects of business. I was given enough freedom to think freely. My parents were there all the time supporting me and encouraging me. I didn't realize the value of it all then, but later on I understood the kind of impact those discussions had upon my thinking. More importantly, they encouraged me to take risks. When working in a public sector was considered safe, I was encouraged to go into a field that was uncharted, like logistics. The willingness to do something on my own has always been there. Some how, those things did not click because of our middle-class background, not having the money, and also because of our inexperience.

Destiny and Lifestyle Distribution

I believe in destiny. I faced bankruptcy many a time in my logistics business; I borrowed money with no assets but somehow I survived. It was destiny which brought people like Ameya to me. Later Ameya became my partner in successive ventures. In May 2001, the most important thing happened - Lifestyle Distributors Private Ltd. Lifestyle Distribution is into business of distribution of various fast moving consumer goods and is one of the prime dealers of products of companies like HUL, P&G, Reckitt Benckiser, Colgate Palmolive and many more.

After that we started a logistics firm in Bhilai, parallel to this we were seeking the opportunities coming across. At that time HUL had very few distributor in Chhattisgarh's rural are a because of which they were having problem to distribute in Kanker region. So they want to have a distributor in this area. They were looking for a firm who can manage their distributorship in this area. This was a great opportunity for us, and we did not miss it. In a business there are multiple challenges across various areas including capital, resources, finding great people, market acceptance, etc., some of them are:

Finance: Finance was the biggest concern for this business as it requires around 3 crore of investment. HUL wants its distributor to have at least inventory of 15 days (worth 1.5 crore) which makes monthly 3 crore turnover. Arranging this was the biggest problem. To resolve this problem I asked my family and friends, from there we arranged 0.5 crore and a major part came by taking loan from bank on the collateral of family house. But the most important contribution to our start-up came from Mr Nijo Ninan, who was a friend of my father, and took great interest in our business plan. He supported our business to a great extent and kept us confirming that finance will not be a major problem.

Government Regulations: Starting business in India is a big headache. In India registering a company is also an Olympian task. Corruption is so pervasive that for each small work you need to bribe which is irritating many times. But to achieve bigger dreams we have to cross these hurdles

Finding people: The new venture was unable to attract the skilled labor which can handle multiple jobs requiring different skills. A work force having ability to handle all sort of tasks related to distribution, will make the business run very efficiently and also will cut costs. The issue was if you want to hire people who are efficient it will be costly to your business and else your operations will hamper at quality end .But finally with the efforts what he did for senior position she had hired smart and efficient persons. For Low skills jobs he had taken people who had low skill but can be taught.

Market Competition: The Industry with many large players having established clients also acted as thwart for operation of Lifestyle Distributions Private Limited. Territory poaching, margin negotiation was some of the issues which were coming because of stiff competition.

Journey so far: Nothing is easy in life. With support from our families and the initial set of employees, our journey so far has been not that bad; in fact, it has been quite satisfying. I believe that any time is the right time and every place is the right place. Even in the worst times, people have started successful companies. I don't think any time is wrong time. I feel you can create your own niche any time and you need to change your plans as per what you see for future. We have won best distributor award of HUL 2009. We are generating profits and investing them back in the company. Starting with the two of us, we now have 150 full-time employees. We have two offices now; one in Raipur and another in Jaipur. The journey is still continuing.

Future plans: We want to become Central India number one distribution company in this segment. We want to be in as many districts as possible and give better service to our consumers. You need to create more jobs and more wealth in this country and the only way to grow is through entrepreneurs. If you look at all the successful economies, you will see that wealth is created by first time entrepreneurs. In India, Infosys, Wipro, Reliance are the best examples. He is a business man with traits like risk taking, good communication, achievement oriented, and good managerial skills. At the initial stage, as craftsman, he handled all the tasks himself. But now he is following the management style of Employee and Employer. Aarish has got a pleasant personality and a strong convincing skill in his speaking style, which he used to his favor to gain trust among retailers and wholesalers

Case Questions:

1. Discuss the problems faced by Mr. Aarish Rathi in starting his business. How did he overcome the problems?

CASE 7: Venture Capital Investment

Suppose XYZ Company, Inc., a start-up, needs $500,000. The company's product appears to have excellent potential. However, because the product is new and unproven, an investment in the company would be extremely risky. Accordingly, it is reasonable to estimate that a venture capitalist would want a potential return of at least ten times his total investment in five years. Management estimates that the company should be able to "go public" at 20 times earnings in five years. Projected after-tax earnings for the fifth year is $1,250,000. Additional long-term financing of $500,000 will be needed at the beginning of the third year.

Scenario I

In the calculations below it is assumed that the venture capitalist who provides the initial financing ($500,000) also provides the subsequent financing ($500,000), and that he wants a return equal to ten times both. However, it should be noted that if the company made satisfactory progress during the first two years, it would be reasonable to assume that the venture capitalist would be satisfied with a lower return on the subsequent financing since it would involve less risk.

Estimate of Total Dollar Return Required	
Total Investment Estimate of Return Required	$ 1,000,000 × 10 $10,000,000
Projected Market Value in Fifth Year	
Projected Earnings Estimate of P/E Ratio	$1,250,000 × 20 $25,000,000
Percentage Ownership Needed in Fifth Year	
Estimate of Total Dollar Return Required Projected Market Value of Company in Fifth Year	$10,000,000 25,000,000 40%

Scenario II

In this set of calculations it is assumed that a second investor provides the subsequent financing ($500,000). The calculations show that the venture capitalist who provides the initial financing ($500,000) would need 20% ownership as of the fifth Year to realize the return he wants. However, since the ownership to be given up for the subsequent financing will reduce his ownership position, he will want more than 20% ownership initially. For example, if it is assumed that 15% ownership will have to be given up for the subsequent financing, the venture capitalist who provides the initial financing would need 23% ownership initially to end up with 20% ownership in the fifth year.

Assume the same facts as Case I, except a second investor provides the subsequent financing for 15% ownership.

Estimate of Total Dollar Return Required	
Total Investment Estimate of Return Required	\$ 500,000 × 10 \$5,000,000
Projected Market Value in Fifth Year	
Projected Earnings Estimate of P/E Ratio	\$1,250,000 × 20 \$25,000,000
Percentage Ownership Needed in Fifth Year	
Estimate of Total Dollar Return Required Projected Market Value of Company in Fifth Year	\$5,000,000 25,000,000 20%

Thus, it appears that the investment (\$500,000) may be attractive to an interested venture capitalist if the principals of XYZ Company, Inc. are willing to give up approximately 23% ownership.

Conclusion

It must be emphasized that the above procedure is highly subjective. And, you should remember that what really matters is how the venture capitalist views the relative attractiveness of a company. Typically, venture capitalists are satisfied with a minority interest. Although a venture capitalist may demand a majority interest, generally they are not interested in operating control. Some of them like to tie the amount of ownership they ultimately get to the performance of the company. For example, a venture capitalist who wants a majority interest initially may give the principals the opportunity to earn part of it back. Such an arrangement can be used to compromise on pricing when there is a significant disagreement between the principals and the venture capitalist.

To entrepreneurs unfamiliar with venture capital, it may appear that the venture capitalist is seeking an extraordinary high return on his investment. However, it is important to understand that, even under the best of circumstances, only a minority of the companies in which the venture capitalists invests will be successful. He is well aware of this, and must make a sufficient return of his successful investments to come out with an acceptable return overall.

APPENDIX: 2

1. Application for of Provisional Registration Certificate of SSI

GOVERNMENT OF ______________

DIRECTORATE OF INDUSTRIES

APPLICATION FORM FOR PROVISIONAL REGISTRATION

AS SMALL-SCALE INDUSTRIES

(TO BE FILLED IN DUPLICATE)

INSTRUCTIONS

1. Write/type in block (capital) letters.
2. Fill up whichever is applicable.
3. Use English alphabets/Arabic numbers while filling up blocks (to help computerisation). Leave one blank after each word.
4. While filling the form, use the following procedure.

   (i) Name of the unit, e.g., KAMAL ENTERPRISES/G.K ENTERPRISES
   K A M A L E N T E R P R I S E S
   G K E N T E R P R I S E S

   (ii) Pin Code: e.g. 110041 — 1 1 0 0 4 1

   (iii) Date: e.g., 23rd June 1959 — 2 3 0 6 5 9

   (iv) Quantity (kg) e.g., 90 Kg. — 0 0 0 0 9 0

   (v) Amount (Rs in thousands) e.g., Rs. 5000/- — 0 0 0 0 5

   (vi) Fill up appropriate codes in the blocks wherever applicable
   Example 1: Yes-1, No-2, NA-3 — 3
   if NA fill up-3
   Example 2: Category: SSI-1, Anc-2,
   Tiny-3, SSSBE-4,EOU-5. — 3
   If Tiny fill up-3 5. Block/boxes marked (*) are to be filled by office.

5. Applicant should sign all copies.

   Abbreviations used:

   SSI: Small-scale Industries, **ANC:** Ancillary Industrial Undertaking, **SSSBE:** Small-scale Service and business enterprise, **TINY:** Tiny enterprise, **EOU:** Export Oriented Unit, **NA:** Not applicable.

FORM

1. Name of the Unit/Applicant.

2. Address for communication.

   Tel: Pin Code:

3. Category of Unit
   SSI-1, ANC-2,
   SSSBE-3, TINY-4, EOU-5.
4. Location:
   Place/Town
   Tehsil/Taluk
   District
   State
5. Type of Organisation:
   Proprietary-1, Partnership-2, Pvt. Company-3, Cooperative-4,
   Others
6. Nature of activity
   Manufacturing/Assembly (01)
   Processing (02)
   Job work (04)
   Repairing/Servicing (08)
   Note: For any combination of activities, add the respective code to get the required code.
7. Main items of manufacture/activities.
   (i) Name
   Code
   (ii) Name
   Code
   (iii) Name
   Code
   (iv) Name
   Code
   (v) Name
   Code

8. Investment in Fixed Assets (₹ in '000)
   (i) Land
   (ii) Building
   (iii) Plant & Machinery
   (iv) Other Fixed Assets
   TOTAL:
9. Investment in Plant & Machinery
   (original value ₹ in '000)

   Note: Should exclude items whose value is not taken into account while computing the investment. Please enclose project profile in case value of investment in Plant and Machinery exceeds ₹ 40 lacs.
10. Power Load H.P.
    (1 H.P. = 0.795 K.W) K.W.
11. Employment
    (i) Management & Office Staff
    (ii) Supervisory and Workers
12. Date of commencement of
    production (estimated)

    Date:

    Signature of Applicant (Authorised Person)

    Name of proprietor/partner/managing director

FOR OFFICE USE ONLY

Application No. NIC Code

Block Code District Code State Code

Location of Unit

(Conforming-1, Non-Conforming-2)

Whether the items of manufacture/activity require an industrial licence.

Yes-1, No-2

(No industrial licence is required for items listed in Schedule II of the licensing notification dated 25.7.1991 if the unit employs less than 50/100 workers with/ without power)

2. Format of Provisional Registration Certificate of SSI

PROVISIONAL REGISTRATION

The application is accepted for Provisional Registration as a SSI/SSSBE Unit for the manufacture of items/activities as stated in the application form.

Provisional Registration No :

Date of issue :

Category of unit (S. No. 3) : ______________________

Signature

Name & Designation of Registering Authority

1. The endorsed application form is a part of the certificate of registration.
2. The provisional registration is valid for a period of five years from the date of issue.
3. The provisional registration will automatically lapse at the end of the validity period or the date of commencement of production, whichever is earlier.
4. If an applicant/unit is unable to set up the unit within the validity period, the applicant/ unit has the option to apply afresh for provisional registration using standard procedure.
5. The provisional registration is given to enable the unit to obtain all acilities/clearance etc. required in the pre-production stage.
6. The provisional registration is subject to any or all conditions that may be imposed by the Registering Authority.

3. Affidavit for Permanent Registration Certificate of SSI

AFFIDAVIT FOR PERMANENT REGISTRATION AS SMALL-SCALE INDUSTRIES

FORMAT

I/We ____________________son/daughter/wife/widow of ___________resident of ____________________________ do hereby solemnly affirm and declare as under:-

1. that I/We have submitted an application dated __________ for permanent registration of the unit as small scale/ancillary/tiny/export oriented unit/Small Scale Service and Business enterprise.
2. that I/We am/are proprietor(s)/partner(s)/Managing Director of the unit whose name and address is given below:-

   Name:____

   Address:______________________________________
3. that all particulars furnished in the application form are factual and correct.
4. that the location of the unit does not violate any locational restrictions for the time being in force and that I/we have obtained the necessary locational clearances from the competent authority.
5. that I/we have obtained all the statutory clearances/No Objection Certificates/permission required to carry out the manufacture/activity under the prevalent laws, regulations and rules in force.
6. that I/We have also obtained the necessary registration/licence, wherever required, under the relevant laws, rules or orders, for the time being in force, for carrying out the said industrial activity.
7. that the unit does not require an industrial licence because:
   (a) the unit employs less than 50/100 workers with/without use of power.
   (b) the items proposed to be manufactured are reserved for exclusive production in the small scale industries sector.
   (c) the unit does not manufacture any item which is included in Schedule-II of Notification No. S. O 477 (E) dated 25.7.1991 and is not reserved for exclusive manufacture in the SSI sector as included in Schedule-III of the above notification.
8. That the original value of investment in plant and machinery installed at the unit is within the limits prescribed for tiny/SSI/SSSBE/ancillary/export oriented unit as per existing provisions.
9. That the units not owned or controlled or a subsidiary or any other industrial undertaking in terms of the Notification No. S.O. 2 (E) dated. 1.1.93.

10. That I/We undertake to inform the registering authority within 30 days of the crossing of the investment limits in plant and machinery and submit the registration certificate for cancellation of registration or deletion of relevant endorsements as Ancillary/EOU/Tiny enterprise/Small-scale Service and Business Enterprise.
11. That I/We understand that if at a future date the said unit does not satisfy any of the conditions laid down in the notification No. S.O.232 (E) dt. 2.4.91, or does not comply with any of the conditions or restrictions for the time being in force, or includes manufacture items that require an industrial licence, then is such an eventuality, I/We shall be liable and required to surrender our registration as a SSI unit.
12. That I/We undertake to inform the Directorate of Industries/Registering authority immediately in case a situation arises as mentioned at para 11 above.
13. That I/We undertake to inform and to keep informed the Directorate of Industries/ Registering Authority on all parameters and changes, if any, as required from time to time.
14. That I/We undertake to refund to the Central or State Government any or all financial incentives or benefits given under various schemes of assistance for small scale industries alongwith 18% interest, as may be demanded by the appropriate authority of Central/ State Govt, in case it is found that the information or particulars submitted to obtain registration were wrong and fraudulent.
15. That I/We fully understand that we have to comply with the above conditions failing which we are liable for action by the Registering authority for cancellation of the Registration as well as under other relevant provisions of the laws and rules in force.

Signature
DEPONENT

VERIFICATION:

Verified that the contents of the affidavit are true to the best of my knowledge and belief.

DEPONENT

Date:

Place:

(*Note) Strike out whichever is not applicable.

4. Format of Permanent Registration Certificate of SSI

CERTIFICATE OF REGISTRATION

ADDITIONAL SHEET – 1

Registration No.

Date of Issue

Addition/Deletion in Plant & Machinery

S.No	Name of Machinery	Added/Deleted	Original Value Rs in '000
1.			
2.			
3.			
4.			
5.			

Revised value of investment in Plant & Machinery (S.NO 13)

Change in location (S.No 7)

Change in constitution/type of organisation (S.No 9)

Signature

Date: Name & Designation of Registering Authority

5. Application Form of PMRY

APPLICATION FORM FOR FINANCIAL ASSISTANCE UNDER PRIME MINISTER'S ROZGAR YOJANA (PMRY) SCHEME FOR EDUCATED UNEMPLOYED PERSONS

1. Name of the Applicant (in block letters)	
2. Sex	Male / Female
3. Father's/Husband's name	
4. Address for correspondence	
Permanent address	
Whether resident certificate enclosed for a minimum period of 3 years where loan is going to be availed	
5. Date of birth and age	
6. Educational qualification (a) Academic (b) Technical	
7. Present annual income of the family (as per the certificate received from Tahsildar office)	
8. Category belongs to	BC/SC/ST/PH/MC/ Ex-SM/General
9. Proposed Activity/Avocation	
10. Previous experience in the line of activity, if any	
11. Place of proposed enterprises, if any, Give details	
12. Details of registration made in the employment exchange (No., date)	
13. Details of the total amount of loan required. (a) Machinery and equipment (b) Other fixed assets (c) Working capital Total	

14. Extent of margin money proposed to be invested by the applicant (5-16.25%)	
15. (a) Whether the applicant availed loan from any banking, financial institutions of State/Central Govt. (b) If yes, whether all were repaid? (c) If not, indicate the balance amount to be paid.	

Certified that all the informations furnished by me are true to my knowledge and I have not borrowed any subsidy linked loan from any Department/Bank/Financial Institutions.

Signature of the Applicant.

Place :

Date :

Details of the certificate to be enclosed

Affix 6x4 cm of passport size photo. Two copies of filled in application of DIC copy and bankers copy should be signed and submitted in person in District Industries Centre, Hyderabad.

(a) Birth certificate or School/College transfer certificate

(b) Educational qualification certificate

(c) Family income certificate, caste certificate & resident certificate obtained from the Tahsildar.

For Office use only

Recommended by the Task Force Committee for availing financial assistance up to ₹__________ (Rupees ____________________ ____________________only)

CHAIRMAN
PMRY TASK FORCE COMMITTEE
-CUM- GENERAL MANAGER, DIC
HYDERABAD

REFERENCES

Anuradha Prased, *"Entrepreneurship Development under TRYSEM,"* Concept Publishing Co. New Delhi 1988.

Barro, Robert J., Determinants of Economic Growth: A Cross-Country Empirical Study. Boston, MA: MIT Press, 1998.

Batra G.S., *"Development of Entrepreneurship"* Deep & Deep Publication, New Delhi, 2009

Donald F. Kuratko, *Entrepreneurship: Theory, Process and Practices,* 2009.

Drucker, P.F., *"Innovation and Entrepreneurship"*, Heinemann, London 1985

Gillis, Malcolm, Perkins, Dwight H., Roemer, Michael, and Donald R. Snodgrass, *Economics of Development.* 4th ed., New York: W. W. Norton & Company, 1996.

Gupta C. B. & Srinivasan N.P., *"Entrepreneurship Development in India"*, Sultan Chand & Sons New Delhi, 2000

Hans J. Plietner, "Entrepreneurs and New Venture Creation" *Journal of Small Business and Entrepreneurship,* Canada 1986.

Hitesh S. Viramgami *"Fundamentals of Entrepreneurship"*, APH Publishing, 2007.

http://dcmsme.gov.in/ssiindia/definition.htm

http://EzineArticles.com/?expert=Alexander_Gordon

http://www.entrepreneurshipisemi.com/index.php

http://www.and.nic.in/C_charter/indust/msmeact2006.pdf

http://www.angelfire.com/ny/tbse/

http://www.nos.org/srsec319/319-20.pdf

http://www.nsic.co.in/performanceach.asp

http://www.tradechakra.com/indian-economy/globalization.html

http://www.unctad.org/en/docs/poitetebd5.en.pdf

http://www.wisegeek.com/what-is-an-entrepreneur.html

http://www.icmrindia.org/

John A.Hornaday, "Research about Living Entrepreneurs," in *Encyclopedia of Entrepreneurship,* ed. Calvin Kent, Donald Sexton, and Karl Vesper Printice Hall, 1982, P.26-27.

Oden, Howard W., *"Managing Corporate Culture, Innovation, and Intrapreneurship"*, Westport, CT: Quorum Books, 1997.

Peter R. Dickson, *Marketing Management* (Fort Worth, TX: The Dryden Press, 1994.

Poornima M. C., *"Entrepreneurship Development Small Business Enterprises"* Pearson Education New Delhi, 2006 S.H. Nagu and G. Richman, *"Entrepreneurial Development in Rural Sector"*, in Samiuddin (ed.) OP.CIT., pp. 55-58.

Sadhak. H., *"The Role of Entrepreneurs in Backward Areas"* Daya Pubishing House New Delhi, 1989.

Sharma K.P. & Poonam Parashar, *"Entrepreneurship"*, F.K. Publication. New Delhi.

Sharma K.P. & Poonam Parashar, *"Entrepreneurship"*, V.K. Enterprises, New Delhi 2010

Todaro, Michael P., *Economic Development.* Reading, PA: Addison-Wesley Publishing Co, 1996. *http://www.aw-wrdsmth.com/FAQ/characteristics_successful_entre.html.*

Vasant Desai, *"Dynamics of Entrepreneurial Development and Management"* Himalaya Publishing House, New Delhi, 2007.

http://dcmsme.gov.in/howtosetup/grgxx01x.htm#PROVISIONALREGISTRATION CERTIFICATE

http://www.sidbiventure.co.in/svc-01r.htm

http://lakamsani.wordpress.com/2010/03/26/different-types-of-entrepreneurs-replicators-innovators-and-bill-gates/

http://www.and.nic.in/C_charter/indust/MSMED_classification.pdf

http://dcmsme.gov.in/MSMED2006.pdf

http://msme.gov.in/msme_aboutus.htm

http://www.nabard.org/pdf/report_financial/

The Harvard International Development Conference, Saturday April 5, 2003.The Democratization of Credit: The Role of Microfinance in Poverty Alleviation. Moderator: Professor Guy Stuart, The Kennedy School of Government, Harvard University.

Finance for the Poor: Microfinance Development Strategy. *Asian Development Bank,* 2000.

Microfinance, Poverty Alleviation, and Improving Food Security: Implications for India. Meyer, Richard, *Rural Finance Program,* The Ohio State University, Dec 2001.

Concept Paper: Microfinance Institutions in India Tiwari, Piyush and Fahad, S.M. Housing *Entrepreneur Development-New Venture Creation;* By Satish Taneja & S.L.Gupta.

Lectures on Entrepreneurship Development By Dr.B.M. Kacholia of Narsee Monjee Insitute of Management Studies, Mumbai.

Entrepreneurship-ICFAI Publication.

Development Finance Corporation, Mumbai.

SHARE Micro-limited, http://www.bellanet.org/partners/mfn/memberSHARE.html. Growing Stronger with our Members; Microfinance at SHARE, M. Udaia Kumar.

Swayam Krishi Sangam, Annual Report 2000-2001. *www.sksindia.com.*

Phuong LyBusiness suits South Asian women VOL 18 NO -244 REGD NO DA 1589 | Dhaka, Tuesday October 12 2010.

Breaking the Gender Barrier: Vinita Gupta on Creating More Women Technology Entrepreneurs.

Published: February 24, 2011 in India Knowledge@Wharton.

Promoting Entrepreneurship and Innovative SMEs in a Global Economy, OECD paper- 2004.

Effective Small Business Management by Richard M. Hodgetts.

Laghu Aur Madhyam Udyam-Samasyen Aur Samadhan, Dal Singar Yadav & Shrimohan Yadav- 2007.

www.niesbud.nic.in.

www.nisiet.gov.in.

www.iie.nic.in.

www.ediindia.org.

www.isedonline.org.

Bhide, Amar V., *The Origin and Evolution of New Business,* Oxford University Press, New York, 2000.

Brandt, Steven C., *The 10 Commandments for Building a Growth Company,* Third Edition, Macmillan Business Books, Delhi 1977.

Desai, Vasant, *Small Scale Enterprises Vols. 1-12,* Mumbai, Himalaya Publishing House, Latest Edition.

Dollinger, Mare J., *Entrepreneurship: Strategies and Resources,* Illinois, Irwin, 1955.

Gupta, C.B. and Khanka, S.S., *Entrepreneurship and Small Business Management,* Sultan Chand and Sons, 2003.

Gupta, C.B., *Business Organization and Management,* Sultan Chand and Sons, Latest Edition.

Holt, David H., *Entrepreneurship: New Venture Creation, Prentice-Hall of India,*New Delhi, Latest Edition.

http://business.gov.in/manage_business/wholesalers_retailers.php

http://exim.indiamart.com/ssi-policies/store-purchase-program.html

Jain, Vijay K, *Marketing Management for Small Units,* Management Publishing Co, 1988

Keough, Jack. "E-Commerce: A Strategic Weapon." *Industrial Distribution,* December 1998.

Kotler, Philip, *Marketing Management: Analysis, Planning, Implementation and Control,* 6th Edition, Prentice Hall of India, 1988.

Kotler. P, 2003, *Marketing Management,* 11th Edition, Pearson Education, p. 534-50 21

Kotler. P, Gray. A, 2005, *Principles of Marketing,* 11th Edition, Pearson Prentice hall, p. 397-419

Marketing Second Edition, By Robert D. Hisrich pp 239-240 Barron's Educational Series, 2000

Merrefield, David. "*Wholesale Changes.*" *Supermarket News,* 21 September 1998.

Olorunniwo, Festus, and Donna Wood. *'Reengineering in the Wholesale and Retail Industries." Industrial Management,* May-June 1998.

Panda, Shiba Charan, *Entrepreneurship Development,* New Delhi, Anmol Publications, Latest Edition.

Patel, V.G., *The Seven Business Crises and How to Beat Them,* Tata-McGraw,New Delhi, 1995.

Rosenbloom, Bert, ed. *Wholesale Distribution Channels: New Insights and Perspectives.* Binghamton, NY: Haworth Press, 1994.

Singh, B.P. and Chhabra, T.N., *Modern Business Organisation,* Kitab Mahal,Latest Edition.

Taneja, Satish and Gupta S.L., *Entrepreneur Development: New Venture Creation,* Galgotia Publishing Company, 2001.

Verma, J.C., and Gurpal Singh, *Small Business and Industry – A handbook for Entrepreneurs,* New Delhi, Sage, 2002.

Sukesh Gauda, *Principles of marketing, retailing vs wholesaling.*